AGGREGATION AND THE MICROFOUNDATIONS OF DYNAMIC MACROECONOMICS

The ASSET Series

This is a book in the ASSET Series. ASSET is the Association of Southern European Economic Theorists, which exists to encourage the development among participating centres of programmes of research into economic problems. The group has from its beginnings enjoyed the support of several national governments and also the European Union in order to promote exchanges of researchers and ideas among institutions that are all based in Southern Europe. The group also distributes its own discussion papers. The books in this series are all derived from work carried out in an ASSET centre.

Participating centres are: Departament d'Economia e Historia Economica, Universitat Autonoma de Barcelona, Spain; Instituto de Economia Publica and Departmento de Fundamentos del Analisis Economico, Facultad de Ciencias Economicas y Empresariales, Universidad del Pais Vasco–Euskal Herriko Unibersitatea, Bilbao, Spain; Departamento de Fundamentos del Analisis Economico, Universidad de Alicante, Spain; Facultat de Cìencies Economiques I Empresarials, Universitat Pompeu Fabra, Barcelona, Spain; Groupe de Recherche en Economie Mathématique et Quantitative, Centre National de la Recherche Scientifique, Ecole des Hautes Etudes en Sciences Sociales et Université des Sciences Sociales de Toulouse, France; Groupement de Recherche en Economie Quantitative d'Aix-Marseille, Centre National de la Recherche Scientifique, Ecole des Hautes Etudes en Sciences Sociales et Universités d'Aix-Marseille II et III, Aix-en-Provence et Marseille, France; Department of Economics, European University Institute, Firenze, Italy; Dipartimento di Scienza Economiche, Universita degli Studi di Bologna, Italy; Department of Economics, Athens University of Economics and Business, Greece; Faculdade de Economia, Universidade Nova de Lisboa, Portugal; Faculdade de Cîencias Econòmicas e Empresarìais, Universidade Catòlica Portuguesa, Lisboa, Portugal; Centre for Economic Design, Boğaziçi University, Istanbul, Turkey; Eitan Berglas School, Faculty of Social Sciences, Tel Aviv University, Israel.

The screening committee for the series consists of S. Barbera, Universitat Autonoma de Barcelona, Spain; L. Cabral, Universidade Nova Lisboa, Portugal; J. Crémer, Groupe de Recherche en Economie Mathématique et Quantitative, Toulouse, France; R. Davidson, Groupement de Recherche en Economie Quantitative d'Aix-Marseille, Marseille, France; J. P. Florens, Groupe de Recherche en Economie Mathématique et Quantitative, Toulouse, France; L. A. Gérard-Varet, Groupement de Recherche en Economie Quantitative d'Aix-Marseille, Marseille, France; A. P. Kirman, Groupement de Recherche en Economie Quantitative d'Aix-Marseille, Marseille, France; T. Kollintzas, Athens University of Economics and Business, Greece; A. Mas Colell, Universitat Pompeu Fabra, Barcelona, Spain.

Aggregation and the Microfoundations of Dynamic Macroeconomics

MARIO FORNI AND MARCO LIPPI

CLARENDON PRESS • OXFORD
1997

Oxford University Press, Great Clarendon Street, Oxford OX2 6DP

Oxford New York
Athens Auckland Bangkok Bogota Bombay
Buenos Aires Calcutta Cape Town Dar es Salaam
Delhi Florence Hong Kong Istanbul Karachi
Kuala Lumpur Madras Madrid Melbourne
Mexico City Nairobi Paris Singapore
Taipei Tokyo Toronto Warsaw

and associated companies in
Berlin Ibadan

Oxford is a trade mark of Oxford University Press

Published in the United States
by Oxford University Press Inc., New York

British Library Cataloguing in Publication Data
Data available

Library of Congress Cataloging in Publication Data
Data available

ISBN 0–19–828800–X

1 3 5 7 9 10 8 6 4 2

Typeset by the Authors
Printed in Great Britain
on acid-free paper by
Biddles Ltd., Guildford and King's Lynn

Contents

Introduction ix

List of Symbols xvi

I. AGGREGATION OF SCALAR PROCESSES

1. Common and Idiosyncratic Components 3
   - *1.1. The Model for the Individual Variables* 3
   - *1.2. A Large Number of Agents* 7
   - *1.3. Large Numbers: a General Result* 8
   - *1.4. A Continuum of Agents* 15
   - *1.5. Autoregressive Relationships among the Microvariables* 17
   - *1.6. Bibliographic Notes* 18

2. How Many Common Shocks? 19
   - *2.1. Perfect Correlation* 19
   - *2.2. Pairwise Singularity* 24
   - *2.3. Pairwise Cointegration* 26
   - *2.4. How Many Common Shocks?* 30
   - *2.5. Dynamic Principal Components* 35
   - *2.6. Further Empirical Evidence* 38
   - *2.7. Bibliographic Notes* 41

3. The Regional Model 43
   - *3.1. From the Individual to the Regional Model* 43
   - *3.2. Specification of the Regional Model* 46
   - *3.3. Estimation and Diagnostic Checking* 48
   - *3.4. Identification of the Common Shocks* 51
   - *3.5. Bibliographic Notes* 52

4. Aggregating the Common Components 53
   - *4.1. The Wold Representation of the Macrovariable* 53
   - *4.2. Identification of the Microparameters* 59

4.3. Bibliographic Notes 62

II. AGGREGATION OF ECONOMIC MODELS

5. Reformulation of Standard Representative-Agent Models 67
5.1. Life Cycle, Permanent Income under Rational Expectations 68
5.2. A Labor Demand Schedule under Rational Expectations 71
5.3. Consumption and Income Again: Error Correction Mechanisms 73
5.4. Rules of Thumb. Non-Fully Rational, Routinized Behaviors 75
5.5. Structural VAR Models. General Equilibrium 77
5.6. Bibliographic Notes 78

6. The Disaggregated Model 79
6.1. The Microparameter Space 80
6.2. The Micromodel 81
6.3. The Population Space 83
6.4. The Disaggregated Model 84
6.5. Further Comments on the Micromodel. Analytic Functions 85
6.6. Negligible Subsets. The Alternative Principle 90
6.7. Non-Redundancy of the Common Shocks 95
6.8. Dependent and Independent Variables 100
6.9. The Micromodel Coefficients as Analytic Functions 103
6.10. Bibliographic Notes 103

7. The Aggregate Model 105
7.1. Definition of the Aggregate Model 105
7.2. Dropping the Idiosyncratic Component 106
7.3. Aggregation of the DI Model 109
7.4. Macrovariables in the Micromodel. General Equilibrium 109
7.5. Populations and Distributions over Γ 110
7.6. Restrictions and Subsets of the Population Space 113
7.7. Bibliographic Notes 114

8. The Rank of the Aggregate Vector 116
8.1. General Statements 116
8.2. The Two-Point Example 117

8.3. A Theorem for the DI Model 118
8.4. More on the Subset of Γ_m where the Model is Singular 120
8.5. Bibliographic Notes 121

9. Cointegration 122
9.1. General Results 122
9.2. Log-Linear Models 126
9.3. An Observation on the Alternative Principle 129
9.4. Bibliographic Notes 129

10. An Extension of the Alternative Principle 130
10.1. From the Spectral Density to the Wold Representation 131
10.2. An Extension of the Alternative Principle 134
10.3. Bibliographic Notes 137

11. Granger Causality 138
11.1. General Results 138
11.2. Discussion of the Two-Point Example 139
11.3. Bibliographic Notes 140

12. Wold Representation: VAR and ARMAX Models 141
12.1. VAR Models 141
12.2. Fundamentalness 148
12.3. ARMAX Models 149
12.4. Interpretation. Overidentifying Restrictions 152
12.5. Bibliographic Notes 153

III. MACROECONOMIC APPLICATIONS

13. Permanent Income and the Error Correction Mechanism 159
13.1. Excess Sensitivity 160
13.2. Cointegration of Consumption and Total Income 164
13.3. Singularity 167
13.4. Consumption Volatility 170
13.5. Complete Information and the Representative Agent 172
13.6. An Explanation for Sensitivity and Smoothness 174
13.7. Micro and Macro Singularity 179

13.8. Reconciling PIH and ECM 182
13.9. An Empirical Exercise 183
13.10. Bibliographic Notes 186

14. Disaggregating the Business Cycle 189
14.1. The Number of Common Shocks 189
14.2. Identification of the Common Technology Shock 190
14.3. Estimation of the Sectoral Model 194
14.4. Diagnostic Checking, Data Sources, and Data Treatment 198
14.5. Summary 200

Conclusions 202

Appendix. Elements of Discrete Time Series Theory 204
A.1. Orthogonal Projections 205
A.2. The Wold Representation 208
A.3. MA Representations of Regular Processes 209
A.4. Non-Fundamentalness and Prediction 215
A.5. Scalar ARMA Processes 215
A.6. Vector Processes 217
A.7. The Spectral Density 219
A.8. Granger Causality and Sims's Theorem 222
A.9. Bibliographic Notes 223

References 225

Index 233

Introduction

Overview

This book studies the problem of aggregation over agents within the area of macroeconomics which is known as the Slutsky–Frisch approach. This field has been dominated in the last 20 years by models based on intertemporal optimization and rational expectations. Such models can be briefly described as follows:

(1) A representative agent maximizes a function depending upon expected values of x_t and y_t, where x_t is a variable (or a vector of variables) independent of the agent's action, whereas y_t is controlled by the agent.

(2) Expectations are rational, i.e. the expected values are not obtained by subjective rules of thumb; rather, they are optimal predictions based on a given information set.

(3) Owing to the usual choice of quadratic functionals in the optimization step, the solution of the model takes on the form of a system of *linear* stochastic difference equations. In the simplest case, x_t, the independent variable, depends on its past values and an exogenous shock, while y_t, the dependent variable, depends on x_t, contemporaneous and past, on past values of y_t itself, and possibly on another shock. The theory behind the optimization problem produces either overidentifying restrictions on the structural parameters, or weaker properties, like cointegration.

(4) Lastly, the model obtained is estimated and the theory is tested using data that are aggregated over the whole population of a country, all the firms of a country, etc.

We are not interested here in distinguishing between the style of work which has been dominant in the US literature—in which steps (1) to (4), in that order, characterize the presentation of empirical macroeconomic studies—and the approach which has had many followers in Europe, in the UK in particular, in which preliminary statistical analysis plays a major role, whereas theory is employed more as an *ex post* interpretation than as an *ex ante* microfoundation; or, lastly, the VAR approach and the more recent structural VAR models. In the same way, our questions and results apply both if the micromodel is in the intertemporal optimization stream, and if agents are supposed to follow routinized behavior or fixed-rule, non-optimal, expectations. Our question is whether any interpretation or microfoundation, or even a comment on an estimated macromodel, retain their sense when the representative-agent fiction is dropped, i.e. when differences among agents are taken into account.

If one grants that agents may differ from one another both by the variable x_t that they face, and by the response of y_t to x_t, then several questions arise:

(a) Given the micromodel, how is the macromodel obtained?

(b) Do the features of the micromodel, as derived from the micro theory, survive aggregation? For example, if x_t and y_t are cointegrated at the micro level, are the corresponding macrovariables cointegrated as well? If x_t is not Granger-caused by y_t at the micro level, does the same property hold for the corresponding macrovariables?

(c) Do the parameters of the macromodel bear a simple relationship to the corresponding parameters of the micromodel?

(d) If the micro theory leads to overidentifying restrictions, can we conclude that the parameters of the macromodel are overidentified?

Our results may be read in two different ways. In the first place, our answer to questions (b), (c), (d), and related issues is strongly negative. If we rule out *ad hoc* assumptions on the distribution of the microparameters over the population, then aggregation spoils any pleasant property of micromodels. This is hardly surprising, as aggregation has already been recognized as a major source of difficulty in many branches of economic theory and empirical economics. However, a complete assessment of the difficulties arising with aggregation of dynamic micromodels has not yet been provided.

On the other hand, the difference between micro- and macromodels, which arises from aggregation, can be a source of reconciliation between theory and empirical data. If independent information on the distribution of the microparameters can be obtained, then a conflict between theory and aggregate data may be shown as the consequence of the representative-agent assumption. In other words, when aggregate data are correctly employed to test the aggregate model—i.e. the model which results from micro theory, aggregation theory, and information on the microparameters—then difficulties that had arisen when directly comparing aggregate data with the micromodel may disappear. Recent results concerning aggregate consumption should be taken as an important step in this direction.

Unfortunately, information on the distribution of the microparameters is typically very difficult to obtain. Moreover, the representative-agent practice has led macroeconomists to concentrate their efforts almost exclusively on micro modeling. By contrast, the message of this book is that macroeconomic modeling and testing would receive a new impetus if a better balance were reached between micro theory, aggregation theory, and empirical research on the distribution of the microparameters over the population.

Plan of the Book

In Part I we begin by reviewing methods and results in aggregation of scalar processes. This part may be also seen as preparing for Parts II and III. Precisely, here we motivate our idea that individual variables are driven by more than one macroeconomic shock. To fix ideas, suppose that the variable is income. We will assume that individual incomes can be decomposed into a common and an idiosyncratic component. Common components are correlated across different agents, whereas idiosyncratic components are, by definition, mutually orthogonal. The difference between our model and the common–idiosyncratic model that one encounters in recent literature is that we assume that the common components are driven by more than one common shock. For this reason, showing that only the common component survives aggregation, as we do in Chapter 1, is not as trivial as usual.

In Chapters 2 and 3 we show that the multi-shock assumption not only is a mathematical generalization of the usual model, but has a solid empirical basis. Using US data for income and wage, disaggregated at state level, we prove that the assumption that one, or even two, macroeconomic shocks drive all micro incomes is untenable. In the same way we can rule out only one permanent shock. In Chapter 3 a method for the estimation of dynamic common–idiosyncratic models with large cross-sectional dimension, based on the results in Chapter 1, is proposed. In Chapter 4 we present some useful results concerning aggregation of the common components.

In Part II we deal with aggregation of economic models. In Chapter 5 we show how well-known representative-agent micromodels can be reformulated to take into account the fact that different agents face different microvariables. In Chapter 6 we give the definition of micromodel as a function associating a vector equation to any point of the microparameter space. Based on the definition of micromodel are the definitions of the disaggregated model and aggregate model given in Chapter 7. The latter is a function associating a vector macroequation with any point of a suitably defined population space. The crucial fact is that the coefficients of the vector macroequation are analytic functions (i.e. functions that admit a Taylor expansion) of the microparameters. This implies that we can apply an Alternative Principle, stating that any restriction on the macroparameters holds either for a negligible subset of the microparameter space (a set of zero Lebesgue measure) or for the whole microparameter space.

In the remaining chapters of Part II we will systematically apply the Alternative Principle to: (i) the rank of the aggregate vector; (ii) cointegration of the aggregate vector; (iii) Granger causality; (iv) aggregate VAR and ARMAX models. Our typical result will be that, given a property holding for the micromodel, if a minimum of heterogeneity is allowed, then the property does not hold for the aggregate variables with the exception of a negligible subset of the microparameter space. Moreover, the dynamics of a macroequation depend on the dynamics of the whole micromodel, not only on the dynamics of the corresponding microequation. Important consequences are firstly that complicated dynamic macroequations may arise in spite of perfectly static microequations. Secondly, the coefficients of a macroequation are functions of the micro coefficients of both corresponding and non-corresponding microequations.

The definitions and results in this part are based on typical partial equilibrium models. However, this approach has been adopted solely to make presentation easier. As we show in Sections 7.4 and 8.3, no particular problems arise in adapting our results to general equilibrium models.

Part III contains two macroeconomic applications. In Chapter 13 we report and elaborate on recent results on aggregate consumption. Using US panel data, within the current common–idiosyncratic model, it is possible to reconcile, to some extent, the permanent income hypothesis with aggregate evidence. In particular, positive autocorrelation and smoothness, relative to income, of aggregate consumption are no longer paradoxical empirical facts. We show that our multi-shock model, suitably specified, leads to explanations for all the remaining discrepancies between micro- and macromodels. This chapter is meant as an example of the positive use of aggregation theory that we have mentioned above.

Chapter 14 is based on Forni and Reichlin (1995, 1996). A common–idiosyncratic model is applied to a data set including output and productivity for 450 American industries from 1958 to 1986. The model is specified and estimated by a new method, exploiting the large numbers result proved in Chapter 1. The main empirical findings are: (i) there are two common shocks driving output and productivity of the 450 sectors; (ii) technological innovations produce positive comovements at business cycle frequencies, but they are not sufficient to explain all cyclical fluctuations; (iii) technological shocks are strongly correlated with the growth rates of the investment in machinery and equipment sectors.

References to the Literature

The book focuses on the consequences of aggregation for dynamic economic models, not on aggregation in general, nor on aggregation in time series analysis. This is the reason why important general contributions may have been overlooked, whereas side remarks or footnotes regarding aggregation of economic models have been mentioned and commented on. In the same way, time aggregation and seasonal adjustment, which produce effects similar to aggregation over agents, have not been considered.

The literature on aggregation of dynamic economic models is rather scanty. Moreover, even when the issue has been considered, *ad hoc* simplifying assumptions are almost invariably introduced. For instance, when heterogeneity of the response of y_t to x_t is allowed then almost invariably x_t is assumed to be the same for all agents, or, as mentioned above, the same up to an idiosyncratic component. In this book we provide a general treatment, in which agents are heterogeneous inasmuch as their responses are heterogeneous and they face variables that, according to the empirical findings in Part I, are driven by many macroeconomic shocks.

There are two ideas upon which the book is developed. The first, that aggregation may produce dramatic differences between micro and macro dynamic shapes of univariate and multivariate economic models, has been explored in Granger (1980), Trivedi (1985), Lippi (1988), Lippi and Forni (1990), Lewbel (1994). The second, that such differences may occur because the macromodel keeps only the common component whereas the idiosyncratic components are washed out by aggregation, has been put forward in Granger (1987), and more recently in Goodfriend (1992), Pischke (1995), Forni and Lippi (1994), Forni and Reichlin (1996). We believe that the book provides a substantial step forward with the general treatment of the common–idiosyncratic model and the empirical analysis of the dimension of the common component in Parts I and III, with the genericity analysis in Part II.

The scope of the book, as stated above, is limited to *linear* macroeconomic models, irrespective of whether they arise from optimization or from different linear models of behavior. Our disaggregated model differs from the representative-agent model in that we allow that microparameters may vary across agents. We do not go further. Thus, for example, we do not consider the recent literature in which aggregation of agents applying S-s rules is studied (as for instance in Caplin, 1985); nor do we deal with models in which agents interact with one another (as in Kirman, 1993). However, we believe that empirical implementation of such non-linear models cannot avoid careful consideration of the issues that we study in Part I. For example, modeling consumers as fixing consumption by an S-s rule, instead of a linear model, still leaves unsettled the question as to how far individual incomes are heterogeneous.

Lastly, for a very important development of the idea that aggregation, though destroying pleasant micro regularities, may *create* properties of the macrovariables that are not typical of the corresponding individual variables, we should mention here Hildenbrand's *Market Demand* (Hildenbrand, 1994).

With some inevitable exceptions, we have managed to confine quotations and comments on the literature to specific sections at the end of each chapter.

Mathematical Prerequisites

All the mathematical results invoked are carefully stated and references are provided. Even though some of the proofs are reported we have not tried to write a self-contained book. Simply, when a result can be proved without introducing a complex formal apparatus, we give the proof. The Appendix contains all the references to the theory of stationary stochastic processes that are needed in the text. The treatment is fairly complete as regards the Wold representation and fundamentalness, whereas for all the results linking the spectral density of a process to its Wold representation we have only indicated the exact reference in Rozanov's book. In Part II we also make reference to the basics of Lebesgue measure, including Fubini's theorem, and some elementary topology. Definitions and results from the theory of analytic functions are less familiar to economists than stochastic processes. For this reason they have been included in the text, in Chapters 6 and 11, rather than in the Appendix.

Notation

Consider the following expression:

$$a_1^i(L)u_{1t} + a_2^i(L)u_{2t}.$$

Here u_{1t} and u_{2t} denote two white-noise processes, while $a_l^i(L)$ denote polynomials (or more general functions) in the lag operator L. The exponent i indicates that the process belongs to the agent i, while the lower index, 1 or 2, refers to the first or the second shock respectively. As an alternative we could have written

$$a_{i1}(L)u_{1t} + a_{i2}(L)u_{2t}.$$

This second notation has no logical drawback, but is too flat. When looking at $a_{il}(L)$, we should make an effort to remember that the first index refers to agents, the second to shocks. In our notation indexes or other variables referring to agents always take the upper position.

Now consider the expression

$$a_1^{\gamma^i}(L)u_{1t} + a_2^{\gamma^i}(L)u_{2t},$$

where γ^i is a vector of microparameters. Here we are saying that the coefficients of the polynomials in front of u_{1t} and u_{2t} are functions of γ^i, where γ^i is the microparameter vector of the agent i. The reason why we use γ^i instead of γ_i is that γ^i has components. The latter will be distinguished by a lower index:

$$\gamma^i = (\gamma_1^i \quad \gamma_2^i \quad \cdots \quad \gamma_s^i).$$

With minor exceptions we have employed lower case letters for the stochastic variables, irrespective of whether they are scalars or vectors, disaggregated or aggregated magnitudes.

The use of exponents to indicate functional dependence is rather unusual and one may feel uneasy with, say, a^x indicating a function of the variable x. We can only say that, in our opinion, all different solutions would have led to even more awkward results.

Some readers will find very inelegant, if not mistaken, the use of expressions like 'the function $f(x)$' instead of 'the function f'. In the same way, the symbol L in the lag operators could have been dropped in many cases. However, with symbols like $a_l^{\gamma^i}(L)$ there is nothing we could drop without complications or ambiguities.

Finally, we use $i = 1, \infty$ or $i = 1, n$ with the meaning of $i = 1, 2, \ldots, \infty$ or $i = 1, 2, \ldots, n$.

Acknowledgements

We are not able to make a formal list of all the colleagues who gave suggestions, encouragement, and criticism during the gestation of the book. However, we owe a special debt to Carlo Giannini and Alan Kirman, to several colleagues at the Dipartimento di Economia Politica, Modena, the Dipartimento di Scienze Economiche, Rome, the Istituto per la Ricerca Sociale, Milan. We are also deeply indebted to Lucrezia Reichlin, who incessantly urged us to go on with the book and kindly allowed us to draw from joint work by her and Mario Forni.

Serious and less serious mistakes were avoided thanks to the patient reading by Carlo Giannini, Clive Granger, Arthur Lewbel, Massimiliano Marcellino, Paolo Zaffaroni, and two anonymous referees. All of their observations were carefully taken into consideration, even though in a few cases we decided to stick to our version.

We also wish to thank Andrew Schuller, for constantly stimulating us to persevere in the project, and Jason Pearce, who supervised the book design, making our struggling with Plain TeX Macros a real pleasure.

Finally, generous financial support from the CNR (Consiglio Nazionale delle Ricerche), Comitato 10, and the MURST (Ministero della Università e della Ricerca Scientifica e Tecnologica), Comitato 13, is gratefully acknowledged.

List of Symbols

Here we list the symbols that have been used in a systematic way throughout the book.

$x_t^i,\ y_t^i,\ c_t^i$	scalar processes relative to agent i; used in Parts I and III
$a_l^i(L),\ b^i(L)$, etc.	scalar polynomials in the lag operator L, relative to agent i (Parts I and III)
$u_t = (\,u_{1t} \quad u_{2t} \quad \cdots \quad u_{ht}\,)$	the vector of common shocks, i.e. the shocks affecting all the individual variables
$\zeta_t^i = a_1^i(L)u_{1t} + \cdots + a_h^i(L)u_{ht}$	the common component of the i-th process (Parts I and III)
ξ_t^i	the idiosyncratic shock of the i-th process (Parts I and III)
$\chi_t^i = b^i(L)\xi_t^i$	the idiosyncratic component of the i-th process (Parts I and III)
$\gamma = (\,\omega \quad \lambda\,)$	the microparameter vector, where $\omega = (\,\omega_1 \quad \cdots \quad \omega_s\,)$ is the vector of individual parameters, while $\lambda = (\,\lambda_1 \quad \cdots \quad \lambda_c\,)$ is the vector of common parameters (Part II)
Γ	the microparameter space (Part II)
γ^i	the microparameter vector of agent i (Part II)
$p = (\,\omega^1 \quad \omega^2 \quad \cdots \quad \omega^m \quad \lambda\,)$	the population microparameter vector (Part II)
p^i	the microparameter vector of the i-th agent in the population p; if $p = (\,\omega^1 \quad \cdots \quad \omega^m \quad \lambda\,)$ then $p^i = (\,\omega^i \quad \lambda\,)$ (Part II)
Γ_m	the population space (Part II)
$a^\gamma(L),\ A^\gamma(L)$, etc.	polynomials and matrices in the lag operator L whose coefficients depend on the microparameter vector γ (Part II)
$x_t^\gamma,\ y_t^\gamma,\ z_t^\gamma$, etc.	scalar or vector processes depending on the microparameter vector γ (Part II)
$a^{\gamma^i}(L),\ A^{\gamma^i}(L)$, etc.	polynomials and matrices in the lag operator L whose coefficients depend on the microparameter vector of the i-th agent (Part II)
$x_t^{\gamma^i},\ y_t^{\gamma^i},\ z_t^{\gamma^i}$, etc.	scalar or vector processes depending on the microparameter vector of the i-th agent (Part II)

$a^{p^i}(L),\ A^{p^i}(L)$, etc.	polynomials and matrices in the lag operator L whose coefficients depend on the microparameter vector of the i-th agent of the population p (Part II)
$x_t^{p^i},\ y_t^{p^i},\ z_t^{p^i}$, etc.	scalar or vector processes depending on the microparameter vector of the i-th agent of the population p (Part II)
$z_t^p,\ x_t^p,\ y_t^p$, etc.	scalar or vector aggregate processes depending on the population p (Parts II and III)
$G^p(L),\ H^p(L)$, etc.	polynomial matrices in L entering the definition of aggregate vectors or scalars, and therefore depending on the population p (Parts II and III)
$i,\ j$	indexes of agents within populations; i also denotes the imaginary unit; we have managed to avoid any possible confusion

I

Aggregation of Scalar Processes

1

Common and Idiosyncratic Components

In this and the following three chapters, which constitute the first part of this book, we analyze univariate aggregation of microvariables whose dynamics typically differ across individuals, like for instance income, wealth, or wage rates. Two main questions are discussed. Firstly, how should dynamic heterogeneity be modeled? Secondly, given the micromodel, what are the consequences of aggregation on the univariate properties of the variables? The results presented here, besides being interesting *per se*, will prove useful in Parts II and III, where the variables just mentioned are embedded within multivariate models based on economic theory.

In the present chapter we introduce our general set-up and discuss the effects of aggregating over a huge number of agents. We assume that there are two kinds of shocks affecting individual variables: idiosyncratic or microeconomic shocks, which are specific to each particular agent and are mutually independent across agents, and common or macroeconomic shocks, which on the contrary are the same for all individuals. We assume more than one common shock and analyze the conditions under which, owing to large numbers, idiosyncratic shocks nearly cancel out in the aggregate, while common shocks, even when negligible at the micro level, completely predominate at the macro level.

1.1. The Model for the Individual Variables

1.1.1. The first question to face when dealing with aggregation problems is how to model individual heterogeneity. Standard time series macroeconomic literature is not very helpful to this end. Almost all existing models adopt the representative-agent hypothesis, i.e. they assume that macroeconomic variables behave as if there were only one agent in the economic system.

However, starting with the celebrated islands model (Lucas, 1973), a few authors have introduced a certain amount of heterogeneity.[1] Usually the

[1] For a partial list see Section 1.6 below.

following individual model is employed: (i) the variable corresponding to agent i, call it x_t^i, is covariance stationary after suitable differencing; (ii) assuming for simplicity that x_t^i is already stationary, x_t^i can be decomposed as

$$x_t^i = a^i \zeta_t + \chi_t^i, \tag{1.1}$$

where ζ_t and χ_t^i are (jointly) stationary, while χ_t^i is orthogonal to ζ_t and χ_t^j at any lead and lag, for $i \neq j$. The orthogonality assumptions motivate the definition of χ_t^i as the *idiosyncratic component*, and of $a^i \zeta_t$ as the *common component.*

Typically, ζ_t is modeled as an ARMA:

$$\zeta_t = a(L) u_t,$$

where u_t is a white-noise process and $a(L)$ is a rational function in the lag operator L. In the same way, the idiosyncratic component is modeled as

$$\chi_t^i = d^i(L) \xi_t^i,$$

where ξ_t^i is a white noise. The white-noise processes u_t and ξ_t^i will be referred to, respectively, as the *common shock* and the *idiosyncratic shock*: u_t may represent, for instance, changes in technology or policy which affect the whole economy, while ξ_t^i is an agent-specific source of variability, like health or tastes.

The model just described, while appealing by its simplicity, imposes very strong restrictions on heterogeneity. Besides the coefficient a^i, heterogeneity is confined within the idiosyncratic term. The response function $a(L)$ to the common shock is identical for all individuals, so that we cannot have, for instance, agents who react immediately and agents who react with some delay. Moreover, we cannot have, for instance, both a permanent and a transitory shock, each affecting different groups of individuals in different ways. In Chapter 2 we shall show that model (1.1) has a very poor empirical performance with US income and wages data. Thus both elementary theoretical considerations and empirical evidence lead to a more general model for the individual processes. The distinction between a common and an idiosyncratic component will be kept. However, we shall assume that the common component of each individual process is affected by more than one shock, and the response functions to the common shocks may differ across individuals. Precisely:

DEFINITION 1.1. The *individual model* is a countable family $\mathcal{F}$ of stationary stochastic variables x_t^i, $i = 1, \infty$. We assume that x_t^i can be decomposed in the following way:

$$\begin{aligned} x_t^i &= \zeta_t^i + \chi_t^i \\ \zeta_t^i &= a_1^i(L) u_{1t} + a_2^i(L) u_{2t} + \cdots + a_h^i(L) u_{ht}, \end{aligned} \tag{1.2}$$

where: (i) the shocks u_{lt}, $l = 1, h$, common shocks henceforth, form an orthonormal white noise (i.e. they are unit variance white noises, mutually orthogonal at any lead and lag); (ii) the response functions $a_l^i(L)$ are rational functions in the lag operator L with no poles of modulus smaller than or equal to unity; (iii) the idiosyncratic component χ_t^i is an ARMA orthogonal at any lead and lag to χ_t^j, $j \neq i$, and ζ_t^j, for any j.

The reason why we assume an infinity of individuals is that we want to analyze the asymptotic behavior of aggregate variables. However, the pure MA structure of (1.2), along with the orthogonality assumption on the idiosyncratic components, allow us to consider without difficulties finite subfamilies of $\mathcal{F}$ (complications arise with autoregressive links among the microvariables x_t^i; see Section 1.5).

REMARK 1.1. If a finite number of individuals were assumed, model (1.2) would be identical to the dynamic factor model (see Section 1.6 for references). In that model the white-noise common shocks are replaced by mutually orthogonal latent factors. A moment's reflection, however, shows that the white-noise condition does not imply loss of generality. Serially correlated common factors can be easily accommodated within our framework: if the l-th factor is $f_{lt} = b_l(L)\eta_{lt}$, $b_l(L)$ being rational, and the i-th response function is $c_l^i(L)$, the factor model can be obtained by setting $u_{lt} = \eta_{lt}$ and $a_l^i(L) = c_l^i(L)b_l(L)$. In the same way, the assumption of unit variance orthogonal common shocks simply normalizes representation (1.2), without loss of generality.

REMARK 1.2. Model (1.2), considered for a finite number m of individuals, has a very important property from the point of view of estimation. When m becomes very large, VAR models become useless since the number of parameters grows as fast as m^2. By contrast, since h is fixed, model (1.2) places a strong restriction on the covariance structure of the vector whose components are the variables x_t^i. As a consequence, the number of parameters in (1.2) grows linearly with m, so that parsimonious specifications of (1.2) can be estimated with disaggregated data, without requiring an unrealistic time span for the time series (for references see Section 1.6 and Chapter 3).

REMARK 1.3. In Definition 1.1 the heterogeneity of the individual response functions $a_l^i(L)$ is not restricted in any way, so that not only can different individuals respond with different time profiles to the same shock, but different signs of the responses are allowed. For instance, suppose that u_{1t} represents improvement in the performances of engines operated by energy source 1, and u_{2t} does the same for energy source 2. A positive u_{1t} causes a shift from engines operated by energy source 1 to those operated by energy source 2. Thus the effects on production in the two sectors (engines of type 1 and 2 respectively) have opposite signs. As another example, natural disasters cause a decrease in production in many industries, but an increase in the sectors which take care of the recovery. In Section 1.3 we shall assume that both signs are allowed, but positive correlation between common components must prevail.

1.1.2. It must be pointed out that we do not make any assumption on the zeros of $a_l^i(L)$. In particular, we do not require the usual condition that $a_l^i(L)$ does not vanish inside the unit circle. We must recall that given

$$x_t = a(L)w_t, \tag{1.3}$$

where w_t is a white noise, then (1.3) is a fundamental representation, and w_t is a fundamental noise, for x_t, if $a(L)$ has no zeros inside the unit circle. If (1.3) is fundamental, then w_t is equal, up to a constant, to the residual of the projection of x_t on its past values, i.e. on the space spanned by x_{t-k}, for $k > 0$, and conversely (see Sections A.2 and A.3 and in particular Theorem A.2 in the Appendix).

Since we do not make assumptions on the zeros of $a_l^i(L)$ we do not assume that u_{lt} is fundamental for ζ_{lt}^i. This may surprise the reader accustomed to the standard presentation of ARMA models, in which roots of the MA polynomials inside the unit circle are strictly forbidden. However, the rationale for this condition has nothing to do with the economic meaning of the variables and their MA representations, but only with the purpose of predicting future values of the variables on the basis of their past values.

To clarify the possibility that an economically meaningful MA representation is not fundamental, let us consider the following example. Suppose that $h = 1$, and that the shock u_t represents the increase in technological knowledge taking place at time t. The common component

$$\zeta_t^i = a^i(L)u_t \tag{1.4}$$

represents the learning by doing process through which u_t gets absorbed by firm i. The coefficients of $a^i(L)$ are non-negative and we assume that they sum to unity, i.e. $a^i(1) = 1$. Furthermore, assume for simplicity that $a^i(L)$ is a finite polynomial of degree s. Now consider the binomial function

$$b(L) = (1+L)^s = \sum_{k=0}^{s} \binom{s}{k} L^k.$$

The following result holds:

THEOREM 1.1. Let $d(L)$ be a fundamental polynomial of degree s. Then

$$\frac{d_k}{d_0} \le b_k = \binom{s}{k}$$

for $k = 0, s$.

Proof. Consider the factorization

$$\begin{aligned}\frac{d(L)}{d_0} &= (1+\alpha_1 L)(1+\alpha_2 L)\cdots(1+\alpha_s L)\\ &= 1 + (\alpha_1+\alpha_2+\cdots+\alpha_s)L + (\alpha_1\alpha_2+\alpha_1\alpha_3+\cdots+\alpha_{s-1}\alpha_s)L^2\\ &\quad + \cdots + (\alpha_1\alpha_2\cdots\alpha_s)L^s.\end{aligned}$$

The result follows from $|\alpha_k| \leq 1$, for $k = 1, s$. Q.E.D.

Returning to the learning process (1.4), if any one of the coefficients of $a^i(L)$ sticks out of the binomial bell, then (1.4) is non-fundamental. On the other hand, the condition of Theorem 1.1 is not particularly plausible for learning processes. It implies for instance that $a_s^i \leq a_0^i$, and that $a_1^i \leq s a_0^i$, and therefore is not consistent with cases in which the first impact is very small as compared to the subsequent coefficients. Several examples of non-fundamentalness could be provided with x_t^i representing incomes, wages, etc. If u_t is a shock to income and we assume that its absorption takes place in two periods, then fundamentalness implies that the first impact is not smaller than the lagged one, and this condition is far from being obviously fulfilled in empirical situations.

We will return to the fundamentalness problem in Chapters 4 and 12, where we will deal with the relationship between fundamentalness and aggregation.

1.2. A Large Number of Agents

An important feature of model (1.2) is that, under some suitable assumptions, the ratio of the variance of the aggregate idiosyncratic component to the variance of the aggregate common component tends to zero as the number of individuals tends to infinity. This result is a simple version of the law of large numbers. Let us begin with the particular case of identical common components, i.e. $\zeta_t^i = \zeta_t$ for all i, and identical variances of the idiosyncratic terms, i.e. $\operatorname{var}(\chi_t^i) = \sigma_\chi^2$ for all i. We shall consider two kinds of aggregates: total variables and per capita variables.

In the first case we have

$$\sum_{i=1}^{m} x_t^i = m\zeta_t + \sum_{i=1}^{m} \chi_t^i.$$

By the orthogonality of the terms χ_t^i, the variance of the second term is $m\sigma_\chi^2$, while that of the first is $m^2\sigma_\zeta^2$. Thus, as m becomes large, the idiosyncratic term $\sum \chi_t^i$ (although big in comparison with χ_t^i) becomes very small in variance as compared to the common term $m\zeta_t$. Precisely, the fraction of the total variance explained by the common term is $R_m^2 = m\sigma_\zeta^2/(m\sigma_\zeta^2 + \sigma_\chi^2)$, and this ratio tends to unity as m goes to infinity.

A similar result emerges when the relevant aggregate is the per capita magnitude $x_t = \sum x_t^i/m$. In this case the idiosyncratic component is $\sum \chi_t^i/m$; when m goes to infinity its variance σ_χ^2/m tends to zero, so that x_t converges in variance to ζ_t.

A numerical example helps to get an idea of the order of magnitude of the effect just described. Let us set $\sigma_\chi^2 = 9$ and $\sigma_\zeta^2 = 1$. Notice that in this case x_t^i is dominated by the idiosyncratic component at the individual level, since R_1^2 is only 0.1. Now assume $m = 1000$ and consider per capita variables. The variance of the idiosyncratic component is 0.009, while that of the common component is 1; the common term explains about 99% of the total variance. If $m = 10000$, R_m^2 is near 0.999.

An interesting consequence of this large numbers effect is that the dynamic features of micro- and macrovariables may be quite different from one another, since the properties of the macrovariables do not depend on the idiosyncratic components, which may have a major impact at the micro level. In particular, the sign of autocorrelation at any lag may be reversed in the aggregate. This is precisely what happens with US labor income: panel data indicate that there is a large, negative first-order autocorrelation in micro incomes (see e.g. Deaton, 1992, other references in Section 1.6), whereas aggregate labor income exhibits a positive first-order autocorrelation, an empirical finding which may seem paradoxical at a first glance. Model (1.2) can provide a simple explanation: the common terms are smooth, but at the micro level they are dominated by the idiosyncratic components, whose serial correlation is negative.

1.3. Large Numbers: a General Result

1.3.1. Let us now return to our convergence results and drop the simplifying assumptions introduced in the previous section. We begin by considering some examples.

EXAMPLE 1.1. Consider the case $h = 1$, $\zeta_t^i = u_{t-i+1}$, and $\mathrm{var}(\chi_t^i) = 1$. In this case the common components are pairwise orthogonal, so that

$$\sum_{i=1}^{m} \mathrm{var}(\zeta_t^i) = \sum_{i=1}^{m} \mathrm{var}(u_{t-i+1}) = m$$

which is equal to the variance of the aggregate idiosyncratic component. Therefore no large numbers effect occurs.

EXAMPLE 1.2. Assume again that $h = 1$, while $\zeta_t^i = 0.5^i u_t$. Here the common components are perfectly correlated; despite this, by taking the common components from 1 to m we get

$$\sum_{i=1}^{m} \zeta_t^i = 2(1 - 0.5^m)u_t,$$

whose variance is bounded as m tends to infinity, so that no large numbers effect can occur.

These examples show that the intuition of a vanishing idiosyncratic component requires some additional conditions. This is what we do in the following two assumptions.

ASSUMPTION 1.1. There exists a positive real μ such that $\mathrm{var}(x_t^i) \leq \mu$ for every individual process in the family $\mathcal{F}$.

ASSUMPTION 1.2. There exist a stationary process U_t and a positive real θ, such that considering the orthogonal projection

$$\zeta_t^i = c^i U_t + G_t^i \qquad (1.5)$$

(with G_t^i orthogonal to U_t), we have $c^i \geq \theta > 0$ with the exception of a finite subset of the family $\mathcal{F}$.

Notice that Assumption 1.2 imposes a lower bound on the variance of ζ_t^i (with a finite number of exceptions), thus excluding the case in Example 1.2. Hence imposing non-negative correlation among the ζ_t^i's does not imply fulfillment of Assumption 1.2. On the other hand, as the following example shows, negative correlation among some, even infinite, of the ζ_t^i's is not ruled out by Assumption 1.2.

EXAMPLE 1.3. Assume that the agents are partitioned into two infinite groups of individuals, namely Odd and Even. Within each group agents have the same common component and the same variance of the idiosyncratic component. Moreover, the common components of the Odd and the Even have the same variance and are negatively correlated, although correlation is not perfect. Formally,

$$x_t^i = \zeta_t^O + \chi_t^i, \qquad \text{for } i = 1, 3, 5, \ldots$$
$$x_t^i = \zeta_t^E + \chi_t^i, \qquad \text{for } i = 2, 4, 6, \ldots$$

with $\mathrm{cov}(\zeta_t^O, \zeta_t^E) = \sigma_{OE} < 0$, $\mathrm{var}(\zeta_t^O) = \mathrm{var}(\zeta_t^E) = \sigma_\zeta^2$, $|\sigma_{OE}| < \sigma_\zeta^2$ (correlation is not perfect). Defining $U_t = (\zeta_t^O + \zeta_t^E)/2$ and projecting ζ_t^i on U_t we get

$$\zeta_t^i = U_t + (-1)^i(\zeta_t^E - \zeta_t^O)/2.$$

Hence Assumption 1.2 is fulfilled.

REMARK 1.4. Assumption 1.2 has a nice geometrical interpretation. Consider the Hilbert space spanned by u_{lt-k}, for $l = 1, h$ and $k \geq 0$. Then consider the hyperplane $\mathcal{U}$ containing all vectors ζ_t such that $\text{cov}(\zeta_t, U_t) = \theta$. $\mathcal{U}$ partitions the space into the half where the covariance between ζ_t and U_t is greater than or equal to θ, and the half where the covariance is smaller than θ. We want only a finite number of agents to lie in the second half for some $\theta > 0$.

If, as hitherto, the individual processes are interpreted as natural magnitudes belonging to economic agents such as consumers or income earners, then aggregate variables are obtained by simply summing (or averaging) over the x_t^i. However, we need not stick to this interpretation. For example, the variables might be prices of different goods, so that aggregation would consist of a weighted average. Moreover, the variables x_t^i might be the per capita variables obtained by aggregating over subgroups of an underlying population. Lastly, when the micromodel is in logarithms, under suitable assumptions the linear approximation to the aggregate variable is a weighted average of the individual logarithms (see Section 9.2). In general, it will be convenient to introduce a sequence of weights N^i, for $i = 1, \infty$. We do not impose any normalization. Rather, we impose bounds ensuring that none of the processes disappears (relatively) when the number of agents grows. Precisely:

ASSUMPTION 1.3. There exist positive reals μ_1 and ν_1 such that $\nu_1 \leq N^i \leq \mu_1$, for any i.

Now let v be an increasing sequence of positive integers:

$$v = \{v_1,\ v_2,\ \ldots\},$$

with $v_k > v_{k-1}$, and

$$\chi_t^{m,v} = \sum_{k=1}^{m} N^{v_k} \chi_t^{v_k} \Big/ \sum_{k=1}^{m} N^{v_k}$$

$$\zeta_t^{m,v} = \sum_{k=1}^{m} N^{v_k} \zeta_t^{v_k} \Big/ \sum_{k=1}^{m} N^{v_k}.$$

Now we can state and prove our result.

THEOREM 1.2. (i) Under Assumptions 1.1 and 1.3

$$\lim_{m \to \infty} \text{var}(\chi_t^{m,v}) = 0,$$

for any increasing sequence v. The convergence is uniform with respect to v. (ii) Under Assumptions 1.2 and 1.3 there exist an integer m_0 and a positive real τ such that

$$\text{var}(\zeta_t^{m,v}) > \tau \tag{1.6}$$

for any increasing sequence v and $m > m_0$. (iii) Assumption 1.2 is also necessary for (1.6). More precisely, if Assumptions 1.1 and 1.3 hold but Assumption 1.2 does not, there exists an increasing sequence v such that $\lim_{m\to\infty} \mathrm{var}(\zeta_t^{m,v}) = 0$.

Proof. Statement (i) follows from

$$\mathrm{var}(\chi_t^{m,v}) < \frac{\mu_1^2 \mu}{\nu_1^2 m}.$$

As for statement (ii), let k_1 be an integer such that (1.5) holds with $c_i \geq \theta > 0$, for $k > k_1$. Without loss of generality let U_t be of unit variance. Assumption 1.2 implies that

$$\mathrm{var}(\zeta_t^{m,v}) \geq \left(\frac{\sum_{k=1}^m c^{v_k} N^{v_k}}{\sum_{k=1}^m N^{v_k}} \right)^2. \tag{1.7}$$

We have

$$\sum_{k=1}^{m} c^{v_k} N^{v_k} = \sum_{k=1}^{k_1} c^{v_k} N^{v_k} + \sum_{k=k_1+1}^{m} c^{v_k} N^{v_k} \geq -H + (m - k_1)\theta\nu_1,$$

where $-H$ is the sum of all terms $N^{v_k} c^{v_k}$ with $c^{v_k} < 0$. The term within brackets in (1.7) is greater than

$$\frac{-H}{\mu_1 m} + \frac{\theta\nu_1(m - k_1)}{\mu_1 m},$$

which is independent of v. The conclusion follows immediately.

Turning to statement (iii), suppose that Assumption 1.2 does not hold. We want to construct an increasing sequence v_k, $k = 1, \infty$, such that

$$\mathrm{var}\left(\sum_{k=1}^{m} N^{v_k} \zeta_t^{v_k} \right) \leq 2m\mu\mu_1^2.$$

This would imply $\lim_{m\to\infty} \mathrm{var}(\zeta_t^{m,v}) = 0$, since $\left(\sum_{k=1}^m N^{v_k}\right)^2 \geq \nu_1^2 m^2$. We proceed by induction. Take $v_1 = 1$. Then assume that indexes v_k, $k \leq m-1$, have been determined in such a way that

$$\mathrm{var}\left(\sum_{k=1}^{m-1} N^{v_k} \zeta_t^{v_k} \right) \leq 2(m-1)\mu\mu_1^2.$$

Let $\tilde{\zeta}_t^{m-1} = \sum_{k=1}^{m-1} N^{v_k} \zeta_t^{v_k}$, and $\tilde{\theta} = 1/[4(m-1)]$. Since Assumption 1.2 does not hold, we can find infinitely many indexes j such that in the orthogonal projection

$$\zeta_t^j = \tilde{c}^j \tilde{\zeta}_t^{m-1} + \tilde{G}_t^m$$

we have $\tilde{c}^j < \tilde{\theta}$. Let us select a j such that $j > v_{m-1}$, and put $v_m = j$. Now

$$\operatorname{var}\left(\sum_{k=1}^{m} N^{v_k}\zeta_t^{v_k}\right) \leq 2(m-1)\mu\mu_1^2 + \mu\mu_1^2 + 4\mu_1^2\tilde{\theta}(m-1)\mu = 2m\mu\mu_1^2.$$

Q.E.D.

REMARK 1.5. Obviously the idiosyncratic component does not vanish for the sequence of non-normalized aggregates $\tilde{x}_t^m = \sum_{k=1}^m N^{v_k}x^{v_k}$. However, consider the ratio

$$R_{m,v}^2 = \frac{\operatorname{var}(\sum_{k=1}^m N^{v_k}\zeta_t^{v_k})}{\operatorname{var}(\sum_{k=1}^m N^{v_k}x_t^{v_k})}.$$

An immediate corollary of Theorem 1.2 is that for any strictly increasing sequence v

$$\lim_{m\to\infty} R_{m,v}^2 = 1,$$

where the convergence is uniform with respect to v.

REMARK 1.6. Statement (i) of Theorem 1.2 still holds under weaker assumptions. Firstly, assume that there exist positive reals H and ρ, with $\rho < 1$, such that $\left|\operatorname{cov}(\chi_t^i, \chi_t^{i+k})\right| \leq H\rho^k$, for $k \geq 0$, and, for simplicity, that $N^i = 1$ for any i. We have

$$\begin{aligned}\operatorname{var}\left(\frac{1}{m}\sum_{i=1}^m \chi_t^i\right) &\leq \frac{1}{m}H + 2\frac{m-1}{m^2}H\rho + \cdots + 2\frac{1}{m^2}H\rho^{m-1}\\ &< \frac{1}{m}H\left(1 + 2\rho\frac{1-\rho^{m-1}}{1-\rho}\right),\end{aligned}$$

which tends to zero as m tends to infinity. Thus statement (i) does not necessarily require orthogonality among the different idiosyncratic components, as we have assumed in Definition 1.1. If the covariance among idiosyncratic components declines sufficiently fast, then they are canceled out by aggregation. Secondly, let S_m be the variance–covariance matrix of $(\chi_t^1 \ \ \chi_t^2 \ \ \cdots \ \ \chi_t^m)$, let ρ_m be the greatest eigenvalue of S_m, and assume that the ratio ρ_m/m tends to zero as m tends to infinity. Now let C_m be the orthonormal matrix such that $C_m S_m C_m'$ is diagonal. The matrix $\rho_m I_m - C_m S_m C_m'$, where I_m is the identity matrix of size m, is positive semidefinite. Therefore the matrix $C_m'\rho_m I_m C_m - S_m = \rho_m I_m - S_m$ is positive semidefinite. As a consequence, if p_m is the column vector whose components are all equal to $1/m$,

$$\operatorname{var}\left(\frac{1}{m}\sum_{i=1}^m \chi_t^i\right) = p_m' S_m p_m \leq \rho_m/m.$$

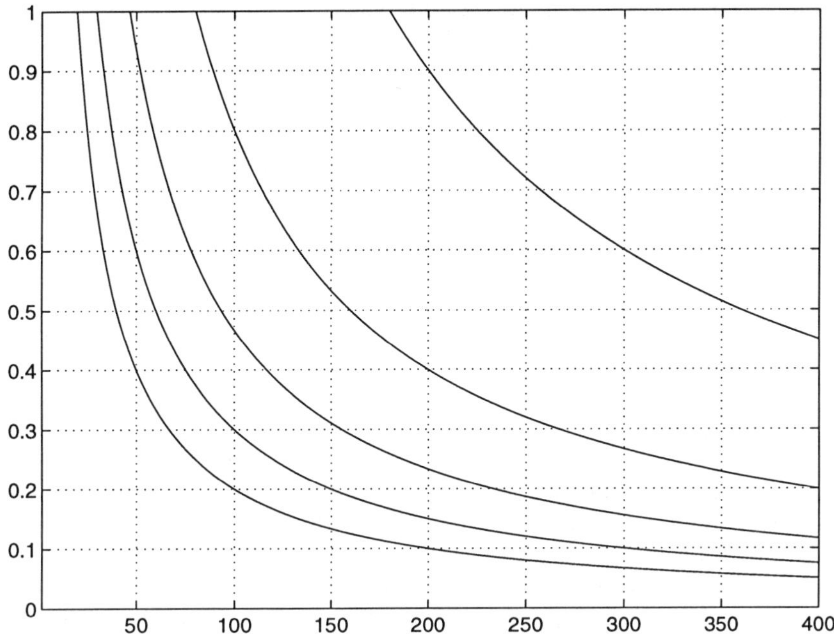

Fig. 1.1. Contour plot of function (1.8)
The contours, from the right to the left, refer to $R^2 = 0.5$, $R^2 = 0.4$, $R^2 = 0.3$, $R^2 = 0.2$, and $R^2 = 0.1$.

If we go back to the case in which S_m is diagonal, we have the trivial fact that unbounded variances of the processes χ_t^i are allowed, provided that the greatest among the first m variances grows slower than m.

1.3.2. One may wonder how large m must be in order to have $R_m^2 = 1$ to a good approximation when there is little correlation among the ζ_t^i's and the idiosyncratic component is large. The following calculation may help to clarify this point. Set $\text{var}(\zeta_t^i) = 1$ and $\text{var}(\chi_t^i) = (1 - R^2)/R^2$ for all i. Now let us assume that the correlation ρ between ζ_t^i and ζ_t^j is positive and identical for any pair i, j, $i \neq j$. Example 1.4 below shows how a model fulfilling the latter condition can be constructed. Assuming $N^i = 1$ for all i we have

$$R_m^2 = \frac{1 + (m-1)\rho}{1/R^2 + (m-1)\rho}. \tag{1.8}$$

Figure 1.1 plots the contours $R_m^2 = 0.95$ of the above function when R^2 is set equal to 0.1, 0.2, 0.3, 0.4, and 0.5; we have ρ on the vertical axis and m on the horizontal axis. In the case of perfect correlation (the top margin of the figure), starting with $R^2 = 0.5$, 20 agents are sufficient to get $R_m^2 > 0.95$. In the case $\rho = 0.2$ and $R^2 = 0.2$ we need $m = 400$.

The following example shows how a sequence with positive constant correlation among any two of its members can be built.

EXAMPLE 1.4. Assume again $h = 1$ and let ρ be a non-negative number smaller than unity. We want to construct a sequence of unit variance linear combinations of the shocks u_{t-k}, $k = 1, \infty$, such that the covariance of any pair of these is ρ. Put

$$\begin{aligned} \zeta_t^1 &= u_t \\ \zeta_t^2 &= \alpha^2 \zeta_t^1 + \beta^2 u_{t-1} \\ &\vdots \\ \zeta_t^i &= \alpha^i (\zeta_t^1 + \zeta_t^2 + \cdots + \zeta_t^{i-1}) + \beta^i u_{t-i+1} \\ &\vdots \end{aligned} \tag{1.9}$$

The existence of coefficients α^i and β^i fulfilling our requirement can be proved by induction. Set $\alpha^2 = \rho$, $\beta^2 = \sqrt{1-\rho^2}$, so that $\mathrm{var}(\zeta_t^2) = 1$ and $\mathrm{corr}(\zeta_t^1, \zeta_t^2) = \rho$. Now suppose that α^i and β^i satisfying the requirement exist for $i < s$. With such coefficients, (1.9) ensures that ζ_t^s has the same correlation $\alpha^s[1 + (s-2)\rho]$ with all the vectors ζ_t^i, $i < s$. Such correlation is equal to ρ if

$$\alpha^s = \frac{\rho}{1 + (s-2)\rho}.$$

By imposing $\mathrm{var}(\zeta_t^s) = 1$ we get

$$(\beta^s)^2 = 1 - \frac{\rho^2(s-1)}{1 + (s-2)\rho}.$$

An easy calculation shows that if $0 \le \rho < 1$, then $0 < (\beta^s)^2 < 1$ for any s. Notice that by setting $\rho = 0$ we reobtain Example 1.1, where Assumption 1.2 is not fulfilled. By contrast, with a positive ρ, Assumption 1.2 is satisfied with $\theta \le \rho$.

REMARK 1.7. Notice that the above construction does not work with $\rho < 0$, since β^s does not exist for all s. Indeed, a constant negative covariance is not possible under Assumption 1.1. Write the variance of $\sum_{i=1}^m \zeta_t^i / m$ as

$$\frac{1}{m^2} \sum_{i=1}^m \mathrm{var}(\zeta_t^i) + \frac{1}{m^2} \sum_{i \neq j} \mathrm{cov}(\zeta_t^i, \zeta_t^j).$$

The first term tends to zero as m goes to infinity. If $\mathrm{cov}(\zeta_t^i, \zeta_t^j) = \rho < 0$, the second term would be

$$\frac{1}{m^2}(m^2 - m)\rho,$$

so that the whole expression would eventually become negative, contradicting the fact that it is a variance.

1.4. A Continuum of Agents

Throughout the book we shall concentrate on methods and results that are valid for finite sets of agents. In the previous section we considered a countably infinite set of agents, but only to pick up finite subsets. Here we briefly review the way in which the definitions of common and idiosyncratic components can be accommodated in the framework of a continuum of agents.

Consider firstly the following example. Let $U = [0, 1]$, and $U^2 = U \times U$. Suppose that each point $i \in U$ represents an agent and that

$$x_t^i = (i - \lambda)u_t + \chi_t^i,$$

where u_t is a unit variance scalar white noise, λ a fixed real number, while χ_t^i is a family of white noises fulfilling $\mathrm{cov}(\chi_t^i, \chi_t^j) = 0$, for $i \neq j$, $\mathrm{var}(\chi_t^i) = \sigma_\chi^2$. The mean of x_t^i is defined as $x_t = \int_U x_t^i di$. We have

$$\mathrm{var}(x_t) = \int_{U^2} \mathrm{cov}(\zeta_t^i, \zeta_t^j) di\, dj + \int_{U^2} \mathrm{cov}(\chi_t^i, \chi_t^j) di\, dj.$$

The second integral is zero, since the covariance $\mathrm{cov}(\chi_t^i, \chi_t^j)$ vanishes outside the diagonal of U^2, which has zero measure. The first integral equals

$$\int_{U^2} (i - \lambda)(j - \lambda) di\, dj = \frac{(1 - 2\lambda)^2}{4}.$$

Notice that the components ζ_t^i can be positively or negatively correlated, according to the coefficients $(i - \lambda)$ in front of u_t, but positive correlation prevails, with the sole exception of $\lambda = 0.5$. It must also be pointed out that since here the number of agents is actually infinite, the fraction of the variance of the aggregated variable due to the idiosyncratic component is zero irrespective of which fraction of the individual variable is explained by the individual idiosyncratic component.

This example can be easily generalized to any distribution $F(i)$ over U. A family

$$x_t^i = \zeta_t^i + \chi_t^i$$

can be defined by giving a collection of functions $c_1(i, j, k)$, $c_2(i, k)$, $i, j \in U$, k integer, and putting

$$\begin{aligned}
&\mathrm{cov}(\zeta_t^i, \zeta_{t-k}^j) = c_1(i, j, k) \\
&\mathrm{cov}(\zeta_t^i, \chi_{t-k}^j) = 0 \\
&\mathrm{cov}(\chi_t^i, \chi_{t-k}^j) = 0, \quad \text{if } i \neq j \\
&\mathrm{cov}(\chi_t^i, \chi_{t-k}^i) = c_2(i, k).
\end{aligned}$$

The functions c_1 and c_2 can be assumed to be F-measurable and fulfilling the positivity conditions for covariance. We have

$$\operatorname{var}(x_t) = \int_{U^2} c_1(i,j,0)dF(i)dF(j) + \int_{U^2} \tilde{c}(i,j)dF(i)dF(j),$$

where $\tilde{c}(i,j)$ equals $c_2(i,0)$ on the diagonal of U^2 and is zero elsewhere. If the diagonal of U^2 has zero F-measure then the aggregate idiosyncratic component has zero variance, i.e. the variance of x_t is equal to the variance of the common component. Notice that the case of a finite set of agents can be accommodated in this framework, with the measure concentrated in a finite number of points. In this case (with a uniform distribution) the diagonal has measure $1/m$, so that the idiosyncratic component gives a decreasing (with m) but positive contribution to $\operatorname{var}(x_t)$.

In Granger (1980) a continuum of agents is considered as the limit of finite populations of m agents as m tends to infinity. The microprocesses are

$$x_t^i = \frac{u_t}{1-\alpha^i L} + \frac{\xi_t^i}{1-\alpha^i L},$$

where u_t and ξ_t^i are scalar white noises fulfilling Definition 1.1. For simplicity we assume that $\operatorname{var}(u_t) = \operatorname{var}(\xi_t^i) = 1$, for any i. In Granger's calculations the spectral density of $m^{-1}\sum_{i=1}^m \xi_t^i/(1-\alpha^i L)$ is approximated by

$$\frac{1}{m}\int_0^1 \frac{1}{|1-\alpha z|^2} p(\alpha)d\alpha, \tag{1.10}$$

where $p(\alpha)$ is a continuous density over U. Using our formulation the limit is

$$\int_{U^2} \frac{1}{1-\alpha z}\frac{1}{1-\beta\bar{z}}\hat{c}(\alpha,\beta)p(\alpha)p(\beta)d\alpha\, d\beta, \tag{1.11}$$

where $\hat{c}$ vanishes outside the diagonal and is equal to unity on the diagonal.

Since $p(\alpha)$ is continuous, the integral (1.11) vanishes independently of whether $p(\alpha)$ is bounded away from unity or not. If α is bounded away from unity, then (1.10) converges to zero, so that the same result turns out both in our formulation and in Granger's. However, if α is not bounded away from unity, so that the idiosyncratic component in Granger's model has no more bounded variance, then (1.10) does not necessarily converge to zero.

For the common component Granger obtains

$$u_t \int_U \frac{1}{1-\alpha L} p(\alpha)d\alpha.$$

Using our formulation, its spectral density is

$$\int_{U^2} \frac{1}{1-\alpha z}\frac{1}{1-\beta\bar{z}}\hat{c}_1(\alpha,\beta,0)p(\alpha)p(\beta)d\alpha\, d\beta = \left|\int_U \frac{1}{1-\alpha z}p(\alpha)d\alpha\right|^2,$$

since $\hat{c}_1$ is equal to unity over U^2.

1.5. Autoregressive Relationships among the Microvariables

Model (1.2) is a moving average representation for a vector with a countable infinity of components, i.e. x_t^i, for $i = 1, \infty$, or $i = -\infty, \infty$ if this second indexation is more convenient. One may be tempted to interpret the moving average (1.2) as a reduced form emerging from a deeper structural representation in which the variables x_t^i are linked by autoregressive relationships. For instance, if x_t^i is agent i's income, then it is reasonable that x_t^i depends on a common source of variation, on an idiosyncratic shock, but also directly on some other agent's income. On the other hand, one can immediately see that when this is the case each individual income depends on some other agent's idiosyncratic shock. Consider for example the following model:

$$x_t^i = \alpha x_{t-1}^i + \alpha x_{t-1}^{i-1} + u_t + \chi_t^i, \tag{1.12}$$

for $i = -\infty, \infty$, where, to fix ideas, we assume that x_t^i is the output of industry i. The product i is necessary for production in industry i and in industry $i-1$. Equation (1.12) has the interpretation that production in industry i at t is driven, *via* inventory replacement, by production at $t-1$ in industries i and $i-1$. Moreover, u_t and χ_t^i are scalar white noises fulfilling Definition 1.1. It is easily seen that if $2\alpha < 1$, the system of infinite equations (1.12) admits the following stationary solutions:

$$x_t^i = \frac{1}{1-2\alpha L}u_t + \frac{1}{1-\alpha L}\chi_t^i + \frac{\alpha L}{1-\alpha L}\chi_t^{i-1} + \frac{\alpha^2 L^2}{1-\alpha L}\chi_t^{i-2} + \cdots.$$

It seems natural to take the term containing u_t as the common component for the variables x_t^i and the sum of the remaining terms as the idiosyncratic component. In this way idiosyncratic components corresponding to different agents, although orthogonal to the common component, are no longer orthogonal to one another. However, it is easily seen that the covariance between the idiosyncratic components of agents i and j declines as fast as $\alpha^{|i-j|}$, so that applying the first result in Remark 1.6, we can conclude that the idiosyncratic component is canceled out by aggregation.

The above consideration can be generalized to the model

$$x_t^i = \sum_{k=-s}^{s} a_{i-k}^i x_{t-1}^{i-k} + u_t + \chi_t^i,$$

in which the product of industry i is employed for production in the $2s+1$ industries 'in the neighborhood' of industry i, provided that there exists a positive real ρ such that

$$\sum_{k=-s}^{s} a_{i-k}^i \leq \rho < 1,$$

for any i, or to other more complicated models. We are not interested in pursuing this analysis here. It will be sufficient to keep in mind that many autoregressive cases can be reduced to moving average models in which covariance among the idiosyncratic components declines geometrically, and that this complication can be easily disposed of as shown in Remark 1.6.

1.6. Bibliographic Notes

Common plus idiosyncratic component representations of heterogeneous variables are used in a number of macroeconomic models, starting with Lucas (1973), Ashenfelter (1978), Lillard and Willis (1978), Altonji and Ashenfelter (1980); more recent examples are Bertola and Caballero (1990), Caballero (1990), Caplin and Leahy (1991), Goodfriend (1992), Forni and Lippi (1994), Pischke (1995).

General dynamic factor or unobservable index models have been introduced in macroeconomics by Sargent and Sims (1977) and Geweke (1977). Important references are Geweke and Singleton (1981), Watson and Engle (1983). These models have been generally employed for analyzing a (relatively small) number of different macroeconomic variables rather than in modeling heterogeneous microvariables.

On fundamentalness in macroeconomic models see Lippi and Reichlin (1993) and the references in Section 12.5 below.

The ideas developed in the present chapter are largely inspired by Granger (1987), where the large numbers implications of the common factors model in a time series framework are amply discussed (see also Granger, 1990). A major difference from our analysis is that Granger's contribution is mainly focused on the single common factor model (1.1).

Chamberlain (1983) and Chamberlain and Rothschild (1983) provide conditions under which a family of stochastic variables x^i, $i = 1, \infty$, possesses a static factor structure: $x^i = \mu^i + \beta_1^i f_1 + \beta_2^i f_2 + \cdots + \beta_h^i f_h + \xi^i$. Precisely, let T_m be the variance–covariance matrix of the vector $(x^1 \quad x^2 \quad \cdots \quad x^m)$, let $\rho_m^{(s)}$ be the s-th eigenvalue of T_m with respect to the descending order. If $\inf_m \rho_m^{(m)} > 0$, $\sup_m \rho_m^{(h)} = \infty$, $\sup_m \rho_m^{(h+1)} < \infty$, then the family has a factor structure with h factors (see Chamberlain, 1983, Theorem 3). The idiosyncratic components ξ^i are orthogonal to the factors but not necessarily to one another. However, if S_m is their variance–covariance matrix, the maximum eigenvalue of S_m remains bounded as m grows (Chamberlain, 1983, p. 1312; Chamberlain and Rothschild, 1983, Theorem 4). This implies that the idiosyncratic component is canceled out by aggregation (Theorem 3 in Chamberlain's paper, or the second argument in our Remark 1.6).

2

How Many Common Shocks?

In the previous chapter we discussed a model with many common shocks and response functions which may differ across agents. Since the simpler model (1.1), with only one common shock, encompasses almost all time series models with heterogeneous agents proposed in recent literature, one may wonder whether such a generalization is really needed.

In the present chapter we conduct an empirical analysis based on US incomes and wages data, in order to get some indication about the number of common shocks. The result is that the single common shock hypothesis is strongly rejected. Moreover, even small numbers of common shocks, like two or three, appear inadequate.

Other evidence on the number of common shocks in macroeconomic data will be presented in Part III. Our purpose here is to show with a paradigmatic case that current models have poor empirical performance, so that a richer heterogeneity not only is theoretically interesting but also has a solid empirical motivation.

2.1. Perfect Correlation

2.1.1. For convenience let us rewrite equation (1.1) here:

$$x_t^i = a^i \zeta_t + \chi_t^i. \tag{2.1}$$

In this section we evaluate the empirical performance of this model.

REMARK 2.1. When (2.1) is fulfilled, we can shift to the one-shock representation

$$x_t^i = a^i a(L) u_t + \chi_t^i,$$

where u_t is a scalar unit variance white noise and $a(L)$ is fundamental. However, this does not necessarily mean that there is only one structural common source of variation in the economy. Going back to model (1.2), we see that (2.1) can be obtained either by assuming $h = 1$, along with response functions identical across agents, up to multiplication by a constant, or by imposing $a_l^i(L) = a^i a_l(L)$ and setting

$$\zeta_t = a_1(L)u_{1t} + a_2(L)u_{2t} + \cdots + a_h(L)u_{ht}.$$

In the latter case, individual incomes may be affected by many independent macroeconomic shocks, such as fiscal policy changes, monetary policy changes, technological improvements, etc., and the responses to different shocks may be different, but different agents react in the same way, up to a scalar, to the shocks. We shall show in Chapter 4 that, if $h > 1$, u_t cannot be given a simple economic interpretation, but turns out to be a complicated linear combination of contemporaneous and past values of the structural shocks u_{lt}.

The first problem we must face in our empirical analysis is lack of individual time series data. Panels are usually too short to give us useful information about the dynamic properties of individual variables. However, there is an indirect way to compare theory and data: equation (2.1) places restrictions on large subaggregates such as economic sectors or regions; regional and sectoral statistics can therefore be used to examine the plausibility of the micromodel.

To clarify this point, let us consider any two large sets of individuals, say regions A and B, and assume that the variable of interest is income. Suppose that individual incomes w_t^i are I(1) and that income changes in deviation from their mean $x_t^i = \Delta w_t^i - \mu^i$ follow model (2.1). Since the idiosyncratic components vanish in the aggregate, averaging over individuals we get

$$x_t^A = \left(\sum_{i\in A} a^i/m^A\right)\zeta_t$$

$$x_t^B = \left(\sum_{i\in B} a^i/m^B\right)\zeta_t.$$

Hence regional per capita income changes x_t^A and x_t^B should be perfectly correlated; by regressing one of them on the other we should get an R^2 equal to unity. The same holds true if total rather than average income is concerned.

2.1.2. We shall check this prediction by using US regional data on total personal income provided by the Bureau of Economic Analysis (July 22, 1993). The data are quarterly, seasonally adjusted, and expressed as annual rates in billions of US dollars. Disaggregation is by state; the period is 1969:I–1992:I. As regards data treatment, we deflated the nominal series with the price index 1987=1, obtained by dividing US total nominal consumption by real consumption. Moreover, we divided by population in order to obtain per capita figures; the quarterly population was constructed by linearly interpolating the annual regional data provided by the BEA (May 26, 1993). Per capita income is expressed in thousands of US dollars.

All the empirical results below are referred to per capita magnitudes. The results obtained for the non-normalized aggregates do not differ in any significant way. However, owing to non-constant population, empirical non-normalized aggregates cannot be immediately accommodated into our model, whereas per capita magnitudes can.

Our model, strictly considered, contains a constant population of infinitely lived agents. However, the model is indistinguishable from one in which agents' births and deaths may occur, provided that the distribution of agents' parameters remains constant: for instance, if the microequation is (2.1), we only need for agents disappearing at t to be replaced by agents having the same coefficients a^i and the same autocovariance structure for the idiosyncratic term.

We can also allow for a growing population. In this case, even though the distribution of agents' parameters is constant, stationarity of the microvariables does not imply stationarity of $\sum x_t^i$. However, $x_t = \sum x_t^i/m_t$ is nearly stationary. Indeed,

$$x_t = \left(\sum_{i=1}^{m_t} a^i/m_t\right)\zeta_t + \sum_{i=1}^{m_t} \chi_t^i/m_t,$$

whose autocovariance at lag k is

$$\frac{\sum_{i=1}^{m_t} a^i}{m_t}\frac{\sum_{i=1}^{m_{t-k}} a^i}{m_{t-k}}\text{cov}(\zeta_t, \zeta_{t-k}) + \text{cov}\left(\sum_{i=1}^{m_t} \chi_t^i/m_t, \sum_{i=1}^{m_{t-k}} \chi_{t-k}^i/m_{t-k}\right).$$

The first term is constant (a constant mean of the a^i's is sufficient). The second depends on t but is negligible for m_t large.

In the same way, under the assumption of distributional invariance of agents' parameters, if the variables w_t^i are I(1) then $\sum w_t^i$ is not I(1), whereas $w_t = \sum w_t^i/m_t$ is I(1), apart from a negligible term. Distributional invariance within each state is therefore what is needed in order to apply the model to our empirical data.

2.1.3. The I(1) representation is not rejected for states' per capita incomes. The DF, ADF(2), and ADF(4) test statistics (with trend) are shown in Figure 2.1 (for the state codes see Table 2.3 at the end of the chapter). The null of a difference–stationary income is rejected at the 5% significance level only for seven states by the DF test, for one state by the ADF(2) test, and for one state by the ADF(4) test. States 22 (Nebraska) and 24 (South Dakota) do not pass two of the three tests; there are no states for which the null is rejected by all the tests.

These results allow us to proceed with our exercise by taking differences and analyzing correlation. Before going on, however, a simple inspection of the graph of some selected series (Figure 2.2) should persuade the reader that correlation among different states is very far from perfect. Massachusetts' per capita income is smooth, whereas North Dakota exhibits a

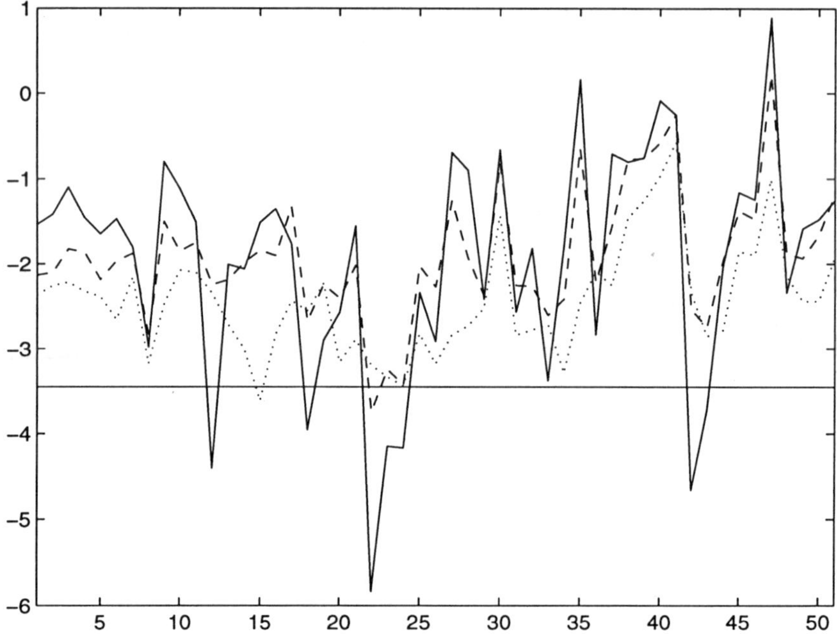

Fig. 2.1. ADF test statistics
DF: solid line. ADF(2): dashed line. ADF(4): dotted line.

large negative autocorrelation in differences; Alaska grows quickly in the middle seventies, when Massachusetts and North Dakota go down, and declines in the eighties, when the other states, including West Virginia, go up. Such different behaviors are clearly inconsistent with perfect positive correlation of income changes.

Now let us take first differences and subtract the mean. Figure 2.3 is a density plot illustrating the R^2 obtained by performing pairwise OLS regressions. Black cells indicate $R^2 > 0.66$; obviously diagonal cells are black, since $R^2 = 1$. Two different gray intensities represent the cases $0.33 < R^2 \leq 0.66$ (dark gray) and $0.05 < R^2 \leq 0.33$ (light gray). Lastly, white cells indicate $R^2 < 0.05$. Obviously the plot is symmetric with respect to the diagonal.

Alaska (state 46) should be considered as a quite particular case, since it appears to be orthogonal to all the other states. But even excluding Alaska, in many cases the R^2, far from being unity, is very close to zero. Out of the 1275 R^2 in the lower-right triangle (excluding the diagonal), 195 (15.3%) are below 0.05, 723 (56.7%) are between 0.05 and 0.33, 338 (26.5%) are between 0.033 and 0.66, while only 19 (1.5%) are above 0.66. The median R^2 is 0.21; the mean is 0.23.

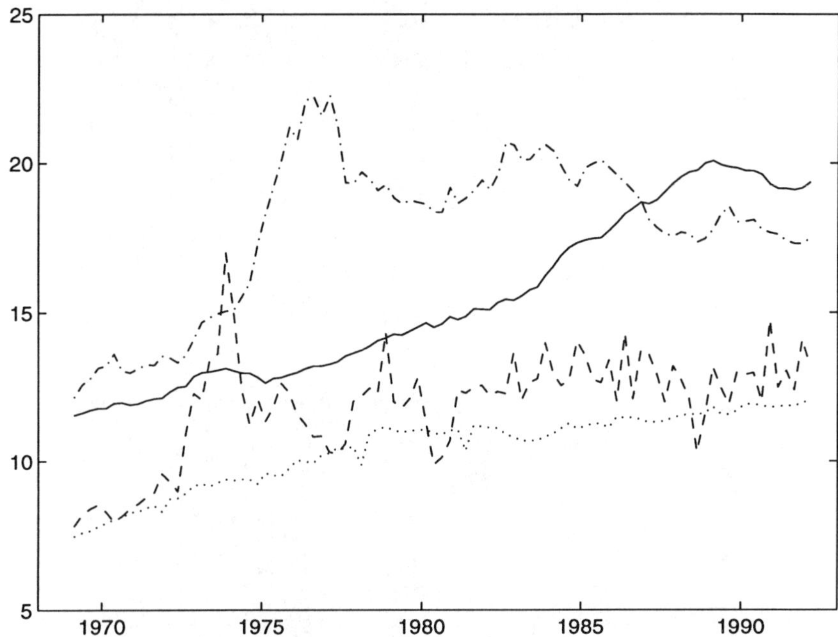

Fig. 2.2. Per capita income of some US states

Massachusetts: solid line. North Dakota: dashed line. West Virginia: dotted line. Alaska: dotted–dashed line.

2.1.4. Is there any test we can apply in order to reject the null hypothesis of perfect correlation? It is not difficult to see that such a test would give a trivial result. Indeed, under the null hypothesis of perfect theoretical correlation the distribution of the empirical R^2 is degenerate, i.e. $R^2 = 1$ with probability 1; hence, if $R^2 < 1$, the null hypothesis is always rejected at any significance level.

However, we should not be so severe as to require $R^2 = 1$. Observed data are subject to measurement errors which may be large in some cases, so that we would observe $R^2 < 1$ even if the true data were perfectly correlated. Besides measurement errors, a non-zero residual may arise from misspecification having little practical importance: it would be hard to conclude that the model is bad for empirical analysis when observing, say, $R^2 = 0.95$ or even $R^2 = 0.9$.

Hence, we are forced to replace formal significance tests with a pragmatic criterion: the model is good if the estimated R^2 reaches some 'acceptance' level. For instance, one could be satisfied with $R^2 = 0.9$. Admittedly, the choice of the critical level is largely a matter of tastes; but surely the large majority of the R^2 represented in Figure 2.3 would not pass the test under whatever reasonable criterion. As regards measurement errors, if they were so large as to account for a substantial fraction of the above results, we

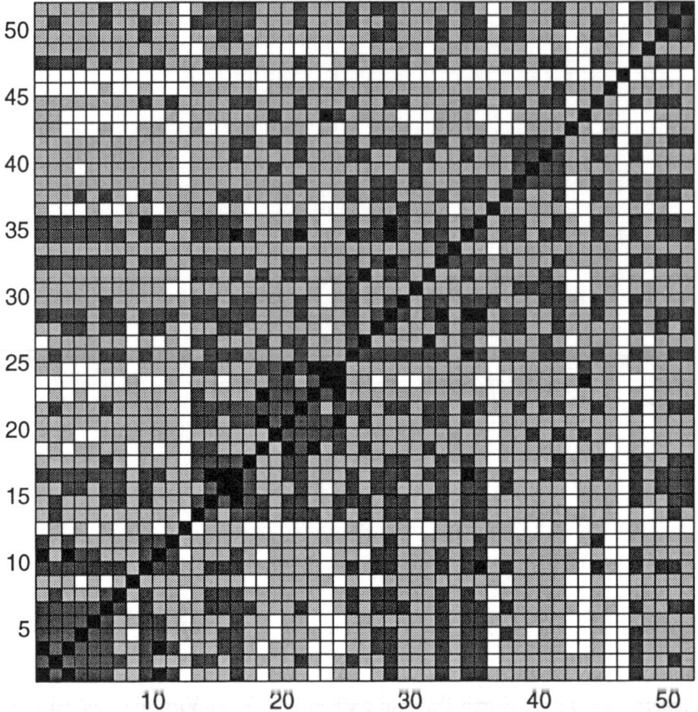

Fig. 2.3. R^2 from pairwise static regressions
White: $R^2 \leq 0.05$. Light gray: $0.05 < R^2 \leq 0.33$. Dark gray: $0.33 < R^2 \leq 0.66$. Black: $R^2 > 0.66$.

should abandon any attempt at empirical analysis.

2.2. Pairwise Singularity

2.2.1. We have seen that model (2.1) is very far from matching the data. In this section we slightly relax the perfect correlation assumption. Precisely, we specify model (1.2) by setting $a_l^i = a^i(L)a_l(L)$:

$$x_t^i = a^i(L)\zeta_t + \chi_t^i$$
$$\zeta_t = a_1(L)u_{1t} + a_2(L)u_{2t} + \cdots + a_h(L)u_{ht},$$

so that we can shift to the representation $x_t^i = a^i(L)a(L)u_t + \chi_t^i$, with only one common shock (see Remark 2.1).

This means that all the vectors

$$(\, \zeta_t^i \quad \zeta_t^j \,) = (\, a^i(L)a(L)u_t \quad a^j(L)a(L)u_t \,)$$

for $i \neq j$ are singular, i.e. the residuals of their joint Wold representation have singular covariance matrix (see Section A.6 in the Appendix). This is equivalent to saying that $(\zeta_t^i \quad \zeta_t^j)$ has singular spectral density matrix (see Theorem A.7 in the Appendix). The same holds for the aggregate variables corresponding to two large subgroups A and B:

$$\begin{aligned} x_t^A &= a^A(L)u_t \\ x_t^B &= a^B(L)u_t, \end{aligned} \tag{2.2}$$

where $a^A(L) = \sum_{i \in A} a^i(L)/m^A$ and $a^B(L) = \sum_{i \in B} a^i(L)/m^B$.

Pairwise singularity is a weaker property than perfect correlation. When two variables are perfectly correlated, regressing one of them on the other gives a null residual. When two variables are singular, we obtain a null residual by regressing one of them on the present, past, and future of the other. To see this, assume for simplicity that in (2.2) $a^B(L)$ does not vanish on the unit circle. In this case we can invert $a^B(L)$ to obtain

$$x_t^A = \frac{a^A(L)}{a^B(L)} x_t^B, \tag{2.3}$$

where the operator $a^A(L)/a^B(L)$ has in general a bilateral power series expansion (see Section A.3 in the Appendix).

EXAMPLE 2.1. If for instance $a^A(L) = 1$ and $a^B(L) = (1 - 2L)/(1 - 0.5L)$, we have

$$\begin{aligned} x_t^A &= \frac{1 - 0.5L}{1 - 2L} x_t^B = \frac{0.25 - 0.5F}{1 - 0.5F} x_t^B \\ &= (0.25 - 0.5F)(1 + 0.5F + 0.5^2F^2 + 0.5^3F^3 + \cdots)x_t^B, \end{aligned} \tag{2.4}$$

where $F = L^{-1}$ is the forward operator $Fx_t^B = x_{t+1}^B$ (see Section A.3 in the Appendix).

We shall return to this example later. Here we merely wanted to show that future values of x_t^B can enter the relation above and must therefore be included in empirical regressions aimed at testing $R^2 = 1$.

REMARK 2.2. As argued in the previous section, in empirical analysis we cannot expect that the estimated R^2 be exactly 1, even when the theoretical R^2 is unity. This problem is more relevant here than in the case of perfect correlation, since here, in addition to measurement errors, we have a further source of spurious residual variance: empirical series are often short, so that in practice we are forced to ignore high-order leads and lags of the variable on the right-hand side also when they are present in the theoretical relation.

EXAMPLE 2.2. To get an idea of this effect let us reconsider the example above. Notice that the coefficients have been chosen in such a way that x_t^B is a white-noise process. In fact, the spectrum of x_t^B is

$$\frac{1 - 0.5e^{-i\phi}}{1 - 2e^{-i\phi}} \frac{1 - 0.5e^{i\phi}}{1 - 2e^{i\phi}} \sigma_u^2 = 4\sigma_u^2.$$

Since the spectrum is constant, x_t^B is serially uncorrelated (see Section A.7 in the Appendix). Inasmuch as x_t^B is white noise, the theoretical parameters of (2.4) remain the same when truncating leads. Hence, if we exclude leads higher than one from the right-hand side of the regression, we get

$$x_t^A = 0.25x_t^B - 0.375x_{t+1}^B + v_t,$$

where v_t is the residual. Since $\text{var}(x_t^B) = 4\sigma_u^2 = 4\text{var}(x_t^A)$, the variance of v_t is 3/16 times the total variance, i.e. the theoretical R^2 is near 0.8. Of course, the problem is potentially even more relevant when $a^B(L)$ vanishes near the unit circle, since in this case we should include many leads and lags to get a good approximation of the theoretical relation (2.3).

2.2.2. In order to implement our analysis we fix a maximum lead and a maximum lag simply by starting with a static regression and adding jointly one lead and one lag until the adjusted R^2, denoted by $\bar{R}^2$, ceases growing.

Results are shown in Figure 2.4. Clearly the inclusion of leads and lags gives little improvement with respect to the figures of the previous section. Out of the 1275 R^2 in the lower-right triangle, 139 (10.9%) are below 0.05, 696 (54.6%) are between 0.05 and 0.33, 411 (32.2%) are between 0.33 and 0.66, 29 (2.3%) are above 0.66. The median R^2 is 0.24; the mean is 0.27.

As regards tests, the considerations in the previous section apply: we cannot test directly for singularity just as we cannot test for perfect correlation. However, in the following section we shall test for pairwise cointegration. Since pairwise singularity is a degenerate case of pairwise cointegration, rejection of the latter implies rejection of both pairwise singularity and perfect correlation.

2.3. Pairwise Cointegration

2.3.1. Let us firstly recall the basic notions on permanent and transitory shocks. Consider the microequation

$$\Delta w_t - \mu = x_t = a_1(L)u_{1t} + a_2(L)u_{2t} + \cdots + a_h(L)u_{ht} + \chi_t,$$

where the index i has been dropped to simplify notation. The shock u_{lt} is permanent for w_t when the associated response function $a_l(L)$ does not

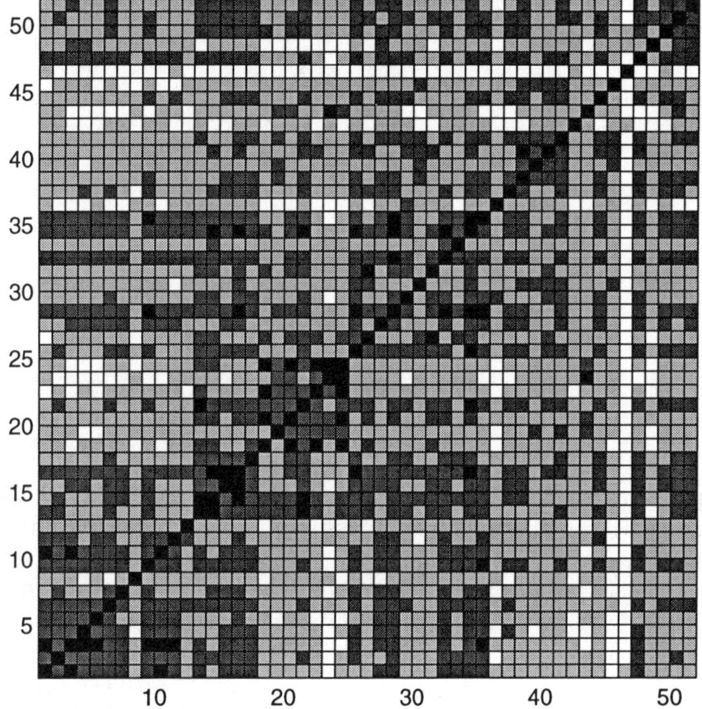

Fig. 2.4. $\bar{R}^2$ from pairwise dynamic regressions
White: $R^2 \leq 0.05$. Light gray: $0.05 < R^2 \leq 0.33$. Dark gray: $0.33 < R^2 \leq 0.66$. Black: $R^2 > 0.66$.

vanish for $L = 1$. On the contrary, if $a_l(1) = 0$, u_{lt} is transitory. For instance, if

$$\Delta w_t = u_{1t} + (1 - L)u_{2t}, \tag{2.5}$$

then u_{1t} is permanent, while u_{2t} is transitory.

The reason for these definitions is that the number $a_l(1)$ measures the long-run effect of a unitary shock u_{lt} on the process w_t. To see this, consider first that

$$w_{t+k} = \mu(k+1) + w_{t-1} + x_t + x_{t+1} + \cdots + x_{t+k}.$$

Then consider two particular realizations of the process x_t, namely x'_t and x''_t, generated by identical shocks, except for $t = \tau$, $l = \lambda$, where $u'_{\lambda\tau} = 1$, $u''_{\lambda\tau} = 0$. Now let $\sum_{s=0}^{\infty} a_{\lambda s} L^s$ be the power series expansion of $a_\lambda(L)$. We have $x'_{\tau-k} - x''_{\tau-k} = 0$ for $k > 0$, so that $w'_{\tau-1} = w''_{\tau-1}$. Moreover,

$$\begin{aligned} x'_\tau - x''_\tau &= a_{\lambda 0} \\ x'_{\tau+1} - x''_{\tau+1} &= a_{\lambda 1} \\ &\vdots \\ x'_{\tau+k} - x''_{\tau+k} &= a_{\lambda k} \\ &\vdots \end{aligned}$$

so that $w'_{\tau+k} - w''_{\tau+k} = \sum_{s=0}^{k} a_{\lambda s}$, and

$$\lim_{k\to\infty} w'_{\tau+k} - w''_{\tau+k} = \sum_{s=0}^{\infty} a_s = a_\lambda(1).$$

In particular, when $a_l(1) = 0$, a unit shock does not modify the level of w in the long run (notice that the assumption $a_l(1) = 0$ is equivalent to assuming that $a_l(L)$ may be factored as $(1-L)b_l(L)$). In (2.5) a unitary value of u_{2t} at τ raises w by 1 at τ but lowers it by the same amount at time $\tau + 1$, so that w comes back to its previous level if no other shocks occur. By contrast, $u_{1\tau} = 1$ changes w by 1 permanently.

2.3.2. Now for convenience let us rewrite model (1.2) for Δw_t^i:

$$\Delta w_t^i = \mu^i + a_1^i(L)u_{1t} + a_2^i(L)u_{2t} + \cdots + a_h^i(L)u_{ht} + \chi_t^i. \tag{2.6}$$

The assumption that w_t^i is I(1) means that either one of the shocks u_{lt} is permanent or the idiosyncratic shock is permanent. For, if all the shocks were transitory, integrating (2.6) we would get a stationary variable plus a deterministic trend, i.e. a trend stationary variable. If the idiosyncratic shock were the only permanent one, the aggregate w_t would be trend stationary, but this is contrary to the ADF tests in Section 2.1. Thus we can assume that at least one of the common shocks is permanent. In this section we shall assume that exactly one of the common shocks is permanent, so that (2.6) can be rewritten as

$$\Delta w_t^i - \mu^i = a_1^i(L)u_{1t} + (1-L)[b_2^i(L)u_{2t} + \cdots + b_h^i(L)u_{ht}] + \chi_t^i. \tag{2.7}$$

Clearly this model is equivalent to one in which there is more than one permanent common shock but the responses to them are as in Section 2.2, or as in Section 2.1.[1] Moreover, rejection of (2.7) implies rejection both of singularity and of perfect correlation.

[1] Incidentally, notice that the common component in Sections 2.1 and 2.2 must be permanent.

When (2.7) holds, the per capita incomes of the two regions A and B are, with an obvious notation,

$$\begin{aligned} x_t^A &= a^A(L)u_{1t} + (1-L)b_2^A(L)u_{2t} + \cdots + (1-L)b_h^A(L)u_{ht} \\ x_t^B &= a^B(L)u_{1t} + (1-L)b_2^B(L)u_{2t} + \cdots + (1-L)b_h^B(L)u_{ht}. \end{aligned} \tag{2.8}$$

Equations (2.8) imply that if w_t^A and w_t^B are I(1) (i.e. both $a^A(1)$ and $a^B(1)$ are non-zero) then they are cointegrated, up to a deterministic trend, with cointegrating vector $(\, a^B(1) \quad -a^A(1)\,)$.[2] To prove this, we must show that the linear combination $\phi_t = a^B(1)w_t^A - a^A(1)w_t^B$ is trend stationary. We have

$$(1-L)\phi_t = \nu + [a^B(1)a^A(L) - a^A(1)a^B(L)]u_{1t} + (1-L)\psi_t, \tag{2.9}$$

where

$$\begin{aligned} \psi_t = {} & a^B(1)[b_2^B(L)u_{2t} + \cdots + b_h^B(L)u_{ht}] \\ & - a^A(1)[b_2^B(L)u_{2t} + \cdots + b_h^B(L)u_{ht}], \end{aligned}$$

and $\nu = a^B(1)\mu^A - a^A\mu^B$. Clearly the operator in square brackets in (2.9) vanishes for $L = 1$, so that it may be factored as $(1-L)c(L)$. Integrating both sides gives

$$\phi_t = \gamma + \nu t + c(L)u_{1t} + \psi_t.$$

Since ψ_t is stationary, ϕ_t is trend stationary.

2.3.3. Figures 2.5 and 2.6 illustrate respectively the results of λ-max and trace pairwise cointegration tests, obtained by following Johansen's procedure; we included two lags in the VAR in levels along with an unrestricted deterministic trend.[3] White cells indicate no cointegration. Light gray indicates that the null hypothesis of no cointegration is rejected at the 10% significance level, but cannot be rejected at the 5% level. Dark gray stands for rejection at the 5%, but not at the 1%, level. Lastly, black means that the probability value of the null is less than 1%.

The overall result is that the large majority of couples are not cointegrated. Excluding the diagonal cells, for which cointegration is trivial, white cells form 67% according to the trace test and 78% according to the maximum eigenvalue test. These figures provide clear-cut evidence against specification (2.7).

[2] Following the terminology in Campbell and Perron (1991), incomes are 'stochastically' cointegrated.

[3] Critical values are taken from Osterwald-Lenum (1992, Table 2). We have obtained similar results also with a restricted trend model (case 2* in Osterwald-Lenum, 1992).

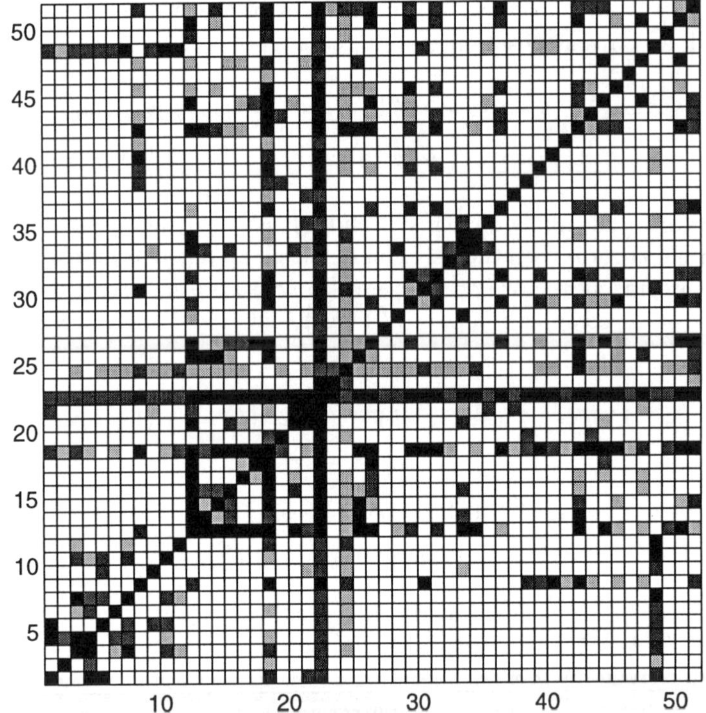

Fig. 2.5. Pairwise cointegration tests (VAR(2), λ-max)
λ-max rank 1 statistic $= \zeta$. White: $\zeta \leq 14.84$. Light gray: $14.84 < \zeta \leq 16.87$. Dark gray: $16.87 < \zeta \leq 21.47$. Black: $\zeta > 21.47$.

2.4. How Many Common Shocks?

2.4.1. In the previous sections we have seen that models in which the common components of individual agents are perfectly correlated, pairwise singular, or pairwise cointegrated, have very poor empirical performances. This may be rephrased by saying that the minimum number of common shocks, or of permanent common shocks, is definitely larger than one. However, the question remains: what is the minimum number of common shocks necessary to get a satisfactory empirical result?[4]

Here we generalize both the cointegration analysis of the previous section and the singularity analysis of Section 2.2, in order to get information about the number of common shocks. Let us consider M subaggregates (states) $G^1, \ldots, G^M$, each being large enough to make the idiosyncratic component

[4] The reason for the expression 'minimum number of common shocks' should be clear: for example, empirical analysis cannot distinguish between the case $h = 1$ and the case in which $h > 1$ but agents respond in the same way, as in Section 2.1.

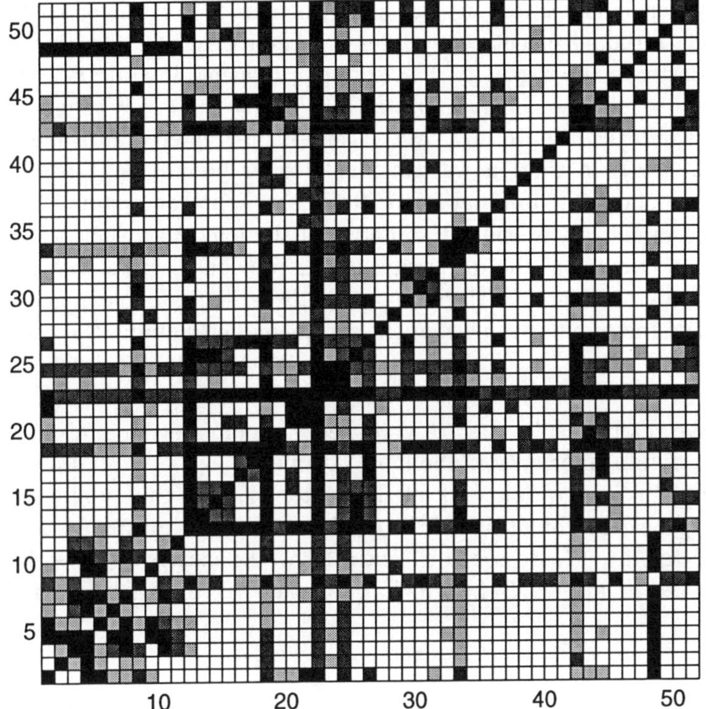

Fig. 2.6. Pairwise cointegration tests (VAR(2), trace)

Trace rank 1 statistic = η. White: $\eta \leq 16.06$. Light gray: $16.06 < \eta \leq 18.17$. Dark gray: $18.17 < \eta \leq 23.46$. Black: $\eta > 23.46$.

negligible. Let us also assume that M is greater than the number of common shocks h.[5] The per capita variable (income change) of state s is

$$x_t^{G^s} = a_1^{G^s}(L)u_{1t} + a_2^{G^s}(L)u_{2t} + \cdots + a_h^{G^s}(L)u_{ht},$$

where $a_l^{G^s}(L) = \sum_{i \in G^s} a_l^i(L)$. With an obvious matrix notation we have

$$X_t = A(L)u_t, \tag{2.10}$$

where X_t is an M-vector and u_t is an h-vector.

Since the components of u_t are mutually orthogonal, the rank r of X_t as a stochastic vector is the rank of the $M \times h$ matrix $A(L)$.[6] Notice that r is not necessarily equal to the number of common shocks: the case $r < h$ corresponds either to the case in which the responses to the shocks are

[5] In the next chapter we shall analyze a model where the number of non-individual shocks is greater than the number of states.

[6] See the observations at the end of Section A.7 in the Appendix.

linearly dependent across agents, as in Sections 2.1 or 2.2, or to the case in which, although agents' responses are heterogeneous, aggregation over states destroys heterogeneity. For example, if agents in state G^s replicate, as a population, the agents in state G^M, for $s = 1, M-1$, then $A(L)$ has rank 1 whatever h is. In any case, r cannot be greater than h (remember that $M > h$), so that, if we can find a lower bound for r, we have an indication about the minimum number of shocks in the system.

In the same way, consider the matrix of the long-run responses $A(1)$: it should be clear from the discussion in the previous section that non-zero columns are associated with permanent shocks, so that we can get a lower bound for the number of permanent shocks by determining the rank r^* of $A(1)$.

2.4.2. We shall consider first r^* and then r. Cointegration analysis can be used to obtain information about r^*. Define W_t by $X_t = \Delta W_t - \mu$. The 'stochastic' cointegration rank of the vector W_t (i.e. the number of independent linear combinations of the entries of W_t that are trend stationary) is equal to $M - r^*$. To see this, notice that the matrix $A(L) - A(1)$ can be factored as $(1-L)B(L)$, so that equation (2.10) can be rewritten as follows:

$$X_t = B(L)\Delta u_t + A(1)u_t.$$

If $A(1)$ has rank r^*, there exists a full rank $M - r^* \times M$ matrix C such that $CA(1) = 0$. By premultiplying the above equation by C and integrating we get $CW_t = \gamma + C\mu t + CB(L)u_t$, which implies that CW_t is trend stationary.

Estimating the cointegration rank of W_t would give an estimate of r^*; unfortunately, testing for the cointegration rank of a 51-dimensional vector is impossible, owing to the insufficient number of observations over time. Therefore we analyzed vectors of lower dimension, by selecting groups of two, three, four, five, and six states: clearly, if a group of q states has zero cointegration rank (i.e. it is not cointegrated), then r^* cannot be less than q.

We did not analyze all of the possible groups of states since they are too many: with $q = 4$, for instance, we have over five million groups. Hence we proceeded as follows. For the case $q = 2$ we simply took the results of Section 2.3. For the cases $q = 3, 4, 5, 6$ we selected at random 1000 groups of states and tested for cointegration by following Johansen's procedure with a VAR(2) model including an unrestricted deterministic trend, as in Section 2.3.

Results are shown in Table 2.1. In the first column we see the percentage of groups that are not cointegrated at the 90% confidence level according to the trace test and the maximum eigenvalue test. The other columns show the percentages of groups such that the null of no cointegration can be rejected respectively with probability value between 0.1 and 0.05, between

Table 2.1. Percentages of cointegrated groups with $q = 2, 3, 4, 5, 6$

Significance level	No coint.	10%	5%	1%	Total
Trace test					
$q = 2$	83.9	4.7	5.9	5.6	100
$q = 3$	52.7	11.6	15.4	20.3	100
$q = 4$	31.9	9.4	19.2	39.5	100
$q = 5$	16.3	9.4	19.8	54.5	100
$q = 6$	7.1	5.0	15.9	72.0	100
Lambda test					
$q = 2$	89.2	3.4	3.8	3.6	100
$q = 3$	60.2	9.8	15.7	14.3	100
$q = 4$	40.4	11.5	22.8	25.3	100
$q = 5$	31.5	12.0	21.4	35.1	100
$q = 6$	23.6	13.2	25.9	37.3	100

0.05 and 0.01, and less than 0.01. Obviously, the larger q, the higher the percentage of cointegrated groups. Notice that almost all the groups of six states appear to be cointegrated according to the trace test.

2.4.3. Now let us return to equation (2.10). Since $A(L)$ has rank r, we can find a white-noise r-vector $\tilde{u}_t$, with unit variance and mutually orthogonal components, and a matrix $\tilde{A}(L)$, such that

$$X_t = \tilde{A}(L)\tilde{u}_t, \tag{2.11}$$

where $\tilde{A}(L)$ is $M \times r$ with rank equal to r.[7] Without loss of generality we can assume that the upper $r \times r$ submatrix of $\tilde{A}(L)$, call it $\hat{A}(L)$, is non-singular, so that, taking the first r components of X_t, we have

$$\hat{X}_t = \hat{A}(L)\tilde{u}_t. \tag{2.12}$$

From (2.12) we get

$$\hat{A}_{\text{ad}}(L)\hat{X}_t = \det \hat{A}(L)\tilde{u}_t. \tag{2.13}$$

If $\det \hat{A}(L)$ does not vanish on the unit circle we can write

$$\tilde{u}_t = \hat{B}(L)\hat{X}_t,$$

where, since $\hat{A}(L)$ is not necessarily fundamental, $\hat{B}(L)$ may contain both positive and negative powers of L. Finally, using (2.11),

$$X_t = \tilde{A}(L)\hat{B}(L)\hat{X}_t.$$

[7] See, again, the observations at the end of Section A.7 in the Appendix.

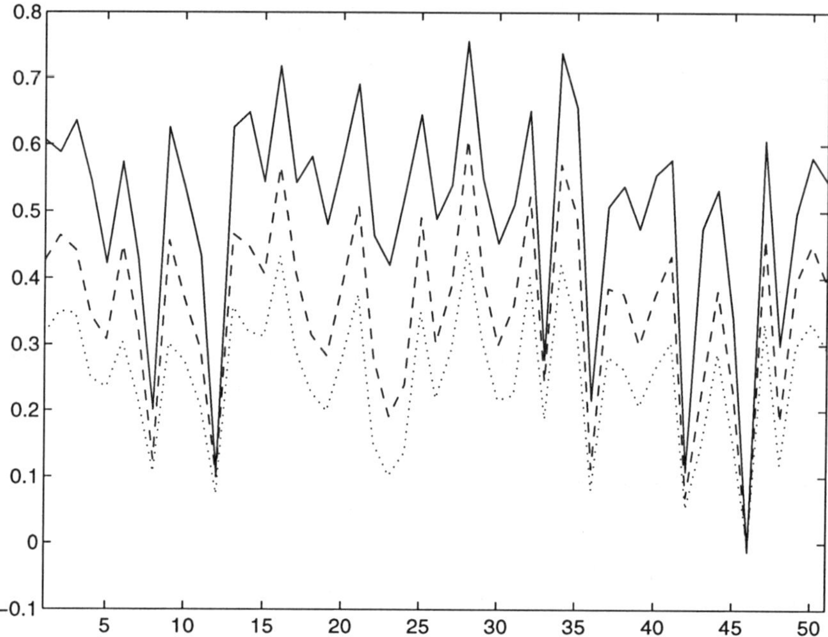

Fig. 2.7. Mean $\bar{R}^2$ with $q = 1, 2, 6$
$q = 1$: dotted line. $q = 2$: dashed line. $q = 6$: solid line.

Thus if a group G of r states constituting a non-singular vector can be found, we should obtain $R^2 = 1$ in the regression of any other state over past, present, and future values of the states in G. This implies that if we find low R^2's using a group of q states, then r must be larger than q.

We performed OLS dynamic regressions by including one, two, three, four, five, and six states on the right-hand side and calculated the goodness of fit. With $q > 1$ a difficulty arises: the states appearing as regressors can be cointegrated (as we have just seen, cointegration is more and more likely as q increases). If cointegration cannot be rejected, regressions may give low R^2's, owing to (near) non-invertibility of the determinant in (2.13).[8]

In order to avoid this problem, we randomly selected 50 six-dimensional 'explanatory' vectors $\hat{X}_t$ whose levels are not cointegrated according to both the trace and the maximum eigenvalue test. We did this for each 'dependent' state, each time excluding the dependent state from the set of possible regressors. Then we performed six regressions for each dependent state and each explanatory vector $\hat{X}_t$, by including on the right-hand side the first regressor $\hat{x}_t^1$, the first two, the first three, and so on.

For each regression we included one lead and one lag of the explanatory

[8] For a discussion of the invertibility problem see Sections A.3 and A.6 in the Appendix.

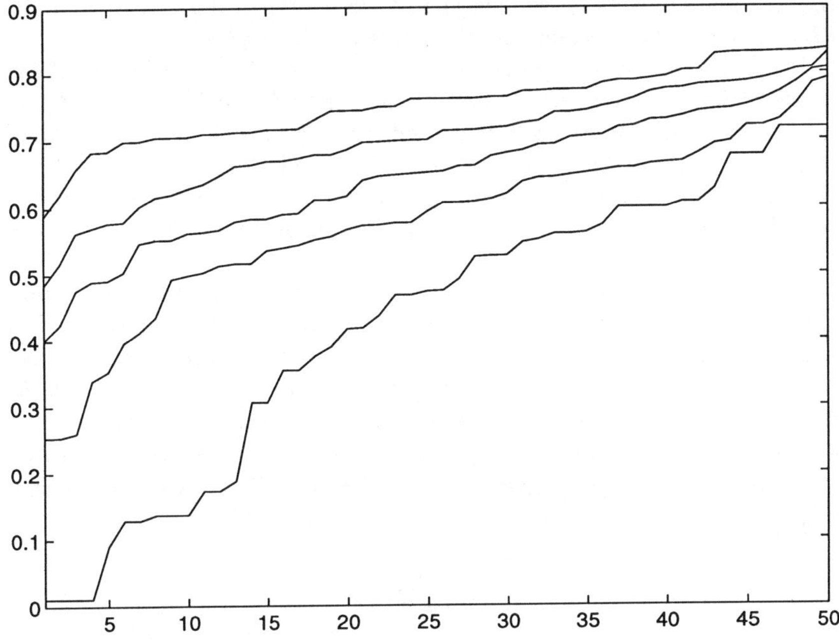

Fig. 2.8. $\bar{R}^2$ for Georgia with $q = 1, 2, 3, 4, 6$

variables. We did not try a more accurate dynamic specification because of the computational difficulties involved; thus when evaluating results the reader should take into account that a better dynamic specification could give better figures.

In Figure 2.7 we report the mean $\bar{R}^2$ for each state with $q = 1, 2, 6$. Notice that there are some states (in particular Alaska (46), Idaho (42), Pennsylvania (12), and District of Columbia (8)) whose explained variance remains very low even with six regressors. For the other states, however, the $\bar{R}^2$ increases from about 0.3 to about 0.6.

In Figure 2.8 we show all the $\bar{R}^2$, ordered by size, for Georgia (28), which is the state reaching the maximum mean $\bar{R}^2$ (over 0.75) with $q = 6$. Notice that, as the number of regressors increases, the curves become flatter and flatter, indicating that the particular choice of the regressors loses importance in determining the explained variance.

2.5. Dynamic Principal Components

2.5.1. Figure 2.8 shows clearly that the goodness of fit varies widely depending on the set of regressors selected, particularly when the number of regressors is low: with $q = 1$, for instance, the $\bar{R}^2$ varies from 0 to about

0.75. What figure should we look at in order to reject the null hypothesis of $h = q$ common shocks against the alternative $h > q$?

Clearly, if there were no measurement errors, we could consider indifferently any set of regressors, since all of them should give $R^2 = 1$ under the null. By contrast, if there are errors, a safer rejection is obtained by looking at the best fit rather than the worst one. Assume for instance that state A is affected by a large measurement error, while the others are not: selecting state A as a regressor can lead us to rejection of the hypothesis $h = q$ even if it is true.

Hence, loosely speaking, we should find the 'best regressors'. Two problems must be solved in order to develop this idea. Firstly, a regressor that works well with Georgia may perform poorly with another 'dependent' state, so that we must define an overall measure for the goodness of fit. A quite natural choice is the ratio of the sum of explained variances to the sum of total variances; that is, if $C(L)\hat{X}_t$ with variance matrix Σ_q is the projection of X_t on the present, past, and future of $\hat{X}_t$, we look for the vector $\hat{X}_t$ which maximizes

$$\hat{R}_q^2 = \frac{\operatorname{trace}\Sigma_q}{\operatorname{trace}\Sigma_X}. \tag{2.14}$$

Notice that $\hat{R}_q^2$ is a weighted sum of states' theoretical R^2's, the weights being the variances of the states.

The second problem is that until now we have considered only explanatory vectors $\hat{X}_t$ whose components are states; but it is quite clear that we could just as well take static linear combinations of states or, more generally, dynamic linear combinations satisfying

$$\hat{X}_t = B(L)X_t, \tag{2.15}$$

where $B(L)$ is a $q \times M$ bilateral linear filter.

The solution to both problems is given by a dynamic generalization of principal component analysis. The elements of the vector $\hat{X}_t$ fulfilling (2.15) that maximizes $\hat{R}_q^2$ are called the principal component series of X_t. Without loss of generality we can order the variables in $\hat{X}_t$ by variance; the j-th element of $\hat{X}_t$ is called the j-th principal component series of X_t.

The principal component series are orthogonal at all leads and lags; denoting by $S_X(\phi)$, $-\pi < \phi \leq \pi$, the spectral density matrix of X_t, and by $\mu_j(\phi)$ the j-th latent root of $S_X(\phi)$, the spectrum of the j-th principal component series is $\mu_j(\phi)$, $-\pi < \phi \leq \pi$. Moreover, denoting by $S_q(\phi)$ the spectral matrix of $C(L)\hat{X}_t$, we have

$$\operatorname{trace} S_q(\phi) = \sum_{j=1}^{q} \mu_j(\phi),$$

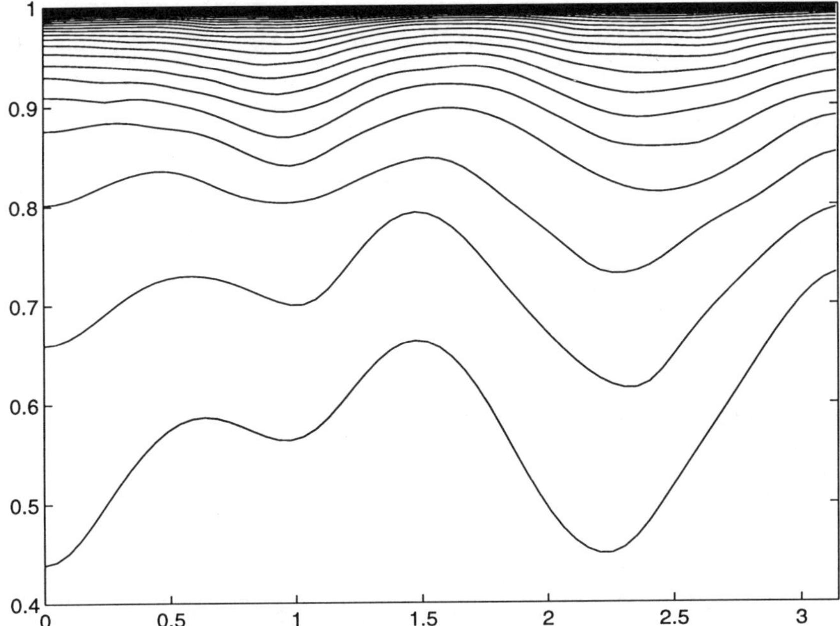

Fig. 2.9. Estimates of $C_q(\phi)$ with $q = 1, 51$

while

$$\operatorname{trace} S_X(\phi) = \sum_{j=1}^{M} \mu_j(\phi). \tag{2.16}$$

Hence, the quantity

$$C_q(\phi) = \frac{\sum_{j=1}^{q} \mu_j(\phi)}{\sum_{j=1}^{M} \mu_j(\phi)} \tag{2.17}$$

is a weighted average of the squared coherences in each state regression, where the weights are the spectra of the dependent states, and measures the overall fit obtained with the first q principal components at each frequency ϕ. Finally, it is easily seen from definition (2.14) that the maximum $\hat{R}_q^2$ is[9]

$$\hat{R}_q^2 = \frac{\int_0^{\pi} \sum_{j=1}^{q} \mu_j(\phi) d\phi}{\int_0^{\pi} \sum_{j=1}^{M} \mu_j(\phi) d\phi}.$$

2.5.2. We estimated $C_q(\phi)$, $q = 1, 50$, by estimating the spectral density matrix of states personal income, calculating the eigenvalues at 129 equally

[9] For further details on principal components in the frequency domain see Brillinger (1981) and the references therein.

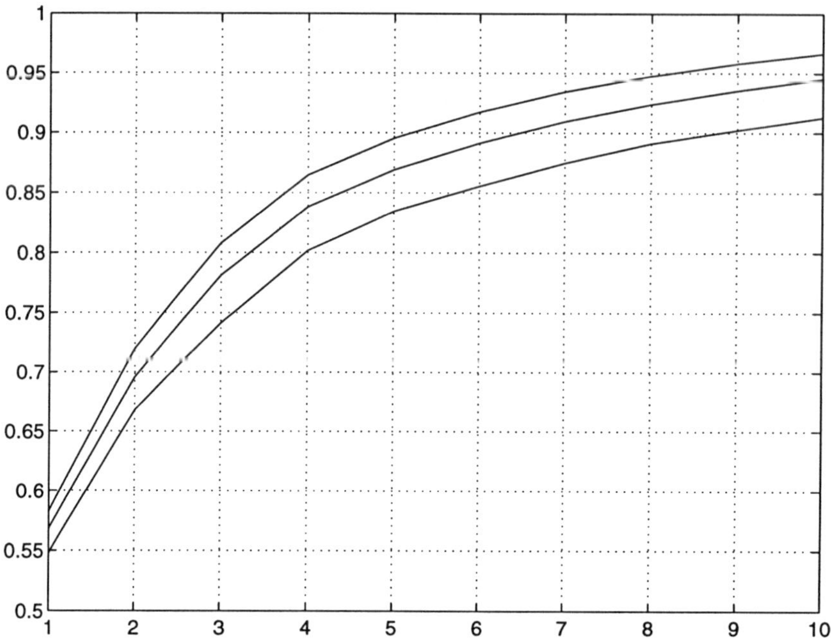

Fig. 2.10. Estimates of $\hat{R}_q^2$ with $q = 1, 10$ and truncation lags 0, 4, 8

spaced frequencies, cumulating, and dividing by the sum. Moreover, we estimated the maximum $\hat{R}_q^2$ by taking the mean of the cumulated eigenvalues over frequencies and dividing by the mean of the sum. The spectral density matrix was estimated by using Bartlett windows of different sizes; the series were not prefiltered. Restriction (2.16) is satisfied by our eigenvalue estimates with a mean error of about 1% with little variation among different frequencies.

Figure 2.9 shows the estimates of $C_q(\phi)$ obtained with truncation lag 8. Figure 2.10 shows the estimates of the maximum $\hat{R}_q^2$ for $q = 1, 10$ with truncation lags 0, 4, and 8. Truncation lag 0 is interesting in that it estimates the explained variance of static principal components. Not surprisingly, the explained variance is much higher than that in the previous section: here we are taking a point of view that is the most favorable for a low-dimensional X_t. Notwithstanding this, the hypothesis $h = 1$ is clearly rejected. Six regressors are needed in order to obtain $\hat{R}^2 > 0.9$.

2.6. Further Empirical Evidence

Until now we have shown only data on personal income. In this section we analyze a different data set, i.e. regional average wages per job.

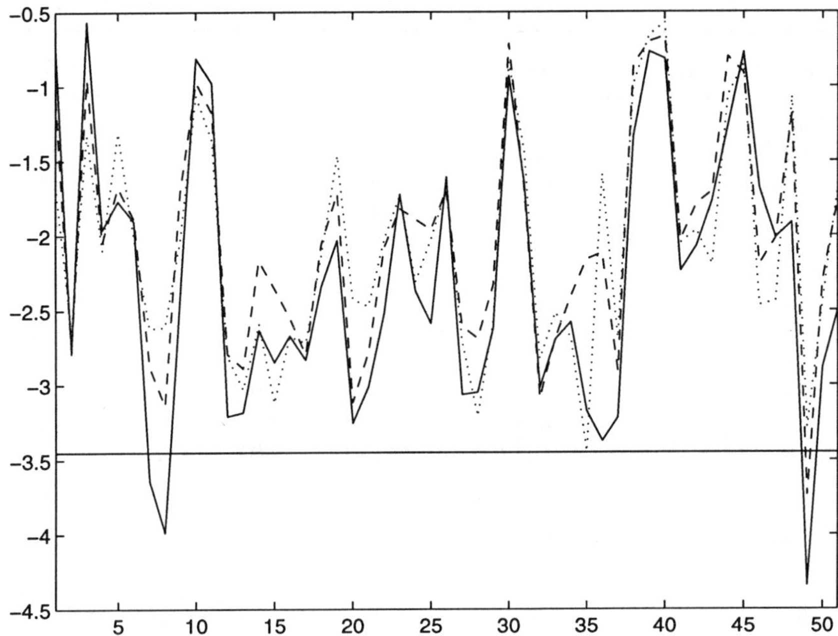

Fig. 2.11. Wages. ADF test statistics
DF: solid line. ADF(2): dashed line. ADF(4): dotted line.

One could reasonably expect that average wages are more homogeneous than per capita incomes, since capital income and labor income of self-employed people are excluded. Surprisingly, wages appear more heterogeneous than incomes, in the sense that more principal components are needed in order to obtain the same percentage of explained variance.

The data are constructed in the following way. Firstly, we took US regional data on wage and salary disbursements provided by the Bureau of Economic Analysis (July 22, 1993). These data are quarterly, seasonally adjusted, at annual rates, and expressed in billions of US dollars. The period is 1969:I–1992:I. Secondly, as we did with incomes, we deflated the nominal series with the price index 1987=1 obtained by dividing US total nominal consumption by real consumption. Lastly, we divided by wage and salary employment; quarterly employment was constructed by linearly interpolating the annual regional data provided by the BEA (May 26, 1993). Average wage per job is expressed in thousands of US dollars.

The DF, ADF(2), and ADF(4) test statistics (with trend) are shown in Figure 2.11. The null of difference–stationary wages is rejected only for three states by the DF test, for one state by the ADF(2) test, and for no states by the ADF(4) test. State 49 (Oregon) does not pass two of the three tests; there are no states for which the null is rejected by all the tests.

Table 2.2. Wages. Percentages of cointegrated groups with $q = 2, 3, 4, 5, 6$

Significance level	No coint.	10%	5%	1%	Total
Trace test					
$q = 2$	82.3	5.3	8.1	4.3	100
$q = 3$	44.3	14.5	24.1	17.1	100
$q = 4$	29.1	15.9	22.3	32.7	100
$q = 5$	14.7	12.8	26.8	45.7	100
$q = 6$	6.3	6.8	21.0	65.9	100
Lambda test					
$q = 2$	88.2	3.6	5.6	2.6	100
$q = 3$	61.5	11.5	16.1	10.9	100
$q = 4$	53.4	11.8	20.0	14.8	100
$q = 5$	46.3	13.9	21.1	18.7	100
$q = 6$	37.2	16.0	24.8	22.0	100

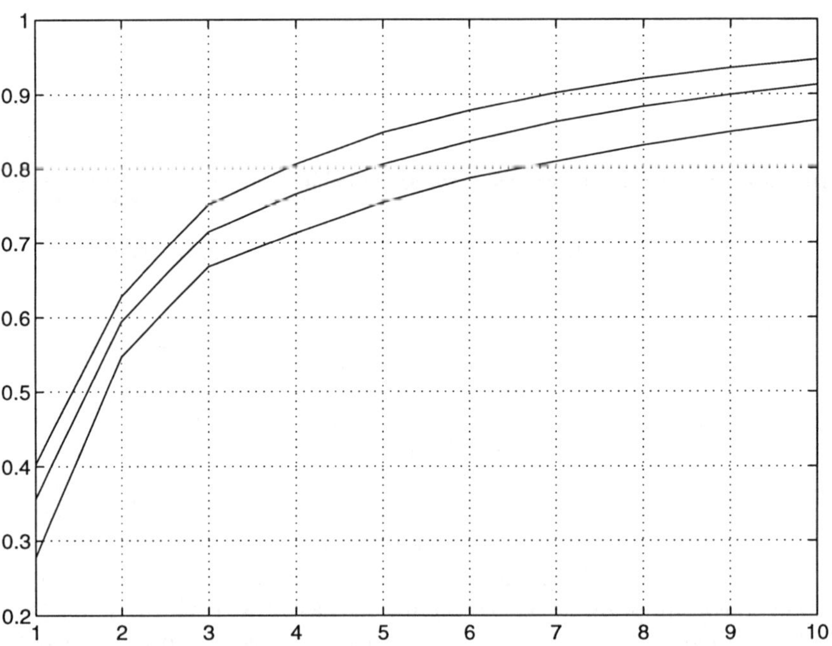

Fig. 2.12. Wage changes. Estimates of $\hat{R}_q^2$ with $q = 1, 10$ and truncation lags 0, 4, 8

According to these results we assume that the average wage per job is I(1) for all the states. Results of cointegration analysis are reported in Table 2.2, which is the same as Table 2.1 with wages in place of incomes. The figures appearing in Table 2.1 do not differ substantially from those of

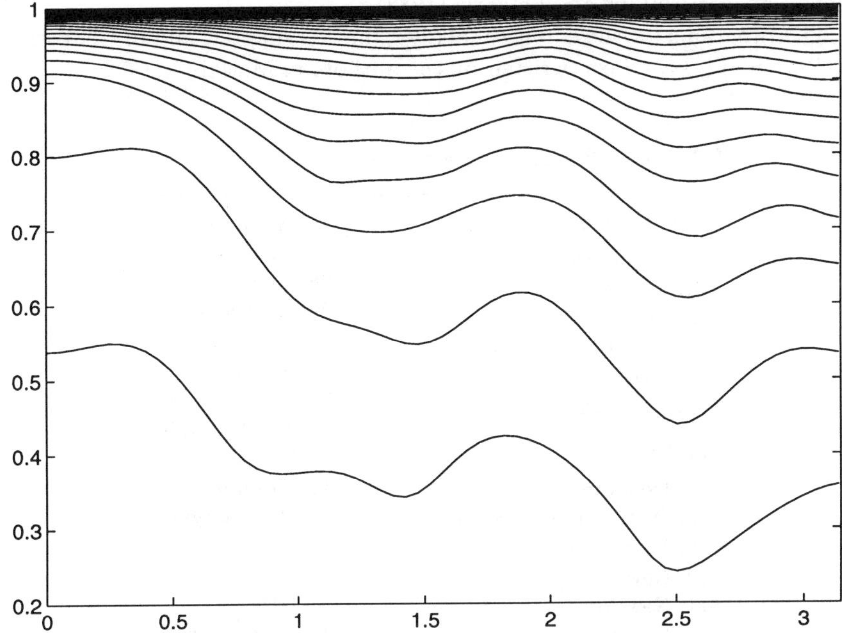

Fig. 2.13. Wage changes. Estimates of $C_q(\phi)$ with $q = 1, 51$

Table 2.2: wages do not appear more cointegrated than incomes.

As regards principal components, Figure 2.12 shows our estimates of the maximum $\hat{R}^2$ with $q = 1, 10$. The comparison with Figure 2.10 indicates that the overall explained variance is lower for wages than for incomes. With $q = 1$ the $\hat{R}^2$ with the largest window size is only 0.4; eight principal components are needed in order to obtain $\hat{R}^2 > 0.9$.

In Figure 2.13 explained variance is decomposed by frequency. Notice that, unlike in Figure 2.9, overall coherency is higher at lower frequencies; this explains why, despite the low $\hat{R}^2$, wages are not less cointegrated than incomes (Table 2.2).

2.7. Bibliographic Notes

A thorough treatment of ADF tests, cointegration, and cointegration tests is found in Banerjee *et al.* (1993). Engle and Granger (1987) and Johansen (1988) are prominent references. 'Stochastic' cointegration is treated in Campbell and Perron (1991) and Johansen (1991); critical values for Johansen's test are given in Osterwald-Lenum (1992).

For principal components in the frequency domain see Brillinger (1981, Chapter 9). For a related analysis focusing on cointegration and cointegration tests, see Phillips and Ouliaris (1988).

The programs for the empirical analysis in this chapter, and in Chapters 3, 13, and 14, have been written by the authors in Matlab.

Table 2.3. Region and state codes

1. New England
   1. Connecticut
   2. Maine
   3. Massachusetts
   4. New Hampshire
   5. Rhode Island
   6. Vermont
2. Mideast
   7. Delaware
   8. District of Columbia
   9. Maryland
   10. New Jersey
   11. New York
   12. Pennsylvania
3. Great Lakes
   13. Illinois
   14. Indiana
   15. Michigan
   16. Ohio
   17. Wisconsin
4. Plains
   18. Iowa
   19. Kansas
   20. Minnesota
   21. Missouri
   22. Nebraska
   23. North Dakota
   24. South Dakota
5. Southeast
   25. Alabama
   26. Arkansas
   27. Florida
   28. Georgia
   29. Kentucky
   30. Louisiana
   31. Mississippi
   32. North Carolina
   33. South Carolina
   34. Tennessee
   35. Virginia
   36. West Virginia
6. Southwest
   37. Arizona
   38. New Mexico
   39. Oklahoma
   40. Texas
7. Rocky Mountain
   41. Colorado
   42. Idaho
   43. Montana
   44. Utah
   45. Wyoming
8. Far West
   46. Alaska
   47. California
   48. Hawaii
   49. Nevada
   50. Oregon
   51. Washington

3

The Regional Model

Until now we have analyzed a model describing individual variables. We have studied regional data, but our aim was mainly to obtain information on the number of common shocks in model (1.2). In the present chapter we shift to a generalization of (1.2).

We assume that individuals are grouped into sets, which we call regions. Non-idiosyncratic shocks are of two kinds: those affecting all the agents of a particular region (local shocks) and those affecting all the agents in the economy (common shocks). Regions are assumed to be small as compared to the whole nation. By aggregating across agents within each region a dynamic factor model identical to (1.2) is obtained, where agents are replaced by regions and individual components are replaced by local components. We will call this model the regional model.

Unlike individual data, sectoral and regional time series data are increasingly available, so that estimation of the regional model is a real possibility for many data sets and countries. We will argue that, if the cross-sectional extension of the data set is large enough, then an estimation strategy based on large numbers can be employed to determine the number of common shocks, the common components, and the regional components. An application to the US personal income data set shows that two common shocks are sufficient to account for the comovement of state data. It must be pointed out that a smaller number of common shocks, as compared to the model in Chapter 2, i.e. two instead of six, is not surprising, since a large fraction of the individual variables' comovement in the regional model is explained by the regional shocks.

3.1. From the Individual to the Regional Model

3.1.1. We have seen in the previous chapter that regressing incomes or wages of US states on a small number of common shocks leaves a substantial fraction of total variance unexplained. Assuming the existence of state-specific shocks is a nice way to justify a large residual without invoking enormous measurement errors.

Although direct application of model (1.2) to regional data is tempting, some problems arise concerning consistency with the individual model. The main question is: how should local shocks be treated at the individual level? Obviously they are not idiosyncratic but, strictly speaking, they cannot be regarded as common either. The reason is that in the individual model (1.2) a finite number of common shocks is assumed, whereas, if we want the convergence results in Theorem 1.2 to hold at the regional level, we need an infinite number of regions and therefore an infinite number of local shocks.

Here we show a possible solution. The idea is to introduce many different populations from which regions are drawn. Within each population, the individual variables follow a model identical to that described in Chapter 1, with local shocks behaving like common shocks; but models differ across populations because local shocks are different.

To be more precise, we redefine the individual model as follows.

DEFINITION 3.1. The *individual model* is a countable family $\mathcal{F}$ of stationary stochastic variables x_t^i, $i = 1, \infty$. $\mathcal{F}$ is partitioned into a countable infinity of subfamilies $\mathcal{F}^s$, $s = 1, \infty$. If $x_t^i \in \mathcal{F}^s$

$$\begin{aligned} x_t^i &= \zeta_t^i + \psi_t^i + \chi_t^i \\ \zeta_t^i &= a_1^i(L)u_{1t} + a_2^i(L)u_{2t} + \cdots + a_h^i(L)u_{ht} \\ \psi_t^i &= b_1^i(L)v_{1t}^s + b_2^i(L)v_{2t}^s + \cdots + b_H^i(L)v_{Ht}^s, \end{aligned} \tag{3.1}$$

where: (i) the shocks u_{lt}, $l = 1, h$, form an orthonormal white-noise vector; (ii) the response functions $a_l^i(L)$ and $b_p^i(L)$ are rational functions in the lag operator L with no poles of modulus less than or equal to unity; (iii) the idiosyncratic component χ_t^i is an ARMA orthogonal at any lead and lag to χ_t^j, $j \neq i$, and ζ_t^j, for any j; (iv) the *local shocks* v_{pt}^s, $p = 1, H$, are unit variance white noises orthogonal at any lead and lag to v_{qt}^r, for $q \neq p$, $r \neq s$, and χ_t^j, ζ_t^j, for all j.

The difference with respect to Definition 1.1 is that here we have an additional component, the *local component* ψ_t^i, driven by shocks which are common within the family $\mathcal{F}^s$ but orthogonal to the local component of $\mathcal{F}^r$, $r \neq s$. Assumptions 1.1, 1.2, and 1.3 can be applied to the above model without any modification.

3.1.2. Now let us fix a positive integer $\tilde{m}$ and consider a sequence G^s, $s = 1, \infty$, where G^s is a non-empty set of m^s integers, with $m^s \leq \tilde{m}$, such that, for $i \in G^s$, $x_t^i \in \mathcal{F}^s$. We shall say that G^s is a *region*.

The motivation for the upper bound $\tilde{m}$ is that we need an infinite set of regions, and we do not want arbitrarily large regions in this set.

By averaging over agents within each region we get the *regional model*[1]

$$\bar{x}_t^s = \bar{\zeta}_t^s + \psi_t^s = \alpha_1^s(L)u_{1t} + \cdots + \alpha_h^s(L)u_{ht} + \phi_t^s, \tag{3.2}$$

where

$$\begin{aligned}
\bar{x}_t^s &= \sum_{i \in G^s} x_t^i / m^s \\
\bar{\zeta}_t^s &= \sum_{i \in G^s} \zeta_t^i / m^s \\
\phi_t^s &= \sum_{i \in G^s} \psi_t^i / m^s + \sum_{i \in G^s} \chi_t^i / m^s \\
\alpha_l^s(L) &= \sum_{i \in G^s} a_l^i(L) / m^s.
\end{aligned}$$

It is easily seen that, by suitably changing symbols, the regional model matches Definition 1.1.

REMARK 3.1. If the number of individuals within each region is large, as is the case with many sectoral and regional time series, idiosyncratic factors are negligible and ϕ_t^s is very close to the average of the individual local components. However, in what follows we do not need to assume large regions; this is the reason why we define the local component as a mixture of both local and idiosyncratic components.

Now let us state and prove the following result.

THEOREM 3.1. (i) If Assumption 1.1 holds for model (3.1), then $\text{var}(\bar{x}_t^s) \leq \mu$ for any s. (ii) If Assumption 1.2 holds for model (3.1), then, in the orthogonal decomposition

$$\bar{\zeta}_t^s = d^s U_t + \Gamma_t^s,$$

we have $d^s \geq \theta > 0$ with the possible exception of a finite number of regions.

Proof. Statement (i) is obvious. As regards (ii), we have $d^s = \sum_{i \in G^s} c^i / m^s$. If $c^i \geq \theta$ for any $i \in G^s$ then $d^s \geq \theta$. Since by Assumption 1.2 the number of individuals violating $c^i \geq \theta$ is finite, the number of regions violating $d^s \geq \theta$ is finite as well. Q.E.D.

Theorem 3.1 states that Assumptions 1.1 and 1.2 carry over to the regional model, so that, by introducing a sequence of regional weights $\bar{N}^s$ fulfilling Assumption 1.3, we can apply the large numbers results in Chapter 1.

[1] We assume here for simplicity that the regional variables of interest are simple averages of the individual variables, but the analysis in this section can be easily extended to more general weighted averages as well as simple and weighted sums.

EXAMPLE 3.1. If $\bar{x}_t^s$ is regional per capita income, an economically interesting sequence of weights is $\bar{N}^s = m^s$, $s = 1, \infty$. National per capita income is obtained by averaging regional incomes with the above weights. Notice that such weights fulfill Assumption 1.3 with $\mu_1 = 1$ and $\nu_1 = \tilde{m}$.

3.1.3. The above model cannot be expected to work well for whatever data set. Two important possible sources of misspecification are: (i) in the true model regional variables are linked by autoregressive relations as in Section 1.5; (ii) the true model is a factor model like (3.2) but individuals are not partitioned in the data according to the true regional partition. Let us briefly discuss (i) and postpone the discussion of (ii) to Section 3.3.

In model (3.2) the variable of region s is completely unaffected by the local component of region r. Cross-sectional linkages are entirely captured by the common components, so that shocks specific to a region or sector cannot influence other regions or sectors indirectly through their effects on their own regional or sectoral variable. This is unsatisfactory, since such autoregressive relations are quite plausible for many regional or sectoral variables. They can arise for instance from demand externalities, input–output relations, technological spillovers, and so on. However, a generalization of model (3.2) to the case of autoregressive linkages could be easily dealt with along the lines of Section 1.5.

3.2. Specification of the Regional Model

3.2.1. Let us consider a data set formed by M regional time series following model (3.2), with M large. In order to specify the model correctly we must firstly identify the number of common shocks h. Consider any partition of the set $\{1, 2, \ldots, M\}$ into the sets $S^1, S^2, \ldots, S^q$ and the vector of averages

$$Y_t = \begin{pmatrix} \sum_{s \in S^1} \bar{N}^s \bar{x}_t^s / \sum_{s \in S^1} \bar{N}^s \\ \vdots \\ \sum_{s \in S^q} \bar{N}^s \bar{x}_t^s / \sum_{s \in S^q} \bar{N}^s \end{pmatrix}.$$

As argued in the previous chapter, if the local components are negligible for all entries in Y_t, the rank of Y_t cannot be greater than h and in general is equal to h. Hence we can apply the dynamic principal component analysis described in Section 2.5 and set $h = r$ if the first r principal components can account for more than a given percentage, say 95%, of the trace of the covariance matrix of Y_t.

Several questions arise. The first is the choice of q. Clearly, q should be as large as possible, since it must be larger than r, which is unknown. However, the larger is q, the smaller are the groups in the partition, and we need large groups in order to wash out the local component. A general method for solving this trade-off is an open question. However, it is clear that if we find $h = q$, then q is too small. Moreover, as shown in Section 3.3, we can obtain some indication about the adequacy of the dimension of the sets S^k after estimation.

Given q, we can partition the data set in several ways. Loosely speaking, in order to ensure that the rank of Y_t is not less than h, the partition should be chosen in such a way as to differentiate the averages as much as possible. This can often be done by exploiting a priori information.

Lastly, we must select the weights $\bar{N}^s$. This problem is particularly relevant when M is not very large or some regions are very big with respect to the average. In this case a good choice, in order to obtain cancellation of the local components, is to assign lower weights to regional variables with larger variance. It is easily seen that under the orthogonality assumption the weights minimizing the variance of the aggregate local components are

$$\bar{N}^s = 1/V^s,$$

where V^s is the variance of the local component of region s. These variances are unknown before estimation. If we do not have prior information it is reasonable to assume V^s proportional to the variance of the regional variable and replace V^s with the sample variance of $\bar{x}_t^s$; these estimates can be used as initial values for the iterative procedure described below.

3.2.2. Now let us illustrate the above strategy with the US per capita personal income data set. We constructed the vector Y_t by averaging over the three groups $S^1 = \{1, \ldots, 17\}$, $S^2 = \{25, \ldots, 40\}$, and $S^3 = \{18, \ldots, 24, 41, \ldots, 51\}$, which roughly correspond to Northeast, South, and Northwest (see state codes in Table 2.3). Since the groups are not very large, we used a weighted average with weights inversely proportional to the variances. Given the three-dimensional vector Y_t, we computed the percentage of the total variance explained at each frequency by the first r principal components, $r = 1, 2$, as in Section 2.5. Figure 3.1 shows that the first two principal components account for about 96% of the total variance, quite uniformly across frequencies, whereas the first accounted for less than 90%, with important differences across frequencies. We interpret this as an indication in favor of two common shocks.

To obtain further evidence against the alternative specification $h = 1$ we used a partition into two groups, with New England, Mideast, and Southeast in the first group (East) and the other states in the second (West), and computed the weighted averages as before. Figure 3.2 shows the coherence between the two aggregates:[2] coherence is high, but not very close to unity, confirming the two common shocks specification. Notice also that coherence is not particularly high at low frequencies; this can be interpreted as

[2] Coherence is computed by using a Bartlett window with lag window size 9.

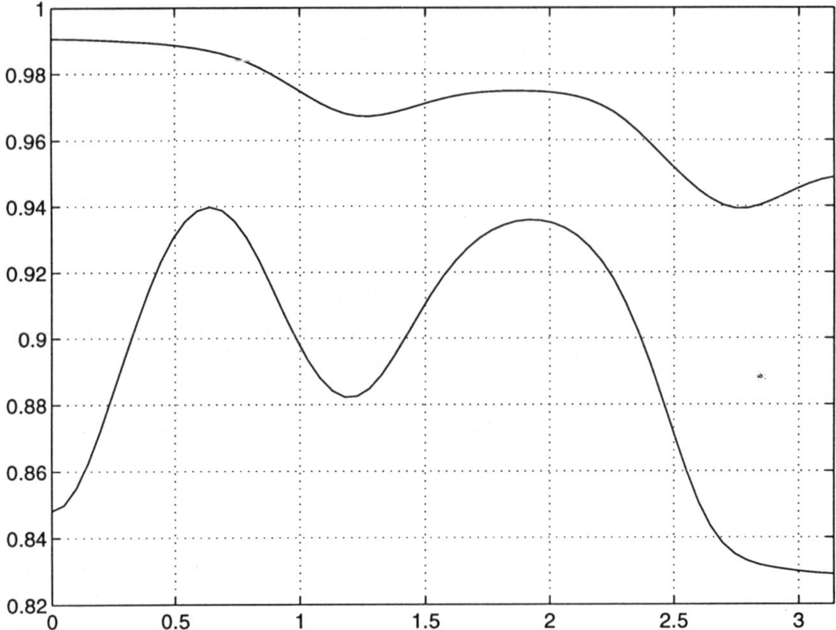

Fig. 3.1. Principal component series of three aggregates: explained variance by frequency

an indication against specifying the common shocks as one permanent and the other transitory.[3]

3.3. Estimation and Diagnostic Checking

3.3.1. Having determined the number of common shocks h, we can estimate the common and the local components as follows. Consider any partition of $\{1, 2, \ldots, M\}$ into the sets $S^1, S^2, \ldots, S^h$ and the h-vector of aggregates

$$Y_t = \begin{pmatrix} \sum_{s \in S^1} \bar{N}^s \bar{x}_t^s / \sum_{s \in S^1} \bar{N}^s \\ \vdots \\ \sum_{s \in S^h} \bar{N}^s \bar{x}_t^s / \sum_{s \in S^h} \bar{N}^s \end{pmatrix}.$$

If Y_t is non-singular, the common components of all regions lie in the linear space spanned by present, past, and future values of the variables in Y_t.

[3] As explained below, the final weights used to form the aggregates are slightly different from those used in this preliminary analysis and are determined within the estimation procedure. Hence after estimation we computed again the principal components for both the three-groups and the two-groups partitions by taking the 'right' weights: once again, the specification with two common shocks was confirmed.

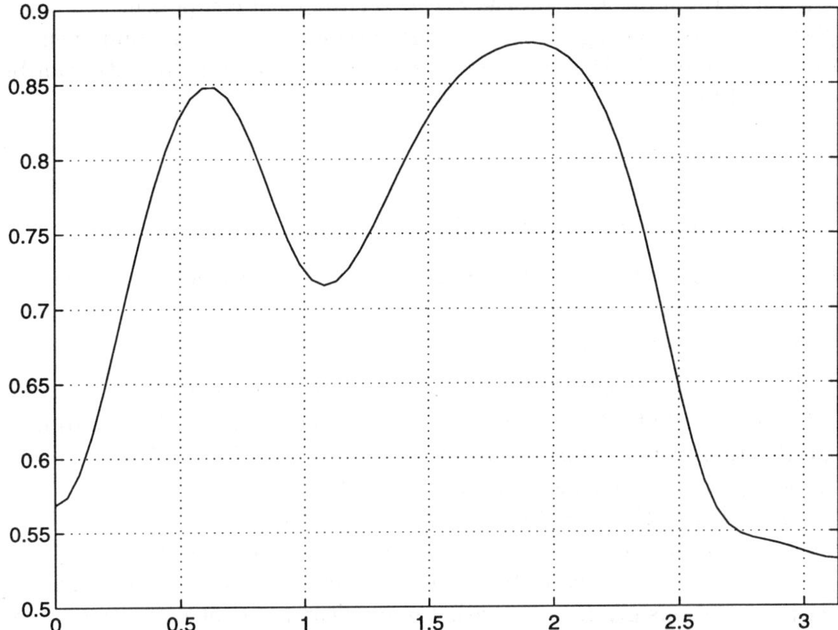

Fig. 3.2. Coherence of two aggregates

By uniqueness of the orthogonal decomposition (see Section A.1 in the Appendix) $\bar{\zeta}_t^s$ is then the projection of $\bar{x}_t^s$ on the above linear space. Hence, although the u_{lt} are unobserved, by ignoring, as usual, high-order leads and lags, we can consistently estimate $\bar{\zeta}_t^s$ by applying OLS equation by equation, with regressors Y_{t-k}, $k = -K, K$.

If M is not very large, we propose the following iterative procedure:

(1) Calculate Y_t by setting $\bar{N}^s = 1/\hat{V}_0^s$, where $\hat{V}_0^s$ is the sample variance of $\bar{x}_t^s$.

(2) Fix a suitable K and, for each s, regress $\bar{x}_t^s$ on the components of Y_{t-k}, $k = -K, K$. Then set $\bar{N}^s = 1/\hat{V}_1^s$, where $\hat{V}_1^s$ is the sample variance of the residual (i.e. the estimated local component) in the s-th regression, and compute Y_t using these weights.

(3) Repeat step (2) until convergence of Y_t is reached. In this way the final vector of weights, $1/\hat{V}^s$, and the final estimates for common and local components are jointly obtained.

REMARK 3.2. Using the above procedure we can analyze the percentage of the total variance explained by the common components. Moreover, we can study the comovements of the common components by spectral analysis as we will do in Chapter 14. However, to obtain a full estimation of (3.2), of the response functions $\alpha_l^s(L)$ in particular, we must identify the common shocks u_{lt}. This is discussed in Section 3.4.

After estimation, we can check whether the local component of Y_{lt} has died out by computing the ratio of the variance of the local component to the variance of Y_{lt}. Under the orthogonality assumption this ratio can be estimated by

$$\frac{1}{\hat{V}} \sum_{s \in S^l} \frac{1}{\hat{V}^s}, \tag{3.3}$$

where $\hat{V}$ is the sample variance of Y_{lt}.

REMARK 3.3. Notice that we cannot simply take the weighted averages of the estimated local components and compute the sample variances, since these averages are zero by construction.

Finally we can check pairwise orthogonality between the local components by means of a Q test. Rejection of orthogonality may be due to misspecification of both type (i) and type (ii), as described in Section 3.1.3. In case (ii), i.e. when data are not partitioned according to the true regional partition, there are two possibilities: (1) the false partition is neither finer nor coarser than the true one; (2) 'false' regions are subsets of the 'true' regions. In both cases the estimates remain consistent, since the sufficient conditions given in Remark 1.6 are clearly satisfied. In case (2) we should be able to identify the true regions by clustering the estimated local components in such a way as to minimize cross-correlations.

3.3.2. Coming to our empirical illustration, we chose H^1 = East and H^2 = West as in 3.2.2. Since the cross-sectional dimension is not very large, we followed the iterative procedure described above, with $K = 3$. We found that the common components account for a large fraction of the total variance in many states, but there are large differences among states: the distribution of the $\bar{R}^2$ ranges from 0.5% of Alaska to 89.6% of Georgia. The mean is 54.8; the median 59.9%.

In order to check the importance of the local components in the aggregates used for estimation we computed the ratio (3.3). The result is good: we have 0.018 for East and 0.025 for West.

It is interesting to see how the variance explained by the local component diminishes as the number of states represented in the aggregate increases. To show this, firstly we reordered states by drawing randomly without replacement from the set of natural numbers $\{1, \ldots, 51\}$ to form the sequence s_k, $k = 1, 51$. Secondly, we computed the ratio (3.3) for the sets $\{s_1, \ldots, s_n\}$, $n = 1, 51$. The experiment was repeated for 50 different reorderings. The result is shown in Figure 3.3 (each line corresponds to a different experiment). With 15 states the variance explained by the local component is less than 5% for all of the experiments. This is comforting since larger explained variances would have invalidated our principal component analysis with groups of 16–18 states.

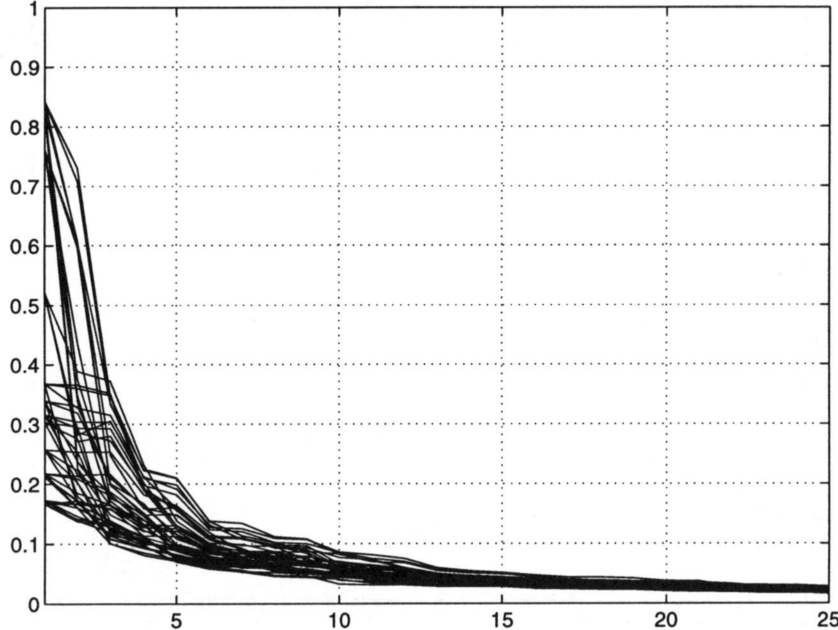

Fig. 3.3. Percentage of variance accounted for by the aggregate local component

Now let us check whether the local components are orthogonal. To this end we applied a Q-test by prewhitening the estimated local components with AR(4) models and computing, for each pair of states, the sum of squared cross-correlations at lags from −3 to 3. Under the null of orthogonality this statistic is distributed as a $\chi^2(7)$. The result is not very good. Both the theoretical and the empirical distributions are shown in Figure 3.4: the null is rejected for about 17% of the pairs at the 5% significance level.

3.4. Identification of the Common Shocks

As mentioned in Remark 3.2, estimation of the regional response functions requires identification of the common shocks u_{lt}. The latter can be achieved by standard structural VAR procedures. The vector of averages Y_t can be represented as $Y_t = C(L)v_t$, where v_t is a fundamental vector of orthonormal residuals. Now, if u_t is fundamental for Y_t, then $u_t = Sv_t$, where S is an orthonormal matrix (see Theorem A.5 in the Appendix). Once $C(L)$ and v_t have been obtained (by estimating a VAR and then orthonormalizing the residuals), S can be selected by imposing economically meaningful restrictions on the response functions $C(L)S^{-1}$. An example of such a pro-

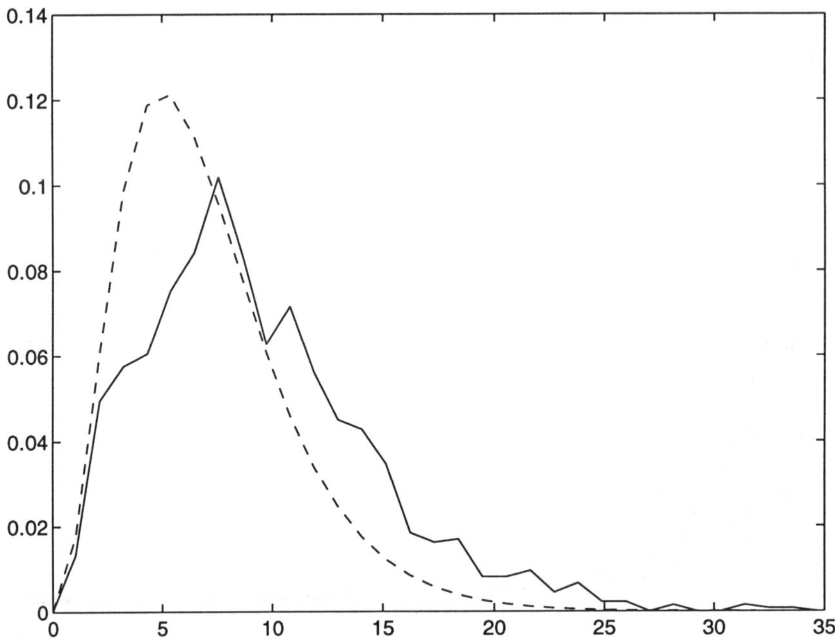

Fig. 3.4. Q-tests for pairwise orthogonality

cedure is provided in Chapter 14 (see also Section 12.1 for a brief overview of structural VAR models). Finally, the regional response functions $\alpha_l^s(L)$ can be estimated by regressing each regional variable on the estimated u_{lt}'s.

Naturally, as just mentioned, if standard structural VAR analysis is employed, then fundamentalness of u_t for Y_t must be assumed. However, since in the regional factor model we typically posses richer information than in structural VAR models, since we have more observed variables than shocks to identify, then, unlike in VAR models, fundamentalness becomes testable. Precisely, fundamentalness implies testable Granger causality restrictions (Forni and Reichlin, 1996). Although interesting for interpretation and identification of the structural shocks, this point will not be developed in this book.

3.5. Bibliographic Notes

Sections 3.2 and 3.3 of this chapter are based on Forni and Reichlin (1996). Factor analytic models with large cross-sectional dimension are studied also in Quah and Sargent (1993), where an estimation procedure based on the EM algorithm is proposed.

4

Aggregating the Common Components

In this chapter we show how the aggregate process can be obtained from the individual processes and analyze the relationship between the aggregate and the individual dynamics. Since the idiosyncratic components play no role in the aggregate, owing to large numbers, we shall concentrate on the common components ζ_t^i and neglect the ξ_t^i's.

It is worth noticing that the results in this chapter can also be applied to aggregation of a small number of individual units, by interpreting the ζ_t^i's as the microvariables rather than the common components. For, if we are not in a large numbers framework, we can drop the distinction between idiosyncratic and common shocks and include the ξ_t^i's in the vector u_t.[1]

In Section 4.1 we study the direct problem: from the individual to the aggregate process. In Section 4.2 we report some tentative solutions to the inverse problem, i.e. the question as to what restrictions make it possible to recover the individual model on the basis of the aggregate model.

4.1. The Wold Representation of the Macrovariable

4.1.1. We shall consider the microvariables

$$\zeta_t^i = a_1^i(L)u_{1t} + a_2^i(L)u_{2t} + \cdots + a_h^i(L)u_{ht}, \tag{4.1}$$

$i = 1, m$, where the response functions in L and the shocks fulfill the assumptions in Definition 1.1. Unlike the previous chapters, the number m is not necessarily large, nor is it assumed that $h > m$ (see interpretation (2) above).

In the present section we shall compare the microvariables (4.1) with the average process $\zeta_t = m^{-1}\sum_{i=1}^m \zeta_t^i$. However, the results can be easily extended to aggregates obtained using any vector N of positive weights. Aggregation of a finite number of ARMA processes is an ARMA process

[1] We shall return in greater detail in Section 7.2 to the cancellation of the idiosyncratic component both in the macro- and the microprocesses.

(see Section A.7 in the Appendix). Let us analyze in some detail the way in which the aggregate ARMA representation can be obtained.

To begin with, consider the simple case in which there is only one common shock, i.e.

$$\zeta_t^i = a^i(L)u_t = \frac{b^i(L)}{c^i(L)}u_t.$$

Multiplying by $c(L) = \prod_i c^i(L)$ and averaging over agents we get

$$\zeta_t = a(L)u_t = \frac{b(L)}{c(L)}u_t,$$

where $b(L) = m^{-1}\sum_i[b^i(L)\prod_{j\neq i} c^j(L)]$. If $b(L)$ does not vanish within the unit circle in the complex plane, the white-noise process u_t is fundamental for ζ_t, so that the Wold representation can be obtained by simply normalizing the above representation, i.e.

$$\zeta_t = \alpha(L)\eta_t,$$

where $\alpha(L) = a(L)/a(0)$ and $\eta_t = a(0)u_t$ (see Theorem A.2 in the Appendix).

However, as we have seen in Section 1.1.2, $a(L)$ can vanish within the unit circle. If u_t is non-fundamental for some ζ_t^i, then clearly u_t can be non-fundamental for the aggregate. But even if all the individual response functions are fundamental, their average may be non-fundamental, i.e. non-fundamentalness may arise from aggregation. Simple examples can be constructed by allowing for negative leading coefficients. For instance, the average of the processes $(4 - 2L)u_t$ and $(-2 - 2L)u_t$ is $(1 - 2L)u_t$, which is non-fundamental. The following example is less obvious, since all the leading coefficients are positive.

EXAMPLE 4.1. Consider the MA(3) processes

$$\zeta_t^1 = (1 + L)^3 u_t = (1 + 3L + 3L^2 + L^3)u_t$$
$$\zeta_t^2 = (1 - L)^3 u_t = (1 - 3L + 3L^2 - L^3)u_t.$$

Here u_t is fundamental for both the variables. Aggregating we get

$$\zeta_t = (1 + 3L^2)u_t = (1 + i\sqrt{3}L)(1 - i\sqrt{3}L)u_t.$$

Both the roots have modulus $1/\sqrt{3} < 1$, so that u_t is non-fundamental for ζ_t.

REMARK 4.1. More generally, if all the response functions $a^i(L)$ are fundamental polynomials of order q with positive leading coefficient and are otherwise unrestricted, $a(L)$ can be non-fundamental if $q \geq 3$. To see this, consider firstly that (provided that the $a^i(0)$ are all positive) $a(L)/a(0)$ is a convex linear combination of the polynomials $a^i(L)/a^i(0)$. The roots of these polynomials can be expressed as functions of the q coefficients in the positive powers of L. Now consider the region in $\mathbb{R}^q$ where all of the roots are in modulus greater than or equal to unity. This region is convex for $q \leq 2$ but not for $q = 3$ (and therefore for $q > 3$). Hence if $q \geq 3$ fundamentalness of $a(L)$ is not a consequence of micro fundamentalness.

4.1.2. If $b(L)$ has p roots within the unit circle, the Wold representation can be obtained by substituting the 'wrong' roots with their reciprocals. Let us assume for the moment $b(0) \neq 0$ and factorize $b(L)$ as

$$b(L) = b(0)\beta(L) \prod_{s=1}^{p} (1 - r_s L),$$

where $|r_s| > 1$, for $s = 1, p$, while $\beta(L)$ does not vanish within the unit circle and fulfills $\beta(0) = 1$. The Wold representation of ζ_t is $\alpha(L)\eta_t$, where

$$\alpha(L) = \frac{\beta(L)}{c(L)} \prod_{s=1}^{p} (1 - r_s^{-1} L)$$

and

$$\eta_t = b(0) \frac{\prod_{s=1}^{p}(1 - r_s L)}{\prod_{s=1}^{p}(1 - r_s^{-1} L)} u_t.$$

Notice that η_t is a white-noise process, since its spectral density

$$b(0)^2 \frac{\prod_{s=1}^{p}(1 - r_s e^{-i\phi})(1 - r_s e^{i\phi})}{\prod_{s=1}^{p}(1 - r_s^{-1} e^{-i\phi})(1 - r_s^{-1} e^{i\phi})} = b(0)^2 \prod_{s=1}^{p} r_s^2$$

is constant.[2]

Lastly, if $b(0)$ vanishes for $L = 0$, we have $a(L) = L^k \tilde{a}(L)$, k being the smallest power of L appearing in $a(L)$ with non-zero coefficient, and we can get the Wold representation by applying the same procedure as before to the representation

$$\zeta_t = \tilde{a}(L)\tilde{u}_t,$$

where $\tilde{u}_t = u_{t-k}$.

EXAMPLE 4.2. As an example, consider the process $\zeta_t = (1 - 2L)u_t$; the Wold representation is

$$\zeta_t = (1 - 0.5L)\eta_t,$$

[2] This is a generalization of the case studied in the Appendix, Section A.3, Case $|\alpha| > 1$. See also Section A.7.

where η_t is

$$\eta_t = \frac{1-2L}{1-0.5L}u_t = \left(1 - \frac{3}{2}L - \frac{3}{4}L^2 - \frac{3}{8}L^3 - \cdots\right)u_t.$$

It is easily seen that η_t is not serially correlated: for $k > 0$

$$\text{cov}(\eta_t, \eta_{t-k}) = -\frac{3}{2^k} + \frac{9}{2^{k+2}}\left(1 + \frac{1}{4} + \frac{1}{4^2} + \cdots\right) = 0.$$

Similarly, the Wold representation of the process in Example 4.1 is

$$\zeta_t = \left(1 + \frac{1}{3}L^2\right)\eta_t,$$

where $\eta_t = [(1+3L^2)/(1+3^{-1}L^2)]u_t$.

4.1.3. Let us go back to the general case $h \geq 1$. Rewrite (4.1) as

$$\zeta_t^i = \frac{b_1^i(L)}{c_1^i(L)}u_{1t} + \frac{b_2^i(L)}{c_2^i(L)}u_{2t} + \cdots + \frac{b_h^i(L)}{c_h^i(L)}u_{ht},$$

where we may assume that $b_l^i(L)$ and $c_l^i(L)$ have no common roots. We have

$$\zeta_t = \frac{b_1(L)}{c_1(L)}u_{1t} + \cdots + \frac{b_h(L)}{c_h(L)}u_{ht}, \tag{4.2}$$

where

$$c_l(L) = \prod_i c_l^i(L), \quad b_l(L) = m^{-1}\sum_i \left[b_l^i(L)\prod_{j\neq i} c_l^j(L)\right], \tag{4.3}$$

for $l = 1, h$. Reducing to the common denominator,

$$c(L)\zeta_t = d_1(L)u_{1t} + \cdots + d_h(L)u_{ht}, \tag{4.4}$$

where

$$c(L) = \prod_l c_l(L), \quad d_l(L) = b_l(L)\prod_{k\neq l} c_k(L), \tag{4.5}$$

for $l = 1, h$. The difficulty here is that, unlike in the previous case, we do not have a univariate representation of $y_t = c(L)\zeta_t$. Let us indicate by $\alpha(L)\eta_t$ the unknown Wold representation of y_t. We must solve the equation

$$|\alpha(e^{-i\phi})|^2\sigma_\eta^2 = |d_1(e^{-i\phi})|^2 + |d_2(e^{-i\phi})|^2 + \cdots + |d_h(e^{-i\phi})|^2,$$

where on the RHS we have the (known) spectral density of y_t, while on the LHS the same spectral density is expressed in terms of the unknowns, i.e. the function $\alpha(L)$ and the variance of η_t. Firstly, let us prove that:

THEOREM 4.1. The function $\alpha(L)$ is a finite polynomial.

Proof. The process y_t is the sum of a finite number of MA processes, whose order is less than the maximum, call it q, among the orders of the polynomials $d_l(L)$. Therefore $\text{cov}(y_t, y_{t-k}) = 0$ for $k > q$. Since η_{t-k}, being fundamental by assumption, lies in the space generated by y_{t-s}, for $s \geq k$, we have $\text{cov}(y_t, \eta_{t-k}) = 0$ for $k > q$. On the other hand,

$$\text{cov}(y_t, \eta_{t-k}) = \text{cov}\left(\sum_{j=1}^{q} \alpha_j \eta_{t-j}, \eta_{t-k}\right) = \alpha_k \sigma_\eta^2,$$

since η_t is a white noise, so that $\alpha_k = 0$ for $k > q$. Q.E.D.

Thus assume that $\alpha(L)$ is a polynomial of order q. Now consider the polynomial in z:

$$G(z) = z^q[d_1(z)d_1(z^{-1}) + d_2(z)d_2(z^{-1}) + \cdots + d_h(z)d_h(z^{-1})], \tag{4.6}$$

where the function within the square brackets is the covariance generating function of y_t. Owing to symmetry, if r is a root of (4.6), then r^{-1} is also a root of (4.6). Therefore we can write

$$G(z) = H_0(1 - r_1 z)(1 - r_2 z) \cdots (1 - r_q z)(z - r_1)(z - r_2) \cdots (z - r_q),$$

with $r_k \leq 1$, for $k = 1, q$. We can put

$$\alpha(L) = (1 - r_1 L)(1 - r_2 L) \cdots (1 - r_q L)$$

and determine η_t as the solution of the equation

$$\alpha(L)\eta_t = d_1(L)u_{1t} + \cdots + d_h(L)u_{ht}.$$

By construction, as in 4.1.2, η_t has a constant spectral density.

REMARK 4.2. Notice that in general the aggregate Wold residual is not an average of the original shocks u_{lt}. Assuming for simplicity that $\alpha(L)$ is invertible, η_t is an infinite linear combination of present and past values of the shocks u_{lt}. Therefore, even if the u_{lt} are 'structural', the fundamental aggregate shock of ζ_t is a complicated construction with no immediate economic interpretation.

EXAMPLE 4.3. As an example of the above procedure, consider the following very simple model with two individuals and two shocks:

$$\zeta_t^1 = 2u_{1t} + 3u_{2t}$$
$$\zeta_t^2 = -2u_{1t-1}.$$

Averaging the two equations gives

$$\zeta_t = (1-L)u_{1t} + \frac{3}{2}u_{2t}.$$

The polynomial $G(z)$ is $-1+(17/4)z-z^2$, which vanishes for $z=1/4$ and $z=4$. The 'right' root is 4; hence the Wold representation of ζ_t is

$$\zeta_t = (1-0.25L)\eta_t = \eta_t - \frac{1}{4}\eta_{t-1},$$

where

$$\eta_t = \frac{1-L}{1-0.25L}u_{1t} + \frac{1.5}{1-0.25L}u_{2t}.$$

4.1.4. The results in 4.1.3 imply some general conclusions about the AR and MA orders of the aggregate process. Calling p_l^i and s_l^i the orders of $c_l^i(L)$ and $b_l^i(L)$ respectively, it is easily seen from the definitions (4.3) that the order of $c_l(L)$ is

$$p_l = \sum_i p_l^i$$

and that of $b_l(L)$ fulfills

$$s_l \le p_l - \min_i(p_l^i - s_l^i).$$

Moreover, the definitions in (4.5) imply that the order of $c(L)$ is

$$p = \sum_l p_l$$

and that of $d_l(L)$ is $q_l = p - p_l + s_l$. Lastly, as we have seen above, the order of $\alpha(L)$ satisfies

$$q \le \max_l q_l = p - \min_l(p_l - s_l).$$

Hence

$$p - q = \min_l(p_l - s_l) \ge \min_{i,l}(p_l^i - s_l^i).$$

The AR and the MA orders of the aggregate may be lower than p and q because $c(L)$ and $\alpha(L)$ may have common roots; but the difference must be equal to $p-q$.

REMARK 4.3. The above results imply that if all of the individual response functions are ARMA(k,w) with $k \ge w$ the aggregate process cannot be either a finite order MA or an AR of order less than $k-w$. For instance, if all of the micro responses are AR(2) the aggregate cannot be MA or white-noise or AR(1).

4.2. Identification of the Microparameters

4.2.1. Now let us deal with the second question to be addressed in this chapter: what can be inferred about the microparameters from the Wold representation of the macroprocess? A moment's reflection shows that in general the same aggregate may come from a wide variety of different sets of individual processes, the more so the greater is the number of shocks h.[3]

The results in Section 4.1.4 can be used to find restrictions on the ARMA orders of the micro response functions. The fact that if the aggregate is AR or ARMA, then the microprocesses cannot be vector MA, is an elementary example. The implication pointed out in Remark 4.4 is less obvious. These restrictions should be taken into account when specifying the dynamics of a disaggregated model such as the one discussed in Chapter 3.

In any case, identification of the microparameters can be obtained only by imposing a richer structure on the microprocesses. A simple but interesting example is that in which there is only one common shock, all the individual response functions are AR(1), but individuals differ as to the lag at which the response begins. Precisely,

$$\zeta_t^i = \frac{bL^{k^i}}{1-cL}u_t,$$

where $k^i \geq 0$ is a non-negative integer. Individuals can be partitioned into M groups containing respectively $N^0, \ldots, N^q$ individuals, where the j-th group contains all the i for which $k^i = j$. The aggregate model is the ARMA

$$(1-cL)\zeta_t = \left(\frac{N^0}{m} + \frac{N^1}{m}L + \cdots + \frac{N^q}{m}L^q\right) bu_t.$$

The polynomial on the RHS reflects the distribution across individuals of the lag between the shock and the first reaction. If this polynomial is fundamental and does not vanish at c, we can in principle recover all the microparameters, i.e. $c, N^0, \ldots, N^q$ and b, by estimating an ARMA model for the aggregate.[4]

The example can be generalized to allow for both higher order AR processes and more than one shock. Notice, however, that the AR nature of individual responses is crucial since, if the micro response functions were

[3] If the idiosyncratic component is dropped as a consequence of a large m, then no information on the micro idiosyncratic components can be obtained from the aggregate process, while if the idiosyncratic shocks have been included among the components of u_t, then h is typically too large to allow identification of the micro structure, unless other assumptions are made.

[4] However, non-fundamental polynomials are not unlikely; see Section 1.1.2.

MA, then the distribution across agents of the lags between the shock and the first reaction would be inextricably confused with the lag distribution of individual responses.

4.2.2. Suppose instead that all individuals react with no lag (i.e. $k^i = 0$) but with heterogeneous AR(1) coefficients. Let us discuss this case in detail. Let

$$\zeta_t^i = \frac{b^i}{1 - c^i L} u_t, \tag{4.7}$$

where $|c^i| < 1$ for all i. Let us partition the individuals into q subgroups, with $c^i = r^k$ in the k-th subgroup and $r^k \neq r^s$ for $k \neq s$. Summing within group s we get

$$\tilde{\zeta}_t^s = \frac{\bar{b}^s N^s}{1 - r^s L} u_t, \tag{4.8}$$

where N^s and $\bar{b}^s$ are, respectively, the number of agents and the average of b^i in group s.

By multiplying each side of the above equality by $c(L) = \prod_{s=1}^q (1 - r^s L)$, summing over groups, and dividing by m we get

$$c(L)\zeta_t = b(L)u_t, \tag{4.9}$$

where

$$b(L) - \frac{1}{m} \sum_{s=1}^{q} \left[\bar{b}^s N^s \prod_{k \neq s} (1 - r^k L) \right].$$

Since the r^s are all different by construction, we have

$$b(1/r^s) = \frac{\bar{b}^s N^s}{m} \prod_{k \neq s} (1 - r^k / r^s) \neq 0 \tag{4.10}$$

for all s, so that $c(L)$ and $b(L)$ have no common roots. Hence, provided that $b(L)$ is fundamental, we can in principle estimate the coefficients of $c(L)$ and $b(L)$. From $c(L)$ we can recover all the autoregressive microparameters r^s. From $b(L)$, using (4.10), we can get the weights of the parameters r^s, i.e. $\bar{b}_s N^s / m$. If in addition $\bar{b}^s = b$ for every s we can find $b, N^1, \ldots, N^q$ and the whole distribution of the parameter c^i is identified.

Keeping the assumption $\bar{b}^s = b$, for any s, the moving average representation of ζ_t has a very close link with the distribution of the parameter c^i. Let us return to equation (4.8) and expand the RHS. We get $\tilde{\zeta}_t^s = bN^s(1 + r^s L + (r^s)^2 L^2 + \cdots)u_t$. Summing over groups and dividing by m gives

$$\begin{aligned} \zeta_t &= \left(1 + \sum_{s=1}^{q} \frac{N^s}{m} r^s L + \sum_{s=1}^{q} \frac{N^s}{m} (r^s)^2 L^2 + \cdots \right) b u_t \\ &= (1 + \mu_1 L + \mu_2 L^2 + \cdots) b u_t, \end{aligned} \tag{4.11}$$

where $\mu_1, \mu_2, \ldots$ are the moments around zero of the distribution of the microparameters.

Naturally, the AR representation of ζ_t provides the same information. Write the AR representation as

$$\zeta_t = d_1\zeta_{t-1} + d_2\zeta_{t-2} + \cdots + bu_t. \tag{4.12}$$

By equating the RHS of the above equation and the last term in (4.11), multiplying by $u_{t-1}/b, u_{t-2}/b, \ldots$, and taking expected values we get

$$\begin{aligned}
d_1 &= \mu_1 \\
d_2 &= \mu_2 - d_1\mu_1 \\
&\vdots \\
d_s &= \mu_s - \sum_{k=1}^{s-1} d_{s-k}\mu_k \\
&\vdots
\end{aligned}$$

Notice that the first coefficient of the AR(∞) representation is the mean while the second coefficient is the variance of the coefficients c^i.

Equations (4.11) and (4.12) provide restrictions for the individual model (4.7) that can be tested by estimating ARMA models for ζ_t. For example, if estimation gives negative even-order coefficients, model (4.7) is rejected. Moreover, since the variance cannot be negative we have $\mu_2 \geq \mu_1^2$. Hence, as already noticed in 4.1.4, we cannot have an aggregate MA(1) process. If $\mu_2 = \mu_1^2$ then the individual coefficients must be equal and the aggregate must be AR(1) with coefficient μ_1 while $\mu_k = \mu_1^k$ for all k (in the same way, in the AR representation we cannot have $d_2 = 0$ along with $d_k \neq 0$ for some $k > 2$). Additional conditions can be derived under the assumption $c^i \geq 0$.[5]

4.2.3. The above results cannot be immediately extended to the case $h > 1$. To illustrate the difficulty, let $h = 2$. The natural generalization of (4.7) is

$$\zeta_t^i = \frac{b_1^i}{1 - c_1^i L} u_{1t} + \frac{b_2^i}{1 - c_2^i L} u_{2t}. \tag{4.13}$$

Application of the results in 4.2.2 requires that ζ_t^i is an AR(1). This occurs if, and only if, the following assumption holds.

ASSUMPTION 4.1. For any i, either $c_1^i = c_2^i$, or one of the coefficients b_l^i vanishes.

[5] See Lewbel (1994, pp. 908–10).

If Assumption 4.1 holds, we may rewrite (4.13) as

$$\zeta_t^i = \frac{1}{1 - c^i L} \eta_t^i,$$

where $\eta_t^i = b_1^i u_{1t} + b_2^i u_{2t}$ and $c^i = \left(c_1^i b_1^i + c_2^i b_2^i\right) / (b_1^i + b_2^i)$. Moreover, if we want to recover the distribution of the parameter c^i another assumption is necessary. The following generalizes $\bar{b}^s = b$, which we have made in 4.2.2.

ASSUMPTION 4.2. The white noise η_t^i and the coefficient c^i are independent, so that

$$\sum_i \frac{1}{m(1 - c^i L)} \eta_t^i = \sum_i \frac{1}{m(1 - c^i L)} \sum_i \frac{\eta_t^i}{m}. \tag{4.14}$$

It is easily seen that if Assumptions 4.1 and 4.2 hold then equation (4.11) holds with $bu_t = \sum_i \eta_t^i / m$.

EXAMPLE 4.4. As an example consider the case in which there are two groups of individuals, B_1 and B_2, such that $\eta_t^i = bu_{1t}$ for $i \in B_1$ and $\eta_t^i = bu_{2t}$ for $i \in B_2$. Moreover, assume that for any individual $i \in B_1$ there is a j in B_2 such that $c^j = c^i$ and vice versa. Clearly in this case condition (4.14) is fulfilled and (4.11) holds with $u_t = (u_{1t} + u_{2t})/2$.

REMARK 4.4. Assumption 4.2 holds if we suppose that c^i and η_t^i are drawn from independent distributions. For independence see Section 7.6.

In general, however, when there are $h > 1$ common shocks equation (4.14) is not fulfilled and the distribution of the microparameters cannot be recovered from the aggregate process alone, even if all the response functions are AR(1). This is hardly surprising: with $h > 1$, unless quite special conditions are fulfilled the identification problem can be solved only in a multivariate framework, i.e. by augmenting the model with other aggregate variables. We shall return to the identification problem in Section 12.4.

4.3. Bibliographic Notes

For the procedure described in Section 4.1.3 see, for example, Rozanov (1967, pp. 43–44).

Theorem 4.1 is due to Lütkepohl (1984). This result is not really necessary here since Rozanov's procedure is self-sufficient. It has been reported because its argument is very simple and elegant. Incidentally, Lütkepohl's theorem put an end to a somewhat involved discussion on the aggregation of ARMA processes; see Anderson (1975, 1978), Rose (1977), Ansley *et al.* (1977).

Section 4.1.4 generalizes the results in Granger and Morris (1976). Section 4.2.1 is an example in the spirit of Trivedi (1985), while Section 4.2.2

is based on Lewbel (1994). Identification of the microparameters from the macroparameters is also studied by Stoker (1984) in a static non-linear framework.

II

Aggregation of Economic Models

5

Reformulation of Standard Representative-Agent Models

In Part I we have dealt with aggregation of scalar stationary (up to suitable differencing) variables. We now enter the core of the book, i.e. aggregation of economic micromodels. The latter contain both dependent (controlled by the agent) and independent variables. Thus we must deal with aggregation of stochastic vectors.

The main empirical result of Part I consists in showing that many crucial economic variables, when considered at the micro level, cannot be modeled as the sum of a common component, equal for all agents up to a scalar, and an idiosyncratic component. For that matter, we have shown that even the weaker assumption that the common components, though not proportional, are all driven by the same shock, is untenable. The empirical analysis of Part I will be the basis for the treatment of the independent variables in the micromodels. For example, if the micromodel describes an agent taking decisions on a variable y_t (dependent), based on the variable x_t (independent), the model for x_t will keep the distinction between a common and an idiosyncratic component, but will allow for the possibility of more than one common shock and for different responses across agents to the common shocks. This is nothing other than equation (1.2), set out in Chapter 1, which we rewrite here for convenience:

$$x_t^i = a_1^i(L)u_{1t} + a_2^i(L)u_{2t} + \cdots + a_h^i(L)u_{ht} + \chi_t^i, \tag{1.2}$$

where the agents are indexed by the integer i, while

$$u_t = (u_{1t} \quad u_{2t} \quad \cdots \quad u_{ht})'$$

is an orthonormal white noise, $h > 1$.

In this chapter we consider, as a first departure from the representative agent, the introduction of models like (1.2) for the independent variable into some well-known representative-agent models. In Chapter 6 we give formal definitions of the microparameter set, the micromodel, the population space, the disaggregated model. In Chapter 7 we give the definition of the aggregate model. In Chapters 8 and 9 we exploit both the difference across the independent variables faced by the agents, and the difference in the responses of different agents, to obtain results regarding, respectively, the rank of the aggregate vector and cointegration for the aggregate variables. In Chapters 11 and 12 we study the consequences of such differences for VAR and ARMAX models.

We start by recalling the current representative-agent version of some well-known examples. Then we replace the independent variable with our model of common plus idiosyncratic components. As we shall see, though arising within different frameworks, all the resulting models can be accommodated in a general and convenient form in which the vector collecting both the dependent and the independent variables evolves according to a vector ARIMA, where the moving average contains both a common and an idiosyncratic component.

Since in this chapter we do not need simultaneous consideration of different agents, indexation of the agents will be dropped.

5.1. Life Cycle, Permanent Income under Rational Expectations

This is quite a familiar model in the representative-agent version. Assuming that labor income has the Wold representation

$$\Delta y_t = a(L)\eta_t,$$

and assuming that the information set of the representative agent consists of the present and past values of income, consumption follows the process

$$\Delta c_t = a(\beta)\eta_t, \tag{5.1}$$

where $\beta = 1/(1+r)$, r being a risk-free rate of interest (see Hall, 1978, and Chapter 13 below).

Now let us drop the representative agent and assume that each agent has a labor income which evolves according to the model

$$\Delta y_t = a_1(L)u_{1t} + a_2(L)u_{2t} + b(L)\xi_t, \tag{5.2}$$

where the polynomials $a_1(L)$, $a_2(L)$, $b(L)$, and the shock ξ_t are agent specific, while the unit variance shocks u_{lt} are common to all agents. For simplicity we have taken $h = 2$.

As soon as individual incomes are modeled as in (5.2), the question as to which information set is employed by each agent to predict future income arises naturally. This problem will be fully analyzed in Chapter 13. Here we limit ourselves to some simple exercises. At one extreme we may suppose that: (a) the agent observes present and past values for each of the three components separately. At the other extreme we can assume that: (b) the agent observes only the variable y_t, without distinguishing amongst its components.

CASE (a). Consumption is easily obtained as

$$\Delta c_t = a_1(\beta)u_{1t} + a_2(\beta)u_{2t} + b(\beta)\xi_t.$$

Thus

$$\begin{pmatrix} \Delta c_t \\ \Delta y_t \end{pmatrix} = \begin{pmatrix} a_1(\beta) & a_2(\beta) \\ a_1(L) & a_2(L) \end{pmatrix} \begin{pmatrix} u_{1t} \\ u_{2t} \end{pmatrix} + \begin{pmatrix} b(\beta) \\ b(L) \end{pmatrix} \xi_t. \tag{5.3}$$

CASE (b). Here some manipulation is required. We must firstly aggregate the different components, then obtain consumption, and finally write consumption in terms of u_t and ξ_t. The assumption is that the agent observes only the variable y_t. This means that he, or she, can only recover the shock of the Wold representation

$$\Delta y_t = a(L)\eta_t, \tag{5.4}$$

which is here normalized by assuming that η_t has unit variance. The shock η_t and the 'deep shocks' u_{1t}, u_{2t}, ξ_t are linked by the equation

$$a(L)\eta_t = a_1(L)u_{1t} + a_2(L)u_{2t} + b(L)\xi_t, \tag{5.5}$$

so that the white noise η_t can be expressed as

$$\eta_t = \frac{a_1(L)u_{1t} + a_2(L)u_{2t} + b(L)\xi_t}{a(L)} \tag{5.6}$$

(see Section 4.1). The application of the consumption equation (5.1) to our individual agent leads immediately to the couple of equations

$$\begin{aligned} \Delta c_t &= a(\beta)\eta_t \\ \Delta y_t &= a(L)\eta_t. \end{aligned} \tag{5.7}$$

By substituting (5.6) into (5.7) we get

$$\begin{pmatrix} a(L) & 0 \\ 0 & 1 \end{pmatrix} \begin{pmatrix} \Delta c_t \\ \Delta y_t \end{pmatrix} = \begin{pmatrix} a(\beta)a_1(L) & a(\beta)a_2(L) \\ a_1(L) & a_2(L) \end{pmatrix} \begin{pmatrix} u_{1t} \\ u_{2t} \end{pmatrix} + \begin{pmatrix} a(\beta)b(L) \\ b(L) \end{pmatrix} \xi_t. \tag{5.8}$$

CASE (c). As an intermediate case we can suppose that the agent is able to distinguish between the idiosyncratic and the common component

$a_1(L)u_{1t}+a_2(L)u_{2t}$, but not between the two components within the latter. Thus he, or she, can make use for prediction of both $b(L)\xi_t$ and

$$d(L)\theta_t = a_1(L)u_{1t} + a_2(L)u_{2t},$$

with corresponding consumption components $b(\beta)\xi_t$ and

$$d(\beta)\theta_t = \frac{d(\beta)}{d(L)} \left(a_1(L)u_{1t} + a_2(L)u_{2t}\right).$$

Summing up:

$$\begin{pmatrix} d(L) & 0 \\ 0 & 1 \end{pmatrix} \begin{pmatrix} \Delta c_t \\ \Delta y_t \end{pmatrix} = \begin{pmatrix} d(\beta)a_1(L) & d(\beta)a_2(L) \\ a_1(L) & a_2(L) \end{pmatrix} u_t + \begin{pmatrix} d(L)b(\beta) \\ b(L) \end{pmatrix} \xi_t. \quad (5.9)$$

It turns out that consumption and income changes have the same common component, up to the factor $d(\beta)/d(L)$, whereas the idiosyncratic components differ for the factor $b(\beta)/b(L)$.

In conclusion, irrespective of the assumptions that we make about the information set of the agent, the application of equation (5.1) and a relatively easy algebraic manipulation leads to representing the vector $(\,c_t \quad y_t\,)'$ as an autoregressive structure, containing the term $(1-L)$, coupled with two moving average terms on the RHS, one in u_t, the other in ξ_t. Naturally, the particular AR and MA matrix polynomials that we obtain depend on the particular assumption on the information set.

Finally, we remark that the representative-agent model is singular, as income and consumption are driven by the same shock η_t. Though driven by three shocks our model is also singular in Case (b). This immediately appears by looking at equation (5.7), or observing that the polynomials in the first row of the RHS of (5.8) are equal to those of the second row up to the factor $a(\beta)$. The models in Cases (a) and (c) may be singular, but not independently of the parameters in the income equation (i.e. the coefficients of the polynomial and the variances of the shocks in (5.2)). In Case (a) a sufficient condition for singularity is

$$a_1(L)/a_1(\beta) = a_2(L)/a_2(\beta) = b(L)/b(\beta).$$

Under (c):

$$d(L)b(\beta) = d(\beta)b(L).$$

In Chapter 8 below we will prove that, irrespective of whether the micromodel is singular or not, aggregation yields a non-singular macromodel provided that both the independent variables and the individual responses can be different across agents.

5.2. A Labor Demand Schedule under Rational Expectations

This example is adapted from Sargent (1978), with considerable simplifications to allow for a straightforward treatment of the problem when we introduce heterogeneity. In the representative-firm version the model is based on the production function

$$(f_0 + p_t)n_t - (f_1/2)n_t^2,$$

where f_0 and f_1 are firm-specific parameters, p_t is a stochastic variable representing productivity, while n_t is the labor employed. The firm is assumed to maximize the present value

$$\begin{aligned} \mathrm{E}_t \sum_{k=0}^{\infty} \beta^k [(f_0 + p_{t+k} - w_{t+k})n_{t+k} - (f_1/2)n_{t+k}^2 \\ - (d/2)(n_{t+k} - n_{t+k-1})^2] \end{aligned} \tag{5.10}$$

where w_t is the real wage rate and β a discount factor (given from outside the model and independent of the firm). The term containing the squared first difference of n_t represents an adjustment cost. d is another firm-specific parameter.

It is assumed that $f_0 > 0$, $f_1 > 0$, $d > 0$, $1 > \beta > 0$. If such inequalities hold the solution for n_t is

$$n_t = \alpha_1 n_{t-1} - \delta \sum_{k=0}^{\infty} \alpha_2^j \mathrm{E}_t(w_{t+k} - p_{t+k} - f_0), \tag{5.11}$$

where α_1, α_2, and δ are non-linear functions of the deep parameters β, f_1, and d. Moreover, α_1 and α_2 are both of modulus smaller than unity (see Sargent, 1978, pp. 1016–18). Lastly, if, as in Sargent's paper, the analysis is limited to the residuals from fitting a linear trend to the variables n_t and w_t, the parameter f_0 can be ignored both in listing the microparameters and in (5.11).

In order to close the model we need a dynamic specification for the independent processes p_t and w_t. A convenient assumption in this exercise is

$$\begin{aligned} p_t &= \rho_0(\eta_t + \rho\eta_{t-1}) \\ w_t &= \tau_0(\epsilon_t + \tau\epsilon_{t-1}), \end{aligned} \tag{5.12}$$

where η_t and ϵ_t are unit variance white noises orthogonal to each other at all leads and lags, $|\rho| < 1$, $|\tau| < 1$. Substituting in (5.11) we obtain

$$\begin{aligned} n_t &= \alpha_1 n_{t-1} \\ &\quad - \delta[\tau_0(\epsilon_t + \tau\epsilon_{t-1}) + \rho_0(\eta_t + \rho\eta_{t-1}) + \alpha_2(\rho_0\rho\eta_t + \tau_0\tau\epsilon_t)] \\ &= \alpha_1 n_{t-1} \\ &\quad - \delta\tau_0[(1 + \alpha_2\tau)\epsilon_t + \tau\epsilon_{t-1}] - \delta\rho_0[(1 + \alpha_2\rho)\eta_t + \rho\eta_{t-1}]. \end{aligned}$$

Thus both w_t (by assumption) and n_t are stationary. The model can be written in vector form as

$$\begin{pmatrix} 1-\alpha_1 L & 0 \\ 0 & 1 \end{pmatrix} \begin{pmatrix} n_t \\ w_t \end{pmatrix} = \begin{pmatrix} g_1 + g_2 L & g_3 + g_4 L \\ 0 & \tau_0(1+\tau L) \end{pmatrix} \begin{pmatrix} \eta_t \\ \epsilon_t \end{pmatrix}. \tag{5.13}$$

Lastly, the RHS can be renormalized by setting

$$\begin{pmatrix} c_t \\ d_t \end{pmatrix} = \begin{pmatrix} g_1 & g_3 \\ 0 & \tau_0 \end{pmatrix} \begin{pmatrix} \eta_t \\ \epsilon_t \end{pmatrix},$$

so that

$$\begin{pmatrix} 1-\alpha_1 L & 0 \\ 0 & 1 \end{pmatrix} \begin{pmatrix} n_t \\ w_t \end{pmatrix} = \begin{pmatrix} 1+\tilde{g}_2 L & \tilde{g}_4 L \\ 0 & (1+\tau L) \end{pmatrix} \begin{pmatrix} c_t \\ d_t \end{pmatrix}, \tag{5.14}$$

where

$$\begin{pmatrix} 1+\tilde{g}_2 L & \tilde{g}_4 L \\ 0 & 1+\tau L \end{pmatrix} = \begin{pmatrix} g_1 + g_2 L & g_3 + g_4 L \\ 0 & \tau_0(1+\tau L) \end{pmatrix} \begin{pmatrix} g_1 & g_3 \\ 0 & \tau_0 \end{pmatrix}^{-1}.$$

Model (5.14) has seven parameters, namely α_1, $\tilde{g}_2$, $\tilde{g}_4$, τ, σ_c^2, σ_d^2, σ_{cd}, which are functions of six deep parameters, those determining the production function and the adjustment cost, namely f_1 and d, and those determining the two exogenous processes τ_0, ρ_0, τ, ρ.[1] This implies that (5.14) can be firstly estimated leaving its parameters free to vary in the region of $\mathbb{R}^7$ which is admissible with regard to stationarity and invertibility (in our case we only need $|\alpha_1| < 1$, $|\tilde{g}_2| < 1$, and $|\tau| < 1$). Subsequently, the model can be reestimated under the restrictions implicit in the functional dependence of the seven parameters in (5.14) on the six structural parameters. Finally, a likelihood ratio can be computed and used as a statistic to test whether the restrictions are rejected by the data or not.

Overidentification and aggregation for this class of models will be analyzed in Section 12.4. For the moment we want to analyze the consequences of dropping the assumption that all firms face the same independent variable. To this purpose model (5.13) is perfectly suitable. For simplicity let us assume that p_t is common to all firms, whereas

$$w_t = (\mu_1 + \nu_1 L)u_{1t} + (\mu_2 + \nu_2 L)u_{2t} + \sigma\xi_t, \tag{5.15}$$

where μ_l, ν_l, and ξ_t are firm specific while u_{1t} and u_{2t} are common shocks (as usual ξ_t and the components of u_t are of unit variance).

[1] Notice that the discount factor β, being given from outside the model, is not listed among the parameters.

As in Section 5.1 we must make an assumption on the information set available to the firms. Let us suppose that only w_t is observed, not its components. Thus, the firm observes the LHS of

$$\tau_0(1+\tau L)\epsilon_t = (\mu_1 + \nu_1 L)u_{1t} + (\mu_2 + \nu_2 L)u_{2t} + \sigma\xi_t, \tag{5.16}$$

where ϵ_t has unit variance. The solution still has the form (5.13), where now we must substitute ϵ_t, as resulting from (5.16), into (5.13). The result is

$$\begin{pmatrix} \tau_0(1+\tau L)(1-\alpha_1 L) & 0 \\ 0 & 1 \end{pmatrix} \begin{pmatrix} n_t \\ w_t \end{pmatrix} = K(L) \begin{pmatrix} \eta_t \\ u_{1t} \\ u_{2t} \end{pmatrix} + H(L)\xi_t,$$

where $K(L)$ is the matrix

$$\begin{pmatrix} \tau_0(g_1+g_2L)(1+\tau L) & (g_3+g_4L)(\mu_1+\nu_1 L) & (g_3+g_4L)(\mu_2+\nu_2 L) \\ 0 & \mu_1+\nu_1 L & \mu_2+\nu_2 L \end{pmatrix},$$

while $H(L)$ is

$$\sigma\begin{pmatrix} (g_3+g_4L) \\ 1 \end{pmatrix}.$$

Thus we have the ARIMA that we were looking for, with the common shocks $(\eta_t \quad u_{1t} \quad u_{2t})$ and the idiosyncratic shock ξ_t on the RHS. The coefficients of the autoregressive and the moving average matrices are (non-linear) functions of the parameters in (5.15), i.e. σ, μ_l, ν_l, $l = 1, 2$, the production function coefficients f_1 and d, and the parameters ρ_0 and ρ (the latter four through g_1, g_2, g_3, and g_4). We recall that ρ_0 and ρ are common to all firms whereas the remaining parameters are individual.

Here, although the assumption on expectations corresponds to Case (b) in Section 5.1, the vector $(n_t \quad w_t)'$ is non-singular unless a particular relationship links the microparameters. However, this depends on the additional source of variation η_t. Assumptions corresponding to Cases (a) or (c) in Section 5.1 lead to different ARIMA models in η_t, u_t, and ξ_t. The latter are, in general, non-singular, owing both to the presence of η_t and the same reasons we have seen in Section 5.1.

5.3. Consumption and Income again: Error Correction Mechanisms

This example, which is adapted from Nickell (1985), is quite similar to the previous one, except that it contains only one source of stochastic variation (as in Section 5.1), and the optimization problem is slightly different. Unlike the model studied in Section 5.1, the consumer here optimizes in two steps. In the first a static utility maximization leads to the preferred ratio between consumption and income under the assumption that both variables follow a steady growth; let κ be that ratio. In the second step the stochastic nature of income is taken into consideration and the following loss function is minimized:

$$\mathrm{E}_t \sum_{k=0}^{\infty} \beta^k [\omega_1 (c_{t+k} - \kappa y_{t+k})^2 + (c_{t+k} - c_{t+k-1})^2 \\ - 2\omega_2 (c_{t+k} - c_{t+k-1})(y_{t+k} - y_{t+k-1})],$$

where the first term accounts for the distance betwen actual and desired consumption, the second measures the preference for smooth consumption, and the third reduces (increases) the loss when consumption and income changes have the same (opposite) sign. As in Section 5.2, the solution is

$$c_t = \alpha c_{t-1} - \delta \sum_{k=0}^{\infty} (b\alpha)^s \mathrm{E}_t y_{t+k},$$

where β, given from outside the model, fulfills $1 > \beta > 0$, while α and δ are functions of ω_1, ω_2, β, and κ, with $|\alpha| < 1$.

If y_t follows the simple I(1) process

$$\Delta y_t - \tau_0(\eta_t - \tau\eta_{t-1}), \tag{5.17}$$

where η_t is a unit variance white noise, the solution is

$$\Delta c_t = a\Delta c_{t-1} + c\Delta y_t + d\Delta y_{t-1} + \rho(\kappa y_{t-1} - c_{t-1}), \tag{5.18}$$

where a, c, d, and ρ are non-linear functions of the deep parameters ω_1, ω_2, β, τ_0, and τ (Nickell, 1985, p. 125). It may be shown that the coefficients of (5.18) are such that Δc_t is stationary. As a consequence, $\kappa y_t - c_t$ is also stationary.

The couple of equations (5.17) and (5.18) can be rewritten in such a way as to highlight the dependence of both Δy_t and Δc_t on η_t. Defining

$$p(L) = (1 - L) - a(1 - L)L + \rho L$$
$$q(L) = c(1 - L) + d(1 - L) + \rho\kappa L$$

we have

$$\begin{pmatrix} p(L) & -q(L) \\ 0 & 1 - L \end{pmatrix} \begin{pmatrix} c_t \\ y_t \end{pmatrix} = \begin{pmatrix} 0 \\ \tau_0(1 - \tau L) \end{pmatrix} \eta_t,$$

i.e.

$$p(L) \begin{pmatrix} \Delta c_t \\ \Delta y_t \end{pmatrix} = \begin{pmatrix} q(L)\tau_0(1 - \tau L) \\ p(L)\tau_0(1 - \tau L) \end{pmatrix} \eta_t. \tag{5.19}$$

The form (5.19) of the model can be employed to analyze its heterogeneous-agent versions. For example, if Δy_t follows an equation like (5.15)

$$\Delta y_t = (\mu_1 + \nu_1 L)u_{1t} + (\mu_2 + \nu_2 L)u_{2t} + \sigma\xi_t, \tag{5.20}$$

and the agent observes only Δy_t, not its components, then the representation in terms of u_t and ξ_t can be immediately obtained along the lines of Sections 5.1 and 5.2. We determine τ and η_t from

$$\tau_0(1 - \tau L)\eta_t = (\mu_1 + \nu_1 L)u_{1t} + (\mu_2 + \nu_2 L)u_{2t} + \sigma\xi_t,$$

with the condition that the variance of η_t is unitary. Substituting in (5.19)

$$p(L)\begin{pmatrix}\Delta c_t\\ \Delta y_t\end{pmatrix} = \begin{pmatrix} q(L)(\mu_1 + \nu_1 L) & q(L)(\mu_2 + \nu_2 L)\\ p(L)(\mu_1 + \nu_1 L) & p(L)(\mu_2 + \nu_2 L)\end{pmatrix}\begin{pmatrix}u_{1t}\\ u_{2t}\end{pmatrix} + \sigma\begin{pmatrix}q(L)\\ p(L)\end{pmatrix}\xi_t. \tag{5.21}$$

Equation (5.18) is a simple example of the error correction mechanism, the term $(\kappa y_{t-1} - c_{t-1})$ being known as the error correction term. In the version we have reported here the joint model of (5.17) and (5.18), or equivalently (5.19), is singular. In fact, (5.18) is an exact relationship between c_t and y_t. There are variants of Nickell's model, see e.g. Hendry and von Ungern-Sternberg (1980), where a motivation for an additional shock in equation (5.18) is provided, so that the model becomes non-singular. Our model (5.21), being obtained under the assumption that the agents see y_t, not its components, and that no additional shock appears in (5.18), is also singular.

5.4. Rules of Thumb. Non-Fully Rational, Routinized Behaviors

The models in the previous three sections belong to the framework of intertemporal optimization under rational expectations. These assumptions, though with considerable variants, have dominated macroeconomic modeling in the last decade.

On the other hand, myopic agents, expectations, and decision rules based on fixed, process-independent, procedures have been widely employed in the past in macroeconomics. It is not our intention here to report in detail the arguments put forward by the scholars who claim that robust rules of thumb are the best agents can do, and that their dismissal has not represented an advance in macroeconomics. Rather, we want to show that such alternative models can be accommodated into our framework without any difficulty.

As a first example, let us recall that the consumption–income equation we have recalled in Section 5.1 is the modern version of a model that in its original formulation by Milton Friedman contains a definition of permanent income as a moving average with exponentially declining coefficients

$$y_{\mathrm{p}t} = (1-\rho)(y_t + \rho y_{t-1} + \rho^2 y_{t-2} + \cdots), \tag{5.22}$$

and the consumption equation

$$c_t = \kappa y_{\mathrm{p}t}. \tag{5.23}$$

Substituting (5.22) into the consumption equation one obtains

$$(1-\rho L)c_t = \kappa y_t. \tag{5.24}$$

The most important difference between (5.24) and the models analyzed in the previous examples is that the coefficients in (5.24) do not depend on the process generating the variable y_t, since κ is derived from a static maximization, while ρ belongs to an adaptive expectations scheme.[2]

In much the same way, the fixed mark-up theory of industrial price formation, as advocated for instance in Coutts *et al.* (1978), can be described as a complicated version of the couple of equations (5.22) and (5.23), with the normal cost playing the role of permanent income.

In general, apart from particular features, deterministic trends, dummies, and other possible variants, these models can be summarized by an equation describing the behavior of a representative agent as an ARMAX (AutoRegressive Moving Average with eXogenous variables):

$$a(L)y_t = b(L)x_t + c(L)\epsilon_t. \tag{5.25}$$

The coefficients of (5.25) may or may not be in some relationship with the coefficients of the process generating the variable x_t. In any case, the attitude behind this class of models usually leads to less demanding conclusions, as compared to the cross-equation restrictions of the rational expectations approach. Usually, equation (5.25) is estimated as a single equation while the implications of the theory consist of restrictions on the coefficients of (5.25) alone. For example, Friedman's permanent income model, and the fixed mark-up theory of prices, both imply a unit long-run elasticity of y_t to x_t. When the models are formulated in the logarithms of the variables, this means $b(1)/a(1) = 1$, which is a testable implication on the coefficients of (5.25) alone.

Now suppose that equation (5.25) is coupled with the following representation for x_t,

$$x_t = a_1(L)u_{1t} + a_2(L)u_{2t} + d(L)\xi_t,$$

[2] See Sargent (1987, pp. 293–94).

and suppose that agents apply their routines directly to x_t, without observing—or without caring about—its components. A representation for the vector $(\,y_t \quad x_t\,)'$ can be obtained as

$$\begin{pmatrix} a(L) & 0 \\ 0 & 1 \end{pmatrix} \begin{pmatrix} y_t \\ x_t \end{pmatrix} = \begin{pmatrix} b(L)a_1(L) & b(L)a_2(L) \\ a_1(L) & a_2(L) \end{pmatrix} \begin{pmatrix} u_{1t} \\ u_{2t} \end{pmatrix} + \begin{pmatrix} c(L) & b(L)d(L) \\ 0 & d(L) \end{pmatrix} \begin{pmatrix} \epsilon_t \\ \xi_t \end{pmatrix}.$$

The lack of distinction between the components of x_t would generate a singular model. Non-singularity is ensured by the disturbance ϵ_t, which is often an *ad hoc* augmentation of the model.

5.5. Structural VAR Models. General Equilibrium

The examples presented in the previous sections belong to the partial equilibrium area. The definitions of micromodel and of aggregate model, which are given in Chapters 6 and 7, are also suited for partial equilibrium models. However, as we shall see in Section 7.4, general equilibrium models require only minor modifications of the definitions. The following is an example of the way in which heterogeneity and aggregation problems can be introduced in a general equilibrium model.

In Blanchard and Quah (1989), a simple structural general equilibrium model for output, unemployment, money, and wage is proposed as a basis for the estimation of a vector autoregression including output and unemployment. The vector autoregressive model has the form

$$\begin{pmatrix} \Delta y_t \\ U_t \end{pmatrix} = \begin{pmatrix} a_{11}(L) & a_{12}(L)(1-L) \\ a_{21}(L) & a_{22}(L) \end{pmatrix} \begin{pmatrix} e_{st} \\ e_{dt} \end{pmatrix},$$

where e_{st} is a shock to productivity, while e_{dt} is a demand shock. Owing to the factor $(1 - L)$, the demand shock has a purely transitory effect on output, whereas the productivity shock has a permanent effect (provided that $a_{11}(1) \neq 0$). In their paper Blanchard and Quah also analyze the model that results if the assumption of 'representative' demand and supply shocks is dropped. We do not need to rewrite the model. We can simply reinterpret e_{dt} and e_{st} as white-noise vectors, instead of scalars. For instance,

$$e_{dt} = (\,e_{dt}^1 \quad e_{dt}^2 \quad \cdots \quad e_{dt}^h\,).$$

In the same way, the functions $a_{ij}(L)$ must be reinterpreted as vectors of functions of suitable dimension. The aggregate variables y_t and U_t thus result as sums of the effects of many different productivity and demand shocks. Naturally, no difficulty arises if we want to distinguish between shocks affecting all the economic units and shocks specific to individual economic units. The aggregation problem in this kind of model will be studied in Chapter 12.

5.6. Bibliographic Notes

For extensive references on Hall's model see Chapter 13 below. For a vast treatment of models based on dynamic objective functions and rational expectations see Hansen and Sargent (1991a). For the microfoundation of error correction mechanisms see, in addition to the works mentioned in Section 5.3, Salmon (1982), Hendry (1995, Chapter 8). For structural VAR models, see Bernanke (1986), Shapiro and Watson (1988), Evans (1989).

6

The Disaggregated Model

Now we want to establish a general framework which includes the examples analyzed in Chapter 5 as particular cases. Unfortunately some complications, both notational and substantive, cannot be avoided. To compensate for them we will proceed by carefully clarifying each step of the construction.

Each of the examples of Chapter 5 produces a function which associates stochastic equations with vectors of microparameters. Some of the microparameters are agent specific, others are common to all agents. For instance, in Section 5.2 μ_1 is an agent-specific parameter whereas ρ_0 is common to all agents. In Section 5.1 all the parameters are agent specific; however, we might change our assumption and suppose that $b(L)$ is agent specific whereas the parameters of $a_1(L)$ and $a_2(L)$ are common to all agents. The microparameter space embodies this distinction, together with the idea of an admissibility region. The micromodel is the function that we have just mentioned: with any point γ of the microparameter space it associates a stochastic equation, i.e. the behavior of an agent whose microparameters are γ. Then we define the population space for a given population size m. A point in the population space is obtained by selecting m points in the microparameter space, each of them with its individual parameters but all with the same common parameters. Finally, the disaggregated model is the application of the micromodel to all the agents of a population, with the additional condition that the idiosyncratic components of different agents are orthogonal to one another.

As anticipated in Section 5.5, the definitions of micromodel and of aggregate model, given in this and the following chapter, are tailored on partial equilibrium models. But this is only a convenience which has been adopted in order to concentrate our attention on the macroparameters as functions of the microparameters. As we will show in Section 7.4, taking into account general equilibrium models would require only a minor modification of the definitions.

6.1. The Microparameter Space

DEFINITION 6.1. The *microparameter space* is a set Γ, with

$$\Gamma \subseteq \mathbb{R}^s \times \mathbb{R}^c.$$

The elements of Γ are couples $(\omega\ \lambda)$, where ω is s-dimensional, while λ is c-dimensional. The coordinates of ω correspond to agent-specific parameters, while the coordinates of λ correspond to parameters common to all agents.

We note that $\mathbb{R}^s \times \mathbb{R}^c$ is a set of couples whose first element is an s-tuple, the second a c-tuple, not a set of $(s+c)$-tuples. Although in many respects $\mathbb{R}^s \times \mathbb{R}^c$ is equivalent to $\mathbb{R}^{s+c}$, the integers s and c are crucial for our definition. If a model has been studied under the assumption that a certain parameter, say λ_1, is common and we want to analyze what would happen if it were agent specific, the microparameter space would no longer be contained in $\mathbb{R}^s \times \mathbb{R}^c$ but in $\mathbb{R}^{s+1} \times \mathbb{R}^{c-1}$. We suppose:

ASSUMPTION 6.1. The set Γ is open and connected.

A subset of a euclidean space which fulfills Assumption 6.1 is called an *open region* (see Apostol, 1974, p. 89).

Let us illustrate Definition 6.1 by means of the model in Section 5.2. In that case the agent-specific parameters are

$$\omega = (\, f_1 \quad d \quad \mu_1 \quad \nu_1 \quad \mu_2 \quad \nu_2 \quad \sigma\,),$$

while

$$\lambda = (\,\rho_0 \quad \rho\,).$$

Thus $s = 7$, $c = 2$. The set Γ can be defined by

$$f_1 > 0,\ d > 0,\ 1 > \rho > 0,\ \mu_l > \nu_l > 0,$$

with no restrictions on σ and ρ_0. Assumption 6.1 is obviously fulfilled.

It is important to remark that s or c may be zero. For instance, c is zero in Section 5.1, and would be zero in Section 5.2 under the assumption that the productivity shocks are firm specific.

The inequalities $\mu_l > \nu_l$ provide an example of the reason why Γ is a subset of a cartesian product, not a cartesian product itself. Another important reason will be given in Remark 6.6 below.

REMARK 6.1. Assuming that Γ is an open set corresponds to the idea that if γ is admissible, then $\gamma + \epsilon$ is admissible as well, provided that $|\epsilon|$ is small enough. Equivalently, any component of γ can vary freely with respect to the others, provided that it remains within the admissibility constraints. In many cases one should allow the set Γ to contain part of its boundary, as is the case when Γ is defined by inequalities and one of them is weak. However, this would complicate our definitions and demonstrations, with no real advantage.

6.2. The Micromodel

The micromodel is a function associating, within a given framework, a vector microequation with every $\gamma \in \Gamma$. Let us begin by describing the framework:

(1) n is the dimension of the microvariables vector.

(2) u_t is an orthonormal white-noise vector of dimension h, the common shocks vector. ξ_t is an orthonormal white-noise vector of dimension r, the idiosyncratic shocks vector. We assume that u_t and ξ_t are orthogonal to one another at all leads and lags.

(3) $D(L)$ is an $n \times n$ diagonal matrix in L with $D_{kk}(L) = (1-L)^{d_k}$.

DEFINITION 6.2. Given n, h, r, $D(L)$, u_t, ξ_t, and the set Γ, a *micromodel* is a function $\mathcal{M}$ associating with any $\gamma = (\omega \quad \lambda) \in \Gamma$:

(I) The polynomial matrices $A^\gamma(L)$, $B^\gamma(L)$, $C^\gamma(L)$, which are respectively $n \times n$, $n \times h$, $n \times r$. The orders of the polynomial matrices are respectively O_A, O_B, O_C, and do not depend on γ.

(II) The vector microequation

$$A^\gamma(L)D(L)z_t = B^\gamma(L)u_t + C^\gamma(L)\xi_t. \tag{6.1}$$

We suppose:

ASSUMPTION 6.2. For all $\gamma \in \Gamma$, the roots of $\det A^\gamma(L)$ lie outside the unit circle.

This implies that there exists a unique stationary process solving

$$A^\gamma(L)w_t = B^\gamma(L)u_t + C^\gamma(L)\xi_t.$$

Denote such a process by w_t^γ. A solution of (6.1) is a process solving $D(L)z_t = w_t^\gamma$ with a given set of initial conditions. Since explicit reference to the initial conditions will never be needed, we will simplify notation by writing z_t^γ to indicate any solution of (6.1). In the same way, to simplify notation, equation (6.1) will be referred to as

$$A^\gamma(L)D(L)z_t^\gamma = B^\gamma(L)u_t + C^\gamma(L)\xi_t. \tag{6.1}$$

ASSUMPTION 6.3. For all $\gamma \in \Gamma$ the k-th component of $D(L)z_t^\gamma$ has positive spectral density at frequency zero.

This means that such a component is integrated of order d_k, i.e. that it is stationary when applying $(1-L)^{d_k}$, non-stationary when applying $(1-L)^{d_k-1}$. Notice that we are not excluding that the spectral density of the vector $D(L)z_t^\gamma$ may be singular at zero. This happens when a cointegration relationship holds among the components.

ASSUMPTION 6.4. In our definition the coefficients of $A^\gamma(L)$, $B^\gamma(L)$, $C^\gamma(L)$ are functions of γ. We assume that all such functions are *analytic* in Γ.

Some illustrations and comments are in order.

REMARK 6.2. Regarding the notation, the symbols $A^\gamma(L)$, $B^\gamma(L)$, and $C^\gamma(L)$ do not contain any reference to $\mathcal{M}$. A different choice in notation would have been complicated and not really necessary. Nevertheless, it must be understood that the functional dependence indicated by $A^\gamma(L)$ is specific to the individual micromodel. For a given Γ, changing the micromodel would change the way in which the coefficients of, say, the autoregressive matrix depend on γ. For instance, if $\tilde{\mathcal{M}}$ were the alternative micromodel, it would be natural to use $\tilde{A}^\gamma(L)$ for the autoregressive matrix.

REMARK 6.3. Regarding the vector z_t^γ, it must be understood that this is the vector containing all the variables entering the agent's decision, both dependent and independent, provided they have an observable aggregate counterpart. For instance, in Section 5.1 agents may base their expectations and decisions on components of their income which have no observable counterpart. However, once the model is written in its final ARIMA form, we have only two observables on the LHS, while the way agents take their decision is embodied in the matrices A, B, and C. Notice that different assumptions on the expectations in Sections 5.1 or 5.2 do not alter Γ, but produce different microequations, i.e. different $\mathcal{M}$'s. In Section 5.1, if the agents observe all the components of their income separately, the coefficients of the micromodel are trivial functions of the microparameters. If, instead, they use only their income, then the resulting functions are more complicated, since the Wold representation of income must firstly be computed, which implies non-linearities in the relationship. The same occurs in the models presented in Sections 5.2 and 5.3.

REMARK 6.4. Representation (6.1) is not unique, in the sense that the same vector process $D(L)z_t^\gamma$ admits different representations fulfilling all the assumptions above. For instance, the matrix $A(0)^\gamma$ cannot be singular by Assumption 6.1. Thus we can multiply both sides of (6.1) by $[A(0)^\gamma]^{-1}$ and obtain another representation of the micromodel. Other representations will be considered in Chapter 7. In any case, a unique representation is altogether outside our interest. Representation (6.1) is to be understood as one amongst the possible translations of the economic relationships linking the microvariables in the form of an ARIMA, i.e. by polynomial matrices in front of z_t^γ, u_t, ξ_t.

REMARK 6.5. Regarding the matrix $D(L)$, in Sections 5.1 and 5.3 we have $d_1 = d_2 = 1$, while in Section 5.2 we have $d_1 = d_2 = 0$. Notice that both in

Section 5.1, under assumption (b), and in Section 5.3, the microvariables are cointegrated, although in a trivial way since the models are singular. In fact, the spectral densities of these models are singular at any frequency. More will be given on this point in Chapter 9.

A detailed comment on Assumption 6.4 is postponed to Section 6.5 below.

6.3. The Population Space

Let the integer m be the size of the populations, i.e. the number of agents. Consider first the cartesian product

$$E = \overbrace{\mathbb{R}^s \times \mathbb{R}^s \times \cdots \times \mathbb{R}^s}^{m \text{ times}} \times \mathbb{R}^c,$$

DEFINITION 6.3. The *population space* Γ_m is the subset of E defined as follows:

$$\Gamma_m = \{(\omega^1 \; \omega^2 \; \cdots \; \omega^m \; \lambda) : (\omega^i \; \lambda) \in \Gamma\}.$$

A point $p \in \Gamma_m$ represents a possible population of size m. Each agent is endowed with his, or her, specific parameters, and all the agents with the same common parameters. Notice that the common parameters may vary from one population to another, i.e. from one vector p to another, but not within a given population, i.e. not across different agents belonging to the same p. Notice also that Γ_m contains populations in which all agents have the same microparameters, populations with a group of agents having the same microparameters ω, while all of the remaining agents have $\tilde{\omega} \neq \omega$, and so on.

DEFINITION 6.4. If $p = (\omega^1 \quad \omega^2 \quad \cdots \quad \omega^m \quad \lambda)$, we shall indicate with p^i, $i = 1, m$, the point $(\omega^i \quad \lambda) \in \Gamma$. Naturally the points p^i form an m-tuple of points of Γ sharing the same λ.

Let us prove that:

THEOREM 6.1. If Γ is an open region then Γ_m is also an open region.

Proof. No loss of generality occurs by setting $m = 2$. Let $\tilde{p} = (\tilde{\omega}^1 \quad \tilde{\omega}^2 \quad \tilde{\lambda})$ and $p = (\omega^1 \quad \omega^2 \quad \lambda)$, with $\tilde{p} \in \Gamma_2$. We have

$$|p - \tilde{p}| = |\omega^1 - \tilde{\omega}^1 \quad \omega^2 - \tilde{\omega}^2 \quad \lambda - \tilde{\lambda}| \geq |p^i - \tilde{p}^i|$$

for $i = 1, 2$. Therefore, if $|p - \tilde{p}| < \epsilon$ and ϵ is sufficiently small, then $(\omega^i \quad \lambda)$ belongs to Γ, $i = 1, 2$. To show that Γ_2 is connected, let us recall that an open subset of $\mathbb{R}^v$ is connected if and only if it is arcwise connected (see Apostol, 1974, p. 89), i.e. if any couple of points in the subset can be joined by a continuous arc lying in the subset. Now consider $\hat{p} = (\hat{\omega}^1 \quad \hat{\omega}^2 \quad \hat{\lambda})$ and $\check{p} = (\check{\omega}^1 \quad \check{\omega}^2 \quad \check{\lambda})$. Then join $\hat{p}$ to $(\hat{\omega}^1 \quad \hat{\omega}^1 \quad \hat{\lambda})$ reproducing the arc joining $(\hat{\omega}^2 \quad \hat{\lambda})$ to $(\hat{\omega}^1 \quad \hat{\lambda})$ in Γ. Then join $(\hat{\omega}^1 \quad \hat{\omega}^1 \quad \hat{\lambda})$ to $(\check{\omega}^1 \quad \check{\omega}^1 \quad \check{\lambda})$, using the arc joining $(\hat{\omega}^1 \quad \hat{\lambda})$ to $(\check{\omega}^1 \quad \check{\lambda})$. Finally join $(\check{\omega}^1 \quad \check{\omega}^1 \quad \check{\lambda})$ to $(\check{\omega}^1 \quad \check{\omega}^2 \quad \check{\lambda})$. Q.E.D.

6.4. The Disaggregated Model

The disaggregated model is a function defined for any $p \in \Gamma_m$. As in Definition 6.2 we need firstly to define a framework. Let

$$u_t, \quad \xi_t^1, \quad \xi_t^2, \quad \ldots, \quad \xi_t^m \tag{6.2}$$

be orthonormal white-noise vectors, where the common shock u_t is h-dimensional while the i-th agent's idiosyncratic shock ξ_t^i is r-dimensional. Suppose:

ASSUMPTION 6.5. The $m+1$ vectors in (6.2) are orthogonal to one another at all leads and lags.

DEFINITION 6.5. Given the population space Γ_m, the micromodel $\mathcal{M}$, and the vectors (6.2), the corresponding *disaggregated model* $\mathcal{DM}$ is the function associating with any

$$p = (\omega^1 \quad \omega^2 \quad \cdots \quad \omega^m \quad \lambda) \in \Gamma_m$$

the m vector microequations

$$A^{p^i}(L)D(L)z_t = B^{p^i}(L)u_t + C^{p^i}(L)\xi_t^i, \tag{6.3}$$

for $i = 1, m$, where $A^{p^i}(L)$, $B^{p^i}(L)$, $C^{p^i}(L)$ depend on $p^i = (\omega^i \quad \lambda)$ according to the function $\mathcal{M}$.

The process solving the i-th equation in (6.3) will be denoted by z_t^{i,p^i}. Such a process is unique up to the initial conditions (see the comment under Assumption 6.2).

One may wonder what the relationship is between the disaggregated model, as defined above, and the *individual model,* as defined in Chapter 1. Firstly, the disaggregated model deals with vectors whereas in Chapter 1 we only consider scalar models; secondly, here we consider finite populations whereas in Chapter 1 we have infinite families. However, infinite families were convenient in Chapter 1 only to establish asymptotic results for the idiosyncratic component. Once the latter have been obtained, a large number of agents will be sufficient if we want to drop the idiosyncratic component, as we argue in detail in Section 7.2. In conclusion, the disaggregated model can be considered as a generalization of the individual model of Chapter 1.

6.5. Further Comments on the Micromodel. Analytic Functions

There are two important points related to the definitions just given which deserve special emphasis.

6.5.1. First of all, each element of Γ_m represents m different individuals, irrespective of whether the subvectors ω^i are different or not. Let us denote by H_m the subset of Γ_m

$$\{(\omega \quad \omega \quad \cdots \quad \omega \quad \lambda),\ (\omega \quad \lambda) \in \Gamma\}.$$

A population belongs to H_m if the parameters of the m agents in the population are equal, not if there is only one agent in the population. This difference can be better appreciated within the definition of the disaggregated model. In fact, since the idiosyncratic shocks ξ_t^i are orthogonal to one another, the agents 1, 2, etc., in a given population are different from one another, even though their parameters may be equal. This is the reason why the processes solving equations (6.3) are indexed by both i and p^i. Even though $p^i = p^j$, the variables z^{i,p^i} and z^{j,p^j} are different if $i \neq j$, owing to the different idiosyncratic components.

6.5.2. Now consider the common shock u_t. In Definition 6.5 this has been assumed as common to all the agents of a population and to all the populations. The second feature of u_t is not really necessary. We might equally be satisfied with the weaker assumption of a shock u_t^λ, i.e. a vector of orthonormal white noises which does not vary within a population but may vary from one population to another. For instance, suppose that ω_1, ω_2, and λ are the microparameters and that the micromodel is

$$x_t^\gamma = (1 + \omega_1 L)u_{1t} + \lambda(1 + \omega_1 L)u_{2t} + \omega_2 \xi_t. \tag{6.4}$$

In this case there is an evident redundancy (this concept will be defined rigorously in Section 6.7 below), i.e. considering a given population, the common component may be rewritten as

$$(1 + \omega_1 L)w_t^\lambda,$$

where

$$w_t^\lambda = \frac{u_{1t} + \lambda u_{2t}}{\sqrt{1 + \lambda^2}}.$$

Here we have different shocks for different λ's, but the same shock within a given population, and this is what really matters.

However, a formal definition, allowing for u_t to vary when λ varies, is not really necessary, as this would only be needed in 6.7, where we discuss redundancy in general. Reference to reparameterizations of the common component with an orthonormal vector of lower dimension depending on λ, but not on the other components of γ, will be sufficient.

6.5.3. Let us now return to Assumptions 6.4 and 6.1. In 6.4 we require that the coefficients of the polynomial matrices A^γ, B^γ, and C^γ be analytic in Γ.

Let us recall the definition of an analytic function.

DEFINITION 6.6. Consider a function $f : \Omega \to \mathbb{R}$, where Ω is an open subset of $\mathbb{R}^v$. Assume that: (a) all the partial derivatives of f exist for any point of Ω. Then, for $\bar{x} \in \Omega$ define

$$a_{k_1 k_2 \cdots k_v}(\bar{x}) = \frac{1}{k_1! k_2! \cdots k_v!} \frac{\partial^{k_1+k_2+\cdots+k_v}}{\partial^{k_1} x_1 \partial^{k_2} x_2 \cdots \partial^{k_v} x_v} f \Big|_{x=\bar{x}}.$$

The Taylor series of f, centered at $\bar{x}$, is

$$\sum_{k_1=0}^{\infty} \sum_{k_2=0}^{\infty} \cdots \sum_{k_v=0}^{\infty} a_{k_1 k_2 \cdots k_v}(\bar{x})(x_1 - \bar{x}_1)^{k_1}(x_2 - \bar{x}_2)^{k_2} \cdots (x_v - \bar{x}_v)^{k_v}.$$

Assume that: (b) given any $\bar{x} \in \Omega$, there exists a neighborhood W of $\bar{x}$ in Ω in which the Taylor series of f, centered at $\bar{x}$, converges absolutely; moreover, for $x \in W$ the Taylor series converges to $f(x)$. Functions for which (a) and (b) hold are called analytic functions. The definition of an analytic function for $f : \Omega \to \mathbb{C}$, where $\mathbb{C}$ is the complex field, goes exactly in the same way.

The following lemmas generalize to analytic functions the fact that two polynomials of v variables that are equal in an open set of $\mathbb{R}^v$ are equal over the whole $\mathbb{R}^v$, and the fact that if $v = 1$ two polynomials can coincide only for a finite number of points (for references see Section 6.10).

LEMMA 6.1. Assume that Ω is open and connected, and that the analytic functions f and g coincide for an open subset of Ω. Then f and g coincide on the whole Ω.

Proof. Let D be the union of all the open sets contained in Ω in which the two functions coincide. Suppose that $D \neq \Omega$ and let $\bar{x}$ be a boundary point of D (if D has no boundary points then its complement has no boundary points either and is therefore open; but this implies non-connectednes of Ω). $\bar{x}$ cannot belong to D since the latter is open. On the other hand, by continuity, all the partial derivatives of $f - g$ at $\bar{x}$ vanish. Therefore, using the Taylor expansion centered at $\bar{x}$, $f - g$ vanishes in a neighborhood around $\bar{x}$. But this implies that $\bar{x} \in D$. Thus assuming that $D \neq \Omega$ leads to a contradiction. Q.E.D.

LEMMA 6.2. Let $v = 1$ and assume that f and g are analytic in the open connected set Ω. If the set where f and g are equal has an accumulation point in Ω, then f and g coincide on the whole Ω.

Proof. Let $h = f - g$. Let $\bar{x}$ be an accumulation point of the subset of Ω where $h = 0$. The first derivative of h at $\bar{x}$ must vanish. Therefore

$$h(x) = \frac{1}{2!}h''(\bar{x})(x - \bar{x})^2 + \cdots.$$

Consider the function $k(x)$, defined as zero at $\bar{x}$, and

$$\frac{h(x)}{x - \bar{x}} = \frac{1}{2!}h''(\bar{x})(x - \bar{x}) + \cdots$$

for $x \neq \bar{x}$. The function k vanishes in the same set in which h vanishes. Therefore its first derivative at $\bar{x}$, i.e. $h''(\bar{x})/2!$, vanishes. By iteration all the derivatives of h vanish at $\bar{x}$. Therefore h vanishes in an open neighborhood of $\bar{x}$ and Lemma 6.1 can be applied. Q.E.D.

Elementary functions and functions obtained by combining elementary functions are analytic. However, caution must be exercised. For instance,

$$\sqrt{x_1^2 + x_2^2}$$

is analytic in $\mathbb{R}^2$ with the exception of the origin, where it does not admit any derivative. In the same way, the roots of the equation

$$ax^2 + bx + c = 0$$

are analytic as functions of $(\,a \quad b \quad c\,) \in \mathbb{R}^3$, with the exception of the plane $a = 0$ and the surface where the discriminant $b^2 - 4ac$ vanishes. More in general:

LEMMA 6.3. Let Ω be an open connected subset of $\mathbb{R}^v$ and let a_l^x, for $l = 0, s$, be analytic functions of x in Ω. Consider the polynomial

$$a_0^x + a_1^x z + a_2^x z^2 + \cdots + a_s^x z^s. \tag{6.5}$$

Suppose that a_s^x and the discriminant of (6.5) never vanish in Ω. Then there exist s functions α_l^x, analytic in Ω, such that

$$a_0^x + a_1^x \alpha_l^x + a_2^x (\alpha_l^x)^2 + \cdots + a_s^x (\alpha_l^x)^s = 0$$

for $l = 1, s$, and any $x \in \Omega$.

We do not report the proof of Lemma 6.3. Suffice it here to recall that the discriminant of a polynomial $p(z)$ is a polynomial in the coefficients of $p(z)$ (a generalization of the familiar $b^2 - 4ac$). The polynomial $p(z)$ has multiple roots if and only if its discriminant vanishes (see Section 6.10 for references).

6.5.4. If the coefficients of the micromodel are analytic in Γ (Assumption 6.4) and Γ is connected (Assumption 6.1), then we can apply a very powerful result that will be presented in Section 6.6. For the moment, we wish to give an example aimed at showing the typical difficulty that may arise with simultaneous fulfillment of Assumptions 6.4 and 6.1.

Let us consider the following univariate model

$$x_t = (a + bL + cL^2)u_t + d\xi_t, \tag{6.6}$$

where u_t and ξ_t are unit variance white noises, and suppose that the information set of an agent is limited to present and past values of x_t. Irrespectively of the way the agent will employ it (in forming expectations for instance), we want to study the Wold representation of x_t, i.e. the LHS of

$$(\alpha + \beta L + \delta L^2)\eta_t = (a + bL + cL^2)u_t + d\xi_t, \tag{6.7}$$

where η_t is a unit variance white noise. More precisely, we want to define the set Γ in such a way that the coefficients α, β, and δ are analytic as functions defined on Γ.

To do this we must follow the details of the procedure by which α, β, and δ are derived.[1] Firstly take the covariance generating function of the RHS of (6.7):

$$ac(z^2 + z^{-2}) + (ab + bc)(z + z^{-1}) + (a^2 + b^2 + c^2 + d^2)$$
$$= \rho_0(z^2 + z^{-2}) + \rho_1(z + z^{-1}) + \rho_2,$$

where

$$\rho_0 = ac, \quad \rho_1 = ab + bc, \quad \rho_2 = a^2 + b^2 + c^2 + d^2.$$

Secondly, set $y = z + z^{-1}$ and consider the equation

$$\rho_0 y^2 + \rho_1 y + (\rho_2 - 2\rho_0) = 0. \tag{6.8}$$

Let q_1 and q_2 be the roots of (6.8) and put

$$\rho_0 y^2 + \rho_1 y + \rho_2 - 2\rho_0 = \rho_0(y - q_1)(y - q_2)$$
$$= \rho_0 z^{-2}(z^2 - q_1 z + 1)(z^2 - q_2 z + 1).$$

[1] This is an application of the procedure described in Section 4.1.

Finally, put $z^2 - q_k z + 1 = (z - m_k)(z - m_k^{-1})$, with $|m_k| < 1$. We can write the covariance generating function as

$$\frac{\rho_0}{m_1 m_2}(1 - m_1 z)(1 - m_1 z^{-1})(1 - m_2 z)(1 - m_2 z^{-1}).$$

Thus

$$\alpha + \beta L + \gamma L^2 = \frac{\rho_0}{m_1 m_2}(1 - m_1 L)(1 - m_2 L),$$

so that

$$\alpha = \frac{\rho_0}{m_1 m_2}, \quad \beta = -\frac{\rho_0}{m_1 m_2}(m_1 + m_2), \quad \delta = \rho_0.$$

Now define $\tilde{\Gamma}$ by $a > 0$, $b > 0$, $c > 0$, $d > 0$. The functions just defined are analytic in $\tilde{\Gamma}$, with the exception of the locus where $\rho_0 = 0$, i.e. $ac = 0$, which is empty, and the locus where the discriminant of (6.8) vanishes, i.e. the subset of Γ

$$\{\gamma : \ \rho_1^2 - 4\rho_0(\rho_2 - 2\rho_0) = 0\}.$$

Going back to the definition of the coefficients ρ_k, this is the set where

$$(ab + bc)^2 - 4ac(a^2 + b^2 + c^2 + d^2) = 0,$$

i.e.

$$b = \sqrt{\frac{4ac(d^2 + a^2 + c^2)}{(a - c)^2}}. \tag{6.9}$$

This is a non-empty hypersurface in $\tilde{\Gamma}$. To simplify the matter further, suppose that a and c are fixed, with $a \neq c$, so that $\tilde{\Gamma}$ is the positive orthant of $\mathbb{R}^2$. The set defined by (6.9) is a curve, call it $\hat{\Gamma}$, which splits $\mathbb{R}^2$ into Γ', the open set above $\hat{\Gamma}$, Γ'', the open set below, and $\hat{\Gamma}$ itself. Taking Γ either as Γ' or as Γ'', both Assumptions 6.4 and 6.1 are fulfilled, whereas 6.4 is not fulfilled in $\tilde{\Gamma}$.

It must be pointed out that in the open set where the discriminant of (6.8) is negative, q_1 and q_2 are complex conjugates. As already pointed out in Definition 6.6, the definition of analytic function presents no problem if the function takes on its values in the complex field. Thus q_1 and q_2 are complex-valued analytic functions of the real variables a, b, c, d. In the same way m_1 and m_2 will be conjugate complex and analytic. As a consequence of conjugacy α, β, and δ are real-valued functions.

Remark 6.6. Naturally, neither Γ' nor Γ'' is a cartesian product. Thus, as anticipated in Section 6.1, we have another important reason for defining Γ as a subset of a cartesian product, not a cartesian product itself. The problem analyzed in the example above arises typically in our models whenever it is necessary to aggregate components and compute the coefficients of a univariate Wold representation (the model in Section 5.1, for instance, under assumptions (b) and (c)). Another source of possible difficulties arises with the solution of the optimization problems on which many of the models under examination are based. For example, in the models of Sections 5.1 and 5.2 a second-order difference equation must be solved, this implying the roots of a second-order algebraic equation. In both cases a double root can be easily ruled out, but this cannot be ensured in general. Lastly, as already observed in Section 6.1, if invertibility and stationarity conditions need to be imposed, the resulting admissibility conditions hold in subsets that are not cartesian products as soon as the polynomial degrees exceed unity.

REMARK 6.7. The example above makes it clear that, although Definitions 6.1 and 6.2 have been given one after another for obvious reasons, the real process leading to a micromodel will be more tortuous. One will begin with a set $\tilde{\Gamma}$, based on straightforward economic considerations. Subsequently, the subset $\hat{\Gamma}$ where analyticity does not hold will be determined. Lastly, Γ will be determined as any one of the open connected components of $\tilde{\Gamma} - \hat{\Gamma}$. The model discussed above represents such a process quite well.

6.6. Negligible Subsets. The Alternative Principle

We have just provided various reasons for the fact that if we want both Assumptions 6.1 and 6.4 then Γ, though contained in a cartesian product, cannot be defined as a cartesian product. In turn, the reason why we want both Assumptions 6.1 and 6.4 is that they allow the proof of a very powerful result, which we shall refer to as the Alternative Principle. Before stating and proving it, let us illustrate its content by way of an example. Consider the micromodel

$$\begin{aligned}(1-L)z_{1t}^{\gamma} &= (1+b_1^{\gamma}L)u_{1t} + (1+b_2^{\gamma}L)u_{2t} \\ (1-L)z_{2t}^{\gamma} &= (1+b_3^{\gamma}L)u_{1t} + (1+b_4^{\gamma}L)u_{2t}.\end{aligned} \tag{6.10}$$

By Assumption 6.3 both the components of z_t^{γ} are I(1) for all $\gamma \in \Gamma$. Now, such components are cointegrated at γ if and only if the matrix whose entries are the polynomials on the RHS of (6.10) is singular for $L = 1$ at γ, i.e.

$$(1+b_1^{\gamma})(1+b_4^{\gamma}) = (1+b_2^{\gamma})(1+b_3^{\gamma}). \tag{6.11}$$

Since the coefficients b_l^{γ} are analytic in Γ and Γ is connected, and since equation (6.11) implies nothing more than elementary algebraic manipulations, then—and this is an application of the Alternative Principle—either cointegration for the components of z_t^{γ} holds for all $\gamma \in \Gamma$, or the subset of Γ for which cointegration holds is negligible. The definition for a negligible subset is the following:

DEFINITION 6.7. A subset of $\mathbb{R}^v$ is *negligible* if it is contained in a set which is closed and has zero Lebesgue measure.

REMARK 6.8. Almost all of our results will heavily exploit the alternative just illustrated by the cointegration example. However, in this case the Alternative Principle leads to a statement regarding the micromodel. Although interesting for the present illustrative purpose, the example is not representative of the applications of the Alternative Principle that we have in mind. In fact, we will see that the coefficients of the aggregate model, as defined in Chapter 7, are analytic in Γ_m. On the other hand, aggregate cointegration, Granger causality, singularity, etc., imply simple algebraic relations among the coefficients of the aggregate model (to be defined in Chapter 7 below). Therefore, cointegration, etc., holds for the aggregate model either everywhere in Γ_m, or for a negligible subset of Γ_m. Equivalently, if we can find a point for which cointegration, etc., does not hold, then cointegration, etc., holds only for a negligible subset of Γ_m.

REMARK 6.9. If Ω is an open region in $\mathbb{R}^v$, negligibility of subsets of Ω relative to Ω is equivalent to negligibility relative to $\mathbb{R}^v$. Naturally, if a subset B of an open region $\Omega \subseteq \mathbb{R}^v$ is negligible, B is also negligible with respect to all measures which are 'diffuse' with respect to the Lebesgue measure. In particular, if the measure μ has a density with respect to the Lebesgue measure then all the Lebesgue negligible subsets of Ω are of zero measure with respect to μ. Notice also that we are not requiring that Ω or B is bounded. Lastly, we observe that a negligible subset of $B \in \Omega$ is nowhere dense in Ω, this meaning that the closure of B in Ω does not contain any open set. Thus, points belonging to B have points not belonging to B in all their neighborhoods, while points not belonging to B possess a neighborhood not containing any point of B.

REMARK 6.10. An important caveat must accompany our use of the term 'negligible'. The reference to the Lebesgue measure or to related diffuse measures in Γ_m has no positive content. Rather, it reflects a state of profound ignorance about the distribution of the microparameters over the populations (we return to this issue in Section 7.6). Fortunately, in all cases when a statement is proved, with the exception of a negligible subset B, we will be able to give an economic interpretation of important subsets of B. For instance, the subset of H_m which has been defined in Section 6.5 as the set of all points

$$(\omega \quad \omega \quad \cdots \quad \omega \quad \lambda),$$

with $(\omega \quad \lambda) \in \Gamma$, will be typically contained in the set B, while Lebesgue negligibility of H_m can be matched with the likelihood that we attribute to equal microparameters for all agents. Unfortunately, however, we shall not be able, with a few exceptions, to interpret the whole B in economic terms. A residual will remain for which no economic interpretation is available, while Lebesgue negligibility is the only information we possess. For an example see Section 8.2.

We shall say that a statement is valid *almost everywhere*, abbreviated a.e., when it holds with the exception of a negligible subset. We are now ready to state and prove the Alternative Principle.

THEOREM 6.2. (ALTERNATIVE PRINCIPLE) Let $\Omega \subset \mathbb{R}^v$ be an open region. Let $f : \Omega \to \mathbb{R}$ be analytic in Ω. Then, either $f(x) = 0$, for any $x \in \Omega$, or the set

$$B = \{x : x \in \Omega, \ f(x) = 0\}$$

is negligible.

Proof. If the closure of B contains an open subset of B then by Lemma 6.1 B coincides with Ω. Thus, if B does not coincide with Ω then B is nowhere dense in Ω. This is not sufficient to prove that B is negligible. In fact, there exist pathological sets which are nowhere dense but non-negligible (see, e.g., Billingsley, 1986, p. 40, Example 3.1). Therefore we must show that the set of the zeros of an analytic function cannot be one of such sets.

For, consider the subset F of Ω whose points have rational coordinates. For every point q of F take the maximum open cube containing q and contained in Ω; call it C_q. The union of the sets C_q is equal to Ω. If the theorem is proved for cubes, then it is proved for Ω. In fact, if $B \cap C_q$ is negligible for all q, then, since the family of the C_q is countable, B is negligible. If, on the contrary, $B \cap C_q = C_q$ for some q, then $B = \Omega$, by Lemma 6.1. Thus let Ω be a cube in $\mathbb{R}^v$. With no loss of generality we can assume

$$\Omega = \{x \in \mathbb{R}^v : \ 0 < x_l < 1, \ l = 1, v\}.$$

If $v = 1$, by Lemma 6.2, B cannot have accumulation points within Ω. Therefore B must be countable and its measure is zero. Let us proceed by induction on the dimension v. Consider the section of the cube obtained by the hyperplane $x_v = a$, call it Ω_a, and the function $f_a : \Omega_a \to \mathbb{R}$, defined as

$$f_a(x_1, x_2, \ldots, x_{v-1}) = f(x_1, x_2, \ldots, x_{v-1}, a).$$

By induction the Principle can be applied to Ω_a and f_a. Let $\mathcal{B}$ be the subset of (0 1) defined as

$$\mathcal{B} = \{a : \ f_a = 0 \text{ for all points of } \Omega_a\}.$$

In words, $\mathcal{B}$ is the subset of the 'vertical' axis such that the function f vanishes over the corresponding section of the cube. If $\mathcal{B}$ has no accumulation points in (0 1) then by Fubini's theorem (Billingsley, 1986, p. 238), the set B has zero measure. Suppose, on the contrary, that $\mathcal{B}$ has an accumulation point $\bar{a}$ in (0 1). Let S be any vertical segment of unit length in Ω and let

$\bar{x} = (\,\bar{x}_1 \quad \cdots \quad \bar{x}_{v-1} \quad \bar{a}\,)$ be its intersection with $\Omega_{\bar{a}}$. S contains an infinity of points accumulating on $\bar{x}$ for which f vanishes. Therefore f vanishes everywhere on S and, by consequence, on Ω. Q.E.D.

A very important alternative formulation of the Principle is:

THEOREM 6.2. (EQUIVALENT FORMULATION) Under the assumptions of the Alternative Principle, if there exists a point $x \in \Omega$ such that $f(x) \neq 0$, then B is negligible in Ω.

A typical application of the Alternative Principle will be one in which we deal with rational functions of L whose coefficients are analytic in Ω. Denote one such function as

$$c^x(L) = \frac{a^x(L)}{b^x(L)}.$$

THEOREM 6.3. Let B be the subset of Ω such that if $x \in B$ then $c^x(L)$ is the zero rational function, i.e. the function which vanishes identically in L. B is either negligible or equal to Ω.

Proof. B is the intersection of the subsets in which the coefficients of $a^x(L)$ vanish. The Alternative Principle applies to each of them. Then, either one of them is negligible, so that the intersection is negligible, or all of them are equal to Ω. Q.E.D.

Another typical situation will be that in which we shall deal with matrices whose entries are rational functions of L:

$$Q(L) = \begin{pmatrix} q_{11}(L) & q_{12}(L) & \cdots & q_{1s}(L) \\ q_{21}(L) & q_{22}(L) & \cdots & q_{2s}(L) \\ & & \vdots & \\ q_{r1}(L) & q_{r2}(L) & \cdots & q_{rs}(L) \end{pmatrix}.$$

The usual definitions of linear dependence of rows and columns, of rank, and the relationship between rank and linear dependence, hold in the same way as they hold for matrices whose entries are real or complex numbers. As a matter of fact, what is required is that the matrices be defined over an *algebraic field*, and rational functions share with real numbers all the algebraic properties of a field (see Section 6.10 for references). Let us briefly review definitions and basic statements:

(1) The columns of $Q(L)$ are linearly dependent if there exists a column vector of rational functions

$$b(L) = (\,b_1(L) \quad b_2(L) \quad \cdots \quad b_s(L)\,)'$$

such that $b(L) \neq 0$, and $Q(L)b(L) = 0$ (here '0' stands, respectively, for the vector whose entries are the zero rational function, and the zero rational function). The same holds for the rows.

(2) The rank of $Q(L)$ is k, with $0 \leq k \leq \min(r, s)$, if there exists a $k \times k$ submatrix of $Q(L)$ which is non-singular (whose determinant is not the zero rational function), whereas no $(k+1) \times (k+1)$ submatrix is non-singular.

(3) Suppose that $k = \text{rank}(Q(L)) < s$. Without loss of generality we can assume that the top-left $k \times k$ submatrix is non-singular. Applying Cramer's rule, the $(k+1)$-th column can be written as a combination of the first k, by way of rational functions (ratios of determinants). Thus if $\text{rank}(Q(L)) < s$, then the columns are linearly dependent. The converse can also be proved by using the standard argument. The same holds for the rows if $k < r$.

THEOREM 6.4. Consider an $r \times s$ matrix $Q^x(L)$ whose entries are rational functions of L, with the coefficients analytic in the open region Ω. Then:

(a) If $r = s$ then $Q^x(L)$ is singular either for a negligible subset of Ω, or for all $x \in \Omega$.

(b) $g(x) = \text{rank}(Q^x(L))$ is constant on $\Omega - N$, where N is a negligible subset of Ω.

(c) Let k be the value of $g(x)$ in $\Omega - N$. There exists a $k \times k$ submatrix of $Q^x(L)$ which is non-singular in all $\Omega - N$.

(d) If $k < s$ there exist a negligible subset N and an s-dimensional column vector

$$b^x(L) = (\, b_1^x(L) \quad b_2^x(L) \quad \cdots \quad b_s^x(L)\,)',$$

whose entries are rational functions with coefficients analytic in Ω, such that $b^x(L) \neq 0$ in $\Omega - N$ and

$$Q^x(L)b^x(L) = 0,$$

for any $x \in \Omega$.

Proof. Statement (a) is nothing other than an application of the Alternative Principle to $\det Q^x(L)$. Now let k be the maximum of $g(x)$ in Ω and let $\tilde{x}$ be such that $k = g(\tilde{x})$. By definition there exists a $k \times k$ submatrix $\hat{Q}^x(L)$ such that $\hat{Q}^{\tilde{x}}(L)$ is non-singular. By (a) $\hat{Q}^x(L)$ can be singular only for a negligible subset of Ω. This proves both (b) and (c). For statement (d), suppose that the submatrix whose existence is ensured in (c) is the $k \times k$ top-left one; call it $P^x(L)$. Now, for $x \in \Omega - N$, obtain the $(k+1)$-th column of the $k \times (k+1)$ top-left submatrix of $Q^x(L)$ from the first k columns by the Cramer rule and let

$$(\, b_1^x(L) \quad b_2^x(L) \quad \cdots \quad b_k^x(L)\,)$$

be the coefficients of the linear combination. The vector

$$b^x(L) = (\, b_1^x(L) \quad b_2^x(L) \quad \cdots \quad b_k^x(L) \quad -1 \quad 0 \quad \cdots \quad 0\,) \det(P^x(L)) \qquad (6.12)$$

does not have a possibly vanishing denominator and is therefore analytic in Ω. Moreover, $Q^x(L)b^x(L) = 0$ everywhere in Ω. Q.E.D.

REMARK 6.11. Statement (c) is worth noticing. The task of keeping the rank of $Q_x(L)$ equal to k for $x \in \Omega - N$ is performed by one single $k \times k$ submatrix. Other $k \times k$ submatrices either do the same job or are singular for all $x \in \Omega$.

6.7. Non-Redundancy of the Common Shocks

6.7.1. We have supposed that u_t, the vector of common shocks, is orthonormal. This implies that none of the common shocks is a linear combination of the others. However, there is another way in which the vector u_t might be considered redundant. Consider firstly the scalar model

$$a^\gamma(L)D(L)x_t^\gamma = b_1^\gamma(L)u_{1t} + b_2^\gamma(L)u_{2t} + \cdots + b_h^\gamma(L)u_{ht} + c^\gamma(L)\xi_t. \tag{6.13}$$

Then isolate the common component

$$\zeta_t^\gamma = b_1^\gamma(L)u_{1t} + b_2^\gamma(L)u_{2t} + \cdots + b_h^\gamma(L)u_{ht}. \tag{6.14}$$

Suppose that for any $\gamma = (\omega \quad \lambda) \in \Gamma$,

$$b_1^\gamma(L) = \kappa^\lambda(L)b_2^\gamma(L), \tag{6.15}$$

i.e. that the response of ζ_t^γ to u_{1t} can be obtained by multiplying the response to u_{2t} by a factor which is a function of L dependent only on λ, not on ω. The model can be rewritten as

$$\begin{aligned}\zeta_t^\gamma &= b_2^\gamma(L)[\kappa^\lambda(L)u_{1t} + u_{2t}] + \cdots + b_h^\gamma(L)u_{ht} \\ &= \tau^\gamma(L)v_t^\lambda + \cdots + b_h^\gamma(L)u_{ht},\end{aligned} \tag{6.16}$$

where v_t^λ depends only on λ, not on ω. This means that $h-1$ shocks, dependent on λ but *independent of* ω, are sufficient to describe the dynamics of ζ_t^γ for any given λ.

The example above suggests a general definition of redundancy:

DEFINITION 6.8. The vector u_t is *redundant* for (6.14) if there exists an h-dimensional vector $q^\lambda(L)$ of rational functions of L such that $q^\lambda(L) \neq 0$ a.e. in Γ and

$$b_1^\gamma(L)q_1^\lambda(L) + b_2^\gamma(L)q_2^\lambda(L) + \cdots + b_h^\gamma(L)q_h^\lambda(L) = 0,$$

for any $\gamma \in \Gamma$.

The following theorem characterizes redundancy in terms of populations of size h.

THEOREM 6.5. Let ζ_t^γ be represented as in (6.14). Consider the following matrix, which is a function defined in Γ_h:

$$\mathcal{Q}^p(L) = \begin{pmatrix} b_1^{p^1}(L) & b_2^{p^1}(L) & \cdots & b_h^{p^1}(L) \\ b_1^{p^2}(L) & b_2^{p^2}(L) & \cdots & b_h^{p^2}(L) \\ & & \vdots & \\ b_1^{p^h}(L) & b_2^{p^h}(L) & \cdots & b_h^{p^h}(L) \end{pmatrix} \tag{6.17}$$

(it must be recalled that if $p = (\,\omega^1 \quad \omega^2 \quad \cdots \quad \omega^h \quad \lambda\,)$, then p^i indicates $(\,\omega^i \quad \lambda\,)$). u_t is redundant for (6.14) if and only if $\mathcal{Q}^p(L)$ is singular for any $p \in \Gamma_h$.

Proof. If u_t is redundant, by Definition 6.8 the matrix $\mathcal{Q}^p(L)$ is singular a.e. in Γ_h and therefore everywhere in Γ_h (Theorem 6.4, a). To prove the converse, assume that $\mathcal{Q}^p(L)$ has rank $k-1$ a.e. in Γ_h, with $1 < k \leq h$ (Theorem 6.4, b). Without loss of generality we can assume that the submatrix

$$\mathcal{P}^p(L) = \begin{pmatrix} b_1^{p^1}(L) & b_2^{p^1}(L) & \cdots & b_k^{p^1}(L) \\ b_1^{p^2}(L) & b_2^{p^2}(L) & \cdots & b_k^{p^2}(L) \\ & & \vdots & \\ b_1^{p^h}(L) & b_2^{p^h}(L) & \cdots & b_k^{p^h}(L) \end{pmatrix}$$

is singular everywhere in Γ_h but that its top-left $(k-1)\times(k-1)$ submatrix, call it $\mathcal{P}_{k-1}^p(L)$, is non-singular a.e. in Γ_h (Theorem 6.4, c). Now consider the system of equations

$$\mathcal{P}^p(L)q^p(L) = 0,$$

where the unknowns are the rational functions $q_l^p(L)$, $l = 1, k$. The latter can be determined by setting $q_k^p(L) = 1$ and applying Cramer's rule to

$$\begin{aligned} b_1^{p^1}(L)q_1^p(L) + b_2^{p^1}(L)q_2^p(L) + \cdots + b_{k-1}^{p^1}(L)q_{k-1}^p(L) &= -b_k^{p^1}(L) \\ b_1^{p^2}(L)q_1^p(L) + b_2^{p^2}(L)q_2^p(L) + \cdots + b_{k-1}^{p^2}(L)q_{k-1}^p(L) &= -b_k^{p^2}(L) \\ &\vdots \\ b_1^{p^{k-1}}(L)q_1^p(L) + b_2^{p^{k-1}}(L)q_2^p(L) + \cdots + b_{k-1}^{p^{k-1}}(L)q_{k-1}^p(L) &= -b_k^{p^{k-1}}(L) \end{aligned} \tag{6.18}$$

while the remaining equation

$$b_1^{p^k}(L)q_1^p(L) + b_2^{p^k}(L)q_2^p(L) + \cdots + b_{k-1}^{p^k}(L)q_{k-1}^p(L) = -b_k^{p^k}(L)$$

holds owing to the singularity of $\mathcal{P}^p(L)$. Now, since $\mathcal{P}^p(L)$ is singular for all $p \in \Gamma_h$, then p^k can be any point in Γ, provided that it forms a population with the points γ^i, for $i = 1, k-1$, i.e. provided that it has the same λ of the points p^i, for $i = 1, k-1$. Thus $q^p(L)$ depends only on λ, and we can rename it $q^\lambda(L)$. The vector equal to $q^\lambda(L) \det \mathcal{P}^p_{k-1}(L)$ for the first k components, and zero for the remaining $h-k$, fulfills Definition 6.8.

Q.E.D.

REMARK 6.12. A corollary to Theorem 6.5 is that the vector fulfilling Definition 6.8 is analytic in Γ.

The following is an equivalent formulation of Theorem 6.5:

THEOREM 6.6. Consider the vector

$$z^p_t = (\, \zeta^{p^1}_t \quad \zeta^{p^2}_t \quad \cdots \quad \zeta^{p^h}_t \,),$$

where $p \in \Gamma_h$. u_t is redundant for ζ^γ_t in (6.14) if and only if the rank of z^p_t is less than h for any $p \in \Gamma_h$.

Proof. $\Sigma_u = I$ and therefore has full rank for any $p \in \Gamma_h$. As a consequence, if the rank of z^p_t is less than h, the rank of (6.17) must be less than h, so that Theorem 6.5 applies. The converse is trivial. Q.E.D.

REMARK 6.13. It must be pointed out that non-redundancy has nothing to do with the dimension of Γ. For instance, if

$$\zeta^\gamma_t = \omega u_{1t} + \omega^2 u_{2t},$$

where ω is scalar, then u_t is non-redundant. In fact, although both a^γ_1 and a^γ_2 depend only on the scalar ω, their ratio is not independent of ω.

6.7.2. Going back to the empirical analysis of Part I, Chapter 2, our results can now be reformulated as follows:

(1) Assume that US individual incomes can be modeled as in (6.13), with the polynomial coefficients parameterized by individual characteristics, the vector ω, and by common parameters.

(2) Our data set is an intermediate aggregation of the individual data corresponding to the actual population.

(3) The data can be employed to check whether the hypothesis that $h = 1$ is reasonable. In fact, given the population size of the US states, $h = 1$ would imply near singularity of the aggregate vector at state level for all $p \in \Gamma_m$, m being the size of the US population, provided that the relative importance of the idiosyncratic component remains within a reasonable range for all $\gamma \in \Gamma$.

(4) The evidence for the actual population is strongly against the hypothesis $h = 1$. Since the rejection is based on the rejection of the singularity of the aggregates at the state level, we also reject that $h > 1$ but redundancy

of u_t for the common component allows a representation with only one common shock.

(5) In conclusion, if we assume that US individual incomes can be modeled as in equation (6.13), then we can also assume that the common component admits a representation with $h > 1$ and u_t non-redundant.

Regarding Chapter 3, our result is that the regional model has two non-redundant common shocks.

6.7.3. Extension of non-redundancy to vector micromodels does not imply any difficulty. Given

$$A^\gamma(L)D(L)z_t^\gamma = B^\gamma(L)u_t + C^\gamma(L)\xi_t,$$

consider the common components vector

$$\zeta_t^\gamma = B^\gamma(L)u_t. \tag{6.19}$$

DEFINITION 6.9. The vector u_t is *redundant* for (6.19) if there exists an h-dimensional (column) vector $q^\lambda(L)$ of rational functions of L, such that $q^\lambda(L) \neq 0$ a.e. in Γ and

$$B^\gamma(L)q^\lambda(L) = 0.$$

Let us point out that non-redundancy of u_t for ζ_t^γ does not imply that u_t is non-redundant for each of the components of the former. On the contrary, in the example

$$\begin{aligned}\zeta_{1t}^\gamma &= \omega u_{1t}\\ \zeta_{2t}^\gamma &= \omega u_{2t},\end{aligned}$$

u_t is non-redundant for ζ_t^γ but redundant for both its components. Redundancy of u_t for ζ_t^γ means redundancy of u_t for each of the components of ζ_t^γ, where redundancy is realized by the same $q^\lambda(L)$ for all the components.

The following theorem will be useful in the analysis of the singularity of the aggregate model (Chapter 8).

THEOREM 6.7. Consider equation (6.19) and suppose that: (i) u_t is non-redundant; (ii) ζ_t^γ is non-singular a.e. in Γ; (iii) $h > n$, i.e. the dimension of u_t is greater than the dimension of ζ_t^γ. Then consider a population $p = (\omega^1 \quad \omega^2 \quad \lambda) \in \Gamma_2$ and the matrix

$$D_l^p(L) = \begin{pmatrix} B^{p^1}(L) \\ \\ b_l^{p^2}(L) \end{pmatrix},$$

where $b_l^{p^2}(L)$ is the l-th row of $B^{p^2}(L)$. There exists an l such that $D_l^p(L)$ has rank $n+1$ for p a.e. in Γ_2.

Proof. It suffices to prove that $D_l^p(L)$ has rank $n+1$ for at least one l and one point of Γ_2. Without loss of generality we can assume that the top-left $n \times n$ submatrix of $B^\gamma(L)$, call it $H^\gamma(L)$, is non-singular a.e. in Γ (Theorem 6.4, c). Assume that p^1 is such that $H^{p^1}(L)$ is non-singular. Let $q^{p^1}(L)$ be the n-dimensional non-zero column vector such that the $(n+1)$-th column of $B^{p^1}(L)$ is equal to $H^{p^1}(L)q^{p^1}(L)$ (Theorem 6.4, d). Now consider

$$\begin{pmatrix} b_{11}^{p^1}(L) & b_{12}^{p^1}(L) & \cdots & b_{1n+1}^{p^1}(L) \\ b_{21}^{p^1}(L) & b_{22}^{p^1}(L) & \cdots & b_{2n+1}^{p^1}(L) \\ & & \vdots & \\ b_{n1}^{p^1}(L) & b_{n2}^{p^1}(L) & \cdots & b_{nn+1}^{p^1}(L) \\ b_{l1}^{p^2}(L) & b_{l2}^{p^2}(L) & \cdots & b_{ln+1}^{p^2}(L) \end{pmatrix}. \tag{6.20}$$

If this matrix is singular, then

$$b_{ln+1}^{p^2}(L) = \begin{pmatrix} b_{l1}^{p^2}(L) & b_{l2}^{p^2}(L) & \cdots & b_{ln}^{p^2}(L) \end{pmatrix} q^{p^1}(L). \tag{6.21}$$

Now, suppose that for any given p^1 (6.21) holds for any p^2 forming a population with p^1 and any l. This means that

$$B^{p^2}(L) \begin{pmatrix} q^{p^1}(L) \\ 0 \\ \vdots \\ 0 \end{pmatrix} = 0$$

for any p^2 forming a population with p^1. In this equation $q^{p^1}(L)$ varies only if the vector λ common to p^1 and p^2 varies. Thus u_t is redundant, contrary to assumption (i). In conclusion, there must exist p^1, p^2, and l such that (6.20) is not singular. Q.E.D.

6.7.4. The definition of redundancy has been given with respect to the micromodel. We can give another definition with reference to each population.

DEFINITION 6.10. Given the population $p \in \Gamma_m$, u_t is *redundant* for the scalar ζ_t^p if there exists an h-dimensional vector $q(L)$ of rational functions in L such that $q(L) \neq 0$ and

$$b_1^{p^i}(L)q_1(L) + b_2^{p^i}(L)q_2(L) + \cdots + b_h^{p^i}(L)q_h(L) = 0,$$

for $i = 1, m$. In the same way, u_t is redundant for the vector ζ_t, relative to p, if there exists an h-dimensional vector $q(L)$ of rational functions in L such that $q(L) \neq 0$ and

$$B^{p^i}(L)q(L) = 0,$$

for $i = 1, m$.

Naturally, even though u_t is non-redundant according to Definition 6.8, or 6.9, the space Γ_m contains populations for which Definition 6.10 holds. For instance, u_t is non-redundant for

$$\zeta_t^\gamma = \lambda(1 + \omega_1 L)u_{1t} + \lambda(1 + \omega_2 L)u_{2t},$$

but is redundant in Γ_2 for the population

$$((1 \quad 1) \quad (0.5 \quad 0.5) \quad \lambda),$$

for any λ.

Regarding the relationship between Definitions 6.8 and 6.9 on the one hand, and Definition 6.10 on the other, the following observations will be sufficient for our purposes. Firstly, if $h \leq m$, redundancy according to Definition 6.8 implies redundancy of u_t for all the populations in Γ_m (see the proof of Theorem 6.5). Conversely, if $\mathcal{S}$ is the subset of Γ_m for which u_t is redundant with respect to a scalar ζ_t^γ, then either $\mathcal{S}$ is negligible, or u_t is redundant according to Definition 6.8. In fact, considering the $m \times h$ matrix

$$\mathcal{Q}_m^p(L) = \begin{pmatrix} b_1^{p^1}(L) & b_2^{p^1}(L) & \cdots & b_h^{p^1}(L) \\ b_1^{p^2}(L) & b_2^{p^2}(L) & \cdots & p_h^{p^2}(L) \\ & & \vdots & \\ b_1^{p^m}(L) & p_2^{p^m}(L) & \cdots & b_h^{p^m}(L) \end{pmatrix},$$

if there exists a $\tilde{p}$ such that the rank of $\mathcal{Q}_m^p(L)$ is h, then the rank of an $h \times h$ submatrix is h a.e. in Γ_m. If such a $\tilde{p}$ does not exist, then the rank of all the $h \times h$ submatrices is less than h everywhere. The conclusion follows from Theorem 6.5.

Secondly, if $m < h$, u_t is redundant for all the populations since the rank of Q_m^p is necessarily less than h. However, this has no consequence on redundancy in the sense of Definition 6.8.

6.8. Dependent and Independent Variables

6.8.1. The definitions given so far are sufficiently general to include, for instance, the micromodel

$$\begin{aligned} y_t^\gamma &= \alpha x_{t-1}^\gamma + a_1 u_{1t} + a_2 u_{2t} + \xi_{1t} \\ x_t^\gamma &= \beta y_{t-1}^\gamma + b_1 u_{1t} + b_2 u_{2t} + \xi_{2t}, \end{aligned} \tag{6.22}$$

whose parameterization can be

$$\omega = (\alpha \quad \beta), \qquad \lambda = (a_1 \quad a_2 \quad b_1 \quad b_2).$$

In this case both the stochastic processes for y_t and x_t depend on all the parameters in ω and λ. On the other hand, all the models of Chapter 5, with the exception of the structural VAR in Section 5.5, allow the distinction between two subgroups of variables: the first group is parameterized by λ and a subvector of ω, and the second group by λ and the whole ω.

In Section 5.2 the wage w_t is parameterized by

$$(\mu_1 \quad \nu_1 \quad \mu_2 \quad \nu_2)$$

while n_t depends also on the additional parameters f_1, d, ρ_0, and ρ_1. In Section 5.3 consumption depends on ω_1 and ω_2, in addition to the parameters of the income process. In Section 5.1 the consumption process depends on the same parameters as the income process. However, this is due, among other reasons, to the decision that β is given from outside the model, and is therefore kept fixed in the model.

In general, the idea that some of the variables are determined independently of the agent's decisions and therefore do not depend on the decision parameters, can be formalized in our framework as follows. The microparameter space is defined as

$$\Gamma \subseteq \mathbb{R}^{s_1} \times \mathbb{R}^{s_2} \times \mathbb{R}^{c}.$$

The elements of Γ are indicated by $\gamma = (\omega \quad \hat{\omega} \quad \lambda)$, where ω, $\hat{\omega}$, and λ are respectively s_1, s_2, and c-dimensional.

Skipping details that can be worked out by the reader, the micromodel is redefined as a function associating with any $\gamma = (\omega \quad \hat{\omega} \quad \lambda) \in \Gamma$ the vector microequation

$$\begin{pmatrix} A^{\gamma}(L) & \tilde{A}^{\gamma}(L) \\ 0 & \mathcal{A}^{\tau}(L) \end{pmatrix} \begin{pmatrix} D(L)y_t^{\gamma} \\ \mathcal{D}(L)x_t^{\tau} \end{pmatrix} = \begin{pmatrix} B^{\gamma}(L) \\ \mathcal{B}^{\tau}(L) \end{pmatrix} u_t + \begin{pmatrix} C^{\gamma}(L) & \tilde{C}^{\gamma}(L) \\ 0 & \mathcal{C}^{\tau}(L) \end{pmatrix} \begin{pmatrix} \epsilon_t \\ \xi_t \end{pmatrix}, \qquad (6.23)$$

where $\tau = (\hat{\omega} \quad \lambda)$. y_t^{γ} is the vector of the dependent variables, x_t^{τ} is the vector of the independent variables, ϵ_t and ξ_t are idiosyncratic disturbances. If Γ is an open region, the projection of Γ on $\mathbb{R}^{s_2} \times \mathbb{R}^{c}$, i.e. the set

$$\hat{\Gamma} = \{(\hat{\omega} \quad \lambda) \; : \; \exists \omega, \; (\omega \quad \hat{\omega} \quad \lambda) \in \Gamma \},$$

is also an open region. Moreover, if all the assumptions on the micromodels are fulfilled for (6.23), the bottom block of the equations in (6.23) defines an autonomous micromodel for x_t^{τ}, which is parameterized on $\hat{\Gamma}$. No additional difficulty arises in defining the population space and the disaggregated model. Model (6.23) will henceforth be referred to as the DI model. For the population space it will be convenient to write

$$(\omega^1 \quad \omega^2 \quad \cdots \quad \omega^m \quad \hat{\omega}^1 \quad \hat{\omega}^2 \quad \cdots \quad \hat{\omega}^m \quad \lambda),$$

so that the parameters defining the independent variables are grouped together. We shall also write

$$(\hat{\omega}^1 \quad \hat{\omega}^2 \quad \cdots \quad \hat{\omega}^m \quad \lambda)$$

to indicate a point in the population space of the independent variables.

6.8.2. It must be pointed out that the notion of the DI model does not bear any definite relationship to Granger causality. For example, consider the model

$$\begin{aligned} y_t^\gamma &= k_1(\mu_1 + \nu_1 L)u_{1t} + k_2(\mu_2 + \nu_2 L)u_{2t} \\ x_t^\tau &= (\mu_1 + \nu_1 L)u_{1t} + (\mu_2 + \nu_2 L)u_{2t}, \end{aligned} \tag{6.24}$$

where $\omega = (\, k_1 \quad k_2 \,)$, $\tau = \hat{\omega} = (\, \mu_1 \quad \mu_2 \quad \nu_1 \quad \nu_2 \,)$, and there are no common parameters. To see whether y_t^γ Granger-causes x_t^τ we can analyze the projection of y_t^γ on present, past, and future values of x_t^τ. The projection is

$$y_t^\gamma = g^\gamma(L)x_t^\gamma + a_t^\gamma,$$

where

$$\begin{aligned} g^\gamma(L) &= \frac{S_{yx}^\gamma(L)}{S_x^\tau(L)} \\ S_{yx}^\gamma(L) &= k_1(\mu_1 + \nu_1 L)(\mu_1 + \nu_1 F) + k_2(\mu_2 + \nu_2 L)(\mu_2 + \nu_2 F) \\ S_x^\tau(L) &= (\mu_1 + \nu_1 L)(\mu_1 + \nu_1 F) + (\mu_2 + \nu_2 L)(\mu_2 + \nu_2 F) \end{aligned}$$

(see Section A.8 in the Appendix). The ratio $g^\gamma(L)$ has no powers of F (y_t^γ does not Granger-cause x_t) if and only if $k_1 = k_2$, or $\mu_1/\mu_2 = \nu_1/\nu_2$, i.e. for a negligible subset of Γ. For, suppose that α is a root of the denominator. If α is a root of both the summands then it is a root of the numerator as well. Otherwise α is a root of the numerator only if $k_1 = k_2$.

The inverse direction of causality can be analyzed in the same way, with the numerator and denominator of the projection given by

$$\begin{aligned} S_{xy}^\gamma(L) &= k_1(\mu_1 + \nu_1 L)(\mu_1 + \nu_1 F) + k_2(\mu_2 + \nu_2 L)(\mu_2 + \nu_2 F) \\ S_y^\gamma(L) &= k_1^2(\mu_1 + \nu_1 L)(\mu_1 + \nu_1 F) + k_2^2(\mu_2 + \nu_2 L)(\mu_2 + \nu_2 F). \end{aligned}$$

The conclusion is that apart from a negligible subset of Γ, Granger causality occurs in both directions.

However, if the first equation of (6.24) is substituted by

$$y_t^\gamma = k[(\mu_1 + \nu_1 L)u_{1t} + (\mu_2 + \nu_2 L)u_{2t}],$$

so that $\omega = k$, then neither y_t^γ Granger-causes x_t^τ, nor x_t^τ Granger-causes y_t^γ. In this case model (6.24) is also singular. Lastly, if the first equation were

$$y_t^\gamma = k(\mu_1 + \nu_1 L)u_{1t}$$

the model would not be singular, y_t^γ would Granger-cause x_t^τ, but not vice versa.

We shall return to singularity and Granger causality in Chapter 8 and 10 respectively, and show that aggregation, although preserving the DI structure, does not preserve singularity and unidirectional Granger causality.

6.9. The Micromodel Coefficients as Analytic Functions

The coefficients of the models presented in Chapter 5, i.e. the coefficients of the ARIMA's in u_t and ξ_t, can be obtained from the microparameters partly by simple algebraic manipulations, and partly by taking roots of polynomials whose coefficients are simple functions of the microparameters. The microparameter space Γ is defined as an open set, this corresponding to the idea that small changes in the components of an admissible γ in all directions leave the point admissible (see Remark 6.1). Moreover, if Γ is carefully defined, so that multiple roots and vanishing leading coefficients are avoided, then, by Lemma 6.3, the coefficients of the micromodel are analytic functions of the microparameters and the Alternative Principle can be applied. In the models presented in Chapter 5 the polynomial roots appear both in the maximization procedure and when the Wold representations are determined. As for maximization, the usual exercises are limited to second-order difference equations and therefore to second-order polynomials, so that the use of our mathematical apparatus might seem a waste of energy. However, the Wold representations considered in Sections 5.1, 5.2, and 5.3 imply the roots of polynomials of arbitrary order. Furthermore, in Chapter 12, when VAR and ARMAX models will be analyzed, multivariate Wold representations will be necessary, the latter implying roots of high-order polynomials. For the latter we do not possess explicit formulas.[2] Thus we have to resort to Lemma 6.3 and the Alternative Principle.

6.10. Bibliographic Notes

For the notion of negligible subsets of $\mathbb{R}^v$ see Debreu (1970, p. 387). See also Mas-Colell (1985, pp. 316–17).

The proofs of Lemmas 6.1 and 6.2 are standard; see, e.g., Smirnov (1964, Vol. III, pp. 64–65 and 323). They have been reported only to provide the reader with an idea of the consequences of the definition of analytic function. For Lemma 6.3 and the definition of discriminant, see, e.g., Ahlfors (1979, pp. 301–3). We could not find a reference for the Alternative Prin-

[2] This is a well-known result of Galois theory. See, e.g., Kaplansky (1972).

ciple. However, the result will hardly surprise the mathematically expert reader.

For linear algebra over a field, see van der Waerden (1953, Vol. II, Chapter XV). See also Vol. II, p. 49, for the field of rational functions.

7

The Aggregate Model

7.1. Definition of the Aggregate Model

Let us begin by rewriting here the i-th equation of the disaggregated model, as defined in Section 6.4:

$$A^{p^i}(L)D(L)z_t = B^{p^i}(L)u_t + C^{p^i}(L)\xi_t^i. \tag{7.1}$$

Now rewrite equation (7.1) as

$$D(L)z_t = \tilde{B}^{p^i}(L)u_t + \tilde{C}^{p^i}(L)\xi_t^i, \tag{7.2}$$

where

$$\tilde{B}^{p^i}(L) = \left[A^{p^i}(L)\right]^{-1} B^{p^i}(L), \quad \tilde{C}^{p^i}(L) = \left[A^{p^i}(L)\right]^{-1} C^{p^i}(L).$$

DEFINITION 7.1. Given the disaggregated model $\mathcal{D}$ and the vector of weights

$$N = (\, N^1 \quad N^2 \quad \cdots \quad N^m \,),$$

the corresponding *aggregate model* is the function associating with any $p \in \Gamma_m$ the macroequation

$$D(L)Z_t = \left(\sum_{i=1}^{m} N^i \tilde{B}^{p^i}(L)\right) u_t + \sum_{i=1}^{m} N^i \tilde{C}^{p^i}(L)\xi_t^i. \tag{7.3}$$

By z_t^p we indicate any solution of (7.3). If z_t^{i,p^i} are solutions of the microequations (7.1), the process

$$\sum_{i=1}^{m} N^i z_t^{i,p^i}$$

is a solution for the macroequation (7.3).

7.2. Dropping the Idiosyncratic Component

Just as in Part I, by letting the size of the population grow, under suitable assumptions on the micromodel, the variance ratio of the common to the idiosyncratic component can be made bigger than any preassigned real number. The following condition reproduces Assumptions 1.1 and 1.2 for the micromodel underlying the aggregate model.

ASSUMPTION 7.1. Consider, for $k = 1, n$, the components of the vector $D(L)z_t^\gamma$, i.e. the variables $D_{kk}(L)z_{kt}^\gamma$ (see Definition 6.2). Now let

$$D_{kk}(L)z_{kt}^\gamma = \zeta_{kt}^\gamma + \chi_{kt}^\gamma$$

be the common–idiosyncratic decomposition for the k-th component of $D(L)z_t^\gamma$. We assume that there exists a positive real μ such that

$$\text{var}(D_{kk}(L)z_{kt}^\gamma) < \mu$$

for any $k = 1, n$ and any $\gamma \in \Gamma$. Moreover, there exist a positive real θ and a stationary stochastic n-dimensional vector U_t, such that in the orthogonal projection

$$D_{kk}(L)\zeta_t^\gamma = c_k^\gamma U_t + G_{kt}^\gamma$$

we have $c_k^\gamma > \theta$ for any $k = 1, n$, and any $\gamma \in \Gamma$.

Notice that here, unlike in Assumption 1.2, we impose the second condition on the whole Γ. But this is obviously necessary since the condition is not on the populations but on the set from where the individuals of the populations are picked up. If the second condition did not hold for the whole Γ, we could form populations for which the idiosyncratic component would not vanish.

Assumption 7.1 may require that we restrict our analysis to subsets of the original Γ. For instance, if for γ' and γ'' we had $D(L)z_t^{\gamma'} = -D(L)z_t^{\gamma''}$, we should isolate either γ' or γ''. In the same way, we should be forced to take only a bounded subset of Γ.

If Assumption 7.1 holds, and if Assumption 1.3 holds for N, then Theorem 1.2 applies uniformly on Γ, i.e. given $\epsilon > 0$, we can find an m_ϵ such that if $m > m_\epsilon$ then, for any $k = 1, n$, and any $p \in \Gamma_m$, the fraction of $\text{var}\left(\sum_{i=1}^m D_{kk}(L)z_{kt}^{p^i}\right)$ which is due to the common component is greater than $1 - \epsilon$.

Henceforth we shall proceed by dropping the idiosyncratic component in the aggregate model. This may be motivated in three ways:

(1) m is a large number and is interpreted strictly as the number of individuals in the populations. Moreover, Assumption 7.1 holds. In this

case we may have $N^i = 1$, for any i, but also different systems of weights, as observed in Section 1.3, if the individual processes represent prices, for instance, or if the weights arise from a linear approximation to a non-linear aggregation procedure.

(2) The number m can also be interpreted as the number (possibly small) of (huge) groups of agents sharing the same γ but not the same idiosyncratic components. In this case we may assume that the idiosyncratic component vanishes within each of the groups, so that Assumption 7.1 is not necessary. The numerosity (absolute or relative) of group i is N^i, while $A^{p^i}(L)$, $B^{p^i}(L)$, and $\tilde{B}^{p^i}(L)$ are common to all the N^i agents in group i.

(3) It must be pointed out that the distinction between common and idiosyncratic shocks makes sense only when we intend to apply large numbers results. If, instead, we are dealing with a small number of processes, we can rewrite the micromodel without any distinction between idiosyncratic and common shocks. For instance, suppose that there is one common shock and the population size is two. In this case there is no point in keeping the distinction. The model can be reformulated with three common shocks, the first agent being affected by the first two shocks (the common and the first idiosyncratic), the second by the first and the third (the common and the second idiosyncratic).

Irrespective of whether we assume the first, the second, or the third point of view, we are going to drop the idiosyncratic component from the aggregate model. It will be very convenient in the remaining chapters of Part II to drop the idiosyncratic component from the micromodel as well (as we have already done in Chapter 4). This will greatly simplify notation and create no harm: when we state something like 'if the micromodel fulfills ...', the reader should take it to mean 'if the common component of the micromodel fulfills ...'. In any case, the difference between our statements and the ones in which the idiosyncratic component is taken into explicit consideration is insignificant, as we show in Sections 8.3.3, 9.1.2, 11.2.2, and 12.3.2 below.

However, the reader should keep in mind that the above notational simplification does not mean that the idiosyncratic term is unimportant. As the examples in Sections 5.1, 5.2, and 5.3 show, the functions of L in front of the common shocks depend in general on the way agents deal with the idiosyncratic components. This point will be further developed in Chapter 13. In conclusion, the disaggregated equation, the aggregated equation, and the aggregated vector will be rewritten respectively as

$$D(L)z_t^{p^i} = \tilde{B}^{p^i}(L)u_t \tag{7.4}$$

$$D(L)z_t^p = \left(\sum_{i=1}^{m} N^i \tilde{B}^{p^i}(L)\right) u_t \tag{7.5}$$

$$z_t^p = \sum_{i=1}^{m} N^i z_t^{p^i}. \tag{7.6}$$

Notice that since here the i-th equation of the disaggregated model (7.4) does not contain the idiosyncratic term, its solution depends only on p^i and has therefore been indicated by $z_t^{p^i}$, instead of z_t^{i,p^i}, both in (7.4) and in (7.6).

Observing that

$$\left[A^{p^i}(L)\right]^{-1} \det A^{p^i}(L) = A_{\text{ad}}^{p^i}(L),$$

the aggregated model can be formulated as an ARIMA:[1]

$$G^p(L)D(L)z_t^p = H^p(L)u_t, \tag{7.7}$$

where

$$G^p(L) = \prod_{i=1}^{m} \det[A^{p^i}(L)]$$

$$H^p(L) = \sum_{i=1}^{m} \frac{N^i G^p(L)}{\det A^{p^i}(L)} A_{\text{ad}}^{p^i}(L) B^{p^i}(L).$$

Finally, let us introduce the spectral density of the aggregate vector:

$$S^p(z) = F^p(z)F^p(\bar{z})', \tag{7.8}$$

where $|z| = 1$ and

$$F^p(L) = \sum_{i=1}^{m} N^i \tilde{B}^{p^i}(L).$$

The following result holds:

THEOREM 7.1. All the coefficients of (7.5), (7.7), and (7.8), as functions of p, are analytic in Γ_m.

This is a trivial statement, as the reader can check by simple inspection of the definitions we have just set up. In fact, all the coefficients appearing in the three formulas are obtained by elementary algebraic manipulations of the coefficients of $A^{p^i}(L)$ and $B^{p^i}(L)$.

Using Theorem 7.1, together with Theorem 6.1, we can apply the Alternative Principle to important issues regarding the aggregate model, such as rank and cointegration. This is done in the following two chapters. Other issues, like Granger causality, VAR, and ARMAX representations, will require a reconsideration of the Alternative Principle and will be dealt with in Chapters 11 and 12.

[1] This is a generalization of the univariate procedure applied in Section 4.1.

7.3. Aggregation of the DI Model

No specific difficulty arises for aggregation of the DI model. First of all we can rewrite (6.23) excluding the idiosyncratic components:

$$\begin{pmatrix} A^{\gamma}(L) & \tilde{A}^{\gamma}(L) \\ 0 & \mathcal{A}^{\tau}(L) \end{pmatrix} \begin{pmatrix} D(L)y_t^{\gamma} \\ \mathcal{D}(L)x_t^{\tau} \end{pmatrix} = \begin{pmatrix} B^{\gamma}(L) \\ \mathcal{B}^{\tau}(L) \end{pmatrix} u_t.$$

Taking the inverse of the autoregressive matrix and multiplying both sides gives

$$\begin{pmatrix} D(L)y_t^{\gamma} \\ \mathcal{D}(L)x_t^{\tau} \end{pmatrix} = \begin{pmatrix} A^{\gamma}(L)^{-1} & Q^{\gamma}(L) \\ 0 & \mathcal{A}^{\tau}(L)^{-1} \end{pmatrix} \begin{pmatrix} B^{\gamma}(L) \\ \mathcal{B}^{\tau}(L) \end{pmatrix} u_t,$$

where $Q^{\gamma}(L) = -A^{\gamma}(L)^{-1}\tilde{A}^{\gamma}(L)\mathcal{A}^{\tau}(L)^{-1}$. As a consequence, aggregation leaves the DI structure untouched, i.e. the aggregate vector x_t^p depends only on

$$(\hat{\omega}^1 \quad \hat{\omega}^2 \quad \cdots \quad \hat{\omega}^m \quad \lambda),$$

not on ω^i, $i = 1, m$.

7.4. Macrovariables in the Micromodel. General Equilibrium

There are models in which the agents are assumed to employ aggregate variables to determine the individual variables. This is the case, for example, when an aggregate variable is used by the agents to improve their prediction of some individual variable. Such models cannot immediately be accommodated in our framework because some individual variables depend on the population. Consider the following two-variable example. The independent variable is

$$x_t^{\tau} = (1 + \nu_1 L)u_{1t} + (1 + \nu_2 L)u_{2t},$$

where $\tau = (\nu_1 \quad \nu_2)$, ν_1 and ν_2 being individual parameters. Suppose that the agent sets the dependent microvariable y_t as

$$\mu_1 x_t^{\tau} + \mu_2 x_{t-1}^p,$$

where μ_1 and μ_2 are individual parameters and x_t^p is the aggregate variable. Here Definition 6.2 does not apply because y_t depends on x_{t-1}^p, which depends on the population. The difficulty can be overcome by directly defining the model for y_t^p and x_t^p. Let

$$p = (\mu^1 \quad \mu^2 \quad \cdots \quad \mu^m \quad \nu^1 \quad \nu^2 \quad \cdots \quad \nu^m),$$

where

$$\mu^i = (\,\mu_1^i \quad \mu_2^i\,)\,, \quad \nu^i = (\,\nu_1^i \quad \nu_2^i\,)\,.$$

Defining $p^i = (\,\mu^i \quad \nu^i\,)$, the aggregate model is

$$\begin{aligned} y_t^p &= \sum_{i=1}^m N^i \mu_1^i x_t^{p^i} + \left(\sum_{i=1}^m N^i \mu_2^i\right) x_{t-1}^p \\ x_t^p &= \sum_{i=1}^m N^i \left[(1+\nu_1^i L)u_{1t} + (1+\nu_2^i L)u_{2t}\right], \end{aligned}$$

i.e. putting $Q^p = \sum N^i \mu_2^i$,

$$\begin{aligned} y_t^p &= \sum_{i=1}^m (N^i \mu_1^i + Q^p L) \left[(1+\nu_1^i L)u_{1t} + (1+\nu_2^i L)u_{2t}\right] \\ x_t^p &= \sum_{i=1}^m N^i \left[(1+\nu_1^i L)u_{1t} + (1+\nu_2^i L)u_{2t}\right]. \end{aligned} \tag{7.9}$$

Evidently Theorem 7.1 applies and, provided that the set where p varies is a region, the Alternative Principle applies as well. Finally, the model can be extended to allow for the presence of lagged values of y_t^p and x_t^p in the determination of both microvariables.

The same difficulty arises with general equilibrium models. Individual variables depend on all the microparameters. However, the same straightforward solution applies. Simply, we define the macromodel directly, and since the macroparameters are analytic in the microparameters the Alternative Principle can be invoked. More will be given on these models in Sections 8.3.2 and 12.1.

7.5. Populations and Distributions over Γ

7.5.1. Let us concentrate on interpretation (2), Section 7.2, of the aggregate model. We have m groups of agents, with identical parameters in each group, with N^i being the number of agents in group i. Since all the results in the next chapters will be independent of N, there is no point in letting N vary. However, considering the weights N^i as variables is useful if we want to compare our framework, based on the population space, with the one based on distributions over Γ, which is often adopted in work on aggregation (see Section 7.7 for references). Redefine the population space as follows:

$$\Theta_m = \Gamma_m \times S_+^{m-1},$$

with $S_+^{m-1} = \{N \in \mathbb{R}^m \;:\; \sum N^i = 1,\; N^i > 0\}$, so that N, after normalization, can vary independently of $p \in \Gamma_m$.

Given $(p \quad N) \in \Theta_m$, we may associate with $(p \quad N)$ the distribution over Γ which is concentrated on the finite set $\{p^i,\ i=1,m\}$, with N^i being the mass concentrated on p^i (naturally if $p^i = p^j$ the mass concentrated on p^i will be $N^i + N^j$, and so on).

The above correspondence, denoted by $\mathcal{F}$, is of course not one-to-one. Permutations of the ω^i and the N^i do not alter the implied distribution. However, $\mathcal{F}$ gives a (non-parsimonious) parameterization for the set Π_m of all the distributions over Γ which are concentrated on finite subsets of Γ containing no more than m points, with the condition that such points share the same λ.

Now assume for simplicity that $D(L) = I$ in the micromodel, so that z_t^γ is stationary and we can avoid referring to the initial conditions. Given $\theta = (p \quad N) \in \Theta_m$, the aggregate vector

$$z_t^p = \sum_{i=1}^{m} N^i z_t^{p^i}$$

can be read as the expectation of $z_t^{p^i}$ with respect to $\mathcal{F}(\theta)$. In the same way, in representation (7.5), which becomes

$$z_t^p = \left(\sum_{i=1}^{m} N^i \tilde{B}^{p^i}(L) \right) u_t,$$

the matrix within the brackets can be read as the expectation of $\tilde{B}^{p^i}(L)$ with respect to $\mathcal{F}(\theta)$.

Alternatively, we might have started with distributions over Γ instead of populations. Precisely, let the micromodel be defined as usual and assume for simplicity that $D(L) = I$. Then consider a family Π of distributions over Γ, parameterized over an open region $\Theta \in \mathbb{R}^v$, with the condition that the distributions of the family are concentrated on subsets of Γ for which λ is constant. Indicate by $P(\theta)$ the generic distribution of the family. The aggregate vector is

$$\begin{aligned} z_t^\theta &= \int_\Gamma z^\gamma dP(\theta) \\ &= \left[\int_\Gamma \tilde{B}^\gamma(L) dP(\theta) \right] u_t + \int_\Gamma \tilde{C}^\gamma(L) \chi_t^\gamma dP(\theta). \end{aligned}$$

The idiosyncratic term can be dropped using either the argument in Section 1.4 (if the distributions $P(\theta)$ are diffuse), or the argument in Sections 1.3 and 7.2 (if the distributions $P(\theta)$ are concentrated), so that the aggregated vector can be rewritten as

$$z_t^\theta = \left[\int_\Gamma \tilde{B}^\gamma(L) dP(\theta) \right] u_t. \tag{7.10}$$

Several important observations are in order.

7.5.2. To avoid possible misunderstandings, it must be pointed out that the number m plays different roles in the set-up that we have adopted in this book, and in the distributional approach. In the first m can represent both the number of agents and the number of groups containing agents with identical parameters (see 7.2, interpretations (1) and (2)). If instead we start with distributions of Π_m, the number m represents the maximum number of steps in the distributions of the family. The number of agents is not given. Rather, the definition of the aggregate vector as the expectation of z_t^γ, relative to a given $d \in \Pi_m$, has the motivation that if we consider M agents independently drawn from the distribution d, then

$$\frac{1}{M}\sum_{i=1}^{M} z_t^{\gamma^i} \to \mathrm{E}(z_t^\gamma),$$

as M tends to infinity. Thus, if $\theta = (\,p \quad N\,)$, and $\tilde{p}$ is a population of M agents drawn from $\mathcal{F}(\theta)$, then when M tends to infinity M^i/M^j tends to N^i/N^j with probability one, where M^i is the number of individuals in $\tilde{p}$ whose parameter vector is p^i.

7.5.3. Assume that the distributions of the family Π are concentrated on finite subsets of Γ with no more than m points. Let us call it an m-family. In this case, being the sum of a finite set of ARIMA vectors, z_t^θ is an ARIMA as well. Moreover, if $P(\theta)$ is analytic in θ, since Θ is assumed to be an open region, we can apply the Alternative Principle to the coefficients of the spectral density of z_t^θ. As a consequence, the results of the following chapters, from 8 to 12, can be adapted to the distributional framework. For example, if we can find a point $\theta \in \Theta$, such that the macromodel is non-cointegrated, then the subset of Θ for which the macromodel is non-cointegrated is negligible.

7.5.4. Consider instead a family Π of distributions that are diffuse on Γ. Then z_t^θ is no longer an ARIMA, unless special conditions are fulfilled. In fact, if a non-trivial polynomial matrix $A^\gamma(L)$ is present in the micromodel, then an MA representation of z_t^θ in terms of rational functions of L may be impossible.[2] Under suitable conditions on the distributions of the family, the spectral density of z_t^θ is analytic in θ and the Alternative Principle can be applied. However, difficulties arise when we want to analyze the Wold representation of z_t^θ, because the algebraic procedure employed in Chapter 11 no longer applies. It is mainly for this reason that we limit ourselves in this book to finite populations.

[2] See Granger (1980), in which aggregation of AR(1) scalar processes produces a process that does not have rational spectral density.

7.6. Restrictions and Subsets of the Population Space

As we have observed in Remark 6.10, when we say that a subset of Γ_m is negligible because it has zero Lebesgue measure, we simply manifest our state of profound ignorance about the distribution of the microparameters over the populations. We do not even choose a measure on the space Γ_m (or $\Gamma_m \times S_+^{m-1}$). Any measure for which sets of zero Lebesgue measure are negligible is acceptable.

It might be argued that this is rather an extreme situation, since in many empirical cases we possess information that can be employed to exclude sizablc subsets of the population space. For example, suppose that we know that ω_1 and ω_2 are negatively correlated. In this case, the relevant population space would be the subset of $\Gamma_m \times S_+^{m-1}$ such that

$$\sum N^i(\omega_1^{p^i} - \bar{\omega}_1)(\omega_2^{p^i} - \bar{\omega}_2) < 0,$$

where $\bar{\omega}_l$, $l = 1, 2$, is the mean of $\omega_l^{p^i}$ over $(p \quad N)$. Other interesting subsets of the population space may be obtained by considering m-families of distributions over Γ. For example, suppose that there is only one microparameter ω, and that $\Gamma = \mathbb{R}$, so that $\Gamma_m = \mathbb{R}^m$. Then assume that

$$\Theta = \{(\theta_1 \quad \theta_2) \in \mathbb{R}^2 \ : \ \theta_1 < \theta_2\},$$

and that $P(\theta)$ is concentrated on the points

$$\omega^i(\theta) = \theta_1 + i\frac{\theta_2 - \theta_1}{m},$$

$i = 1, m$, with weights $N^i = 1/m$. The distributions of the family approximate the uniform distribution on $[\theta_1, \theta_2]$. Since $\omega^i(\theta)$ is analytic in θ_1 and θ_2, and since $\tilde{B}^{\gamma}(L)$ is analytic in γ, the coefficients of

$$\frac{1}{m}\sum_{i=1}^{m} \tilde{B}^{\omega^i(\theta)}(L)$$

are analytic in θ. It must be pointed out that while θ varies in Θ, the vector

$$((\omega^1(\theta) \quad \omega^2(\theta) \quad \cdots \quad \omega^m(\theta)) \quad (\tfrac{1}{m} \quad \tfrac{1}{m} \quad \cdots \quad \tfrac{1}{m}))$$

describes a two-dimensional manifold in $\Gamma_m \times S_+^{m-1}$.

Both when a subset of $\Gamma_m \times S_+^{m-1}$ is obtained directly, and when it is obtained through an m-family, the argument in Section 7.5.3 applies, i.e. all the results that can be obtained by applying the Alternative Principle can be adapted, with $\Gamma_m \times S_+^{m-1}$ substituted either by a subset of $\Gamma_m \times S_+^{m-1}$ or by another parameter space. What is needed is that the relevant macro coefficients be analytic as functions of the microparameters.

However, restrictions with a solid empirical or theoretical basis should not be confused with restrictions that are introduced to avoid some of the complications of aggregation. For instance, suppose that the micromodel is

$$\begin{aligned} y_t^\gamma &= \omega_1 x_t^\tau \\ x_t^\tau &= (1+\omega_2 L)u_{1t} + (1+\omega_3 L)u_{2t}, \end{aligned}$$

where $\tau = (\omega_2 \quad \omega_3)$, while there are no common parameters. If we assume that ω_1 and τ are drawn from independent distributions, then obviously

$$y_t^p = \bar{\omega}_1^p x_t^p,$$

so that the macroequation has precisely the same shape as the corresponding microequation. Now, at the risk of being pedantic, we must recall that assuming independence is a very heavy restriction, as it implies zero correlation and therefore a reduction of dimension in the population space. Let us also observe that a state of profound ignorance about the relationship between two parameters does *not* translate into the assumption of independent distributions. The correct translation is into a diffuse measure over the space of all possible distributions.

As a last observation on restrictions we must remind the reader that information on the distribution of the microparameters may be very difficult, if not impossible, to obtain. In our micromodels we are not dealing only with, say, propensity to consume and income. Dynamic micromodels, as the examples discussed in Chapter 5 show, are determined by very deep microparameters. It would be hard to say, a priori, what the relationship is between one of the parameters of the loss function in the model of Section 5.3, and the parameters of the polynomials in L in the common component of income. But even an empirical investigation on such a relationship seems hard to set out.

In conclusion, we will stick to Γ_m as our parameter space, and consider subsets of zero Lebesgue measure as negligible. This is convenient, as the next chapters will show, whereas restrictions, when motivated, are easy to deal with.

7.7. Bibliographic Notes

For aggregation based on distributions over a given microparameter space, see Granger (1980), Stoker (1982, 1984), Lewbel (1994). Both Granger and Lewbel analyze aggregation of $(1-\alpha^i L)x_t^i = \epsilon_t^i$, under the assumption that

α^i and ϵ_t^i are independently distributed. In this case independence, although considerably simplifying aggregation, does not produce a trivial result. In fact, the aggregate model is not obtained by averaging the autoregressive coefficients (see Section 4.2 and also 8.4). A typical example of independence as a means to avoid, or to postpone, the complications of aggregation is in Friedman's *A Theory of the Consumption Function* (Friedman, 1957). The ratio of permanent consumption to permanent income is assumed to be independent of income, so that aggregate consumption emerges as aggregate income times the average ratio (pp. 18–19).

8

The Rank of the Aggregate Vector

8.1. General Statements

In Chapters 6 and 7 we have given general definitions of the micromodel and aggregate model. In the remaining chapters of Part II we shall consider convenient specifications or simplifications, which allow a simple application of the Alternative Principle. The reader will be easily convinced that generalization to more complex cases or to additional problems is straightforward.

We shall begin by analyzing one of those circumstances in which aggregation is not bad. Precisely, we shall prove that if a 'small amount' of heterogeneity across agents is allowed, then, even though the micromodel is everywhere singular, the aggregate vector has full rank with the exception of a negligible subset of Γ_m. This means that even when the micromodel, resulting from the application of some economic theory, is singular, we do not necessarily need to invoke the rather *ad hoc* assumption of measurement errors to justify the fact that the empirical aggregate vector is very far from being singular.

Singularity or non-singularity is a property of the stationary vectors $D(L)z_t^\gamma$ or $D(L)z_t^p$. Therefore in the present chapter we can assume, with no loss of generality, that $D(L) = I$. Let us begin with the following statements:

THEOREM 8.1. If $h < n$, i.e. the number of common shocks is smaller than the number of variables, then z_t^γ and z_t^p are singular everywhere in Γ and Γ_m respectively. If $h \geq n$ and there exists a point $p \in \Gamma_m$ for which z_t^p is non-singular, then z_t^p is singular for a negligible subset of Γ_m.

Proof. The singularity of z_t^p means that the determinant of the spectral density (7.8) vanishes identically in z. In turn this means that all the coefficients of the powers of z in (7.8) vanish. Theorem 7.1 and the Alternative Principle lead to the result. Q.E.D.

THEOREM 8.2. If $h \geq n$ and there exists a point $\gamma \in \Gamma$ such that z_t^γ is non singular, then z_t^p is singular for a negligible subset of Γ_m.

Proof. Let $\gamma = (\omega \quad \lambda)$ and consider $\tilde{p} = (\omega \quad \omega \quad \cdots \quad \omega \quad \lambda)$. $z_t^{\tilde{p}}$ is obviously non-singular. Q.E.D.

8.2. The Two-Point Example

Both Theorems 8.1 and 8.2 are trivial applications of the Alternative Principle. With the next theorem we introduce a method to build a point in Γ_m which triggers the Alternative Principle into action. The idea is very simple and will often be applied henceforth. Let us employ a simple example. The model is

$$\begin{aligned} y_t^\gamma &= \kappa^\gamma(L)x_t^\gamma \\ x_t^\gamma &= b_1^\gamma(L)u_{1t} + b_2^\gamma(L)u_{2t}, \end{aligned}$$

i.e.

$$\begin{aligned} y_t^\gamma &= \kappa^\gamma(L)[b_1^\gamma(L)u_{1t} + b_2^\gamma(L)u_{2t}] \\ x_t^\gamma &= b_1^\gamma(L)u_{1t} + b_2^\gamma(L)u_{2t}. \end{aligned}$$

We leave completely unspecified the polynomials appearing in the model and Γ. In any case, given any specification, the micromodel is typically singular independently of which γ is chosen. Assume $m = 2$. The aggregate model can be written as

$$\begin{pmatrix} y_t^p \\ x_t^p \end{pmatrix} = \begin{pmatrix} N^1\kappa^{p^1}(L) & N^2\kappa^{p^2}(L) \\ N^1 & N^2 \end{pmatrix} \begin{pmatrix} b_1^{p^1}(L) & b_2^{p^1}(L) \\ b_1^{p^2}(L) & b_2^{p^2}(L) \end{pmatrix} \begin{pmatrix} u_{1t} \\ u_{2t} \end{pmatrix}. \tag{8.1}$$

The first matrix on the RHS is singular only if $\kappa^{p^1}(L) = \kappa^{p^2}(L)$. If Γ contains the points $\gamma' = (\omega' \quad \lambda)$ and $\gamma'' = (\omega'' \quad \lambda)$ such that $\kappa^{\gamma'}(L) \neq \kappa^{\gamma''}(L)$, then the matrix is non-singular a.e. on Γ_2. Suppose that such γ' and γ'' exist and call B_1 the negligible subset of Γ_2 where $\kappa^{p^1}(L) = \kappa^{p^2}(L)$. Naturally B_1 contains the subset $H_2 \subseteq \Gamma_2$ whose elements are the homogeneous populations, i.e. the subset of the populations $(\omega \quad \omega \quad \lambda)$.

In addition to non-singularity of the first matrix, non-singularity of the aggregate vector requires that the rank of the second matrix on the RHS of (8.1) be 2. In fact, if the second matrix were of rank 1 everywhere in Γ_2, the matrix $\mathcal{Q}^p(L)$, which has been introduced in Theorem 6.5 and is defined on Γ_2, would be singular everywhere in Γ_2. If we assume that u_t is non-redundant, the second matrix has rank 2 a.e. on Γ_2. Call B_2 the set where the second matrix has rank less than 2. The set $B = B_1 \cup B_2$ is negligible.

REMARK 8.1. As already observed, the set H_2 is obviously contained in B_1. However, the set B_1 may contain points that do not belong to H_2. For example, consider the model in Section 5.1, Case (b). The function $\kappa(L)$ is $a(\beta)/a(L)$, where $a(L)$ is defined in equation (5.5). Assuming that the functions $a_l(L)$ are first-order polynomials, it is easy to verify that different points of Γ may produce the same $a(L)$. In this case, as anticipated in Remark 6.10, the set B_1 contains points for which we have no economic interpretation. We shall return in Section 8.4 to the subset of Γ_m where the model is singular.

The above argument can be extended without difficulty to Γ_m, for any m. Take a point

$$(\omega' \quad \omega'' \quad \lambda) \in \Gamma_2 - B.$$

Then consider $\hat{p} = (\omega' \quad \omega'' \quad \cdots \quad \omega'' \quad \lambda)$, where ω'' is replicated $m-1$ times. The aggregate vector corresponding to $\hat{p}$ is

$$\begin{pmatrix} y_t^{\hat{p}} \\ x_t^{\hat{p}} \end{pmatrix} = \begin{pmatrix} N^1 \kappa^{\gamma'}(L) & \tilde{N}\kappa^{\gamma''}(L) \\ N^1 & \tilde{N} \end{pmatrix} \begin{pmatrix} b_1^{\gamma'}(L) & b_2^{\gamma'}(L) \\ b_1^{\gamma''}(L) & b_2^{\gamma''}(L) \end{pmatrix} \begin{pmatrix} u_{1t} \\ u_{2t} \end{pmatrix},$$

with $\tilde{N} = N^2 + \cdots + N^m$, $\gamma' = (\omega' \quad \lambda)$, $\gamma'' = (\omega'' \quad \lambda)$, and is evidently non-singular. Therefore the subset of Γ_m for which the aggregate vector is singular is negligible.

Here we have the paradigm of many of our results. Important aggregation effects arise when: (i) agents' responses to the independent variables may be different; (ii) the independent variables are not equal, nor proportional, nor driven by the same unique shock ($h \geq 2$ and non-redundancy of u_t). A couple of agents which are different in both respects is sufficient for a result valid a.e. in Γ_m.

REMARK 8.2. Remark 6.13 on non-redundancy and the dimension of Γ applies here as well. Our result does not depend on the dimension of Γ, i.e. on the fact that we have many or few microparameters. For example, suppose that we have only one microparameter, ω, that $\kappa^{\gamma}(L) = \omega$, and

$$b_1^{\gamma}(L) = \omega, \quad b_2^{\gamma}(L) = \omega^2.$$

All the same u_t is non-redundant and $\kappa^{p^1}(L) = \kappa^{p^2}(L)$ only for $p \in H_2$, which is a negligible subset of Γ_2.

8.3. A Theorem for the DI Model

8.3.1. The analysis of the above example can be generalized in many ways. The following seems sufficient to cover many economically interesting cases.

Consider the micromodel

$$\begin{aligned} a^{\gamma}(L)y_t^{\gamma} &= \kappa_1^{\gamma}(L)x_{1t}^{\gamma} + \kappa_2^{\gamma}(L)x_{2t}^{\gamma} + \cdots + \kappa_{n-1}^{\gamma}(L)x_{n-1t}^{\gamma} \\ A^{\gamma}(L)x_t^{\gamma} &= B^{\gamma}(L)u_t, \end{aligned} \tag{8.2}$$

where y_t^γ is a scalar while x_t^γ is $(n-1)$-dimensional. Naturally the model is singular for γ everywhere in Γ. Notice that (8.2) can be rewritten in the DI form

$$\begin{pmatrix} \alpha^\gamma(L) & -\kappa^\gamma(L) \\ 0 & A^\gamma(L) \end{pmatrix} \begin{pmatrix} y_t^\gamma \\ x_t^\gamma \end{pmatrix} = \begin{pmatrix} 0 \\ B^\gamma(L) \end{pmatrix} u_t,$$

where $\kappa^\gamma(L) = (\,\kappa_1^\gamma(L) \quad \kappa_2^\gamma(L) \quad \cdots \quad \kappa_{n-1}^\gamma(L)\,)$.

THEOREM 8.3. Assume that in (8.2) we have (i) $h \geq n$; (ii) x_t^γ is non-singular a.e. in Γ; (iii) u_t is non-redundant for x_t; (iv) there exist two points $\gamma' = (\,\omega' \quad \lambda\,)$ and $\gamma'' = (\,\omega'' \quad \lambda\,)$ such that for at least one l, $l = 1, n-1$, $\kappa_l^{\gamma'}(L) \neq \kappa_l^{\gamma''}(L)$. Then $z_t^p = (\,y_t^p \quad x_t^p\,)'$ is non-singular a.e. in Γ_m.

Proof. As observed above, we only need to prove the theorem in Γ_2. Firstly define $K_l^\gamma(L) = \alpha^\gamma(L)^{-1}\kappa_l^\gamma(L)$ and rewrite the model as follows:

$$\begin{pmatrix} y_t^\gamma \\ x_t^\gamma \end{pmatrix} = \begin{pmatrix} K_1^\gamma(L) & K_2^\gamma(L) & \cdots & K_{n-1}^\gamma(L) \\ & & I_{n-1} & \end{pmatrix} A^\gamma(L)^{-1}B^\gamma(L)u_t.$$

Define the matrices

$$E^\gamma(L) = A^\gamma(L)^{-1}B^\gamma(L)$$

$$\tilde{G}^p(L) = \begin{pmatrix} N^1 E^{p^1}(L) \\ N^2 E^{p^2}(L) \end{pmatrix}$$

and

$$G^p(L) = \begin{pmatrix} K_1^{p^1}(L) & \cdots & K_{n-1}^{p^1}(L) & K_1^{p^2}(L) & \cdots & K_{n-1}^{p^2}(L) \\ & I_{n-1} & & & I_{n-1} & \end{pmatrix}.$$

The aggregate model is

$$\begin{pmatrix} y_t^p \\ x_t^p \end{pmatrix} = G^p(L)\tilde{G}^p(L)u_t.$$

Without loss of generality assume that the set $B_1 \subset \Gamma_2$ where $K_1^{p^1}(L) = K_1^{p^2}(L)$ is negligible (i.e. $l = 1$ in assumption (iv)). Since the determinant of the submatrix of $G^p(L)$ obtained by taking the first n columns is $K_1^{p^1}(L) - K_1^{p^2}(L)$, such a submatrix is non-singular a.e. in Γ_2. By assumption (iii) and Theorem 6.7, one of the matrices of $\tilde{G}^p(L)$ obtained by augmenting the upper $(n-1) \times h$ submatrix with one of the last $n-1$ rows must have rank n a.e. in Γ_2. Thus, the rank of $G^p(L)\tilde{G}^p(L)$ is n a.e. in Γ_2. Q.E.D.

8.3.2. Theorem 8.2 applies in a natural way to the models introduced in Section 7.4. In the same way, the analysis developed for model (8.1) and its generalization in Theorem 8.3 apply with slight modifications. Rewriting model (7.9) for $m = 2$ will be sufficient as an illustration:

$$\begin{pmatrix} y_t^p \\ x_t^p \end{pmatrix} = \begin{pmatrix} N^1\mu_1^1 + Q^pL & N^2\mu_1^2 + Q^pL \\ N^1 & N^2 \end{pmatrix} \begin{pmatrix} 1+\nu_1^1 L & 1+\nu_2^1 L \\ 1+\nu_1^2 L & 1+\nu_2^2 L \end{pmatrix} \begin{pmatrix} u_{1t} \\ u_{2t} \end{pmatrix}.$$

In addition to non-redundancy of u_t for x_t, a sufficient condition for aggregate non-singularity a.e. in Γ_2, and therefore in Γ_m, is the existence of a $p = (\omega_1 \quad \omega_2 \quad \lambda)$ such that $\mu_1^1 \neq \mu_1^2$.

8.3.3. Let us return to the complete micromodel, i.e. restore the idiosyncratic component. The following example will be sufficient for a brief discussion:

$$\begin{aligned} y_t^\gamma &= \kappa^\gamma(L)[b_1\gamma(L)u_{1t} + b_2^\gamma(L)u_{2t}] + \tilde{\kappa}^\gamma(L)\chi_t^\gamma \\ x_t^\gamma &= b_1\gamma(L)u_{1t} + b_2^\gamma(L)u_{2t} + \chi_t^\gamma. \end{aligned}$$

Firstly, suppose that $b_2^\gamma(L) = 0$ for any $\gamma \in \Gamma$, i.e. that there is only one common shock. Theorem 8.1, first statement, undergoes a modification since z_t^γ is not necessarily singular. However, dropping χ_t^γ in the aggregate model ensures that z_t^p is singular, which is the really important conclusion. The second statement of Theorem 8.1 holds with no modification. In Theorem 8.2 we only need to assume that there exists a point $\gamma \in \Gamma$ such that the common component of z_t^γ is non-singular. Theorem 8.3 holds with no modification.

8.4. More on the Subset of Γ_m where the Model is Singular

As already observed in Remark 8.1, if B is the subset of Γ_m for which z_t^p is singular, we may be unable to give an economic interpretation of the whole B. However, we may be interested in an indirect characterization of B. Consider for example a further simplification of the model analyzed in Section 8.2:

$$\begin{aligned} y_t^\gamma &= \kappa^\gamma(L)x_t^\gamma \\ x_t^\gamma &= b_1^\gamma(L)u_{1t} + b_2^\gamma(L)u_{2t}. \end{aligned}$$

Assume $\sum N^i = 1$. Naturally, if p is such that $\kappa^{p^i}(L)$ and $x_t^{p^i}$ are independent, i.e. if

$$\sum N^i\kappa^{p^i}(L)x_t^{p^i} = \left(\sum N^i\kappa^{p^i}(L)\right)\left(\sum N^i x_t^{p^i}\right) = \left(\sum N^i\kappa^{p^i}(L)\right)x_t^p, \quad (8.3)$$

then the model is singular. However, the converse is not true. Analysis of Γ_2 will be sufficient. Equation (8.3) can be rewritten as

$$\sum N^i\kappa^{p^i}(L)(b_1^{p^i}(L)u_{1t} + b_2^{p^i}(L)u_{2t}) = K^p(L)\sum N^i(b_1^{p^i}(L)u_{1t} + b_2^{p^i}(L)u_{2t}),$$

with $K^p(L) = \sum N^i \kappa^{p^i}(L)$. Orthonormality of u_t implies

$$\sum N^i \kappa^{p^i}(L) b_j^{p^i}(L) = K^p(L) \sum N^i b_j^{p^i}(L)$$

for $j = 1, 2$, i.e.

$$\begin{aligned} N^1(\kappa^{p^1}(L) - K^p(L))b_1^{p^1}(L) + N^2(\kappa^{p^2}(L) - K^p(L))b_1^{p^2}(L) = 0 \\ N^1(\kappa^{p^1}(L) - K^p(L))b_2^{p^1}(L) + N^2(\kappa^{p^2}(L) - K^p(L))b_2^{p^2}(L) = 0. \end{aligned} \tag{8.4}$$

Non-redundancy of u_t for x_t^γ and the fact that $\kappa^{p^1}(L) \neq \kappa^{p^2}(L)$ for at least a p imply that equations (8.4) hold only for a negligible subset of Γ_2. However, if $\kappa^{p^1}(L) \neq \kappa^{p^2}(L)$, equations (8.4) imply not only that u_t is redundant for x_t^γ with respect to the population p (which is the condition for singularity of the aggregate vector), but also that such redundancy is realized by a particular vector which depends on the polynomials $\kappa^{p^i}(L)$.

Incidentally, the same technique can be used to analyze the independence assumption made in Section 4.2.3. Let us rewrite the model, with a slight modification, as

$$\zeta_t^\gamma = \frac{1}{1 - cL}(b_1 u_{1t} + b_2 u_{2t}),$$

where $\gamma = \omega = (c \quad b_1 \quad b_2)$. Then consider the representation

$$\zeta_t^\gamma = \frac{1}{1 - cL}\eta_t^\gamma,$$

with $\eta_t^\gamma = b_1 u_{1t} + b_2 u_{2t}$. Now, if u_t is non-redundant for ζ_t^γ, then η_t and $(1 - cL)^{-1}$ are not correlated for a negligible subset of Γ_m.

8.5. Bibliographic Notes

As we have seen, the micromodel in Section 5.1 is singular under suitable assumptions on the information set. In the same way, the micromodel in Section 5.3 is singular if agents base their prediction of income on a univariate model (as is assumed in Section 5.3). The fact that singularity is not an exception in micro theory has been pointed out, e.g. in Hansen and Sargent (1991b, pp. 82–83). As a possible way out of this difficulty the authors assume that the econometrician only has data on a subset of the variables observed and employed by the representative agent. Another possible way to reconcile theory and data is to introduce measurement errors (see e.g. Sargent, 1989). In this chapter we have seen that aggregation of heterogeneous agents provides a natural solution to the problem. From a time series theoretical point of view, our solution is close to Hansen and Sargent's. However, we do not need any assumption on the information set of the agents.

9

Cointegration

9.1. General Results

9.1.1. As another important application of our method let us consider the problem of whether micro cointegration implies macro cointegration. We do not want to deal with the problem at a high level of generality. However, the reader will be easily convinced that our results, obtained in the two-variable case, can be extended to any number of variables.

Let us consider the two-variable micromodel

$$\begin{aligned}(1-L)y_t^\gamma &= b_{11}^\gamma(L)v_{1t} + \cdots + b_{1h_1}^\gamma(L)v_{h_1t} \\ &\qquad + (1-L)[d_{11}^\gamma(L)w_{1t} + \cdots + d_{1h_2}^\gamma(L)w_{h_2t}] \\ (1-L)x_t^\gamma &= b_{21}^\gamma(L)v_{1t} + \cdots + b_{2h_1}^\gamma(L)v_{h_1t} \\ &\qquad + (1-L)[d_{21}^\gamma(L)w_{1t} + \cdots + c_{2h_2}^\gamma(L)w_{h_2t}],\end{aligned} \tag{9.1}$$

where $(\, v_t \quad w_t \,)$ is an (h_1+h_2)-dimensional orthonormal white noise, while the $b_{kl}^\gamma(L)$'s and the $c_{kl}^\gamma(L)$'s are assumed to be rational functions of L whose denominators have no roots inside or on the unit circle. This means that (9.1) may be thought of as the result of premultiplication by the autoregressive matrix. We suppose:

ASSUMPTION 9.1. $b_{kl}^\gamma(L)$ does not vanish at $L=1$ for any $\gamma \in \Gamma$, for $k=1,2$, and $l=1,h_1$. Thus y_t^γ and x_t^γ are both I(1), and are both driven by h_1 permanent shocks and by h_2 transitory shocks.

Let us firstly recall some elementary algebra. Given the rational function $b(L)$, we may write

$$b(L) = (1-L)\tilde{b}(L) + R, \tag{9.2}$$

where R is uniquely determined as the constant $b(1)$, while

$$\tilde{b}(L) = \frac{1}{1-L}[b(L) - b(1)] \tag{9.3}$$

Notice that $[b(L)-b(1)]$ contains the factor $(1-L)$, so formula (9.3) makes sense. By using (9.2) the micromodel can be rewritten as

$$\begin{aligned}(1-L)y_t^\gamma &= R_{11}^\gamma v_{1t} + R_{12}^\gamma v_{2t} + \cdots + R_{1h_1}^\gamma v_{h_1t} + (1-L)S_{xt}^\gamma \\ (1-L)x_t^\gamma &= R_{21}^\gamma v_{1t} + R_{22}^\gamma v_{2t} + \cdots + R_{2h_1}^\gamma v_{h_1t} + (1-L)S_{yt}^\gamma,\end{aligned}$$

where S^{γ}_{xt} and S^{γ}_{yt} are stationary variables. Notice that the assumption $b^{\gamma}_{kl}(1) \neq 0$ implies that none of the R^{γ}_{kl} can vanish for any $\gamma \in \Gamma$.

By definition, cointegration of the micromodel at γ means that there exists a scalar c^{γ} such that $y^{\gamma}_t - c^{\gamma} x^{\gamma}_t$ is stationary. Notice that c^{γ} cannot be zero, otherwise y^{γ}_t would be stationary, contrary to Assumption 9.1.

THEOREM 9.1. If $h_1 = 1$ the micromodel is cointegrated for any $\gamma \in \Gamma$. If $h_1 > 1$ then the micromodel is cointegrated either everywhere in Γ or for a negligible subset of Γ.

Proof. The first statement is trivial: simply put $c^{\gamma} = R^{\gamma}_{11}/R^{\gamma}_{21}$. For the second, observe that cointegration is equivalent to

$$\frac{R^{\gamma}_{11}}{R^{\gamma}_{21}} = \frac{R^{\gamma}_{12}}{R^{\gamma}_{22}} = \cdots = \frac{R^{\gamma}_{1h_1}}{R^{\gamma}_{2h_1}},$$

and the functions R^{γ}_{kl} are analytic in Γ. Q.E.D.

Let us now consider the aggregation of model (9.1) over the populations of Γ_m. Assume firstly that $h_1 = 1$, i.e. only one permanent shock. In this case the aggregated model is cointegrated with cointegration coefficient

$$\begin{aligned} c^p &= \frac{N^1 R^{p^1}_{11} + N^2 R^{p^2}_{11} + \cdots + N^m R^{p^m}_{11}}{N^1 R^{p^1}_{21} + N^2 R^{p^2}_{21} + \cdots + N^m R^{p^m}_{21}} \\ &= \frac{N^1 R^{p_1}_{21} c^{p^1} + N^2 R^{p^2}_{21} c^{p^2} + \cdots + N^m R^{p^m}_{21} c^{p^m}}{N^1 R^{p^1}_{21} + N^2 R^{p^2}_{21} + \cdots + N^m R^{p^m}_{21}}. \end{aligned} \tag{9.4}$$

REMARK 9.1. It must be pointed out that when $h_1 = 1$ the micromodel is cointegrated for any $\gamma \in \Gamma$. Moreover, the aggregated model is cointegrated for any $p \in \Gamma_m$ irrespective of whether the micro cointegration coefficients are equal across the p^i or not. As formula (9.4) shows, the macro cointegration coefficient is a weighted average of the micro cointegration coefficients.

Assume now that $h_1 > 1$ and define

$$\begin{aligned} C^{\gamma}_{1t} &= R^{\gamma}_{11} v_{1t} + R^{\gamma}_{12} v_{2t} + \cdots + R^{\gamma}_{1h_1} v_{h_1 t} \\ C^{\gamma}_{2t} &= R^{\gamma}_{21} v_{1t} + R^{\gamma}_{22} v_{2t} + \cdots + R^{\gamma}_{2h_1} v_{h_1 t}. \end{aligned} \tag{9.5}$$

Macro cointegration occurs for the following subsets of Γ_m:

(i) The subset containing the populations p such that the micromodel is cointegrated for p^i, $i = 1, m$, and c^{p^i} is constant across the agents of p.

(ii) The subset of the populations p for which there exists a scalar white noise V^p_t such that $C^{p^i}_{1t} = A^{p^i}_1 V^p_t$ and $C^{p^i}_{2t} = A^{p^i}_2 V^p_t$. Notice that V^p_t depends on p but not on i. This is a strong redundancy.

REMARK 9.2. Notice that both the sets under (i) and (ii) either are negligible or coincide with the whole Γ_m. Unfortunately conditions (i) and (ii) do not characterize the populations for which aggregate cointegration occurs. Consider the case $m = 2$, $h_1 = 2$, $N^i = 1$. Aggregate cointegration is equivalent to

$$\det \begin{pmatrix} R_{11}^{p^1} + R_{11}^{p^2} & R_{12}^{p^1} + R_{12}^{p^2} \\ R_{21}^{p^1} + R_{21}^{p^2} & R_{22}^{p^1} + R_{22}^{p^2} \end{pmatrix} = 0. \tag{9.6}$$

Assuming that

$$(R_{11}^{\gamma} \quad R_{12}^{\gamma} \quad R_{21}^{\gamma} \quad R_{22}^{\gamma})$$

varies in an open set of $\mathbb{R}^4$, aggregate cointegration defines a subset of dimension 7 in $\mathbb{R}^8$. On the other hand, as the reader can check, both the sets defined by (i) and (ii) have dimension lower than 7.

REMARK 9.3. Notice also that aggregate cointegration does not require cointegration of the micromodels. For instance, if the matrix in (9.6) is

$$\begin{pmatrix} 2+2 & 2+1 \\ 3+1 & 2+1 \end{pmatrix},$$

we have macro cointegration but not micro cointegration.

The following two theorems give quite a clear picture of aggregate cointegration.

THEOREM 9.2. Let B be the subset of Γ_m in which the aggregated model is cointegrated. Then either B is negligible or $B = \Gamma_m$. In any case, B contains the populations defined in (i) and in (ii). However, B, even when negligible, may contain points that do not correspond to definitions (i) or (ii).

Proof. If $h_1 = 1$ then $B = \Gamma_m$. If $h_1 > 1$, then aggregate cointegration is equivalent to

$$\frac{\sum N^i R_{11}^{p^i}}{\sum N^i R_{21}^{p^i}} = \frac{\sum N^i R_{12}^{p^i}}{\sum N^i R_{22}^{p^i}} = \cdots = \frac{\sum N^i R_{1h_1}^{p^i}}{\sum N^i R_{2h_1}^{p^i}}.$$

The conclusion follows from the Alternative Principle. For the last statement, see Remark 9.2. Q.E.D.

THEOREM 9.3. Suppose that v_t is non-redundant for C_{1t}^{γ} (or for C_{2t}^{γ} but not necessarily for both). Then the aggregate model is cointegrated for any $p \in \Gamma_m$ if and only if one of the following conditions holds: (a) $h_1 = 1$; (b) the micromodel is cointegrated for any $\gamma \in \Gamma$ and the cointegration coefficient depends only on λ (i.e. it does not vary within the populations).

Proof. Trivially if condition (a) or (b) holds then we have macro cointegration over the whole Γ_m. To prove necessity, observe firstly that if the micromodel is not cointegrated for a $\gamma = (\omega \quad \lambda)$, then the macromodel is not cointegrated for

$$(\omega \quad \omega \quad \cdots \quad \omega \quad \lambda).$$

Thus, for the Alternative Principle, the macromodel is cointegrated for a negligible subset of Γ_m. Hence cointegration of the micromodel is necessary. Now let us assume that $h_1 > 1$, that cointegration holds for the micromodel for any $\gamma \in \Gamma$, but that there exist $\gamma^1 = (\omega^1 \quad \lambda)$ and $\gamma^2 = (\omega^2 \quad \lambda)$ such that $c^{\gamma^1} \neq c^{\gamma^2}$. We must show that there exists a $p \in \Gamma_m$ for which macro cointegration does not hold. Suppose that v_t is non-redundant for C^{γ}_{2t} (the case of v_t non-redundant for C^{γ}_{1t} can be treated in the same way). This implies that for p a.e. in Γ_2, $c^{p^1} \neq c^{p^2}$. By the usual argument we can limit ourselves to considering Γ_2. Macro cointegration in Γ_2 is equivalent to

$$\frac{N^1 c^{p^1} R^{p^1}_{21} + N^2 c^{p^2} R^{p^2}_{21}}{N^1 R^{p^1}_{21} + N^2 R^{p^2}_{21}} = \frac{N^1 c^{p^1} R^{p^1}_{22} + N^2 c^{p^2} R^{p^2}_{22}}{N^1 R^{p^1}_{22} + N^2 R^{p^2}_{22}} = \cdots .$$

In particular, the matrix

$$\begin{pmatrix} N^1 c^{p^1} & N^2 c^{p^2} \\ N^1 & N^2 \end{pmatrix} \begin{pmatrix} R^{p^1}_{21} & R^{p^1}_{22} \\ R^{p^2}_{21} & R^{p^2}_{22} \end{pmatrix}$$

must be singular. The first matrix is non-singular a.e. in Γ_2. Non-redundancy of v_t for C^{γ}_{2t} ensures non-singularity of the second almost everywhere in Γ_2. Q.E.D.

Let us illustrate the above analysis by the model in Section 5.3. Firstly rewrite the common component of (5.21):

$$\begin{aligned} (1-L)c^{\gamma}_t &= K^{\gamma}(L)[(\mu_1 + \nu_1 L)u_{1t} + (\mu_2 + \nu_2 L)u_{2t}] \\ (1-L)y^{\gamma}_t &= (\mu_1 + \nu_1 L)u_{1t} + (\mu_2 + \nu_2 L)u_{2t}, \end{aligned}$$

where $K^{\gamma}(L) = q^{\gamma}(L)/p^{\gamma}(L)$. As regards parameterization, let

$$\begin{aligned} \omega &= (\kappa \quad \omega_1 \quad \omega_2 \quad \mu_1 \quad \mu_2 \quad \nu_1 \quad \nu_2) \\ \lambda &= \sigma. \end{aligned}$$

The two-dimensional vector u_t is non-redundant for y^{γ}_t. Moreover, different polynomials $K^{\gamma}(L)$ corresponding to different agents in the same population are easily found (see the procedure by which the polynomials $q^{\gamma}(L)$ and $p^{\gamma}(L)$ are obtained in Section 5.3). By Theorem 8.3, the macromodel is non-singular a.e. in Γ_m although the micromodel is singular everywhere in Γ. Moreover, since κ, i.e. the micro cointegration coefficient, can vary within populations, we must also conclude that aggregate consumption and income are cointegrated only for a negligible subset of Γ_m.

Suppose that, instead, we keep the propensity to consume κ fixed across the agents of the same population, so that

$$\omega = (\omega_1 \quad \omega_2 \quad \mu_1 \quad \mu_2 \quad \nu_1 \quad \nu_2)$$
$$\lambda = (\kappa \quad \sigma).$$

No difficulty arises in finding different polynomials $K^\gamma(L)$ corresponding to different agents in the same population. Therefore in this case the macromodel is non-singular and cointegrated a.e. in Γ_m.

9.1.2 As in Section 8.3.3 we will resort to a very simple example for a brief discussion of cointegration when the idiosyncratic component is reinserted in the micromodel:

$$\begin{aligned}(1-L)y_t^\gamma &= b_{11}^\gamma(L)u_{1t} + b_{12}^\gamma(L)u_{2t} + c_1^\gamma(L)\xi_{1t}^\gamma \\ (1-L)x_t^\gamma &= b_{21}^\gamma(L)u_{1t} + b_{22}^\gamma(L)u_{2t} + c_2^\gamma(L)\xi_{2t}^\gamma,\end{aligned} \tag{9.7}$$

where ξ_{1t}^γ and ξ_{2t}^γ are idiosyncratic shocks. Naturally cointegration of the aggregate vector depends only on the common components, and we only need to modify the statements above by substituting 'the common component of y_t^γ and x_t^γ' where we have referred to y_t^γ and x_t^γ. However, it is worthwhile noting that when there is only one common shock, or u_t is redundant for the common component, it may happen that the aggregate model is cointegrated whereas the micromodel is not. For example, suppose that in (9.7) $b_{k2}(1) = 0$ for any $\gamma \in \Gamma$. Then the micromodel is cointegrated if and only if

$$\det \begin{pmatrix} b_{11}^\gamma(1) & c_1^\gamma(1) \\ b_{21}^\gamma(1) & c_2^\gamma(1) \end{pmatrix} = 0.$$

If there exists a point in Γ such that this equality does not hold, then although the micromodel is not cointegrated a.e. in Γ, the aggregate model is cointegrated everywhere in Γ_m.

9.2. Log-Linear Models

Several models employed for econometric estimation and testing are linear in the logarithms of the aggregates. The corresponding micromodels, when explicitly mentioned, derive from optimization exercises in which agents use the logs of the microvariables: for instance, the micromodel in Section 5.3 could be derived in just the same way if the variables in the loss function were the logs instead of the natural values of consumption and income. Naturally, the distance between actual and desired consumption would be

$$\log c_t - \log \kappa - \log y_t,$$

while the remaining terms of the loss function would be $\log c_t - \log c_{t-1}$ (the rate of change of consumption) and $(\log c_t - \log c_{t-1})(\log y_t - \log y_{t-1})$. The difficulty arises when dealing with aggregation. Since we do not want to give a fully formal treatment of this case, let us consider a very simplified framework and notation. Suppose that we have only two income variables, whose logs are denoted by $\hat{y}_t^1$ and $\hat{y}_t^2$, and whose dynamics are given by

$$\hat{y}_t^i = \hat{y}_{t-1}^i + S_t^i, \tag{9.8}$$

where the variables S_t^i are zero-mean stationary. Furthermore, indicate by $\hat{c}_t^i$ the logs of the corresponding consumption variables and assume that

$$\hat{c}_t^i = \hat{k}^i + \hat{y}_t^i + T_t^i, \tag{9.9}$$

with T_t^i zero-mean stationary. Equations (9.9) establish that consumption and income, in logs, are cointegrated with cointegration vector $(1 \quad -1)$, for $l = 1, 2$. Finally, assume that the two log-income variables are cointegrated with cointegration vector $(1 \quad -1)$, i.e.

$$\hat{y}_t^2 = \hat{k} + \hat{y}_t^1 + U_t, \tag{9.10}$$

where U_t is zero-mean stationary. In terms of natural magnitudes, we are assuming that the rate of growth of both incomes is zero mean and stationary; the ratio of consumption to income is stationary for $i = 1, 2$; moreover, the ratio of income 1 to income 2 is also stationary. This assumpion is crucial, as we shall see below. The aggregate variables are

$$\begin{aligned} c_t &= \exp \hat{c}_t^1 + \exp \hat{c}_t^2 \\ y_t &= \exp \hat{y}_t^1 + \exp \hat{y}_t^2. \end{aligned}$$

Their relationship with the microvariables is non-linear. However, under our assumptions, the variables $\Delta \log c_t$ and $\Delta \log y_t$ can be approximated using a suitable Taylor expansion. Moreover, it can be shown that the approximations of c_t and y_t are cointegrated. For, consider firstly

$$\Delta \log y_t = \log \frac{y_t}{y_{t-1}} = \log \frac{\exp \hat{y}_t^1 + \exp \hat{y}_t^2}{\exp \hat{y}_{t-1}^1 + \exp \hat{y}_{t-1}^2}.$$

Dividing numerator and denominator by $\exp \hat{y}_{t-1}^1$ we obtain

$$\begin{aligned} &\log \frac{\exp(\hat{y}_t^1 - \hat{y}_{t-1}^1) + \exp(\hat{y}_t^2 - \hat{y}_{t-1}^1)}{1 + \exp(\hat{y}_{t-1}^2 - \hat{y}_{t-1}^1)} \\ &= \log \frac{\exp \Delta \hat{y}_t^1 + \exp \Delta \hat{y}_t^2 \exp(\hat{\kappa} + U_{t-1})}{1 + \exp(\hat{\kappa} + U_{t-1})}. \end{aligned} \tag{9.11}$$

Now, the first-order Taylor approximation of the function

$$\log \frac{\exp z_1 + \exp z_2 \exp z_3}{1 + \exp z_3},$$

centered at $(\,0 \quad 0 \quad a\,)$, is

$$\frac{1}{1+\exp a} z_1 + \frac{\exp a}{1 + \exp a} z_2$$

(the third derivative being zero). Thus, if $\Delta \log y_t$ is expanded around the means of $\Delta \hat{y}_t^1$, $\Delta \hat{y}_t^2$, and $y_t^2 - y_t^1$, i.e. around $(\,0 \quad 0 \quad \hat{\kappa}\,)$, we get

$$\Delta \log y_t \approx \check{y}_t = \frac{1}{1+\exp \hat{\kappa}} \Delta \hat{y}_t^1 + \frac{\exp \hat{\kappa}}{1+\exp \hat{\kappa}} \Delta \hat{y}_t^2. \tag{9.12}$$

In the same way

$$\Delta \log c_t \approx \check{c}_t = \frac{1}{1+\exp(\hat{\kappa}^1 - \hat{\kappa}^2 + \hat{\kappa})} \Delta \hat{c}_t^1 + \frac{\exp(\hat{\kappa}^1 - \hat{\kappa}^2 + \hat{\kappa})}{1+\exp(\hat{\kappa}^1 - \hat{\kappa}^2 + \hat{\kappa})} \Delta \hat{c}_t^2. \tag{9.13}$$

Both in (9.12) and in (9.13), the approximations are weighted averages of the micro log-variations. The weights are equal only when $\hat{\kappa}^1 = \hat{\kappa}^2$, i.e. when the propensities to consume are equal. Let us indicate by μ^1 and μ^2 the weights in (9.12), with ν^1 and ν^2 the weights in (9.13). Consider

$$\begin{aligned}
\check{y}_t - \check{c}_t &= \mu^1 \Delta \hat{y}_t^1 + \mu^2 \Delta \hat{y}_t^2 - \nu^1 \Delta \hat{c}_t^1 - \nu^2 \Delta \hat{c}_t^2 \\
&= (\mu^1 - \nu^1) \Delta \hat{y}_t^1 + (\mu^2 - \nu^2) \Delta \hat{y}_t^2 + \Delta V_t,
\end{aligned} \tag{9.14}$$

where V_t is a stationary variable. Finally, using (9.10) we have

$$\Delta(\log y_t - \log c_t) \approx \check{y}_t - \check{c}_t = (\mu^1 - \nu^1 + \mu^2 - \nu^2) \Delta \hat{y}_t^1 + \Delta W_t = \Delta W_t,$$

where W_t is stationary. Thus, approximately, the variable $\log y_t - \log c_t$ is stationary.

REMARK 9.4. It must be pointed out that cointegration of the approximated aggregates has been obtained under very strict conditions. Not only have we assumed that the micro cointegration vectors are equal across individuals and equal to $(\,1 \quad -1\,)$, we have also assumed that different incomes are pairwise cointegrated with cointegration vector $(\,1 \quad -1\,)$. Looking at (9.14) one may think that this assumption could be relaxed if the propensities to consume are equal, so that the weights μ^i are equal to the weights ν^i. But this would be a mistake. If $\hat{y}_t^2 - \hat{y}_t^1$ is not stationary, then neither is the variable $\Delta \log y_t$. For, consider again expression (9.11) and transform it into

$$\log \frac{\exp \Delta \hat{y}_t^1 + \exp(\hat{y}_{t-1}^2 - \hat{y}_{t-1}^1) \exp \Delta \hat{y}_t^2}{1 + \exp(\hat{y}_{t-1}^2 - \hat{y}_{t-1}^1)}.$$

9.3. An Observation on the Alternative Principle

The results of the last chapters can be rephrased in the following form. Firstly we write an equation like

$$f(p) = 0, \tag{9.15}$$

where $p \in \Gamma_m$ and f may be the determinant of the aggregate spectral density in Chapter 8, or the determinant of the spectral density at $L = 1$ in Chapter 9. Secondly, we want to know how big the subset of Γ_m is where (9.15) holds. The answer is that if there are at least two non-redundant shocks (two permanent non-redundant shocks in the case of cointegration), and the responses of the agents are not all equal, then (9.15) does not hold on the whole Γ_m. Now, if f were a simple expression among microparameters, implying elementary algebraic manipulations (sums, products, powers), then we could conclude that (9.15) holds for a negligible subset of Γ_m. Unfortunately, (9.15) results from algebraic manipulations both of the microparameters and the roots of polynomials whose coefficients are algebraic manipulations of the microparameters. If these polynomials were of order 2 (or 3, or 4), then, as already noted in Section 6.9, we might conclude straightforwardly in the same way on the basis of an elementary analysis. However, the polynomials may be of any order whatsoever, so that we do not possess formulas for the roots, but only the information that they are analytic functions of the coefficients.[1] Therefore we must invoke the Alternative Principle.

9.4. Bibliographic Notes

Cointegration under aggregation has been studied in Lippi (1988), Gonzalo (1989), Lippi (1989), Gonzalo (1993). Lippi (1988) claims that micro cointegrated variables aggregate to cointegrated macrovariables only if the micro cointegrating vectors are equal for all individuals. Gonzalo (1989) points out that a single permanent shock gives macro cointegration even though the micro cointegrating vectors are not equal. The conditions under which macro cointegration occurs are carefully stated in Gonzalo (1993) for an n-dimensional vector. In our Theorem 9.3 we show that, in the case $n = 2$, if the micro cointegration vector is not constant and there are at least two non-redundant permanent shocks, then Gonzalo's conditions hold only for a negligible subset of Γ_m. Generalization to higher dimensional vectors is straightforward. Section 9.2 is based on Lippi (1988). For an exact result on log-linear models, see Lewbel (1992).

[1] See the footnote in Section 6.9.

10

An Extension of the Alternative Principle

In Chapters 8 and 9 we have studied some of the properties of the aggregated model that can be analyzed on the basis of its MA representation in terms of the vector u_t. We now turn to problems involving the roots of the spectral density or the Wold representation of the aggregated vector. Such roots must be considered when we study Granger causality, while the Wold representation is necessary when we aim to study a vector autoregressive (VAR) model or an ARMAX linking the aggregate variables.

The problem to be addressed can be illustrated by the following example. Suppose that the micromodel is

$$\begin{pmatrix} y_t^\gamma \\ x_t^\gamma \end{pmatrix} = \begin{pmatrix} b_{11}^\gamma(L) & b_{12}^\gamma(L) & b_{13}^\gamma(L) \\ b_{21}^\gamma(L) & b_{22}^\gamma(L) & b_{23}^\gamma(L) \end{pmatrix} \begin{pmatrix} u_{1t} \\ u_{2t} \\ u_{3t} \end{pmatrix},$$

so that the aggregate model is

$$\begin{pmatrix} y_t^p \\ x_t^p \end{pmatrix} = \sum_{i=1}^{m} N^i B^{p^i}(L) u_t. \tag{10.1}$$

The Wold representation of the aggregate vector is an MA:

$$\begin{pmatrix} y_t^p \\ x_t^p \end{pmatrix} = \Phi^p(L) \begin{pmatrix} w_{1t}^p \\ w_{2t}^p \end{pmatrix}, \tag{10.2}$$

where $\Phi^p(0) = I$, $\det \Phi^p(L)$ has no roots of modulus less that unity, $\Phi^p(L)$ has no poles of modulus less than or equal to unity, and w_t^p is a two-dimensional white noise.

Naturally, whatever our specific aim may be, we are interested in knowing whether the coefficients of the matrix $\Phi^p(L)$ are well-behaved functions of $p \in \Gamma_m$. We shall see that, under the assumptions set up in Chapter 6 for the micromodel, and an additional assumption, such coefficients are analytic functions of p, so that the Alternative Principle can be applied. This problem will be studied in the present chapter. In Chapter 11 we study Granger causality, while in Chapter 12 we shall analyze VAR and ARMAX models.

10.1. From the Spectral Density to the Wold Representation

In Section 6.5.4 we have already discussed an elementary example of the problem we want to deal with. At the cost of some repetition, let us start with a generalized version of that problem. Consider the univariate model

$$x_t^\gamma = b_1^\gamma(L)u_{1t} + b_2^\gamma(L)u_{2t} + \cdots + b_h^\gamma(L)u_{ht}, \tag{10.3}$$

where the $b_l^\gamma(L)$'s are polynomials in L of degree s, whose coefficients are polynomial functions of $\gamma \in \Gamma$. The covariance generating function of x_t^γ is

$$S^\gamma(z) = b_1^\gamma(z)b_1^\gamma(z^{-1}) + b_2^\gamma(z)b_2^\gamma(z^{-1}) + \cdots + b_h^\gamma(z)b_h^\gamma(z^{-1}). \tag{10.4}$$

Consider

$$z^s S^\gamma(z), \tag{10.5}$$

which is a polynomial of degree $2s$. Since (10.5) is symmetric, if it vanishes at α, it vanishes at α^{-1} as well. Therefore, s of its roots are of modulus less than or equal to unity, while the remaining roots are the reciprocals. Let

$$(\alpha_1^\gamma \quad \alpha_2^\gamma \quad \cdots \quad \alpha_s^\gamma)$$

be the roots lying inside the closed unit circle. We have

$$S^\gamma(z) = b^\gamma(1-\alpha_1^\gamma z)(1-\alpha_2^\gamma z)\cdots(1-\alpha_s^\gamma z)(1-\alpha_1^\gamma z^{-1})(1-\alpha_2^\gamma z^{-1})\cdots(1-\alpha_s^\gamma z^{-1}).$$

The Wold representation of x_t^γ is

$$\begin{aligned} x_t^\gamma &= \sqrt{b^\gamma}(1-\alpha_1^\gamma L)(1-\alpha_2^\gamma L)\cdots(1-\alpha_s^\gamma L)\eta_t \\ &= (a_0^\gamma + a_1^\gamma L + \cdots + a_s^\gamma L)\eta_t, \end{aligned} \tag{10.6}$$

with $\sigma_\eta^2 = 1$. Now, by Lemma 6.3, the coefficients of (10.6) are analytic functions of γ, provided that the leading coefficient of (10.5) does not vanish, and there are no multiple roots. The first condition is violated if the s-th autocorrelation of x_t^γ vanishes. In turn, this occurs if all the leading coefficients of the polynomials $b_l^\gamma(L)$ vanish simultaneously, or the zero-lag coefficients vanish simultaneously, or cancellations across the summands in (10.4) occur. The second condition is violated if the discriminant of (10.5) vanishes.

When a model based on economic grounds is given, it appears perfectly sound to assume that both the first and the second condition are violated only for negligible subsets of Γ. Assuming for simplicity that the first condition is never violated, we can define Γ' and Γ'' as the subsets where the discriminant is, respectively, positive or negative. Limiting the analysis to Γ' or Γ'' we can apply the Alternative Principle.

This is the way we have dealt with the problem in the previous chapters. Considering the models in Sections 5.1, 5.2, 5.3, under the assumption that the agents see only their individual independent variables, not their components, the micromodel involves the coefficients of a Wold representation. Therefore, the assumption that the coefficients of the micromodel are analytic holds if we take as Γ one of the sets delimited by the discriminant of an algebraic equation. On the other hand, if one considers the results obtained in Chapters 8 and 9, the above limitation appears as evidently harmless. As a matter of fact, the Alternative Principle is applicable in both the half spaces delimited by the zeros of the discriminant and in the corresponding subregions of Γ_m. In the same way, the non-redundancy of u_t or the existence of particular points in Γ_2, both of which have been repeatedly invoked, has the same plausiblity both if Γ is the half space where the discriminant is non-positive and if Γ is the one where the discriminant is non-negative.

Having settled this, in the present chapter we must deal with a further problem of leading coefficients and multiple roots. In fact, since now we need the coefficients of the Wold representation of the *aggregate* vector, we must extract roots of further algebraic equations whose coefficients are simple algebraic manipulations of the coefficients of the micromodel. As a consequence, the coefficients of the Wold representation will be analytic functions of $p \in \Gamma_m$, provided that the leading coefficients and the discriminants of these algebraic equations do not vanish.

Let us go back to (10.1) and reproduce the procedure by which it is possible to get representation (10.2) (see Section 10.3 for references).

STEP 1. Consider the spectral density of the aggregate vector:

$$S^p(z) = \begin{pmatrix} S^p_y(z) & S^p_{yx}(z) \\ S^p_{xy}(z) & S^p_x(z) \end{pmatrix}.$$

STEP 2. Transform $S^p(z)$ into

$$\begin{pmatrix} 1 & 0 \\ \dfrac{S^p_{yx}(z^{-1})}{S^p_y(z)} & 1 \end{pmatrix} \begin{pmatrix} S^p_y(z) & 0 \\ 0 & \dfrac{D^p(z)}{S^p_y(z)} \end{pmatrix} \begin{pmatrix} 1 & \dfrac{S^p_{yx}(z)}{S^p_y(z^{-1})} \\ 0 & 1 \end{pmatrix},$$

where $D^p(z) = \det S^p(z)$ (we must recall that $S^p_y(z) = S^p_y(z^{-1})$).

STEP 3. Split $S^p_y(z)$ and $D^p(z)$ as

$$S^p_y(z) = V^p(z)V^p(z^{-1})$$
$$D^p(z) = W^p(z)W^p(z^{-1}),$$

where

$$V^p(z) = \sqrt{b^p}(1-\alpha_1^p z)(1-\alpha_2^p z)\cdots(1-\alpha_s^p z)$$
$$W^p(z) = \sqrt{B^p}(1-\beta_1^p z)(1-\beta_2^p z)\cdots(1-\beta_k^p z),$$

the α_l^p's and the β_l^p's being the roots of modulus less than or equal to unity of, respectively, $z^s S_y^p(z)$ and $z^k D^p(z)$.

STEP 4. Consider the representation

$$S^p(z) = \begin{pmatrix} V^p(z^{-1}) & 0 \\ \dfrac{S_{yx}^p(z^{-1})}{V^p(z)} & \dfrac{W^p(z)}{V^p(z)} \end{pmatrix} \begin{pmatrix} V^p(z) & \dfrac{S_{yx}^p(z)}{V^p(z^{-1})} \\ 0 & \dfrac{W^p(z^{-1})}{V^p(z^{-1})} \end{pmatrix}, \tag{10.7}$$

which derives from the splitting

$$\begin{pmatrix} S_y^p(z) & 0 \\ 0 & \dfrac{D^p(z)}{S_y^p(z)} \end{pmatrix} = \begin{pmatrix} V^p(z^{-1}) & 0 \\ 0 & \dfrac{W^p(z)}{V^p(z)} \end{pmatrix} \begin{pmatrix} V^p(z) & 0 \\ 0 & \dfrac{W^p(z^{-1})}{V^p(z^{-1})} \end{pmatrix}.$$

STEP 5. By inserting between the two matrices in (10.7) the matrix product

$$\begin{pmatrix} z^r & 0 \\ 0 & 1 \end{pmatrix} \begin{pmatrix} z^{-r} & 0 \\ 0 & 1 \end{pmatrix},$$

where r is the smallest integer such that $z^r V^p(z^{-1})$ and $z^r S_{xy}^p(z^{-1})$ contain no powers of z^{-1}, we finally get

$$S^p(z) = \Phi_1^p(z)\Phi_1^p(z^{-1})',$$

where

$$\Phi_1^p(z) = \begin{pmatrix} z^r V^p(z^{-1}) & 0 \\ \dfrac{z^r S_{xy}^p(z^{-1})}{V^p(z)} & \dfrac{W^p(z)}{V^p(z)} \end{pmatrix}.$$

If $\Phi^p(L)$ had no poles of modulus less than or equal to unity, and $\det \Phi^p(L)$ had no roots of modulus less than unity, then the Wold representation would have been reached. But this is not the case since

$$\det \Phi_1^p(z) = \frac{W(z) z^r V^p(z^{-1})}{V^p(z)}$$

has roots inside the unit circle, namely the roots of $z^r V^p(z^{-1})$. For this reason, the procedure that leads to the Wold representation cannot stop here. However, the remaining steps are nothing other than elementary algebraic manipulations of $\Phi_1^p(L)$, not implying further extractions of roots. We will not give such steps explicitly here. The information that we want to convey to the reader is that the coefficients of the Wold representation which is eventually obtained depend both on p and on the roots α_l^p and β_l^p. Such coefficients are therefore analytic in Γ_m with the exception of the points of Γ_m where either the discriminant or the leading coefficient of $z^s S_x^p(z)$ or $z^k D^p(z)$ vanishes.

Naturally the solution adopted in Chapter 6 could be reproduced here. We could take a region of Γ_m where neither the leading coefficients nor the discriminants of the aforementioned polynomials vanish. However, this second limitation of the space does not appear very elegant. We prefer to expend some effort in showing that the Alternative Principle can be applied in spite of the difficulties just illustrated. This will be done below. Let us suggest to the reader not interested in mathematical details that he, or she, simply read the statements of Theorems 10.1 and 10.2 and skip directly to the next chapter.

10.2. An Extension of the Alternative Principle

Let us begin by recalling that the definition of an analytic function (Definition 6.5) can be extended without difficulty if Ω is an open subset of $\mathbb{C}^v$, where $\mathbb{C}$ is the complex field. The following lemma generalizes Lemmas 6.2 and 6.3 (see Section 10.3 for references).

LEMMA 10.1. (a) Let $v = 1$ and assume that f and g are analytic in the open region $\Omega \subseteq \mathbb{C}$. If the set where $f = g$ has an accumulation point in Ω, then $f = g$ on the whole Ω. (b) Let Ω be an open connected subset of $\mathbb{C}^v$ and let a_l^x be analytic functions of $x \in \Omega$, for $l = 0, s$. Consider the polynomial

$$a_0^x + a_1^x z + \cdots + a_s^x z^s. \tag{10.8}$$

Suppose that a_s^x and the discriminant of (10.8) do not vanish in Ω. Then there exist s functions α_l^x, analytic in Ω, such that

$$a_0^x + a_1^x \alpha_1^x + \cdots + a_s^x (\alpha_s^x)^s = 0,$$

for $l = 1, s$, for any $x \in \Omega$.

We are now ready to prove an Alternative Principle for a function which is not analytic on the whole Ω.

THEOREM 10.1. Let Ω be an open region in $\mathbb{R}^v$. Consider the polynomial

$$g^x(z) = b_0^x + b_1^x z + \cdots + b_s^x z^s,$$

where the coefficients b_l^x are polynomial functions of $x \in \Omega$. Both the leading coefficient and the discriminant of $g^x(z)$ are polynomials in x and therefore vanish either everywhere in Ω or in a negligible subset of Ω. Assume that the second alternative holds and call Q the negligible subset of Ω where the first or the second polynomial vanishes. Now let f be a polynomial function of $v+s$ variables, and define B as the subset of $\Omega - Q$ in which

$$G(x_1, x_2, \ldots, x_v) = f(x_1, x_2, \ldots, x_v, \alpha_1(x), \alpha_2(x), \ldots, \alpha_s(x)) = 0,$$

where $\alpha_l(x)$, $l = 1, s$, are the s distinct roots of $g^x(z)$. Then either B is negligible in Ω or $B = \Omega - Q$.

Proof. By slightly modifying the reasoning employed in the proof of the Alternative Principle (Theorem 6.2) we can assume that Ω is the unit radius open ball $\{x : |x| < 1\}$. Assume that $\tilde{x} \in \Omega - Q$ and that

$$f(\tilde{x}_1, \tilde{x}_2, \ldots, \tilde{x}_v, \alpha_1(\tilde{x}), \alpha_2(\tilde{x}), \ldots, \alpha_s(\tilde{x})) \neq 0.$$

Let y be any point of the boundary of Ω, i.e. a point of $\hat{\Omega} = \{t : |t| = 1\}$, and let $I(\tilde{x}, y)$ be the straight segment joining $\tilde{x}$ and y, including $\tilde{x}$ and excluding y. Define $\mu(y)$ as the measure of the subset of $I(\tilde{x}, y)$ where f vanishes. By Fubini's theorem, after a change of coordinates, the Lebesgue measure of B is the integral of $\mu(y)$ with respect to the measure on $\hat{\Omega}$. Thus it is sufficient to prove that $\mu(y) = 0$ for any y. In turn, this is equivalent to proving the theorem for the case $v = 1$.

Assume, without loss of generality, that $\Omega = (0, 1)$, that $\tilde{x}$ does not belong to Q, and that G does not vanish at $\tilde{x}$. The set Ω can be viewed as a subset of the complex plane $\mathbb{C}$. The polynomials b_l^x, $l = 1, s$, can be naturally defined for any complex value of x. Since b_s^x and the discriminant of $g^x(z)$ vanish by assumption only for a finite subset of Ω (this is the specification of the assumption of the theorem for $v = 1$), they vanish only for a finite subset of $\mathbb{C}$, call it $\tilde{Q}$. For $x \in \mathbb{C} - \tilde{Q}$, the $\alpha_l(x)$'s, $l = 1, s$, are analytic functions of x (Lemma 10.1, b). Naturally, the polynomial f can be calculated for complex values of x and the function

$$G(x) = f(x, \alpha_1(x), \alpha_2(x), \ldots, \alpha_s(x))$$

is analytic in $\mathbb{C} - \tilde{Q}$. Since $G(\tilde{x}) \neq 0$, and since $\mathbb{C} - \tilde{Q}$ is connected (as already mentioned in the proof of Theorem 6.1, connectedness is equivalent to arcwise connectedness), the subset $\tilde{B}$ where G vanishes cannot possess accumulation points within any bounded subset of $\mathbb{C} - \tilde{Q}$ (Lemma 10.1, a). As a consequence, $\tilde{B} \cap [1/n, 1 - 1/n]$ must be a finite set, and therefore $B = \tilde{B} \cap \Omega$ must be countable. Q.E.D.

REMARK 10.1. The difference between this theorem and the Alternative Principle as stated in Theorem 6.2 is that the function G is not analytic in the whole Ω, but only in $\Omega - Q$, which is not necessarily connected. Nevertheless we were able to 'connect' the set passing by the complex field.

Let us go back to the discussion in Section 10.1 and consider a statement that implies a polynomial equation $F(\gamma)$ among the coefficients of (10.6). Theorem 10.1 implies that if there exists a $\tilde{\gamma}$ such that $F(\tilde{\gamma}) \neq 0$, then the subset of Γ where $F(\gamma) = 0$ is negligible, where Γ now includes the points where the discriminant of (10.5) is positive, negative, or zero. In the same way, the results in Chapters 8 and 9 could be restated without imposing, as we do in Assumption 6.4, that the micromodel coefficients be analytic in the whole Γ. It would be sufficient to assume that the leading coefficients or the discriminants emerging in the micromodel construction vanish in negligible subsets. For, the step from the micro- to the macromodel only implies elementary manipulations of the micromodel coefficients.

However, we do not want to modify the definitions of Chapter 6. The main reason why we have presented Theorem 10.1 here is that it represents a simpler version of the following theorem, which is the statement that we really need in order to apply the Alternative Principle to the coefficients of the Wold representation of the aggregate vector.

THEOREM 10.2. Let Ω be an open region in $\mathbb{R}^v$. Consider the polynomial

$$g^x(z) = b_0^x + b_1^x z + \cdots + b_s^x z^s,$$

where the coefficients b_l^x are analytic functions of $x \in \Omega$. Both the leading coefficient and the discriminant of $g^x(z)$ are analytic functions of x and therefore vanish either everywhere in Ω or in a negligible subset of Ω. Assume that the second alternative holds and call Q the negligible subset of Ω where the first or the second polynomial vanishes. Now let f be a polynomial function of $v + s$ variables, and define B as the subset of $\Omega - Q$ in which

$$G(x_1, x_2, \ldots, x_v) = f(x_1, x_2, \ldots, x_v, \alpha_1(x), \alpha_2(x), \ldots, \alpha_s(x)) = 0,$$

where $\alpha_l(x)$, $l = 1, s$, are the s distinct roots of $g^x(z)$. Then either B is negligible in Ω or $B = \Omega - Q$.

Proof. The difference with Theorem 10.1 is just that here the functions b_l^x are analytic functions, not necessarily polynomials. As in Theorem 10.1, we can prove the theorem for $\Omega = (0, 1)$. Assume that $\tilde{x}$ does not belong to Q and that $G(\tilde{x}) \neq 0$. The functions b_l^x possess an absolutely convergent Taylor expansion for any $x \in \Omega$. Therefore they can be extended to an open connected subset $\tilde{\Omega}$, where $\Omega \subset \tilde{\Omega} \subseteq \mathbb{C}$. Call $\tilde{Q}$ the subset of $\tilde{\Omega}$ where either the leading coefficient or the discriminant of $g^x(z)$ vanishes. $\tilde{Q}$ has no accumulation points in $\tilde{\Omega}$ (since it has no accumulation points in Ω), and $\tilde{\Omega} - \tilde{Q}$ is connected. The roots $\alpha_l(x)$ are analytic functions of the coefficients of $g^x(z)$ (Lemma 10.1, b) and therefore analytic functions of x in the open connected set $\tilde{\Omega} - \tilde{Q}$. The conclusion follows as in the proof of Theorem 10.1. Q.E.D.

There is a slight difference between the Alternative Principle of Theorem 10.2 and the Alternative Principle of Theorem 6.2. Application of Theorem 10.2 allows us to say that a given statement is valid either for a negligible subset or for a set whose complement is negligible, whereas when Theorem 6.2 is applicable we say that a statement is valid either for a negligible subset or for the whole region. A slight modification with respect to Theorem 6.2 is also necessary for the equivalent formulation:

THEOREM 10.2. (EQUIVALENT FORMULATION) Under the assumptions of Theorem 10.2, if there exists a point $x \in \Omega - Q$ such that $G(x) \neq 0$, then B is negligible.

Proof. The function G does not vanish in an open neighborhood of x. Then the set where G does not vanish cannot be negligible. Q.E.D.

The application of Theorem 10.2 to our aggregate model requires a further assumption. The following seems to be easily acceptable.

ASSUMPTION 10.1. Let $S^\gamma(z)$ be the $n \times n$ spectral density matrix of the vector $D(L)z_t^\gamma$. Consider the diagonal elements $S_{ll}^\gamma(z)$, $l = 1, n$, the determinant $\det S^\gamma(z)$, and the polynomials

$$g_l^\gamma(z) = z^{s_l} S_{ll}^\gamma(z), \quad q^\gamma(z) = z^d \det S^\gamma(z),$$

where s_l and d are the minimal integers necessary to eliminate negative powers of z. We assume that the leading coefficients or the discriminants of the polynomials $g_l^\gamma(z)$ and $q^\gamma(z)$ vanish in a negligible subset of Γ.

If Assumption 10.1 is fulfilled, then the leading coefficients and the discriminants of the polynomials that we must consider in order to obtain the Wold representation of the aggregate vector do not vanish for H_m, i.e. for the subset of Γ_m where the agents have equal microparameters. Therefore they vanish in a negligible subset of Γ_m and Theorem 10.2 can be applied.

10.3. Bibliographic Notes

For the procedure in Section 10.1, see Theorem A.9 in the Appendix, and the reference to Rozanov (1967) in Section A.9. For Lemma 10.1 see the references for Lemmas 6.1, 6.2, and 6.3 in Section 6.10. As with the Alternative Principle in Chapter 6, we could not find a reference for Theorems 10.1 and 10.2.

11

Granger Causality

11.1. General Results

Granger causality is a relationship between the components of $D(L)z_t^\gamma$ or $D(L)z_t^p$. Therefore, as in Chapter 8, there is no loss of generality in assuming $D(L) = I$. Let us further simplify the matter by considering a two-variable model. With no loss of generality we can write the model as

$$\begin{aligned} A^\gamma(L)y_t^\gamma &= b_{11}^\gamma(L)u_{1t} + b_{12}^\gamma(L)u_{2t} + \cdots + b_{1h}^\gamma(L)u_{ht} \\ A^\gamma(L)x_t^\gamma &= b_{21}^\gamma(L)u_{1t} + b_{22}^\gamma(L)u_{2t} + \cdots + b_{2h}^\gamma(L)u_{ht}, \end{aligned} \tag{11.1}$$

where $A(L)^\gamma$ and the $b_{kl}^\gamma(L)$'s are polynomials in L (this form can be obtained, if necessary, by multiplying the LHS by the adjoint of the autoregressive matrix). Granger causality, both in the micromodel and in the aggregate model, can be studied by analyzing the spectral density. By Sims's theorem (see Section A.8 in the Appendix), the variable y_t^γ, or y_t^p, Granger-causes the variable x_t^γ, or x_t^p, if the orthogonal projection of the first on the whole process of the second is not identical with the projection on present and past values only. The same is true for the opposite direction of causality. Let us concentrate on the aggregate variables. We have indicated the spectral density by $S^p(z)$. In our case, with obvious notation

$$S^p(z) = \begin{pmatrix} S_y^p(z) & S_{yx}^p(z) \\ S_{xy}^p(z) & S_x^p(z) \end{pmatrix}.$$

The function $g^p(L)$ in the projection

$$y_t^p = g^p(L)x_t^p + U_t^p$$

is determined as

$$g^p(L) = \frac{S_{yx}^p(L)}{S_x^p(L)},$$

where both denominator and numerator may contain powers both of L and $F = L^{-1}$ (see Section A.8 in the Appendix). Assuming that $S_x^p(L)$ has no roots of unit modulus, $g^p(L)$ admits a Laurent expansion in an annulus defined by $R_1 < |z| < R_2$, where $R_1 < 1 < R_2$. The expansion is

$$g^p(L) = \sum_{l=-\infty}^{+\infty} H_l^p L^l,$$

where the coefficients H_l^p are obtained by expanding backward for the roots of $S_x^p(L)$ whose modulus is greater than unity, and forward for the roots whose modulus is smaller than unity.

THEOREM 11.1. Assume that: (1) the micromodel (11.1) fulfills Assumption 10.1; (2) the subset of Γ_m for which $S_x^p(L)$ or $S_y^p(L)$ have roots of unit modulus is negligible. Let Q be the subset of Γ_m for which the leading coefficient or the discriminant of $S^p(z)$ vanishes. If there exists a point in $\Gamma_m - Q$ for which x_t^p Granger-causes y_t^p, then the subset for which x_t^p does not Granger-cause y_t^p is negligible. The same statement holds for Granger causality in the opposite direction.

Proof. By Assumption 10.1, Q is negligible. Excluding the negligible subset where $S_x^p(L)$ has unit modulus roots, the coefficients H_l^p are elementary functions of the coefficients of (11.1) and the roots of $S_x^p(L)$. On the other hand, Granger non-causality is equivalent to equating H_l^p to zero, for l negative. The proof follows from application of Theorem 10.2 to the functions H_l^p. Q.E.D.

REMARK 11.1. Notice that Theorem 11.1 holds for the micromodel as well. Moreover, Theorem 11.1 can be proved by directly applying Theorem 10.2 to the coefficients of the Wold representation of the aggregate vector, instead of the bilateral projections.

11.2. Discussion of the Two-Point Example

11.2.1. As in Chapters 8 and 9, we would like to provide a theorem establishing that under plausible assumptions there exists a point in $\Gamma_m - Q$ for which y_t^p Granger-cause x_t^p and/or vice versa. This is trivial if there exists a point of Γ for which Granger causality occurs. The interesting case is therefore that in which Granger causality is unidirectional at the micro level. Consider the model

$$\begin{aligned} y_t^\gamma &= \kappa^\gamma(L)x_t^\gamma \\ A^\gamma(L)x_t^\gamma &= b_{21}^\gamma(L)u_{1t} + b_{22}^\gamma(L)u_{2t} + \cdots + b_{2h}^\gamma(L)u_{ht}, \end{aligned}$$

i.e.

$$\begin{aligned} A^\gamma(L)y_t^\gamma &= \kappa^\gamma(L)[b_{21}^\gamma(L)u_{1t} + b_{22}^\gamma(L)u_{2t} + \cdots + b_{2h}^\gamma(L)u_{ht}] \\ A^\gamma(L)x_t^\gamma &= b_{21}^\gamma(L)u_{1t} + b_{22}^\gamma(L)u_{2t} + \cdots + b_{2h}^\gamma(L)u_{ht}. \end{aligned} \tag{11.2}$$

Notice that model (11.2) is singular for any $\gamma \in \Gamma$. Moreover, since y_{t-1}^γ lies in the space spanned by x_{t-k}^γ, $k > 0$, y_t^γ fails to Granger-cause x_t^γ.

Given a population $p = (\omega^1 \quad \omega^2 \quad \lambda) \in \Gamma_2$, assuming $h = 2$ and $N^i = 1$ for simplicity, the projection of $y\,_t^p$ over the whole process x_t^p is $g^p(L)x_t^p$, where $g^p(L)$ is the ratio of

$$(\kappa^{p^1}(L)b_{21}^{p^1}(L)+\kappa^{p^2}(L)b_{21}^{p^2}(L))(b_{21}^{p^1}(F)+b_{21}^{p^2}(F)) \\ +(\kappa^{p^1}(L)b_{22}^{p^1}(L)+\kappa^{p^2}(L)b_{22}^{p^2}(L))(b_{22}^{p^1}(F)+b_{22}^{p^2}(F))$$

to

$$(b_{21}^{p^1}(L)+b_{21}^{p^2}(L))(b_{21}^{p^1}(F)+b_{21}^{p^2}(F))+(b_{22}^{p^1}(L)+b_{22}^{p^2}(L))(b_{22}^{p^1}(F)+b_{22}^{p^2}(F)).$$

The denominator can be written as

$$Q^\gamma(1-\alpha_1^p L)(1-\alpha_2^p L)\cdots(1-\alpha_s^p L)(1-\alpha_1^p F)(1-\alpha_2^p F)\cdots(1-\alpha_s^p F),$$

with $|\alpha_l^p|<1$, $l=1,s$. Multiplying both numerator and denominator by L^s we obtain the ratio of two polynomials in L. The condition for absence of Granger causality from y_t^p to x_t^p is that all the factors $L-\alpha_l^p$ of the denominator belong to the numerator as well. Such cancellation occurs either if $\kappa^{p^1}(L)=\kappa^{p^2}(L)$, or if u_t is redundant for x_t^γ, so that x_t^γ can be rewritten as $c^\gamma(L)w_t^\lambda$ (notice that in both cases the aggregate vector becomes singular as well). However, if u_t is non-redundant and the functions κ are not equal, the cancellation appears as very unlikely. A detailed development of this point would be tedious and add very little to what the reader can expect on the basis of the previous chapters, i.e. that different responses and non-redundancy produce important aggregation effects: in our case aggregate Granger causality a.e. in Γ_m, in spite of lack of Granger causality at the micro level.

11.2.2. No changes occur in the above reasoning if we add idiosyncratic components in both the equations (11.2): Granger causality is unidirectional in the micromodel, while the aggregate model can be studied in terms of the common component only. Theorem 11.1 deals only with the aggregate variables and therefore its statements are not affected by the possible presence of the idiosyncratic components.

11.3. Bibliographic Notes

Granger causality for aggregate variables, in spite of microvariables for which the corresponding Granger causality does not occur, has been pointed out in Lippi (1988) and Granger (1990). Similar phenomena can emerge with time aggregation, seasonal adjustment, aggregation of unobserved components, omitted variables, errors in variables; see Sims (1971, 1974), Tiao and Wei (1976), Nerlove *et al.* (1979), Lütkepohl (1982), Forni (1990).

12

Wold Representation: VAR and ARMAX Models

12.1. VAR Models

Vector autoregressive models have been extensively employed in macroeconomics since Sims (1980).

VAR analysis, summarily described, consists of two distinct steps. Firstly a vector autoregressive model is estimated:

$$A(L)z_t = \epsilon_t, \tag{12.1}$$

where $A(0) = I$ and ϵ_t is a vector white noise. Since $B(L) = A(L)^{-1}$ is invertible by definition and therefore fundamental, the MA representation

$$z_t = B(L)\epsilon_t$$

may be thought of as an approximation of the Wold representation of x_t. Secondly, identifying criteria are introduced which allow the determination of structural shocks and impulse response functions. Such criteria are usually based on economic theory, econometric testing, and any other kind of available information. In the early eighties VAR models were mainly identified by recursive schemes: for instance, the first variable affects all the others at time t, whereas none of the others affects the first at time t, the second affects all the remaining ones at time t whereas the latter do not affect the second at time t, etc. In turn, the contemporaneous causal ordering was usually based on the strength of lagged causality.

More recently, the criteria proposed have been more closely linked to economic theory and the resulting VAR models labeled as structural VAR. According to the criteria employed, structural VAR models may be just identified, underidentified, or overidentified.

Let us begin by considering a micromodel containing two microvariables y_t^γ and x_t^γ. Furthermore, assume that the common shocks vector can be partitioned into two subvectors:

$$u_t = \begin{pmatrix} v_{1t} & v_{2t} & \cdots & v_{h_1t} & w_{1t} & w_{2t} & \cdots & w_{h_2t} \end{pmatrix}'.$$

As for the interpretation of the variables, suppose for example that y_t^γ represents employment at the firm level, x_t^γ represents the wage rate at the firm level, the components of $v_t = (v_{1t} \quad \cdots \quad v_{h_1 t})$ are technological shocks, and the components of $w_t = (w_{1t} \quad \cdots \quad w_{h_2 t})$ are shocks to the wage. Firms react to both causes of variation according to the model

$$\begin{pmatrix} \Delta y_t^\gamma \\ \Delta x_t^\gamma \end{pmatrix} = \begin{pmatrix} b_{11}^\gamma(L) & b_{12}^\gamma(L) \\ L b_{21}^\gamma(L) & b_{22}^\gamma(L) \end{pmatrix} \begin{pmatrix} v_t \\ w_t \end{pmatrix}, \tag{12.2}$$

where the $b_{kl}^\gamma(L)$'s are row vectors of rational functions of dimension h_1 for $l = 1$, and dimension h_2 for $l = 2$. We are not assuming any particular property for the micromodel, except that the shocks to technology affect the wage rate with a one-period lag.

Now consider the aggregate model (assuming $N^i = 1$ for simplicity)

$$\begin{pmatrix} \Delta y_t^p \\ \Delta x_t^p \end{pmatrix} = \begin{pmatrix} a_{11}^p(L) & a_{12}^p(L) \\ L a_{21}^p(L) & a_{22}^p(L) \end{pmatrix} \begin{pmatrix} v_t \\ w_t \end{pmatrix} = a^p(L) u_t, \tag{12.3}$$

where $a_{kl}^p(L) = \sum b_{kl}^{p^i}(L)$, and the standard Wold representation

$$\begin{pmatrix} \Delta y_t^p \\ \Delta x_t^p \end{pmatrix} = \begin{pmatrix} C_{11}^p(L) & C_{12}^p(L) \\ C_{21}^p(L) & C_{22}^p(L) \end{pmatrix} \begin{pmatrix} E_t \\ F_t \end{pmatrix}, \tag{12.4}$$

with $C^p(0) = I$. Alternatively, representation (12.4) may result from a general equilibrium model and therefore be defined directly as a function of p, as in Section 7.4.

The first question is whether there exists an identification rule which, when applied to (12.4), gives a result that can be considered as *consistent* with the micromodel. In our case the obvious candidate is the following rule:

IDENTIFICATION RULE. (a) The shocks of the aggregate model are orthonormal; (b) one of the shocks of the aggregate model has no contemporaneous impact on x_t.

This criterion just identifies the macromodel

$$\begin{pmatrix} \Delta y_t^p \\ \Delta x_t^p \end{pmatrix} = \begin{pmatrix} A_{11}^p(L) & A_{12}^p(L) \\ L A_{21}^p(L) & A_{22}^p(L) \end{pmatrix} \begin{pmatrix} V_t \\ W_t \end{pmatrix},$$

where the dependence of V_t and W_t on p has been dropped here and will be dropped henceforth for simplicity.

Now compare the two representations:

$$\begin{pmatrix} A_{11}^p(L) & A_{12}^p(L) \\ L A_{21}^p(L) & A_{22}^p(L) \end{pmatrix} \begin{pmatrix} V_t \\ W_t \end{pmatrix} = \begin{pmatrix} a_{11}^p(L) & a_{12}^p(L) \\ L a_{21}^p(L) & a_{22}^p(L) \end{pmatrix} \begin{pmatrix} v_t \\ w_t \end{pmatrix}. \tag{12.5}$$

Two problems must be addressed:

PROBLEM 1. Can we recover the polynomial $A^p_{kl}(L)$ by using the coefficients of $a^p_{kl}(L)$ alone?

PROBLEM 2. Can we recover the aggregate shock V_t (W_t) by using only the components of v_t (w_t)?

Let us now define two special subsets of Γ_m:

DEFINITION 12.1. The set $D \subseteq \Gamma_m$ is the subset of all points such that there exists a 2×2 matrix of rational functions $d^p(L)$ with the properties: (a) $d^p(L)$ has no poles of modulus smaller than or equal to unity; (b) $d^p(L)$ is fundamental, i.e. $\det(d^p(L))$ has no roots of modulus smaller than unity; (c) the last h_2 entries in the first row and the first h_1 entries in the second row of $d^p(L)a^p(L)$ vanish. Moreover, define $\tilde{D}$ as the subset of Γ_m for which there exists a 2×2 non-zero matrix of rational functions fulfilling only (a) and (c).

Property (c) implies that

$$\begin{aligned} a^p_{11,1}(L)a^p_{21,s}(L) - a^p_{11,s}(L)a^p_{21,1}(L) &= 0 \\ a^p_{12,1}(L)a^p_{22,s}(L) - a^p_{12,s}(L)a^p_{22,1}(L) &= 0, \end{aligned} \tag{12.6}$$

for all s, i.e. that

$$\frac{a^p_{11,1}(L)}{a^p_{21,1}(L)} = \frac{a^p_{11,s}(L)}{a^p_{21,s}(L)} \qquad \frac{a^p_{12,1}(L)}{a^p_{22,1}(L)} = \frac{a^p_{12,s}(L)}{a^p_{22,s}(L)}$$

for all s, where $a_{kl,s}$ stands for the s-th component of the vector a_{kl}. In other words, (c) requires that the responses of y^p_t to the shocks v_{st} differ from the responses of x^p_t by the same multiplicative scalar function of L, and the same must hold for the responses to the shocks in w_{st}.

REMARK 12.1. Notice that either $\tilde{D} = \Gamma_m$ or $\tilde{D}$ is negligible. Since Definition 12.1 deals only with sums of polynomials $b^\gamma_{kl,s}(L)$, then this statement is based on Theorem 6.2. Moreover, in general D does not coincide with $\tilde{D}$, since the points of D must fulfill (b), which is equivalent to the fundamentalness of

$$a^p_{11,s}(L)a^p_{22,s}(L) - La^p_{12,s}(L)a^p_{21,s}(L),$$

for all s.

We have:

THEOREM 12.1. Assume that $p \in D$ and that $a^p_{11}(0) \neq 0$. Then:

(I) $A^p_{kl}(z)A^p_{kl}(z^{-1}) = a^p_{kl}(z)a^p_{kl}(z^{-1})'$, for $k, l = 1, 2$ (recall that the LHS is the covariance generating function of $A^p_{kl}(L)V_t$ if $l = 1$, and of $A^p_{kl}(L)W_t$ if $l = 2$). Therefore $A^p_{kl}(L)$ can be recovered by means of $a^p_{kl}(L)$ alone.

(II) V_t is a linear combination of the components of v_t only, and the same holds for W_t and w_t.

Proof. Start with (12.5). Multiply both sides by $d^p(L)$:

$$d^p(L)A^p(L)\begin{pmatrix} V_t \\ W_t \end{pmatrix} = d^p(L)a^p(L)\begin{pmatrix} v_t \\ w_t \end{pmatrix} = \begin{pmatrix} q^p_1(L) & 0 \\ 0 & q^p_2(L) \end{pmatrix}\begin{pmatrix} v_t \\ w_t \end{pmatrix}.$$

Now let the LHS's of

$$Q^p_1(L)\hat{V}_t = q^p_1(L)v_t \qquad Q^p_2(L)\hat{W}_t = q^p_2(L)w_t$$

be fundamental scalar representations, with the shocks of unit variance. Since $\hat{V}_t$ and $\hat{W}_t$ are orthogonal at all leads and lags, $(\hat{V}_t \quad \hat{W}_t)$ is a vector white noise. Both sides of

$$d^p(L)A^p(L)\begin{pmatrix} V_t \\ W_t \end{pmatrix} = \begin{pmatrix} Q^p_1(L) & 0 \\ 0 & Q^p_2(L) \end{pmatrix}\begin{pmatrix} \hat{V}_t \\ \hat{W}_t \end{pmatrix}$$

are fundamental vector representations. Therefore, by Theorem A.5 in the Appendix

$$\begin{pmatrix} \hat{V}_t \\ \hat{W}_t \end{pmatrix} = M^p\begin{pmatrix} V_t \\ W_t \end{pmatrix}, \quad d^p(L)A^p(L) = \begin{pmatrix} Q^p_1(L) & 0 \\ 0 & Q^p_2(L) \end{pmatrix} M^p,$$

with M^p orthonormal. Since

$$d^p_{21}(L)a^p_{11}(L) + d^p_{22}(L)a^p_{21}(L)L = 0,$$

and since $a^p_{11}(L)$ does not contain the factor L by assumption, then $d^p_{21}(L)$ must contain the factor L, so that the matrix $d^p(L)A^p(L)$ contains the factor L in the lower left entry. The latter is equal to $Q^p_2(L)M^p_{21}$. Since $Q^p_2(L)$ is fundamental, then $M^p_{21} = 0$. Orthonormality implies $M^p_{12} = 0$, so that M^p is diagonal, and (II) is proved. Now consider (12.5) again:

$$\begin{aligned} A^p_{11}(L)V_t + A^p_{12}(L)W_t &= a^p_{11}(L)v_t + a^p_{12}(L)w_t \\ A^p_{21}(L)LV_t + A^p_{22}(L)W_t &= a^p_{21}(L)Lv_t + a^p_{12}(L)w_t. \end{aligned}$$

V_t, being a combination of the components of v_t only, is orthogonal to w_t, while, for the same reason, W_t is orthogonal to v_t. Thus $A^p_{11}(L)V_t = a^p_{11}(L)v_t$, etc., and (I) is proved. Q.E.D.

Statement (II) of Theorem 12.1 admits a converse.

THEOREM 12.2. Let

$$\begin{pmatrix} B_{11}^p(L) & B_{12}^p(L) \\ B_{21}^p(L) & B_{22}^p(L) \end{pmatrix} \begin{pmatrix} V_t \\ W_t \end{pmatrix} = \begin{pmatrix} a_{11}^p(L) & a_{12}^p(L) \\ a_{21}^p(L)L & a_{22}^p(L) \end{pmatrix} \begin{pmatrix} v_t \\ w_t \end{pmatrix}. \tag{12.7}$$

If V_t is a combination of v_t only, and W_t is a combination of w_t only, then p belongs to $\tilde{D}$ (Definition 12.1). If, in addition, $a_{11}^p(0) \neq 0$, then $B_{21}^p(0) = 0$.

Proof. Multiply both sides of (12.7) by $B_{\text{ad}}^p(L)$:

$$\det B^p(L) \begin{pmatrix} V_t \\ W_t \end{pmatrix} = B_{\text{ad}}^p(L) a^p(L) \begin{pmatrix} v_t \\ w_t \end{pmatrix}.$$

Since V_t is orthogonal to w_t and W_t is orthogonal to v_t, then the matrix on the RHS must be block diagonal (see Definition 12.1), so that $B_{\text{ad}}^p(L)$ fulfills (a) and (c). The lower left block of the matrix on the RHS is

$$-B_{21}^p(L)a_{11}^p(L) + B_{11}^p(L)a_{21}^p(L)L.$$

If $a_{11}^p(0) \neq 0$, then $B_{21}^p(0) = 0$. Q.E.D.

REMARK 12.2. Notice that the matrix $B^p(L)$ of Theorem 12.2 is not necessarily fundamental. More will be given on this in Section 12.2.

REMARK 12.3. A consequence of Theorem 12.2 is that the identification rule assumed for the macromodel is the only one that guarantees that Problem 2 has a positive answer for the points of $\tilde{D}$.

Theorems 12.1 and 12.2 can be straightforwardly generalized to different micromodels and higher dimensional vectors. A micromodel that we have already reported in Section 5.5 is the structural VAR introduced in Blanchard and Quah (1989). With a slight change in notation with respect to Section 5.5, the model is

$$\begin{pmatrix} \Delta y_t^\gamma \\ x_t^\gamma \end{pmatrix} = \begin{pmatrix} b_{11}^\gamma(L) & b_{12}^\gamma(L)(1-L) \\ b_{21}^\gamma(L) & b_{22}^\gamma(L) \end{pmatrix} \begin{pmatrix} v_t \\ w_t \end{pmatrix}, \tag{12.8}$$

where y_t^γ is I(1) while x_t^γ is stationary. In this case the micro shocks in w_t have only a transitory effect on y_t. In the same way as in model (12.2) we choose for the aggregate VAR the identification criterion that is 'consistent' with (12.8), i.e. we impose that one of the macro shocks has only a transitory effect on y_t^p. Using this rule, Theorems 12.1 and 12.2 hold, provided that $1 - L$ is substituted for L.

Going back to a recursive scheme, consider the micromodel

$$\begin{pmatrix} x_{1t}^\gamma \\ x_{2t}^\gamma \\ \vdots \\ x_{nt}^\gamma \end{pmatrix} = b^\gamma(L) \begin{pmatrix} v_{1t} \\ v_{2t} \\ \vdots \\ v_{nt} \end{pmatrix},$$

where $b^{\gamma}_{kl}(L)$ contains the factor L if $l > k$. Using the same recursion for the aggregate vector, Theorems 12.1 and 12.2 hold. However, it must be pointed out that the condition that $d^p(L)a^p(L)$ is block diagonal implies that $a^p_{11}(L)$ is proportional to *all* the vectors $a^p_{k1}(L)$, for $k > 1$, etc.

There are two important observations on Theorems 12.1 and 12.2. Firstly, as the following example shows, statement (I) of Theorem 12.1, i.e. that $A^p_{kl}(L)$ can be recovered by the coefficients of $a^p_{kl}(L)$ alone, does not imply that $p \in \tilde{D}$.

EXAMPLE 12.1. Consider

$$\begin{aligned} v_t &= (\,v_{1t} \quad v_{2t}\,)' \\ w_t &= (\,w_{1t} \quad w_{2t}\,)' \\ a_{11} &= (\,\sqrt{2} \quad \sqrt{2}L\,) \\ a_{12} &= (\,1-L \quad 0\,) \\ a_{21} &= \begin{pmatrix} \frac{\sqrt{2}}{2} & \frac{\sqrt{2}}{2} \end{pmatrix} \\ a_{22} &= (\,0 \quad 1\,). \end{aligned}$$

We have

$$\begin{aligned} 2V_t + (1-L)W_t &= \sqrt{2}v_{1t} + \sqrt{2}v_{2t-1} + (1-L)w_{1t} \\ V_t - W_t &= \frac{\sqrt{2}}{2}v_{1t} + \frac{\sqrt{2}}{2}v_{2t} + w_{2t}. \end{aligned}$$

The reader may easily check that the LHS is a valid fundamental MA representation of the vector on the RHS, and that

$$A_{kl}(z)A_{kl}(z^{-1}) = a_{kl}(z)a_{kl}(z^{-1})'.$$

However, neither $a_{11}(L)$ and $a_{21}(L)$ nor $a_{12}(L)$ and $a_{22}(L)$ are proportional.

Secondly, the following example shows that proportionality is not sufficient for consistent aggregation. Fundamentalness is requested as well.

EXAMPLE 12.2. Specify the RHS of (12.3) as

$$\begin{pmatrix} 1 & 1 \\ \alpha L & 1 \end{pmatrix} \begin{pmatrix} v_t \\ w_t \end{pmatrix},$$

where v_t and w_t are unidimensional so that proportionality occurs trivially. However, if $\alpha > 1$ we cannot put $V_t = v_t$ and $W_t = w_t$. The fundamental representation is

$$\begin{pmatrix} \dfrac{\sqrt{\alpha^2+1}}{2} & \sqrt{\dfrac{2}{\alpha^2+1}} \\ \dfrac{\sqrt{\alpha^2+1}}{2}L & \alpha\sqrt{\dfrac{2}{\alpha^2+1}} \end{pmatrix} \begin{pmatrix} V_t \\ W_t \end{pmatrix},$$

with $\det A(L) = \alpha - L$. Clearly all the coefficients of $A(L)$ depend on α. Moreover, V_t depends on both v_t and w_t.

Combining Theorems 12.1 and 12.2 with the observation on the Lebesgue measure of the set D (Remark 12.1), we have:

THEOREM 12.3. Consider the micromodel (12.2). If there exists a point in Γ_m for which equations (12.6) do not hold, then the subset of Γ_m where Problem 2 has a positive answer is negligible.

Notice that Theorem 12.3 is still based on the Alternative Principle in the version given in Chapter 6. In fact, equations (12.6), whose fulfillment is a necessary condition for a positive answer to Problem 2, imply elementary restrictions of the kind analyzed in Chapters 8 and 9. The following theorem, instead, requires an application of Theorem 10.2.

THEOREM 12.4. Suppose that Assumption 10.1 is fulfilled for model (12.2). Let $\hat{D}$ be the subset of Γ_m for which

$$A^p_{kl}(z)A^p_{kl}(z^{-1}) = a^p_{kl}(z)a^p_{kl}(z^{-1})' \tag{12.9}$$

for $k, l = 1, 2$. Then either $\hat{D}$ is negligible or $\Gamma_m - \hat{D}$ is negligible.

Proof. Equation (12.9) can be rewritten as a list of equations among the coefficients of the functions of z written on both sides. On the RHS we have the functions of p appearing in the micromodel, whereas on the LHS we have the coefficients of the Wold representation of the aggregate vector. Assumption 10.1 triggers the application of Theorem 10.2. Q.E.D.

Notice that $\hat{D}$ contains D, i.e. the subset of Theorem 12.1, but can be bigger, as Example 12.1 has shown.

Explicit construction of points for which equations (12.6) or (12.9) do not hold is possible with the following specification of model (12.2):

$$\begin{pmatrix} \Delta y^\gamma_t \\ \Delta x^\gamma_t \end{pmatrix} = \begin{pmatrix} b^\gamma_{11}(L) & \kappa^\gamma(L)b^\gamma_{22}(L) \\ 0 & b^\gamma_{22}(L) \end{pmatrix} \begin{pmatrix} v_t \\ w_t \end{pmatrix}, \tag{12.10}$$

with $\kappa^\gamma(L)$ scalar. Equivalently

$$\begin{aligned} \Delta y^\gamma_t &= \kappa^\gamma(L)\Delta x^\gamma_t + b^\gamma_{11}(L)v_t \\ \Delta x^\gamma_t &= b^\gamma_{22}(L)w_t. \end{aligned} \tag{12.11}$$

In this specification the wage rate does not depend on technology shocks, while employment depends on the shocks w_t through the wage rate, without distinction among the different components in w_t. This is precisely the shape of the model in Section 5.2.

THEOREM 12.5. Assume that h_2 (i.e. the dimension of w_t) is greater than unity, that w_t is non-redundant for Δx^γ_t, and that there exist $\gamma' = (\omega' \quad \lambda)$

and $\gamma'' = (\omega'' \quad \lambda)$ in Γ such that $\kappa^{\gamma'}(L) \neq \kappa^{\gamma''}(L)$. Moreover, assume that the population $(\gamma' \quad \gamma'' \quad \lambda)$ does not belong to the subset Q of Γ_2 where the relevant leading coefficients or discriminant vanish (see Section 10.2). Then the subset $\tilde{D}$ of Γ_m (Definition 12.1) is negligible.

Proof. Since $a_{21}^p(L) = 0$, we only need to prove that the vector

$$\begin{pmatrix} a_{12}^p(L) \\ a_{22}^p(L) \end{pmatrix} w_t$$

is singular only for a negligible subset of Γ_m. This has been done in Theorem 8.4. Q.E.D.

12.2. Fundamentalness

The reason why condition (b) in Definition 12.1, i.e. that $d^p(L)$ is fundamental, is necessary for consistent aggregation in VAR analysis deserves further discussion. Suppose that $p \in \tilde{D}$, i.e. that (a) and (c) in Definition 12.1, but not necessarily (b), hold. The matrix $a(L)$ can be rewritten as

$$\begin{pmatrix} a_{11}^p(L) & a_{12}^p(L) \\ L\tilde{d}^p(L)a_{11}^p(L) & \hat{d}^p(L)a_{12}^p(L) \end{pmatrix}$$

with $\tilde{d}^p(L)$ and $\hat{d}^p(L)$ scalars. Putting

$$K_1^p(L)V_t = a_{11}^p(L)v_t, \quad K_2^p(L)W_t = a_{12}^p(L)w_t,$$

with $K_1^p(L)$ and $K_2^p(L)$ fundamental, we have

$$\begin{pmatrix} \Delta y_t^p \\ \Delta x_t^p \end{pmatrix} = \begin{pmatrix} K_1^p(L) & K_2^p(L) \\ L\tilde{d}^p(L)K_1^p(L) & \hat{d}^p(L)K_2^p(L) \end{pmatrix} \begin{pmatrix} V_t \\ W_t \end{pmatrix}, \tag{12.12}$$

and this is a representation for which statements (I) and (II) in Theorem 12.1 hold. However, this MA representation is not the Wold representation unless it is fundamental, i.e. unless $\hat{d}^p(L) - L\tilde{d}^p(L)$ is fundamental. If this is not the case we have a conflict. On the one hand, consistent aggregation leads to (12.12), which is not fundamental. As a consequence (12.12) is not the MA representation resulting (approximately) from inverting the estimated VAR. On the other hand, transforming (12.12) to achieve fundamentalness would destroy both statements (I) and (II) of Theorem 12.1, as Example 12.2 has shown.

Fundamentalness has no special motivation in the micro theory or in empirical observations. We have argued in Chapter 1, Section 1.1.2, that structural shocks driving the univariate processes entering the micromodels as independent variables need not be fundamental. Moreover, several authors have argued that structural shocks driving multivariate models based on rational expectations are not necessarily fundamental (see Section 12.5 below). The assumption of fundamentalness, which is implicit in standard VAR and ARMAX analysis (see Section 12.3 below), is therefore no more than a practical rule to achieve identification. Given the data, VAR estimation is equivalent to an estimation of the covariance structure of the underlying vector process. Among all the infinite MA representations corresponding to that covariance structure, the fundamental one is chosen. But there is still an infinity of fundamental MA representations, obtained by inserting an invertible constant matrix between $B(L)$ and ϵ_t. The choice of such a matrix is usually based either on economic theory (as in structural VAR analysis) or on statistical considerations (as in Sims's recursive schemes). However, if the structural shocks were non-fundamental, the last identification step, although correct, could do nothing to mend the damage caused by incorrectly choosing the fundamental representation.

12.3. ARMAX Models

12.3.1. Let us specify model (12.10) by supposing that:

ASSUMPTION 12.2. (1) v_t is one-dimensional, w_t is two-dimensional. (2) Let $\Gamma = \mathbb{R}^8$, and

$$\begin{aligned} b^{\gamma}_{11}(L) &= \omega_1 + \omega_2 L \\ b^{\gamma}_{22,1}(L) &= \omega_3 + \omega_4 L \\ b^{\gamma}_{22,2}(L) &= \omega_5 + \omega_6 L \\ \kappa^{\gamma}(L) &= \omega_7 + \omega_8 L. \end{aligned}$$

In other words, we are assuming that all the functions in (12.10) are polynomials of degree 1. Their coefficients are free to vary with respect to one another. There are no common parameters. The model has the DI structure, with Δx^{γ}_t parameterized with ω_3, ω_4, ω_5, and ω_6. To be completely consistent with our definition of a micromodel we should rule out from $\mathbb{R}^8$ the subset where the spectral density of Δy^{γ}_t or Δx^{γ}_t vanishes. However, its inclusion is completely harmless.

Now consider the subset $\check{\Gamma} \subset \Gamma$ defined by $\omega_1 = \omega_2 = 0$. We want to analyze aggregation for $\check{\Gamma}_2$. Let $p = (\,\gamma^1 \quad \gamma^2\,)$. We can write the aggregated vector as

$$\begin{pmatrix} \Delta y^p_t \\ \Delta x^p_t \end{pmatrix} = \begin{pmatrix} \kappa^{\gamma^1}(L) & \kappa^{\gamma^2}(L) \\ 1 & 1 \end{pmatrix} \begin{pmatrix} \omega^1_3 + \omega^1_4 L & \omega^1_5 + \omega^1_6 L \\ \omega^2_3 + \omega^2_4 L & \omega^2_5 + \omega^2_6 L \end{pmatrix} \begin{pmatrix} w_{1t} \\ w_{2t} \end{pmatrix}. \tag{12.13}$$

Let $\hat{\Gamma}_2$ be the subset of $\check{\Gamma}_2$ where both the matrices in (12.13) are fundamental. If $p \in \hat{\Gamma}_2$ we can determine the representation of the aggregate vector fulfilling our identification criterion by simply inserting the factor $Q^p(Q^p)'$ in front of w_t, with Q^p orthonormal and such that the resulting matrix in L vanishes at zero in the lower left entry. Precisely

$$\begin{pmatrix} \Delta y_t^p \\ \Delta x_t^p \end{pmatrix} = \begin{pmatrix} A_{11}^p(L) & A_{12}^p(L) \\ A_{21}^p(L)L & A_{22}^p(L) \end{pmatrix} \begin{pmatrix} V_t \\ W_t \end{pmatrix}, \tag{12.14}$$

where

$$\begin{aligned} A_{21}^p(L)L &= [(\omega_3^1 + \omega_4^1 L) + (\omega_3^2 + \omega_4^2 L)]\mu - [(\omega_5^1 + \omega_6^1 L) + (\omega_5^2 + \omega_6^2 L)]\nu \\ A_{22}^p(L) &= [(\omega_3^1 + \omega_4^1 L) + (\omega_3^2 + \omega_4^2 L)]\mu + [(\omega_5^1 + \omega_6^1 L) + (\omega_5^2 + \omega_6^2 L)]\nu \\ A_{11}^p(L) &= [(\omega_7^1 + \omega_8^1 L)(\omega_3^1 + \omega_4^1 L) + (\omega_7^2 + \omega_8^2 L)(\omega_3^2 + \omega_4^2 L)]\mu \\ &\quad - [(\omega_7^1 + \omega_8^1 L)(\omega_5^1 + \omega_6^1 L) + (\omega_7^2 + \omega_8^2 L)(\omega_5^2 + \omega_6^2 L)]\nu \\ A_{12}^p(L) &= [(\omega_7^1 + \omega_8^1 L)(\omega_3^1 + \omega_4^1 L) + (\omega_7^2 + \omega_8^2 L)(\omega_3^2 + \omega_4^2 L)]\mu \\ &\quad + [(\omega_7^1 + \omega_8^1 L)(\omega_5^1 + \omega_6^1 L) + (\omega_7^2 + \omega_8^2 L)(\omega_5^2 + \omega_6^2 L)]\nu \\ \mu &= (\omega_5^1 + \omega_5^2)/\rho, \quad \nu = (\omega_3^1 + \omega_3^2)/\rho, \end{aligned} \tag{12.15}$$

and ρ is such that $\mu^2 + \nu^2 = 1$.

The MA representation (12.14) can be rewritten in the ARMA form:

$$\begin{aligned} A_{22}^p(L)\Delta y_t^p &= A_{12}^p(L)\Delta x_t^p + K^p(L)V_t \\ A_{11}^p(L)\Delta x_t^p &= A_{21}^p(L)\Delta y_{t-1}^p + K^p(L)W_t, \end{aligned} \tag{12.16}$$

where $K^p(L) = \det A^p(L)$. The first equation in (12.16) is the aggregated ARMAX and can be compared to the micro ARMAX in the first line of (12.11). Using the equations for the coefficients of the entries of $A^p(L)$, it is very easy to find a point in $\hat{\Gamma}_2$ such that:

(A) The dynamics of the aggregated ARMAX contain both the lagged Δy_t^p and Δx_t^p, whereas the micro ARMAX contains only lagged Δx_t^γ. Moreover, the point of $\hat{\Gamma}_2$ can be chosen in such a way that firstly $A_{22}^p(L)$ is not a factor of $A_{12}^p(L)$ nor of $K^p(L)$, and secondly $A_{12}^p(L)$ is not a factor of $K^p(L)$.

(B) The coefficients of the polynomials in the aggregate ARMAX depend on ω_l^k, for $k = 1, 2$, $l = 3, 6$. Precisely, the derivatives of such coefficients with respect to the microparameters ω_l^k, for $k = 1, 2$, $l = 3, 6$, do not vanish, contrary to what happens in the micromodel.

(C) A point for which effects (A) and (B) occur can be found even though the micromodel is static, i.e. if we limit our analysis to the subset $\tilde{\Gamma} \in \Gamma$ where $\gamma_8 = 0$.

(D) Consider the set $\check{\Gamma} \subset \Gamma$ where $\omega_1 = \omega_2 = \omega_8 = 0$, and $\omega_7 = 1$. y_t^γ and x_t^γ are cointegrated with cointegration vector $(1 \quad -1)$ for any $\gamma \in \check{\Gamma}$. However, such cointegration is trivial since the micromodel is singular, and because the adjustment takes place in one single time period: in fact, the first equation of the model is $\Delta y_t^\gamma = \Delta x_t^\gamma$. Aggregation produces a non-singular vector. Δy_t^p and Δx_t^p are cointegrated with cointegration vector $(1 \quad -1)$. Moreover, equations (12.16) and (12.15) show that the macro-model has the shape of a non-trivial error correction mechanism, with the adjustment occuring asymptotically.

Assumption 10.1 obviously holds for model (12.6). Moreover, it is easy to show that there exist points in $\hat{\Gamma}_m$ for which the relevant discriminant and leading coefficients do not vanish. Therefore Theorem 10.2 can be applied, so that effects (A) and (B) occur in Γ_m with the exception of a negligible subset. (In the same way, taking the subset of $\tilde{\Gamma}_m \in \Gamma_m$ where $\omega_8 = 0$, (A) and (B) hold with the exception of a subset negligible in $\tilde{\Gamma}_m$.)

REMARK 12.4. Since the spectral densities that must be split to get the Wold representation of the model in the present section are of order 2, an elementary analysis would be sufficient to obtain (A), (B), and (C) except for a negligible subset of Γ_m. However, such results can be viewed as a paradigm for a model in which $b_{11}^\gamma(L)$ and $b_{22}^\gamma(L)$ are any vectors of rational functions. In this case the micro ARMAX would be

$$\Delta x_t^\gamma = (\omega_7 + \omega_8 L)\Delta x_t^\gamma + b_{11}(L)v_t,$$

in which the independent variable is linked to the dependent variable by a polynomial of order 1, plus an ARMA disturbance, whereas the aggregated model has in general the shape of the first of equations (12.16), with (A), (B), and (C) holding.

12.3.2. Both the problems discussed in this section and in Section 12.1 can be easily dealt with if the idiosyncratic component is taken explicitly into consideration. Theorems 12.3, 12.4, and 12.5 hold with no modification since they refer to aggregate functions of L. As regards statements (A) to (D) in this section, consider model (12.11) augmented with idiosyncratic components:

$$\begin{aligned} \Delta y_t^\gamma &= \kappa^\gamma(L)\Delta x_t^\gamma + b_{11}^\gamma(L)v_t + c_1^\gamma(L)\xi_{1t}^\gamma \\ \Delta x_t^\gamma &= b_{22}^\gamma(L)w_t + c_2^\gamma(L)\xi_{2t}^\gamma. \end{aligned}$$

Statement (A) holds with a slight modification: the micromodel is a finite distributed lag with an ARMA disturbance, whereas the macromodel is a general ARMAX. Similar slight modifications are necessary for the other statements.

12.4. Interpretation. Overidentifying Restrictions

12.4.1. We can now draw some conclusions to the long discussion of the relationship between macro- and micromodels. Suppose that we start with a VAR or an ARMAX model which has been estimated using macro data. What we have learnt is that the estimated coefficients cannot be interpreted as averages of corresponding micro coefficients. Rather, static microequations may turn into dynamic macroequations, singular micromodels become non-singular macromodels, unidirectional micromodels become feedback macromodels, etc. Therefore, the interpretation of aggregate dynamics as giving information on micro behaviors has no ground, unless we want to assume that micro homogeneity prevails.

12.4.2. Suppose instead that we start with a micromodel providing restrictions on the coefficients of the dynamic representation of the micro vector. In principle, we can deal with aggregation, i.e. we can study whether the micro restrictions produce macro restrictions that are testable with aggregate data. By way of example, consider again the consumption model in Section 5.1. Write the income as

$$\Delta y_t^\gamma = (\omega_1 + \omega_2 L)u_{1t} + (\omega_3 + \omega_4 L)u_{2t},$$

with $\gamma = (\omega_1 \quad \omega_2 \quad \omega_3 \quad \omega_4)$. Under the assumption that the agent observes y_t^γ, not its components, we have

$$\begin{aligned} \Delta y_t^\gamma &= (a^\gamma + b^\gamma L)\eta_t^\gamma \\ \Delta c_t^\gamma &= c^\gamma \eta_t^\gamma = (a^\gamma + b^\gamma \beta)\eta_t^\gamma, \end{aligned} \tag{12.17}$$

with $\sigma_\eta^2 = 1$. Notice that the micromodel (12.17) is overidentified: the representation of $(y_t^\gamma \quad c_t^\gamma)$ has three parameters, but c^γ is given once a^γ and b^γ are given.

We now want to see whether the aggregate model is overidentified. Let us firstly consider the subset of Γ_m whose populations can be divided into two groups of agents, A and B. The income of agents in A is affected only by u_{1t}, and the income of agents in B only by u_{2t}. Moreover, the two groups are homogeneous. Thus the aggregate model is parameterized by

$$p = ((\omega_1^1 \quad \omega_2^1 \quad 0 \quad 0) \quad (0 \quad 0 \quad \omega_3^2 \quad \omega_4^2)).$$

The aggregate vector is

$$\begin{aligned} \Delta y_t^p &= (\omega_1^1 + \omega_2^1 L)u_{1t} + (\omega_3^2 + \omega_4^2 L)u_{2t} \\ \Delta c_t^p &= (\omega_1^1 + \omega_2^1 \beta)u_{1t} + (\omega_3^2 + \omega_4^2 \beta)u_{2t}. \end{aligned}$$

This dynamic representation has six parameters which depend on only four microparameters. Therefore the macromodel is overidentified. However, this result depends crucially on the fact that we did not allow the populations to vary freely in Γ_2. If we drop the restriction on p the aggregate dynamic representation becomes

$$\begin{aligned}\Delta y_t^p &= [(\omega_1^1 + \omega_1^2) + (\omega_2^1 + \omega_2^2 L)]u_{1t} + [(\omega_3^1 + \omega_3^2) + (\omega_4^1 + \omega_4^2)]u_{2t} \\ \Delta c_t^p &= (a^{p^1} + b^{p^1}\beta)\eta_t^{p^1} + (a^{p^2} + b^{p^2}\beta)\eta_t^{p^2},\end{aligned} \tag{12.18}$$

where the coefficients in the second equations are obtained from[1]

$$\begin{aligned}(a^{p^i} + b^{p^i} z)(a^{p^i} + b^{p^i} z^{-1}) &= (\omega_1^i + \omega_2^i z)(\omega_1^i + \omega_2^i z^{-1}) \\ &\quad + (\omega_3^i + \omega_4^i z)(\omega_3^i + \omega_4^i z^{-1}) \\ \eta_t^{p^i} &= \frac{(\omega_1^i + \omega_2^i L)u_{1t} + (\omega_3^i + \omega_4^i L)u_{2t}}{a^{p^i} + b^{p^i} L}.\end{aligned} \tag{12.19}$$

System (12.18) still has six parameters, which now depend on eight microparameters. Moreover, as a close inspection of (12.18) and (12.19) shows, when p varies in Γ_2 the macroparameters describe a six-dimensional subset of $\mathbb{R}^6$. Therefore, if p is allowed to vary freely in Γ_2, then aggregation destroys overidentifying restrictions.

In conclusion, overidentifying restrictions at the micro level do not automatically produce overidentifying restrictions for the macroequations. Whether or not macro restrictions occur depends on both the micromodel and the set in which the populations may vary.

12.5. Bibliographic Notes

For identification of structural VAR models, see the works mentioned in Section 5.6, and Giannini (1992).

The fact that macro shocks can result from the combination of corresponding and non-corresponding micro shocks is implicit in our treatment of singularity in Chapter 8. Mixing of micro shocks and of micro coefficients through aggregation has been pointed out in Lippi (1988), Lippi and Forni (1990), Blanchard and Quah (1989), and Geweke (1978) for temporal aggregation. The presentation in Section 12.1 owes much to Blanchard and Quah (1989, pp. 669–72). However, in their theorem on p. 670, Blanchard and Quah claim that conditions (a) and (c) (see our Definition 12.1) are necessary and sufficient for excluding mixing of the micro shocks, which is only partially correct: (a) and (c) are necessary, as Theorem 12.2 shows,

[1] See Chapter 4, Section 4.2.

but not sufficient, as Example 12.2 shows. Indeed, also fundamentalness, i.e. condition (b), is requested in Theorem 12.1.

For the reasons why fundamentalness is not a necessary consequence of economic modeling see for instance Hansen and Sargent (1980, 1991b), Quah (1990), Lippi and Reichlin (1993).

The consequences of aggregation on the dynamic shape of single-equation ARMAX models is studied in Trivedi (1985), Lippi (1988), and Lippi and Forni (1990). See also Nickell (1985) for an example in which all agents face the same independent variable. From a different viewpoint, aggregation as a source of macro dynamics has been pointed out in Stoker (1986).

Important effects on the dynamics of VAR, VARMA (vector ARMA), or single-equation ARMAX models, owing to seasonal adjustment or time aggregation, are noted, more or less explicitly, in the works by Sims, Geweke, Tiao and Wei, mentioned in Section 11.3, and in some works in which different models for forecasting aggregate variables are compared; see, e.g., Lütkepohl (1987), Lee *et al.* (1990).

Both the results on mixing of the VAR coefficients and the effect labeled as (B) in Section 12.3 can be compared to the well-known Lucas effect (Lucas, 1976). The latter occurs in the micromodel, and is due to rational expectations, whereas the mixing observed in this chapter, which is due to aggregation, is independent of whether the Lucas effect occurs in the micromodel or not and is therefore more general than the Lucas effect. Using the terminology in Engle *et al.* (1983), aggregation can destroy structural invariance.

Identification of the micro structure underlying the macromodel, in a time series context, has been studied in Lewbel (1994). The possibility of identifying the micro structure, under the assumption that all agents face the same independent variable, is also pointed out in Sargent (1978, p. 1016, footnote).

Lastly, a comment is needed upon the relationship between the way we define the macroequations in this chapter and the analysis of aggregation in Theil's 1954 book. Theil starts with a microequation like

$$y_t^i = a^i x_t^i + \epsilon_t^i. \tag{12.20}$$

The corresponding macroequation in Theil's book is the orthogonal projection of the aggregate variable y_t on the aggregate variable x_t, i.e. the equation

$$y_t = Ax_t + E_t, \tag{12.21}$$

which has by definition the same dynamic shape of (12.20). Theil's aggregation analysis then consists in studying the relationship between A on the one hand, and the coefficients a^i and the correlations among the x_t^i's on the other hand. Thus, although contamination effects are shown as a consequence of aggregation in Theil's analysis, the dynamics of the micro- and the macroequation are equal by definition. By contrast, our macroequation is the projection of y_t on x_t, the past of x_t, and the past of y_t. In this way we can compare the dynamics of the micromodel with the result obtained by an econometrician estimating either a VAR or an ARMAX model, in which the residual, unlike E_t in (12.21), is orthogonal to x_t, the past of x_t, and the past of y_t.

III

Macroeconomic Applications

13

Permanent Income and the Error Correction Mechanism

In this part we present two applications of the aggregation theory developed in Parts I and II. Chapter 14 contains another application of the method proposed in Part I to determine the number of common components to a large panel of time series. In this chapter, which is mainly based on Forni and Lippi (1994), we return to the consumption model sketched in Section 5.1, i.e. the permanent income hypothesis under rational expectations (PIH), as it was worked out by Hall in 1978.

Hall's model, in its simplest representative-agent version, implies that: (i) aggregate consumption is a random walk independent of past income changes; (ii) if income is I(1) and its measure of persistence is greater than unity, then consumption is more volatile than income; (iii) if labor income is I(1) then total income and consumption are cointegrated by the vector $(1 \quad -1)$; (iv) if predictions are univariate then income and consumption are singular.

As regards empirical evidence, testing for cointegration gives mixed results, while implications (i), (ii), and (iv) are strongly rejected. Poor empirical performance has led to a great deal of work aimed at reconciling the theory with reality. In particular, many papers have been written in order to explain rejection of (i) and (ii), which have become known respectively as 'excess sensitivity' and 'excess smoothness'.

We shall show here that, when individual incomes are heterogeneous, the results obtained depend on which assumption we make about the consumers' information set. If consumers are fully informed about the macrovariables, we get exactly the same results as in the representative-agent model. By contrast, if incomplete information is assumed, properties (i), (ii), and (iv) do not hold at the macro level, so that cointegration is the sole aggregate implication of the permanent income hypothesis. Moreover, we show that aggregate income and consumption follow an error correction mechanism (ECM) with a general dynamic shape, so that the PIH with heterogeneous consumers can provide a microfoundation for the ECM model of consumption.

We do not assume deep knowledge of the PIH model, so that the first four sections are devoted to a detailed analysis of the main theoretical implications and empirical shortcomings of the model in its representative-agent version. The discussion on singularity (Section 13.3 below) and consumption volatility (Section 13.4) should also be perused by the reader already acquainted with the theory.

13.1. Excess Sensitivity

13.1.1. Let us begin by illustrating the main features of Hall's model in its simplest formulation. For the moment we consider only one consumer, so that we drop any reference to the microparameter vector or the superscript i. Our consumer is infinitely lived and maximizes at time $t = 0$ the expected utility of consumption

$$\mathrm{E}_0 \sum_{t=0}^{\infty} \theta^t u(c_t), \tag{13.1}$$

subject to the sequence of budget constraints

$$A_{t+1} = (1+r)A_t + y_t - c_t. \tag{13.2}$$

In equations (13.1) and (13.2) r is the interest rate, which is assumed constant, θ is an individual utility discount factor, c_t is consumption, A_t is assets, and y_t is labor income, taken as exogenous. E_0 is expectation at time $t = 0$ conditional to the information set I_0. We do not make specific assumptions on I_t for the moment, except that I_t includes at least y_{t-k}, $k \geq 0$.

The simplest way to solve the optimization problem above is to solve the budget constraint for c_t and substitute in equation (13.1), so obtaining

$$\mathrm{E}_0 \sum_{t=0}^{\infty} \theta^t u(A_t/\beta + y_t - A_{t+1}),$$

where β is the discount factor $(1+r)^{-1}$. The consumer now has to maximize the above expression with respect to the sequence $\{A_t\}_{t=1}^{\infty}$, with A_0 given. Equating to zero the derivative with respect to A_1 gives one first-order condition, i.e.

$$\theta \mathrm{E}_0 u'(c_1) = \beta u'(c_0).$$

At times $t = 1, 2, \ldots$ the consumer will be facing problems similar to (13.1) with $A_1, A_2, \ldots$ given and information sets $I_1, I_2, \ldots$ respectively. This gives the system of Euler equations

$$\theta \mathrm{E}_{t-1} u'(c_t) = \beta u'(c_{t-1}).$$

To simplify matters further, let us assume quadratic utility, so that marginal utility is linear. If marginal utility is not linear we can hope that a linear approximation will be a good approximation for our purposes. Moreover, let us assume that the 'impatience' parameter θ is equal to the market discount factor β. Under these hypotheses, the above equations become

$$\mathrm{E}_{t-1}c_t = c_{t-1}, \tag{13.3}$$

i.e. optimal consumption is a martingale.

This is the most famed result of Hall's model. The Euler equations for optimal consumption have a testable implication: the change in consumption at time t is independent of all the variables included in the information set at time $t-1$. In particular, consumption is independent of its own past and the past of labor income. The intuition is that, with a constant interest rate and absence of liquidity constraints, rational agents should never change consumption, unless they receive new information about their future income.

A significant correlation between consumption change and past income change has been referred to in the literature as 'excess sensitivity' of consumption. Sensitivity has been tested employing both macro and panel data by many authors, beginning with Flavin (1981). Independence of consumption change from past information has generally been rejected by the data. However, the micro evidence is different from the macro one, indicating substantial aggregation effects. Firstly, at the micro level evidence is somewhat mixed, while rejection at the macro level is strong. Secondly, excess sensitivity has opposite signs: aggregate consumption change is positively correlated with past aggregate income change, while the correlation is negative (and smaller) in the micro data. Moreover, individual income appears to be negatively autocorrelated, while aggregate income is positively autocorrelated.

13.1.2. Let us now present some empirical evidence concerning aggregate US data. We use here the national income and product accounts (NIPA) quarterly data from 1947:1 to 1991:4. All the data are seasonally adjusted, at quarterly rates, taken in per capita terms and expressed in thousands of 1987 dollars. Labor income y_t is constructed following Pischke (1995).[1] As regards consumption, it may seem the most natural choice to take total consumption expenditures (c_t). However, c_t includes durables, while in the theory consumption is treated as if it were made up solely of non-durables

[1] Define W = wage and salary disbursements; O = other labor income; I = personal interest income; D = personal dividend income; R = rental income of persons; P = proprietors' income; T = transfer payments to persons; C = personal contributions for social insurance; τ = personal tax and non-tax payments; N = personal non-tax payments to state and local governments; $q = (W+O)/(W+O+I+D+R)$. Then $y_t = W + O + T - C - N + q(P - \tau)$. Following Blinder and Deaton (1985), the 1975 tax rebate is removed from the income data; the numbers for this correction are taken from Blinder (1981).

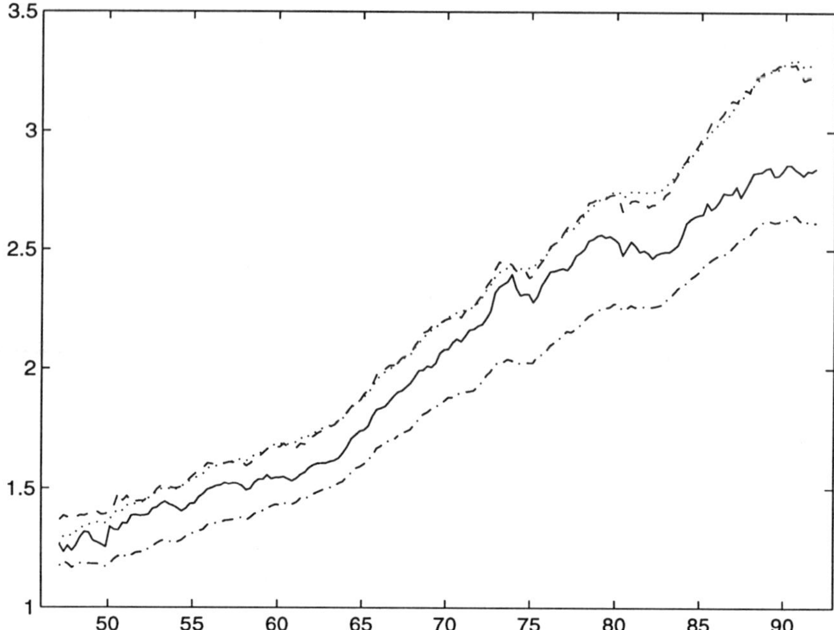

Fig. 13.1. US labor income and consumption
y_t: solid line. c_t: dashed line. c_t': dotted line. c_t'': dotted–dashed line.

and services. The literature provides two solutions for this problem. One is to construct a measure of total consumption that includes an estimate of the service flows for consumer durables in place of purchases. We call this measure c_t'.[2]

Table 13.1. Unit root tests for labor income and consumption

Variable	DF	ADF(1)	ADF(2)	ADF(3)	95% critical value
y_t	−1.846	−1.827	−1.958	−1.935	−3.436
c_t	−2.342	−2.557	−2.619	−2.690	−3.436
c_t'	−1.771	−2.344	−2.294	−2.432	−3.436
c_t''	−2.778	−3.097	−2.725	−2.486	−3.436

[2] The stock of durables is calculated by accumulating the spending flow, starting with the NIPA net stock of consumer durables for the end of 1946, and assuming a depreciation rate of 5% per quarter. To calculate the imputed rent, we assumed a user cost of 6% per quarter. Consumption on clothing and shoes is treated in a similar way, but assuming a depreciation rate of 20%, a zero initial value, and a user cost of 21% per quarter. Consumption c_t' is the imputed rent on durables, clothing, and shoes plus expenditures on services and non-durables other than clothing and shoes.

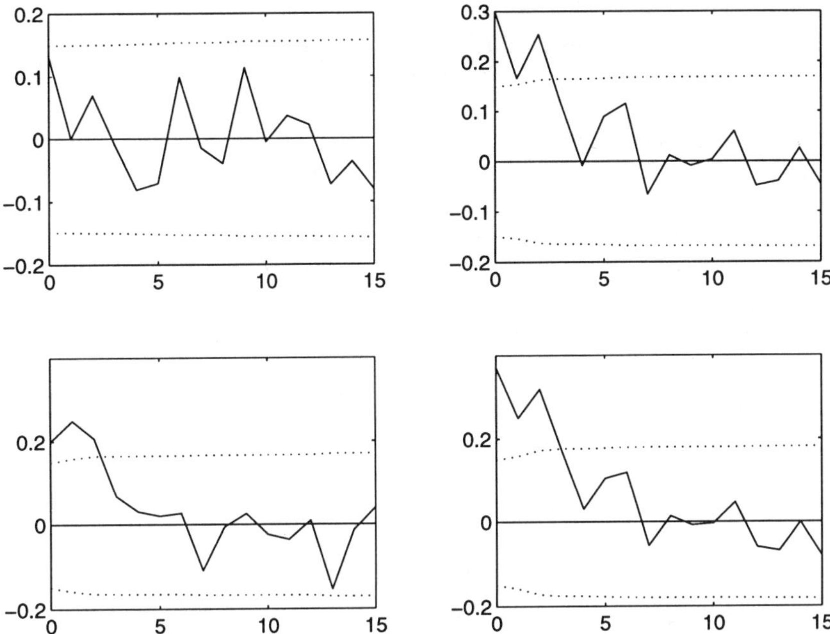

Fig. 13.2. Sample autocorrelation functions

The other solution is simply to ignore durables and take only expenditures on non-durables and services; we call this measure c''_t.[3] The series y_t, c_t, c'_t, and c''_t are plotted in Figure 13.1. Let us begin by testing for the unit root hypothesis in labor income and consumption. As shown in Table 13.1, there is no evidence against the null hypothesis of a unit root in the four series y_t, c_t, c'_t, and c''_t, when compared with the trend stationary alternative. The I(1) evidence for consumption is consistent with the assumption $\theta = \beta$, i.e. that the rate of time preference is equal to the interest rate. Now let us take the first differences Δy_t, Δc_t, $\Delta c'_t$, and $\Delta c''_t$ and look at the sample autocorrelation functions (SACF) reported in Figure 13.2. Consumption change exhibits significant positive autocorrelation at lags from 1 to 3, according to all of the measures of consumption employed. Notice also that positive autocorrelation is much greater than that of labor income, which is essentially a white-noise process. Similar results hold for the sample cross-correlation functions: consumption change is positively correlated with past labor income change, particularly at lags 1 and 2.

[3] Clothing and shoes are treated as durables.

13.2. Cointegration of Consumption and Total Income

13.2.1. In the same year as Hall's paper, Davidson *et al.* (1978) inaugurated a separate line of research on consumption, based on error correction mechanisms and cointegration. The ECM has generally been considered as conflicting with the PIH, but the relationship between the two models has long been somewhat obscure.[4] Campbell (1987) contributes to clarifying the issue by showing that Hall's model implies cointegration between consumption and *total income*, defined as the sum of labor income and capital income.

Cointegration can be shown in the following way. Solving the budget constraint (13.2) forward gives[5]

$$A_t = \frac{\beta}{1-\beta F}c_t - \frac{\beta}{1-\beta F}y_t. \tag{13.4}$$

Taking expectations at time t on both sides and noting that the martingale property of consumption implies $\mathrm{E}_t c_{t+k} = c_t,\ k \geq 0$, we get

$$c_t = r\left[A_t + \mathrm{E}_t\frac{\beta}{1-\beta F}y_t\right]. \tag{13.5}$$

Equation (13.5) clearly illustrates how modern permanent income theory reinterprets Friedman's original intuition. The expression in square brackets on the RHS is total wealth, which includes both assets and human wealth, defined as the present value of the expected labor income stream. Consumption equals permanent income, defined as the flow of rental income from total wealth.

Now let us take the first differences of (13.4) and multiply by F. We get

$$s_t = \frac{\beta F}{1-\beta F}\Delta c_t - \frac{\beta F}{1-\beta F}\Delta y_t, \tag{13.6}$$

where $s_t = \Delta A_{t+1}$ is saving. By applying expectations at time t on both sides and remembering that expectation at time t of future consumption changes is zero, we get

$$s_t = -\mathrm{E}_t\frac{\beta F}{1-\beta F}\Delta y_t. \tag{13.7}$$

[4] For instance, in Engle and Granger (1987) cointegration of income and consumption is interpreted as evidence against the PIH.

[5] The budget constraint can be rewritten as $(1-\beta^{-1}L)A_t = y_t - c_t$. Since $\beta^{-1} > 1$, the inverse of $(1-\beta^{-1}L)$ is an operator in F (see Section A.3 in the Appendix).

Equation (13.7) is Campbell's 'saving for a rainy day' equation: savings anticipate future income falls. An important implication of (13.7) is that if the change in labor income is stationary, then saving is the conditional expectation of a stationary variable and therefore is stationary. Defining total income x_t as the sum of capital income and labor income, i.e.

$$x_t = rA_t + y_t, \tag{13.8}$$

it is easily seen from the budget constraint (13.2) that

$$x_t - c_t = s_t. \tag{13.9}$$

Since c_t and x_t are I(1)[6] while s_t is stationary, total income and consumption are cointegrated, with cointegrating vector $(1 \quad -1)$.

As is well known, cointegration entails the existence of an ECM relation linking income and consumption. However, it must be stressed that the consumption equation is different from that of Davidson *et al.* (1978), because it has a very special form. Since Δc_t is a pure innovation, all the coefficients in the consumption equation must be zero. It is total income, not consumption, that adjusts toward equilibrium, by means of the movements in capital income induced by savings. We shall return to this point in Section 13.8.

13.2.2. Let us now come to empirical data. In order to test for cointegration we need firstly an estimate for total disposable income x_t. The latter is obtained by making some adjustments to NIPA definitions.[7] In relation with c'_t we use x'_t, which is the sum of x_t and our estimate of net interests on durables, clothing, and shoes. By subtracting consumption we get two measures of savings: $s_t = x_t - c_t$ and $s'_t = x'_t - c'_t$. Let us ignore c''_t for the moment.

[6] Notice that the fact that consumption is a random walk is not implied by the martingale property (13.3) alone, since (13.3) does not guarantee that the variance of Δc_t is invariant over time. Nevertheless, the I(1) property of consumption and total income can be derived from stationarity of Δy_t. For consider the equality $\Delta c_t = rs_{t-1} + \Delta y_t$, which is obtained by taking differences in (13.8). Since both Δy_t and s_{t-1} are stationary, the linear combination Δx_t is stationary as well. Hence x_t is either I(1) or stationary (possibly with a linear deterministic trend). But if x_t were stationary c_t should also be stationary by equation (13.9), a fact that is contradicted by the martingale property of consumption. It follows that both x_t and c_t are I(1).

It should be stressed that we have assumed stationarity of Δy_t, not that y_t is $I(1)$. Hence the cointegration result along with the observations above hold true even in the case of a trend stationary y_t. Notice in particular that total income cannot be trend stationary under the PIH even if y_t is trend stationary.

[7] We follow Blinder and Deaton (1985). The 1975 tax rebate is removed, as explained in footnote 1. Moreover, personal 'non-tax' payments to state and local governments are added to both consumption and income. Lastly, interest paid by consumers to business is subtracted from disposable income.

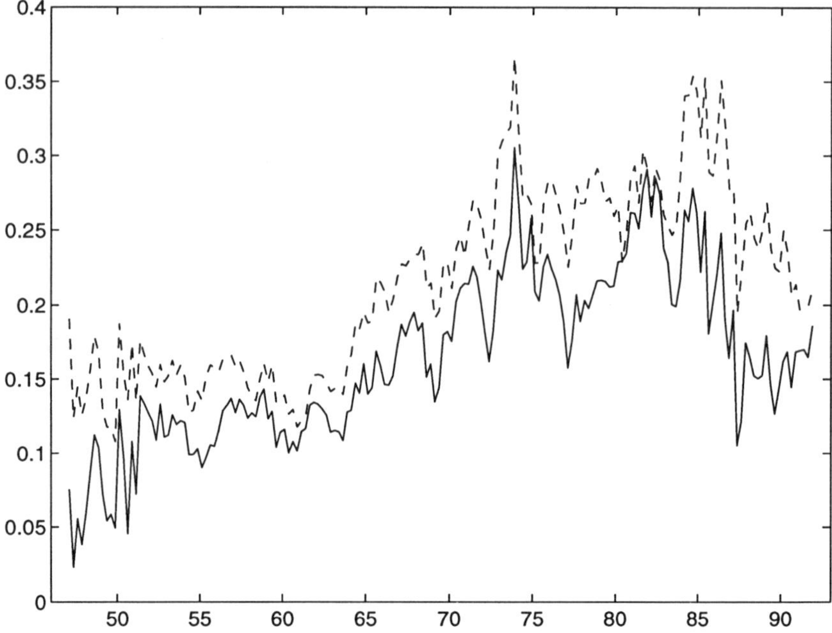

Fig. 13.3. US per capita savings
s_t: solid line. s'_t: dashed line.

Table 13.2. Unit root tests for total income and saving

Variable	DF	ADF(1)	ADF(2)	ADF(3)	95% critical value
With trend					
x_t	−2.441	−2.296	−2.373	−2.294	−3.436
x'_t	−2.415	−2.283	−2.365	−2.295	−3.436
Without trend					
s_t	−3.015	−2.817	−2.422	−2.594	−2.878
s'_t	−2.363	−2.293	−1.966	−2.061	−2.878

Figure 13.3 shows the two measures of saving s_t, s'_t. Neither of them seems stationary. This impression is confirmed by the ADF tests reported in Table 13.2. As regards s_t, the unit root hypothesis is rejected by the Dickey–Fuller test at the 5% level but cannot be rejected by the augmented Dickey–Fuller test with one lag or more. s'_t is I(1) according to both the DF and the ADF test with any number of lags. Hence cointegration is not supported by the data over the whole period 1947:1 to 1991:4.

However, both the series in Figure 13.3 look much more stationary if we concentrate attention on the subperiod starting in the mid-sixties. Indeed, within the period 1964:1 to 1991:4, the hypothesis of a unit root in s_t is rejected at the 5% level by the DF and the ADF(1) tests, while s'_t is stationary according to all the tests (see Table 13.3).

Table 13.3. Unit root tests, 1964:1 to 1991:4

Variable	DF	ADF(1)	ADF(2)	ADF(3)	95% critical value
With trend					
c_t	−1.315	−1.877	−2.362	−3.231	−3.450
x_t	−2.313	−2.713	−2.411	−2.863	−3.450
c'_t	−1.278	−2.206	−2.493	−3.505	−3.450
x'_t	−2.329	−2.742	−2.450	−2.914	−3.450
Without trend					
s_t	−3.417	−3.007	−2.566	−2.657	−2.887
s'_t	−3.312	−3.348	−2.935	−2.977	−2.887

What about c''_t? Clearly, we cannot hope that $x_t - c''_t$ is stationary, since c''_t does not include durables. However, following Campbell (1987), we can assume that, if consumption were made up solely of non-durables and services, total consumption would be a multiple of c''_t. Under this assumption, x_t and c''_t should be cointegrated, with cointegrating vector possibly different from $(1 \quad -1)$. By following Johansen's procedure (with two lags in the VAR) we obtain the rank 1 trace statistic 27.19 and the λ-max statistic 27.68, indicating that the null of no cointegration can be rejected at the 1% significance level.

In conclusion, evidence on cointegration is mixed. If we use c_t or c'_t, we can test for stationarity of saving, which is equivalent to testing for cointegration with cointegrating vector $(1 \quad -1)$. We cannot reject the null of non-stationarity of saving for the whole period 1947:1 to 1991:4, but we can for the period 1964:1 to 1991:4. If we use c''_t, we can only test for cointegration: the null of no cointegration can be rejected at the standard significance level.

13.3. Singularity

13.3.1. To proceed further we must specify the variables contained in the information set I_t of the representative agent. The simplest assumptions in the literature are the following. Firstly, labor income y_t follows the model

$$\Delta y_t = a(L)\eta_t, \tag{13.10}$$

where η_t is white noise and $a(L)$ is a rational function (since we are interested in the second moments of the processes, we are assuming that η_t

and Δy_t have zero mean). Secondly, the representative agent observes only the present and the past of η_t. Lastly we assume normality of η_t, so that conditional expectation and linear projection coincide. We do not assume fundamentalness of η_t.

Equation (13.10) can be used to obtain explicit expressions for consumption, saving, and total income. Let us begin with consumption. Taking differences of the budget constraint (13.2) gives

$$\Delta c_t = \Delta y_t - s_t + (1+r)s_{t-1}. \tag{13.11}$$

From the saving equation (13.7) we get

$$\Delta y_t - s_t = \mathrm{E}_t\left(\Delta y_t + \frac{\beta F}{1-\beta F}\Delta y_t\right) = \mathrm{E}_t\frac{1}{1-\beta F}\Delta y_t$$

and

$$(1+r)s_{t-1} = -\mathrm{E}_{t-1}\frac{1}{1-\beta F}\Delta y_t.$$

Substituting in (13.11) gives

$$\Delta c_t = (\mathrm{E}_t - \mathrm{E}_{t-1})\frac{1}{1-\beta F}\Delta y_t. \tag{13.12}$$

Since the consumer knows the past of η_t, (13.10) implies

$$\mathrm{E}_t\Delta y_{t+k} = \mathrm{E}_t\sum_{s=0}^{\infty} a_s\eta_{t+k-s} = a_k\eta_t + a_{k+1}\eta_{t-1} + a_{k+2}\eta_{t-2} + \cdots$$

$$\mathrm{E}_{t-1}\Delta y_{t+k} = a_{k+1}\eta_{t-1} + a_{k+2}\eta_{t-2} + \cdots$$

so that

$$(\mathrm{E}_t - \mathrm{E}_{t-1})\Delta y_{t+k} = a_k\eta_t.$$

Hence from (13.12) we get

$$\Delta c_t = \left(\sum_{k=0}^{\infty} a_k\beta^k\right)\eta_t = a(\beta)\eta_t. \tag{13.13}$$

Combining (13.11), (13.10), and (13.13) gives saving:

$$s_t = \beta\frac{a(L) - a(\beta)}{\beta - L}\eta_t. \tag{13.14}$$

REMARK 13.1. Notice that the expression on the RHS in (13.14) is a linear combination of the present and past of income innovation, even if the denominator vanishes for $L = \beta < 1$. In fact the numerator also vanishes for $L = \beta$, so that the expression has no poles of modulus less than one.

Lastly, taking the first difference of (13.14) and adding (13.13) the change in total income $\Delta x_t = \Delta s_t + \Delta c_t$ is found to be

$$\Delta x_t = h(L)\eta_t, \tag{13.15}$$

where

$$h(L) = \frac{\beta a(L)(1-L) - (1-\beta)a(\beta)L}{\beta - L}.$$

Notice that $h(1) = a(\beta)$, so that consumption change is $h(1)\eta_t$, i.e. the revision in the long-run expectation of total income.

The labor income equation (13.10) along with the equations obtained for consumption, saving, and total income have an important implication. All these variables are linear combinations of the present and past of the same white noise η_t, i.e. they are pairwise singular.

13.3.2. As regards data, we shall concentrate on labor income and consumption. As we have seen in Chapter 2, singularity implies that by regressing consumption change on the present, past, and future of labor income change we should get a zero residual. This is clearly contradicted by our data set: as shown in Table 13.4, the $\bar{R}^2$ obtained by including 15 leads and 15 lags of Δy_t is about 0.4 for Δc_t and $\Delta c_t''$ and 0.45 for $\Delta c_t'$.

Table 13.4. $\bar{R}^2$ obtained by regressing consumption changes on Δy_{t+s}, $s = -k, h$

	$k=h=0$	$k=h=5$	$k=h=10$	$k=h=15$	$k=15, h=0$
Δc_t	0.193	0.356	0.395	0.396	0.293
$\Delta c_t'$	0.225	0.441	0.459	0.456	0.325
$\Delta c_t''$	0.210	0.397	0.406	0.404	0.263

The empirical puzzle is even more serious if we make the usual assumption that η_t is fundamental for Δy_t, which amounts to assuming that the representative consumer observes only the past of labor income. In such a case Δc_t should be an exact linear combination of the present and past of labor income change, i.e. the future of Δy_t should not help in predicting consumption. The last column of Table 13.4 shows the $\bar{R}^2$ resulting from the regression of Δc_t, $\Delta c_t'$, and $\Delta c_t''$ on $\Delta y_t, \Delta y_{t-1}, \ldots, \Delta y_{t-15}$. When the leads of Δy_t are not included among the regressors, the explained variance does not exceed one-third of total variance.

As we shall see in the following sections, singularity of labor income and consumption (as well as singularity of total income and consumption) is not a general feature of the representative-agent PIH model. Singularity depends on the assumption of univariate predictions that we have made at the beginning of the present section and disappears when two or more (non-singular) variables enter the information set.[8]

13.4. Consumption Volatility

13.4.1. A further empirical puzzle of the PIH has been pointed out by Deaton (1987). Deaton observes that, according to the theory, consumption should be more volatile than income when income is positively autocorrelated, as is the case with US data. This is paradoxical, since the early permanent income theory was intended to explain precisely the fact that consumption changes are very small as compared with income changes. The empirical evidence that the variance of consumption changes is much less than that of income changes is known as 'excess smoothness'.

To illustrate Deaton's paradox let us return to equation (13.13). The variance of Δc_t is $a(\beta)^2\sigma_\eta^2$. If β is near to unity then $a(\beta)$ is approximately equal to $a(1)$, so that

$$\frac{\mathrm{var}(\Delta c_t)}{\mathrm{var}(\Delta y_t)} = \frac{a(\beta)^2\sigma_\eta^2}{\mathrm{var}(\Delta y_t)} \approx \frac{a(1)^2\sigma_\eta^2}{\mathrm{var}(\Delta y_t)},$$

where the approximate equality sign means that the equality holds true in the limit for r approaching zero. The expression on the RHS is Cochrane's persistence measure applied to labor income.[9] If persistence is greater than one or nearly one, as indicated by many of the existing estimates with US data, then the volatility of consumption implied by the theory is much higher than that exhibited by empirical data.

The shortcoming of Deaton's argument is that it relies on the assumption that consumers make univariate predictions. If the consumers' information set is larger, the implied variance of consumption is smaller. To see this, combine equations (13.7) and (13.6) to get

$$\frac{\beta F}{1-\beta F}\Delta c_t = \frac{\beta F}{1-\beta F}\Delta y_t - \mathrm{E}_t\frac{\beta F}{1-\beta F}\Delta y_t.$$

[8] Some further observations may be useful in order to avoid possible misunderstandings about singularity. Firstly, the fact that the vector $(\Delta y_t\ \Delta x_t\ \Delta c_t\ s_t)$ does not have full rank is an obvious consequence of the accounting identity (13.9). This identity is fulfilled by the observed vector, which has rank 3, so that there are no empirical puzzles here. Secondly, the theoretical rank of the vector is further reduced by the budget constraint (13.11), which embodies the assumption of a constant interest rate. Indeed, equation (13.11), along with (13.9), entails rank 2. This is a general result of the PIH, in the sense that rank 3 cannot be obtained by relaxing the assumption of univariate prediction.

[9] See Cochrane (1988).

This equation says that the process on the LHS is a prediction error. Hence its variance decreases when the information set becomes larger. The same property must hold also for consumption change, since the variance of Δc_t is equal, up to a constant, to the variance of the prediction error above. Hence with superior information we could have a smooth consumption even if labor income is persistent.

This criticism can be avoided by focusing on total income rather than labor income. Consider the equation

$$\Delta x_t = \Delta c_t + \Delta s_t,$$

which decomposes total income change in the white-noise component Δc_t and the superstationary component Δs_t. Such a decomposition implies

$$\mathrm{var}(\Delta c_t) = S_{\Delta x}(0);$$

that is, the variance of consumption change is equal to the spectral density of total income change evaluated at the zero frequency. For, simply equate the spectra and notice, firstly, that Δc_t is white noise, and, secondly, that the spectrum of Δs_t and the cross-spectra of Δs_t and Δc_t vanish at the zero frequency because s_t is already stationary. It follows that

$$\frac{\mathrm{var}(\Delta c_t)}{\mathrm{var}(\Delta x_t)} = \frac{S_{\Delta x}(0)}{\mathrm{var}(\Delta x_t)}, \tag{13.16}$$

i.e. the ratio of the variance of consumption change to the variance of total income change is equal to Cochrane's persistence of total income. In the same way, the relative volatility of consumption can be related to Beveridge and Nelson's persistence of total income.[10] Equation (13.16) holds true irrespective of which particular value the interest rate takes on, not just in the limit for r approaching unity. Moreover, it does not depend on univariate predictions (we do not make any assumption on I_t in the derivation above).

13.4.2. Some empirical evidence on total income persistence and consumption volatility is reported in Table 13.5, where Bartlett non-parametric estimates of Cochrane persistence for x_t and x'_t are presented. These are compared with the ratio of the variance of consumption change to that of income change, reported in the last column. ψ is the ratio $\mathrm{var}(\Delta c_t)/\mathrm{var}(\Delta x_t)$, while $\psi' = \mathrm{var}(\Delta c'_t)/\mathrm{var}(\Delta x'_t)$ and $\psi'' = \mathrm{var}(\Delta c''_t)/\mathrm{var}(\Delta x_t)$. Persistence estimates of x_t range from 0.93 to 0.98 while those of x'_t range from 0.93 to 1.00. As is usual with non-parametric estimates, standard errors are

[10] See Beveridge and Nelson (1981).

Table 13.5. Cochrane persistence of total income (standard errors in brackets)

Window size	10	20	30	40	60	ψ	ψ'	ψ''
Δx_t	0.98	0.93	0.96	0.97	0.93	0.52	–	0.22
	(0.27)	(0.36)	(0.46)	(0.53)	(0.79)			
$\Delta x'_t$	1.00	0.95	0.97	0.98	0.93	–	0.19	–
	(0.27)	(0.36)	(0.46)	(0.53)	(0.62)			

quite large; however, with lag window size 20, ψ' is outside the standard confidence interval while ψ'' is on the border.

A stronger rejection of (13.16) can be obtained by using parametric estimates. In conclusion, the representative-agent PIH model cannot produce both the observed volatility of consumption and the estimated persistence of income: either consumption is excessively 'smooth' or total income is excessively persistent.

13.5. Complete Information and the Representative Agent

Hitherto we have shown some of the main features and difficulties of the PIH representative-agent model. Let us now relax the representative-agent hypothesis and see what happens when explicitly aggregating heterogeneous PIH consumers. Since in this chapter we do not focus on the relationship between microparameters and individual microequations, we simplify notation and go back to Part I. So we write, for example, $b^i(L)$ instead of $b^{p^i}(L)$.

To begin with, let us assume a very simple disaggregated model, where individual labor income is driven by only one common shock:

$$\Delta y_t^i = b^i(L)u_t + c^i(L)\xi_t^i. \tag{13.17}$$

When aggregating over m agents the idiosyncratic components cancel out, so that per capita income is

$$\Delta y_t = b(L)u_t, \tag{13.18}$$

where $b(L) = m^{-1}\sum_i b^i(L)$. As noted in Section 1.2, the model can explain the finding that micro incomes are negatively autocorrelated whereas macro income is positively autocorrelated, provided that we assume non-smooth and large idiosyncratic components.

Let us now deal with consumption. The first problem we must face is the definition of the information set employed by agents in order to predict their incomes. In the present section we assume that macro information is *complete*: that is, agent i sees all of the common shocks appearing in its labor income equation. In our one-shock model, this means simply that agents see u_t. Moreover, let us assume that consumer i also observes the idiosyncratic shock ξ_t^i. This assumption is removed below.

Straightforward application of the steps in Section 13.3 gives

$$\Delta c_t^i = b^i(\beta)u_t + c^i(\beta)\xi_t^i.$$

Aggregating over individuals leads to the macroequation

$$\Delta c_t = b(\beta)u_t, \tag{13.19}$$

where c_t is per capita consumption.

Now let us modify the information concerning the idiosyncratic component, while retaining the assumption that agents see the common shock u_t. For instance, let us assume that consumer i cannot see the idiosyncratic shock ξ_t^i but only the idiosyncratic component $c^i(L)\xi_t^i$. Clearly, if ξ_t^i is fundamental nothing changes in the information set. However, if ξ_t^i is not fundamental, observing the idiosyncratic component gives strictly less information than observing ξ_t^i.[11] In this case the relevant model for prediction is obtained from (13.17) by substituting for $c^i(L)\xi_t^i$ the fundamental representation of the idiosyncratic component, say $\hat{c}^i(L)\hat{\xi}_t^i$. Individual consumption becomes $\Delta c_t^i = b^i(\beta)u_t + \hat{c}^i(\beta)\hat{\xi}_t^i$. The important point here is that only the idiosyncratic component of micro consumption is modified. When averaging over consumers idiosyncratic components vanish, so that aggregate consumption is still given by (13.19).

Other assumptions about prediction of the idiosyncratic component could be made. But, if information concerning the common component of income is complete, nothing changes at the macro level.

Equation (13.19), along with (13.18), makes a macromodel which is identical in all relevant respects to the representative-agent model. This leads us to the following quite interesting result: when information concerning the common component is complete, the micro implications of the PIH model hold true at the macro level. We can rephrase this by saying that, despite consumers' heterogeneity, completeness of aggregate information implies that the representative agent exists, i.e. per capita consumption is identical to the consumption of a PIH agent whose labor income is per capita labor income.

This result can be easily extended to the general case of h common shocks: if consumers are able to discern all of the common shocks, then the correct macromodel may be derived by assuming a representative consumer whose information space is spanned by the present and the past of the common shocks.

[11] See Section A.4 in the Appendix.

13.6. An Explanation for Sensitivity and Smoothness

13.6.1. We now come to the case of incomplete information. As we have already seen in Section 5.1, several interesting alternatives arise. Here we shall consider: (i) consumer i cannot see the shocks u_t and ξ_t^i but only the components $\zeta_t^i = b^i(L)u_t$ and $\chi_t^i = c^i(L)\xi_t^i$; (ii) consumer i observes only Δy_t^i at the micro level, but observes the macrovariable Δy_t; (iii) the same as in (ii), but Δy_t is observed only with some lag; (iv) only Δy_t^i is observed.

Let us consider case (i). If $b^i(L)$ is fundamental for all i, observing ζ_t^i is the same as observing u_t, so that nothing changes at the macro level. By contrast, if $b^i(L)$ is not fundamental for some i, macro information is not complete and aggregation effects arise. We shall limit ourselves to the following example.

Example 13.1. Assume that there are two equally sized groups of consumers. Income is $\Delta y_t^i = u_t + \xi_t^i$ if i belongs to type A and $\Delta y_t^i = 2u_{t-1} + \xi_t^i$ if i belongs to type B. Type B consumers observe only u_{t-1}, not u_t, in addition to their idiosyncratic component, so that their consumption is $2u_{t-1} + \xi_t^i$ instead of $2\beta u_t + \xi_t^i$, as would be the case if u_t were observed. Agents belonging to type A consume $u_t + \xi_t^i$, so that average consumption is equal to average income:

$$\Delta c_t = \Delta y_t = (0.5 + L)u_t.$$

Aggregate consumption change is positively correlated with both its own past and the past of income change.

Case (ii) is somewhat more complicated. This case, too, hinges on fundamentalness. If (13.18) is fundamental, Δy_t gives the same information as u_t, so that the representative-consumer result holds. If it is not, the information set including the present and the past of Δy_t and Δy_t^i contains less information than that including the present and the past of u_t and ξ_t^i. To see this, consider the equation

$$\begin{pmatrix} \Delta y_t^i \\ \Delta y_t \end{pmatrix} = \begin{pmatrix} b^i(L) & c^i(L) \\ b(L) & 0 \end{pmatrix} \begin{pmatrix} u_t \\ \xi_t^i \end{pmatrix}.$$

Since the determinant of the matrix on the RHS vanishes in the zeros of $b(L)$, if $b(L)$ is not fundamental the above representation is not the fundamental joint representation of $(\Delta y_t^i \quad \Delta y_t)$.[12]

[12] Non-fundamentalness of the representation above may also be due to a non-fundamental $c^i(L)$. In this case, however, u_t can be recovered from the present and the past of Δy_t, so that macro information is complete and we have the representative-agent result.

Clearly, in case (ii) consumption of all individuals must be independent of past aggregate income changes, since past aggregate income changes are included in the information set of all agents at time $t-1$. Hence consumption must be independent of past income at the macro level, just as in the representative-agent model. However, the following example shows that the random walk result breaks down.

EXAMPLE 13.2. Micro incomes are as in Example 13.1. Following the procedure in Section 10.1, one obtains that for type B consumers the joint Wold representation of $(\,\Delta y_t^i \quad \Delta y_t\,)$ is

$$\begin{pmatrix} \Delta y_t^i \\ \Delta y_t \end{pmatrix} = \begin{pmatrix} 1-\dfrac{3}{4}L & \dfrac{5}{2}L \\ -\dfrac{3}{8}L & 1+\dfrac{5}{4}L \end{pmatrix} \begin{pmatrix} \epsilon_t^i \\ a_t^i \end{pmatrix},$$

where

$$\begin{pmatrix} \epsilon_t^i \\ a_t^i \end{pmatrix} = \begin{pmatrix} \dfrac{3L}{4+2L} & \dfrac{4+5L}{4+2L} \\ \dfrac{4+5L}{4+8L} & \dfrac{3L}{8+4L} \end{pmatrix} \begin{pmatrix} u_t \\ \xi_t^i \end{pmatrix}.$$

Notice that agents have private information on their common component. Average consumption for type B consumers is

$$\frac{5\beta+(3+4\beta)L}{4+2L}u_t.$$

In the same way type A average consumption is u_t, so that

$$\Delta c_t = \frac{4+5\beta+(5+4\beta)L}{4+2L}u_t.$$

The departure from the representative-agent model becomes more serious in case (iii), in which the assumption is that macro data are accessible only with some lag (for instance, because time is required in order to update national accounts). In this case both autocorrelation of consumption and excess sensitivity can be obtained in the macromodel, as shown by the following example.

EXAMPLE 13.3. Let us assume $\Delta y_t^i = [1+(1/2)L]u_t + \xi_t^i$ for all i. Only the present and the past of Δy_t^i and $\Delta y_{t-1} = [L+(1/2)L^2]u_t$ are observed, so that prediction is based on the joint Wold representation

$$\begin{pmatrix} \Delta y_t^i \\ \Delta y_{t-1} \end{pmatrix} = \begin{pmatrix} 1+\dfrac{1}{4}L & -\dfrac{1}{4}L \\ \dfrac{1}{2}L+\dfrac{1}{4}L^2 & 1+\dfrac{1}{4}L-\dfrac{1}{8}L^2 \end{pmatrix} \begin{pmatrix} \epsilon_t^i \\ a_t^i \end{pmatrix},$$

where

$$\begin{pmatrix} \epsilon_t^i \\ a_t^i \end{pmatrix} = \begin{pmatrix} 1+\frac{1}{4}L & 1-\frac{1}{4}L \\ \frac{1}{2}L & -\frac{1}{2}L \end{pmatrix} \begin{pmatrix} u_t \\ \xi_t^i \end{pmatrix}.$$

Individual consumption is

$$\Delta c_t^i = \left(1+\frac{1}{4}\beta+\frac{1}{4}L\right)u_t + \left(1+\frac{1}{4}\beta-\frac{1}{4}L\right)\xi_t^i,$$

so that aggregate consumption is

$$\Delta c_t = \left(1+\frac{1}{4}\beta+\frac{1}{4}L\right)u_t.$$

Both autocorrelation and correlation with lagged income are non-zero.

Let us now deal with case (iv). Here a problem arises. Since information concerning macrovariables is publicly available at low cost and can help prediction, it is not clear why Δy_t should be excluded from the consumers' information set. However, it can be argued that the value of aggregate information is insignificant at the micro level because the fraction of the variance of micro incomes explained by the macro income is very small.[13] In this case univariate prediction performs almost as well as prediction based both on Δy_t and Δy_t^i. Obviously, when the variance of the common component approaches zero, Δy_t becomes completely uninformative and the two predictions are identical. As long as the cost of acquiring and/or processing aggregate information is non-zero, ignoring aggregate information could be the better choice for consumers.

Besides, case (iv) is attractive since, while being the simplest example of incomplete information, it gives rise to similar results as the more complicated models arising from cases (i), (ii), and (iii). Hence we shall discuss it in some detail below.

13.6.2. In case (iv), the relevant model for prediction is the univariate Wold representation of Δy_t^i

$$\Delta y_t^i = a^i(L)\eta_t^i, \tag{13.20}$$

which can be determined by solving

$$a^i(L)\eta_t^i = b^i(L)u_t + c^i(L)\xi_t^i$$

in the unknowns $a^i(L)$ and η_t^i along the lines of Section 4.1.

[13] See Altonji and Ashenfelter (1980), Pischke (1995).

Consumption and total income for agent i are obtained by straightforward application of formulas in Section 13.3. Consumption is

$$\Delta c_t^i = a^i(\beta)\eta_t^i \tag{13.13'}$$

while total income is

$$\Delta x_t^i = h^i(L)\eta_t^i, \tag{13.15'}$$

where

$$h^i(L) = \frac{\beta a^i(L)(1-L) - (1-\beta)a^i(\beta)L}{\beta - L}.$$

Since[14]

$$\eta_t^i = \frac{b^i(L)}{a^i(L)}u_t + \frac{c^i(L)}{a^i(L)}\xi_t^i, \tag{13.21}$$

we obtain

$$\Delta c_t^i = \frac{a^i(\beta)b^i(L)}{a^i(L)}u_t + \frac{a^i(\beta)c^i(L)}{a^i(L)}\xi_t^i. \tag{13.22}$$

As for the macromodel, we have

$$\Delta c_t = \delta(L)u_t, \tag{13.23}$$

where

$$\delta(L) = m^{-1}\sum_i a^i(\beta)b^i(L)/a^i(L).$$

Therefore consumption change is serially correlated, unless special constraints on the polynomials $a^i(L)$ and $b^i(L)$ hold. Even though no formal specification of the micromodel has been given, the reader will easily accept that such constraints correspond either to a negligible subset or to the whole population space. Aggregate total income is

$$\Delta x_t = \kappa(L)u_t, \tag{13.24}$$

where

$$\kappa(L) = m^{-1}\sum_i h^i(L)b^i(L)/a^i(L).$$

Analysis of (13.18), (13.23), and (13.24) shows that in general aggregate consumption change is correlated with past labor and total income changes. However, the signs of such correlations are ambiguous, unless we are able to make precise assumptions on the micro response functions $b^i(L)$ and $c^i(L)$. On the other hand, we know that individual labor incomes exhibit

[14] Notice that both $b^i(L)/a^i(L)$ and $c^i(L)/a^i(L)$ in (13.21) have no poles of unit modulus even when $a^i(L)$ vanishes on the unit circle. This is because if $a^i(z)$ vanishes at z^*, $|z^*| = 1$, then the spectral density function of Δy_t^i vanishes at z^*, which in turn implies that both $b^i(L)$ and $c^i(L)$ vanish at z^*.

large low-order negative autocorrelations while aggregate labor income is positively autocorrelated. The following MA(1) specification shows that microparameters consistent with the above empirical findings can produce both positive sensitivity and smoothness at the macro level.

13.6.3. Let us parameterize the micromodel in the following way. All the microparameters are common to all agents: $b^i(L) = b(L) = \lambda_1 + \lambda_2 L$, $c^i(L) = c(L) = \lambda_3 - \lambda_4 L$. Moreover, $\lambda_1, \lambda_2, \lambda_3$, and λ_4 are positive and fulfill $\lambda_1\lambda_2 < \lambda_3\lambda_4$. The last inequality ensures that $\text{cov}(\Delta y_t^i, \Delta y_{t-1}^i) < 0$, so that in the Wold representation $\Delta y_t^i = a^i(L)\eta_t^i$ we have $a^i(L) = 1 - aL$ with $a > 0$. The assumption $\lambda_1 > 0$ guarantees that Δy_t is positively autocorrelated.

Within this specification we have

$$\delta(L) = (1 - a\beta)\frac{\lambda_1 + \lambda_2 L}{1 - aL},$$

whose expansion has positive coefficients for all the powers of L. Hence $\text{cov}(\Delta c_t, \Delta c_{t-k}) > 0$ for all k and $\text{cov}(\Delta y_t, \Delta y_{t-k}) > 0$ for all k. To get some intuition for this result, consider that a positive common shock to individual incomes induces further increments in future incomes, since $\lambda_2 > 0$. Imperfectly informed consumers initially understate its long-run effect, since they observe η_t^i, whose first-impact effect is corrected downward in $t+1$. But a positive u_t induces positive changes in future univariate income innovations:

$$\eta_t^i = \frac{\lambda_1 + \lambda_2 L}{1 - aL}u_t + \frac{\lambda_3 + \lambda_4 L}{1 - aL}\xi_t^i.$$

When the latter are observed, consumption is corrected upward, so that aggregate income changes are positively correlated with the past of u_t (and hence with the past of Δc_t and Δy_t).

As regards smoothness, we have

$$\kappa(L) = (1 - a\beta L)\frac{\lambda_1 + \lambda_2 L}{1 - aL},$$

so that

$$\Delta c_t = \frac{1 - a\beta}{1 - a\beta L}\Delta x_t.$$

Therefore the spectrum of Δc_t is equal to that of Δx_t multiplied by

$$\frac{(1 - a\beta)^2}{|1 - a\beta e^{-i\phi}|^2} = \frac{(1 - a\beta)^2}{1 + a^2\beta^2 - 2a\beta\cos\phi}.$$

This expression is equal to 1 for $\phi = 0$ and less than 1 everywhere for $0 < \phi < \pi$. It follows that the spectrum of Δc_t is less than that of Δx_t for $0 < \phi < \pi$, this implying $\text{var}(\Delta c_t) < \text{var}(\Delta x_t)$.

REMARK 13.2. Notice that in the above example we have aggregation effects notwithstanding the fact that all consumers have the same parameters for the income process. The idiosyncratic shocks are sufficient to prevent the representative-agent outcome.

EXAMPLE 13.4. Assume $\lambda_1 = 1$, $\lambda_2 = 0.5$, $\lambda_3 = 2\sqrt{10}$, $\lambda_4 = \sqrt{10}$. Following the procedure in Section 4.1, the Wold representation of the micro incomes is found to be $\Delta y_t^i = (1-(6/13)L)\eta_t^i$, so that individual consumption is $\Delta c_t^i = (1-(6/13)\beta)\eta_t^i$. The first-impact effect of u_t on individual consumption is lower than in the case of perfect information. The 'error' is $(25\beta/26)u_t$, whose variance is only about 1/12 of the variance of consumption change, because of the large idiosyncratic component. This can provide a rationale for incomplete information if acquiring and/or processing information on u_t is not free. Per capita labor income is $\Delta y_t = (1+0.5L)u_t$, while per capita consumption is

$$\Delta c_t = (6.5-3\beta)\frac{1+0.5L}{6.5-3L}u_t,$$

which entails positive autocorrelation and cross-correlation with Δy_t at every lag. Total income is

$$\Delta x_t = (6.5-3\beta L)\frac{1+0.5L}{6.5-3L}u_t.$$

The variance of consumption change is about 0.63, while that of total income change is about 1.25 if β is nearly one. Hence consumption is smooth.

13.7. Micro and Macro Singularity

13.7.1. Univariate predictions have the unappealing consequence that the micromodel is singular. Moreover, it is quite plausible that individuals possess and use more information than the present and past of their income alone in predicting their future labor income stream. By adding idiosyncratic shocks without altering macro information, we can easily avoid micro singularity, while retaining for the macromodel exactly the same results as in the previous section. This is so because, as already observed, the macromodel is not affected by information exclusively involving the idiosyncratic component.

Let us assume that the labor income of agent i is driven by two mutually orthogonal idiosyncratic shocks:

$$\Delta y_t^i = b^i(L)u_t + c^i(L)\xi_t^i + \theta^i(L)\psi_t^i.$$

We also assume for simplicity that $\theta^i(L)$ is fundamental.

The consumer can see Δy_t^i and the component $\theta^i(L)\psi_t^i$ (or, which is the same, the shock ψ_t^i). In other words, the consumer observes the component $b^i(L)u_t + c^i(L)\xi_t^i$, but cannot distinguish the two terms $b^i(L)u_t$ and $c^i(L)\xi_t^i$. We can assume for instance that ψ_t^i is transitory, while both u_t and ξ_t^i are permanent; the consumer can discriminate between the transitory and the permanent components of his, or her, labor income, but cannot discern the common and the idiosyncratic parts of the permanent component.

With these assumptions, the relevant model for prediction is

$$\Delta y_t^i = a^i(L)\eta_t^i + \theta^i(L)\psi_t^i,$$

where $a^i(L)\eta_t^i$ is the Wold representation of $b^i(L)u_t + c^i(L)\xi_t^i$ as in Section 13.6, with η_t^i given by (13.21). Individual consumption is

$$\Delta c_t^i = a^i(\beta)\eta_t^i + \theta^i(\beta)\psi_t^i = \frac{a^i(\beta)b^i(L)}{a^i(L)}u_t + \frac{a^i(\beta)c^i(L)}{a^i(L)}\xi_t^i + \theta^i(\beta)\psi_t^i.$$

Therefore income and consumption are no longer singular in the micromodel.

REMARK 13.3. Notice that, besides singularity, bivariate information destroys cointegration of consumption and labor income unless $a^i(1)\theta^i(\beta) = a^i(\beta)\theta^i(1)$. This result can be easily extended to the case of $h > 1$ common shocks. In non-singular micromodels labor income and consumption are not cointegrated. We shall return to this point later.

The common components of both labor income and consumption are unchanged with respect to the model in Section 13.6, so that the macromodel for labor income and consumption is still given by equations (13.18) and (13.23). Hence, in spite of micro non-singularity, the macromodel is still singular. We have already seen a similar outcome in Section 13.5. With complete information, individual variables are non-singular, whereas aggregate variables are singular.

13.7.2. Until now we have maintained the unrealistic assumption that micro incomes are driven by only one common shock. Though useful for showing the effects of aggregation on the volatility and the correlation properties of consumption, this assumption must be relaxed in order to obtain macro non-singularity and analyze cointegration. To make things simple we shall drop the second idiosyncratic shock and assume only two common shocks. Results can be easily extended to the general case of h common shocks. Under these assumptions individual labor income becomes

$$\Delta y_t^i = b_1^i(L)u_{1t} + b_2^i(L)u_{2t} + c^i(L)\xi_t^i, \tag{13.25}$$

so that per capita labor income is

$$\Delta y_t = b_1(L)u_{1t} + b_2(L)u_{2t}, \tag{13.26}$$

where $b_1(L) = m^{-1} \sum_i b_1^i(L)$ and $b_2(L) = m^{-1} \sum_i b_2^i(L)$.

We assume univariate predictions, having in mind that adding idiosyncratic information would not alter our macro results. Once again the micromodel for prediction is the Wold representation

$$\Delta y_t^i = a^i(L)\eta_t^i,$$

where now $a^i(L)$ and η_t^i are found by solving

$$a^i(L)\eta_t^i = b_1^i(L)u_{1t} + b_2^i(L)u_{2t} + c^i(L)\xi_t^i. \tag{13.27}$$

Individual consumption and total income are still given by equations (13.13′) and (13.15′). By substituting for η_t^i from (13.27) and averaging over individuals we get

$$\Delta c_t = \delta_1(L)u_{1t} + \delta_2(L)u_{2t}, \tag{13.28}$$

where

$$\delta_l(L) = m^{-1} \sum_i a^i(\beta) b_l^i(L)/a^i(L), \qquad l = 1, 2;$$

and

$$\Delta x_t = \kappa_1(L)u_{1t} + \kappa_2(L)u_{2t}, \tag{13.29}$$

where

$$\kappa_l(L) = m^{-1} \sum_i h^i(L) b_l^i(L)/a^i(L), \qquad l = 1, 2,$$

$h^i(L)$ being as in (13.15′).

Now let us consider the matrix of the response functions for consumption and labor income changes obtained from (13.28) and (13.26):

$$m^{-1} \begin{pmatrix} \sum a^i(\beta) b_1^i(L)/a^i(L) & \sum a^i(\beta) b_2^i(L)/a^i(L) \\ \sum b_1^i(L) & \sum b_2^i(L) \end{pmatrix}. \tag{13.30}$$

In general the rows are not proportional, so that the aggregate model is non-singular. More precisely, we can apply Theorem 8.3 here. If the common shocks are non-redundant and $a^i(\beta)/a^i(L)$ is not constant in the microparameter space Γ, then the vector $(\,\Delta c_t \quad \Delta y_t\,)$ is non-singular almost everywhere in the population space Γ_m. Moreover, it is seen from (13.27) that $a^i(\beta)/a^i(L)$ cannot be constant in Γ, unless we force $c^i(L)$ to compensate for the differences in the ratio $b_1^i(L)/b_2^i(L)$ implied by non-redundancy. Hence, in spite of micro singularity, non-singular macrovariables are achieved if the common component of individual labor income is driven by at least two non-redundant shocks.

The model above and that in 13.7.1 have opposite outcomes. In the former aggregation produces non-singularity, while in the latter non-singular microvariables sum up to singular macrovariables. This is so because micro singularity and macro singularity have quite different causes. Micro singularity is linked to the dimension of the information space. When information is one-dimensional we have singularity, while non-singularity is obtained by multivariate information. Obviously, the same is true at the macro level within representative-agent models. By contrast, when heterogeneity is assumed, macro singularity is linked to the number of common shocks. If there is only one common shock we have singularity, whereas when $h > 1$ singularity is unlikely.

13.8. Reconciling PIH and ECM

Let us analyze cointegration within the model with two common shocks. We can distinguish two cases. Firstly, $b_1^i(1) \neq 0$, $b_2^i(1) = 0$, for all i. In this case, the determinant of (13.30) vanishes for $L = 1$, implying that aggregate consumption and labor income are cointegrated. The reason for this is that in the micromodel both income and consumption are driven by only one common permanent shock (see Theorem 9.3, case (a)). The fact that labor income and consumption are cointegrated in the micromodel, owing to singularity, does not play any role in determining macro cointegration. As noted in Remark 13.3, the addition of a second idiosyncratic shock would imply non-cointegration in the micromodel without changing (13.30). The interesting point here is that we may have non-cointegrated microvariables aggregating to cointegrated macrovariables, via cancellation of idiosyncratic trends (see Section 9.1.2).

The second case is when both u_{1t} and u_{2t} have a permanent effect. Aggregate consumption and labor income are not cointegrated, unless the parameters of individual incomes take on very particular values. More precisely, by Theorem 9.3, if Γ is specified in such a way that neither $b_1^i(1)/b_2^i(1)$ nor $a^i(\beta)/a^i(1)$ are constant in Γ, then macro cointegration occurs only for a negligible subset of Γ_m.

Unlike consumption and labor income, consumption and total income are cointegrated independently of the number of common permanent shocks. Indeed, equations (13.28) and (13.29) give the bivariate MA representation

$$\begin{pmatrix} \Delta c_t \\ \Delta x_t \end{pmatrix} = \begin{pmatrix} \delta_1(L) & \delta_2(L) \\ \kappa_1(L) & \kappa_2(L) \end{pmatrix} \begin{pmatrix} u_{1t} \\ u_{2t} \end{pmatrix}. \tag{13.31}$$

We have

$$\delta_1(1) = \kappa_1(1) = m^{-1} \sum_i a_i(\beta) b_1^i(1)/a^i(1)$$

$$\delta_2(1) = \kappa_2(1) = m^{-1} \sum_i a^i(\beta) b_2^i(1)/a^i(1).$$

Hence, Δc_t and Δx_t are cointegrated with cointegrating vector $(1 \quad -1)$.[15] Cointegration is preserved in the macromodel because the cointegrating vectors are the same for all consumers (see Theorem 9.3, case (b)). Put another way, aggregation preserves stationarity of saving, along with difference–stationarity of consumption and total income.

Looking back at the results in the previous sections, we can conclude that stationarity of savings is the sole property of the representative-agent PIH model which is retained when both heterogeneity and incomplete information are assumed. Since consumption is no longer a random walk orthogonal to past income changes, the ECM implied by the PIH under heterogeneity and incomplete information has a general dynamic shape, i.e. the coefficients appearing in the consumption equation are not necessarily all zero, as is the case when the representative agent is assumed. As a consequence, the ECM model of consumption and the PIH are reconciled. In order to fill the often-lamented lack of theoretical grounds for the ECM model of consumption we do not need to resort to adjustment costs in the consumer's objective function as is done by Salmon (1982) and Nickell (1985). Heterogeneous, imperfectly informed PIH consumers can provide the desired microfoundation.

13.9. An Empirical Exercise

As we have seen in Section 13.2, US savings are stationary within the period 1964:1 to 1991:4, so that one might be tempted to estimate model (13.31) over this period. However, two difficulties arise. Firstly, as shown in Chapter 2, evidence from regional data suggests that micro incomes are driven by more than two common shocks. This problem could be solved by shifting to the regional model proposed in Chapter 3, where two macroeconomic shocks seem sufficient. The second difficulty is that, as shown in Chapter 4, the microparameters are not identified, unless we are able to impose a good deal of structure on the joint distribution of the microparameters amongst agents. Unfortunately, existing empirical studies on micro data are useless for the latter purpose, owing to their poor specification of heterogeneity and dynamics.

Hence we are not able to construct a model providing a convincing representation for the microvariables. Nevertheless, it can be useful to show that model (13.31) can reproduce the correlation properties of US macro income and consumption. For this unpretentious aim, the following exer-

[15] Going back to (13.30), notice that the determinant vanishes for $L = \beta < 1$, so that (13.28)–(13.26) cannot be a fundamental representation for labor income and consumption. By contrast, the determinant of the matrix in (13.31) does not vanish for $L = \beta$. Indeed, the determinant is $\beta(1 - L)/(\beta - L)$ times the determinant of (13.30), so that it has exactly the same roots except for β, which is replaced by 1.

cise, in which the two-common-shocks assumption is retained and highly artificial identifying restrictions are imposed, will be sufficient.

We assume that there are two types of workers (for instance, self-employed and employees): let us call them A and B. The income of type A workers responds only to u_{1t}, whereas the income of type B workers responds only to u_{2t}. We have

$$\Delta y_t^i = \frac{1}{1 - b^A L} u_{1t} + c^A(L)\xi_t^i$$

if i belongs to type A and

$$\Delta y_t^i = \frac{1}{1 - b^B L} u_{2t} + c^B(L)\xi_t^i$$

if i belongs to group B. For simplicity of notation we do not assume here unitary variance of the shocks and normalize by assuming unitary leading coefficients.

The idiosyncratic components are assumed to be such that the univariate Wold representations are

$$\Delta y_t^i = (1 - a^A L)\eta_t^i$$
$$\Delta y_t^i = (1 - a^B L)\eta_t^i,$$

for type A and type B respectively, where b^A, a^A, b^B, and a^B are, according to empirical findings, all positive and less than unity.

The resulting joint model of aggregate consumption and total income is

$$\begin{pmatrix} \Delta c_t \\ \Delta x_t \end{pmatrix} = \begin{pmatrix} \dfrac{1 - a^A\beta}{(1 - a^A L)(1 - b^A L)} & \dfrac{1 - a^B\beta}{(1 - a^B L)(1 - b^B L)} \\ \dfrac{1 - a^A\beta L}{(1 - a^A L)(1 - b^A L)} & \dfrac{1 - a^B\beta L}{(1 - a^B L)(1 - b^B L)} \end{pmatrix} \begin{pmatrix} p_t \\ q_t \end{pmatrix}, \tag{13.32}$$

where $p_t = (M/m)u_{1t}$, $q_t = [(m - M)/m]u_{2t}$, M and $m - M$ being the numbers of type A and B agents respectively. The implied ECM is

$$\begin{pmatrix} 1 - \delta_1 L - \delta_2 L^2 & -\theta L \\ -\phi_1 L - \phi_2 L^2 & 1 - \psi L \end{pmatrix} \begin{pmatrix} \Delta c_t \\ \Delta x_t \end{pmatrix} = \begin{pmatrix} \mu \\ \nu \end{pmatrix} s_{t-1} + \begin{pmatrix} v_t \\ w_t \end{pmatrix}, \tag{13.33}$$

where

$$\delta_1 = \frac{(1 - a^A\beta)(a^B b^A \beta + a^A a^B \beta + a^A b^A - a^A a^B b^A \beta)}{\beta(a^B - a^A)} - \frac{(1 - a^B\beta)(a^A b^B \beta + a^A a^B \beta + a^B b^B - a^A a^B b^B \beta)}{\beta(a^B - a^A)}$$

$$\delta_2 = \frac{(1-a^B\beta)a^A a^B b^B - (1-a^A\beta)a^A a^B b^A}{a^B - a^A}$$

$$\theta = -\frac{(1-a^A\beta)(1-a^B\beta)(a^A b^A - a^B b^B)}{\beta(a^B - a^A)}$$

$$\phi_1 = -\psi + \frac{b^A a^B - a^A b^B}{a^B - a^A}$$

$$\phi_2 = \frac{a^A a^B (b^B - b^A)}{a^B - a^A}$$

$$\psi = \frac{(1-a^A\beta)a^B b^B - (1-a^B\beta)a^A b^A}{\beta(a^B - a^A)}$$

$$\mu = \frac{(1-a^A\beta)(1-a^B\beta)[(1-a^A)(1-b^A) - (1-a^B)(1-b^B)]}{\beta(a^B - a^A)}$$

$$\nu = \frac{(1-a^B\beta)(1-a^A)(1-b^A) - (1-a^A\beta)(1-a^B)(1-b^B)}{\beta(a^B - a^A)},$$

and

$$\begin{pmatrix} v_t \\ w_t \end{pmatrix} = \begin{pmatrix} (1-a^A\beta)p_t + (1-a^B\beta)q_t \\ p_t + q_t \end{pmatrix}.$$

We estimated model (13.32), which is equivalent to estimating (13.33) under the restrictions implied by the functional relationships listed above. We also estimated model (13.33) without restrictions and with the restrictions implied by the PIH in its representative-agent version, i.e. $\delta_1 = \delta_2 = \theta = \mu = 0$. The parameter β was fixed at 0.99, which implies a quarterly real interest rate near to 1%. The results are reported in Table 13.6.

The first column shows the estimates for the parameters of model (13.32) obtained when using c_t and x_t, along with the implied parameters of model (13.33). The second column shows the estimates for the free model (13.33). The third column shows the estimates for Campbell's representative-agent ECM. Table 13.7 shows the same estimates when using c_t' and x_t'.

Excess sensitivity is clearly confirmed. The restrictions implied by the representative-agent version of the PIH model are rejected by both data sets. Rejection is very strong when using the second (and more interesting) data set. The LR test gives a probability value of less than 0.001.

Model (13.32) fits the data notably better, especially with c_t' and x_t'. The only shortcoming is the significantly negative estimate of the parameter a^A both using c_t, x_t, and using c_t', x_t', so that the negative autocorrelation for micro incomes, observed in empirical data, holds for only one of the groups. Model (13.32) cannot be rejected against the free model by the LR test at the 5% level with the second data set, and at the 2.5% level with the first.

REMARK 13.4. It must be pointed out that in this exercise we have somewhat modified our attitude toward the population space, as compared to

Table 13.6. Estimates of (13.32), free ECM, and Campbell's representative-agent ECM with c_t, x_t (standard errors in brackets)

	Model (13.32)	Free ECM	Campbell's ECM
b^A	0.62 (0.09)		
a^A	−0.47 (0.09)		
b^B	−0.08 (0.10)		
a^B	0.93 (0.04)		
$10^3\sigma_P^2$	0.16 (0.03)		
$10^3\sigma_Q^2$	0.53 (0.07)		
δ_1	0.15	0.18 (0.10)	—
δ_2	0.28	0.14 (0.10)	—
θ	0.02	0.08 (0.08)	—
ϕ_1	0.45	0.42 (0.13)	0.33 (0.13)
ϕ_2	0.22	0.02 (0.13)	−0.05 (0.12)
ψ	−0.07	0.04 (0.10)	0.00 (0.09)
μ	0.04	0.02 (0.04)	—
ν	−0.05	−0.15 (0.06)	−0.16 (0.05)
$10^3\sigma_v^2$	0.33	0.31 (0.04)	0.35 (0.05)
$10^3\sigma_w^2$	0.68	0.53 (0.07)	0.53 (0.07)
$10^3\sigma_{vw}$	0.27	0.16 (0.04)	0.17 (0.05)
LR Statistic	12.2	—	12.0
$\chi^2_{0.05}$	11.1	—	9.5
Restrictions	5	—	4

Parameters δ_1, δ_2, θ, and μ are restricted to zero in Campbell's model.

Part II. There we assumed the largest population space. Here we have sacrificed generality for the possibility of identification. Unfortunately we do not possess independent information on the distribution of the microparameters to justify our assumption. Therefore the exercise must be interpreted as showing that if information leading to sufficient restrictions could be acquired, then nothing in principle would prevent estimation of the microparameter distribution underlying the aggregate data.

13.10. Bibliographic Notes

For a comprehensive treatment of the PIH see Deaton (1992). A partial list of prominent theoretical and empirical contributions includes Hall (1978), Flavin (1981), Davidson and Hendry (1981), Galí (1991), Hall and Mishkin (1982), Hayashi (1985), Stock and West (1988), West (1988a), Campbell and Deaton (1989), Zeldes (1989), Runkle (1991), Attanasio and Weber (1992), in addition to the works quoted below.

Table 13.7. Estimates of (13.32), free ECM, and Campbell's representative-agent ECM with c_t', x_t' (standard errors in brackets)

	Model (13.32)	Free ECM	Campbell's ECM
b^A	0.65 (0.09)		
a^A	−0.28 (0.11)		
b^B	0.00 (0.10)		
a^B	0.95 (0.03)		
$10^3\sigma_P^2$	0.06 (0.01)		
$10^3\sigma_Q^2$	0.55 (0.08)		
δ_1	0.36	0.41 (0.10)	—
δ_2	0.18	0.10 (0.10)	—
θ	0.01	0.01 (0.04)	—
ϕ_1	0.49	0.79 (0.24)	0.45 (0.24)
ϕ_2	0.14	−0.13 (0.24)	−0.21 (0.22)
ψ	0.01	0.09 (0.10)	0.08 (0.09)
μ	0.03	0.01 (0.02)	—
ν	−0.03	−0.17 (0.05)	−0.17 (0.05)
$10^3\sigma_v^2$	0.09	0.09 (0.01)	0.12 (0.02)
$10^3\sigma_w^2$	0.61	0.53 (0.07)	0.55 (0.08)
$10^3\sigma_{vw}$	0.11	0.08 (0.02)	0.10 (0.03)
LR Statistic	10.8	—	28.7
$\chi^2_{0.05}$	11.1	—	9.5
Restrictions	5	—	4

Parameters δ_1, δ_2, θ, and μ are restricted to zero in Campbell's model.

Major references for ECM, cointegration, and consumption are Davidson *et al.* (1978), Salmon (1982), Nickell (1985), Engle and Granger (1987). Cointegration in the PIH model was firstly noticed by Campbell (1987).

Singularity of the PIH representative-agent model has received little attention in the literature; see, however, Sargent (1989), Hansen and Sargent (1991b), Quah (1990), Forni and Lippi (1994).

The debate on consumption volatility was originated by Deaton (1987); the discussion in Section 13.4 is partly based on Forni (1996). The argument to show that superior information reduces consumption volatility is due to West (1988b). Quah (1990) claims that excess smoothness is explained by allowing for multivariate prediction. With similar arguments Christiano and Eichenbaum (1990) assert that income persistence is not related to consumption volatility. Both claims are not true when Deaton's paradox is reformulated as in Section 13.4.

Section 13.6 was inspired by Lippi (1990), Goodfriend (1992), and Pischke (1995). A different line of research introducing heterogeneity in consumption theory is based on overlapping generations; important refer-

ences are Clarida (1991), Galí (1990), Attanasio and Weber (1991).
Sections 13.7, 13.8, and 13.9 are based on Forni and Lippi (1994).

14

Disaggregating the Business Cycle

In this chapter, the method introduced in Chapter 3 is applied to a data set on the output and productivity of 450 American industries from 1958 to 1986. The objective is to learn about both the sources and the manifestation of the business cycle.

It is found that two common shocks provide a fairly adequate description of the comovements of the 450 sectors. A criterion to identify the technology shock from the bivariate vector of common shocks is proposed, based on the innocuous idea that shocks to technology are mainly positive. This suggests an identifying restriction, namely that the technology shock is that for which the absolute sum of the negative realizations is minimized.

Estimation of a bivariate MA model of cross-sectional average output and productivity indicates that the aggregate technology shock explains 55% of the variance of output and 93% of the variance of productivity at the macro level.

In order to identify the nature of the business cycle, positive and negative comovements among common shocks at business cycle frequencies are analyzed. In addition, a measure of the importance of substitution effects among sectors is proposed.

Both the technology shock and the other common shock produce positive comovements of output at business cycle frequencies. However, in the long run the technology shock has mainly substitution effects, while the other shock has mainly complementarity effects.

These findings are compatible with a view of the business cycle whereby some of the cyclical fluctuations are real, but at least one other common shock is important.

14.1. The Number of Common Shocks

Let us start from the following dynamic factor model

$$\Delta x_t^i = \alpha^i(L)u_t + \beta^i(L)\xi_{xt}^i \tag{14.1}$$

$$\Delta p_t^i = \gamma^i(L)u_t + \delta^i(L)\xi_{pt}^i, \tag{14.2}$$

where x_t^i and p_t^i are the log of output and labor productivity respectively; labor productivity is defined as the log of output minus the log of hours worked; $i = 1, m$ is the index for sectors; $\alpha^i(L)$, $\beta^i(L)$, $\gamma^i(L)$, and $\delta^i(L)$ are vectors of rational functions in the lag operator L.

The model has the following features:

(1) u_t is an h-dimensional white-noise vector of shocks common to productivity and output.

(2) ξ_{xt}^i and ξ_{pt}^i are two vectors of white-noise shocks which are sector and variable specific.

(3) All shocks have unit variance and are mutually orthogonal at all leads and lags.

Before estimating the model, we must identify the number h of common shocks. We employed the method introduced in Section 3.2. Precisely, we partitioned the set $\{1, \ldots, 450\}$ into the subsets $\{1, \ldots, 150\}$, $\{151, \ldots, 300\}$, and $\{301, \ldots, 450\}$. Then we formed a six-dimensional vector Y_t by taking, for each subset, the simple averages of output and productivity. We then estimated, for $r = 1, 6$, the ratios

$$\frac{\sum_{s=1}^{r} \mu_s(\phi)}{\sum_{s=1}^{6} \mu_s(\phi)},$$

where $\mu_s(\phi)$ is the spectral density of the s-th principal component of Y_t (see Section 2.5).[1]

Results are reported in Figure 14.1. The first principal component explains less than 95% of the variance of the aggregates in Y_t at all frequencies and only about 80% at low and high frequencies. By contrast, the first two principal components account for more than 95% of total variance at both long-run and cyclical frequencies. For $r = 2$, the overall measure of fit given by the ratio

$$\frac{\int_0^\pi \sum_{s=1}^{r} \mu_s(\phi) d\phi}{\int_0^\pi \sum_{s=1}^{6} \mu_s(\phi) d\phi}$$

is 0.954. From this we conclude that a model with two common shocks can provide a suitable description of our data set.

14.2. Identification of the Common Technology Shock

Having found that the number of common shocks is two, we estimated by maximum likelihood the common shocks by jointly modeling average output and productivity with an MA(2) specification.

[1] The spectra were estimated by using a Bartlett window with lag window size equal to five.

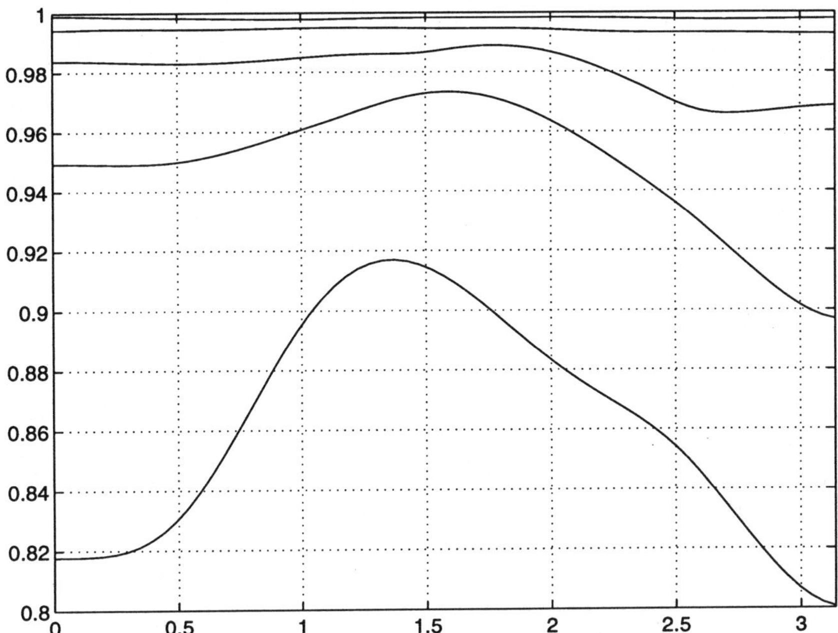

Fig. 14.1. Variance of Y_t explained by the first two principal components at different frequencies

This strategy differs from the usual estimation of VAR models. The reason why we choose an MA model, in spite of a more difficult estimation procedure, is that the MA shape, unlike the AR shape, is preserved by aggregation, as shown in Chapter 4. Thus the model in this section and the one in the next are perfectly consistent.

Regarding identification, let us briefly return to the procedure that we have already recalled in Sections 3.4 and 12.1 (see also Section A.6 in the Appendix). Define $\Delta x_t = m^{-1} \sum_i \Delta x_t^i$, $\Delta p_t = m^{-1} \sum_i \Delta p_t^i$, and $z_t = [\Delta x_t \quad \Delta p_t]'$. Let

$$z_t = A(L) w_t$$

be a fundamental representation of z_t with w_t orthonormal. If the structural representation were

$$z_t = B(L) u_t,$$

with u_t and $B(L)$ fundamental, then $B(L)u_t = [A(L)S][S^{-1}w_t]$, where

$$S = \begin{pmatrix} \sin\theta & \cos\theta \\ -\cos\theta & \sin\theta \end{pmatrix}.$$

Here we propose to choose the value of θ for which one of the components of u_t, labeled technology, has minimum absolute sum of negative values. In

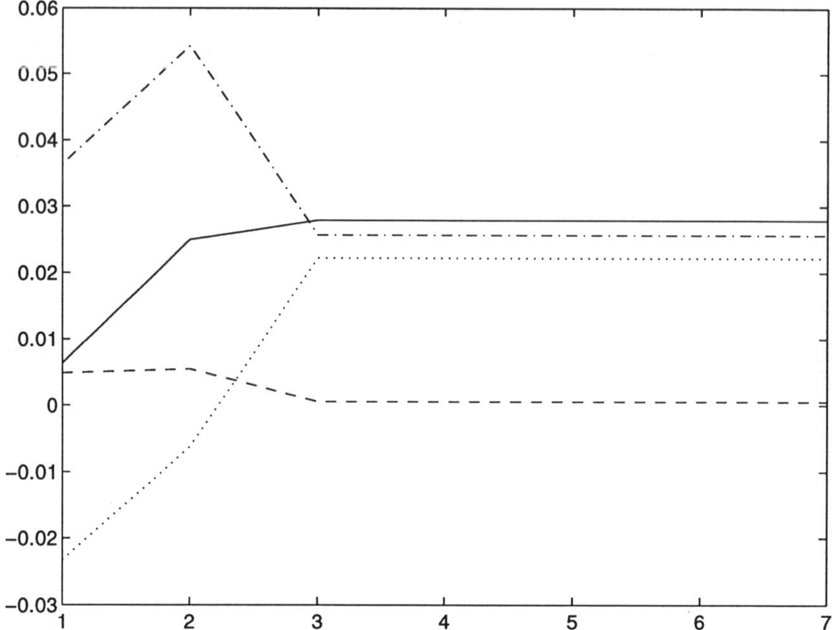

Fig. 14.2. Impulse response functions: our identification
u_t^{NT} on output: dotted–dashed line. u_t^T on productivity: solid line. u_t^{NT} on productivity: dashed line. u_t^T on output: dotted line.

the absence of precise theoretical restrictions, this assumption seems less controversial than the common one of long-run demand neutrality and corresponds to the observation that technology shocks are generally positive.

Let us denote by u_t^T the shock to technology and by u_t^{NT} the other shock. Then define u_t^{T-} as equal to u_t^T if $u_t^T \leq 0$, and equal to zero if $u_t^T > 0$. Put

$$g = \sum_t \mid u_t^{T-} \mid .$$

Our identification strategy corresponds to choosing θ so as to minimize g.[2]

Results are reported in Figure 14.2. Given our identification restrictions, the picture emerging from aggregate estimates is one whereby the common technology shock has a long-run positive effect on both output and productivity, but affects output negatively in the short run. This suggests that when innovations in technology occur, firms reorganize their production process so that in the first year output will grow less than on average.

[2] Note that $z_t = B(L)u_t = B(1)\alpha + B(L)(u_t - \alpha)$, where $\alpha = \mathrm{E}u_t$. If the elements of z_t are not cointegrated $B(1)$ is invertible and $\alpha = B(1)^{-1}\mathrm{E}z_t$. Therefore, given θ, we can identify $u_t - \alpha$ and $B(L)$, while from $B(L)$ we can identify α and u_t.

Productivity, however, even in the first year, grows faster than on average because of the immediate negative impact that the technology innovation has on the demand for labor.

Variance decomposition results indicate that the technological component explains the main bulk, 93%, of the variance of productivity, and 55% of the variance of output. Hence, for aggregate productivity, cyclical fluctuations can only be originated by technology innovations.

It should be observed that the shape of the impulse of the technology shock on productivity reproduces the S shape that has been used in the literature to describe slow diffusion of the innovation throughout the economy (see e.g. Griliches, 1957; Mansfield, 1973; Jovanovic and Lach, 1989, 1990). This should be taken as informal support for our method of identification of the technology shock.[3]

As described, the focus of our identification strategy has been on the technology shock, while we cannot give an economic meaning to the other shock. From the analysis of its dynamic effect, we get a confusing picture. It has an almost neutral long-run effect on productivity (dashed line), but a positive one on output (dotted–dashed line). If we interpreted it as 'demand', we would have to claim that demand is non-neutral with respect to output in the long run because of some hysteresis effects; an explanation based on increasing returns, on the other hand, would contradict the long-run neutrality on productivity.

An alternative explanation would be that the shock represents the effect of hours worked, i.e. it is a shock to supply of labor. To check for this explanation we computed correlation coefficients between the shock and the 450 sectoral rates of growth of real wages. We found that 92% of the correlations are positive, which indicates that either we cannot interpret the shock as supply of labor or the standard view of the labor market, characterized by a positive-sloped supply of labor and a negative-sloped demand for labor, is not correct.

A third possibility is suggested by the findings in King *et al.* (1991), which indicate that real interest rate shocks are an important source of permanent fluctuations in output. To check whether we can interpret the second shock as a real interest rate shock we computed the correlation between our non-technology shock and the real interest rate, but we found it to be insignificant.

[3] In the present exercise we obtain the S shape as an empirical result. An alternative strategy would have been to follow Lippi and Reichlin (1994b) and identify the technology shock as the shock with an S-shaped impulse by minimizing the distance between the empirical impulse and an S-shaped function.

14.3. Estimation of the Sectoral Model

Having identified u_t, we are now in a position to estimate its dynamic impact over time and compare it across the different sectors. To capture the notion of slow diffusion of technology shocks across firms we impose, consistently with the aggregate model, an MA(2) structure for the two common components:

$$\Delta x_t^i = [\psi_{0x}^i + \psi_{1x}^i L + \psi_{2x}^i L^2]u_t^T + [\phi_{0x}^i + \phi_{1x}^i L + \phi_{2x}^i L^2]u_t^{NT} + \chi_{xt}^i \quad (14.3)$$

$$\Delta p_t^i = [\psi_{0p}^i + \psi_{1p}^i L + \psi_{2p}^i L^2]u_t^T + [\phi_{0p}^i + \phi_{1p}^i L + \phi_{2p}^i L^2]u_t^{NT} + \chi_{pt}^i. \quad (14.4)$$

Since χ_{xt}^i and χ_{pt}^i, the sectoral components, are orthogonal to $u_t = [u_t^T \quad u_t^{NT}]$, and the latter is common to all sectors, we can estimate (14.3) and (14.4) equation by equation by OLS.

Some questions are in order. Firstly, how important is the common dynamic component of output and productivity, and are the comovements between sectoral outputs mainly positive or negative? The answers should give us an idea of the relative role of the substitution versus the complementarity effects of the two shocks. Secondly, what is the relationship between technical change and sectoral growth? These problems will be addressed in the next two subsections.

14.3.1. Firstly, we want to assess the relative importance of the common component. Our results indicate that productivity has a larger sectoral component than output. Figure 14.3 reports the distribution (normalized to have area equal to one) of the adjusted R^2 for the 450 regressions of, respectively, sectoral output (dashed line) and sectoral productivity (solid line) against the common shocks. The mean of the adjusted R^2 for these regressions is 0.30 for output and 0.14 for productivity.

Several studies have indicated that the bulk of output and productivity dynamics is explained by sectoral reallocation and not by fluctuations associated with the business cycle (see, e.g., Lilien, 1982). Sectoral reallocation effects should generate negative comovements amongst sectors. Therefore, a natural way to quantify their contribution to fluctuations is to measure the importance of negative comovements over positive comovements in the common dynamic component.

The real business cycle literature has shown that positive comovements at business cycle frequencies can be generated by technology shocks. Moreover, in a multi-sector model Long and Plosser (1983) have suggested that sectoral shocks propagate through input–output linkages. Such a model would predict that the technology shock generates positive comovements at business cycle frequencies and negative comovements in the long run (substitution or reallocation effects). In a monetary model *à la* Lucas (1972),

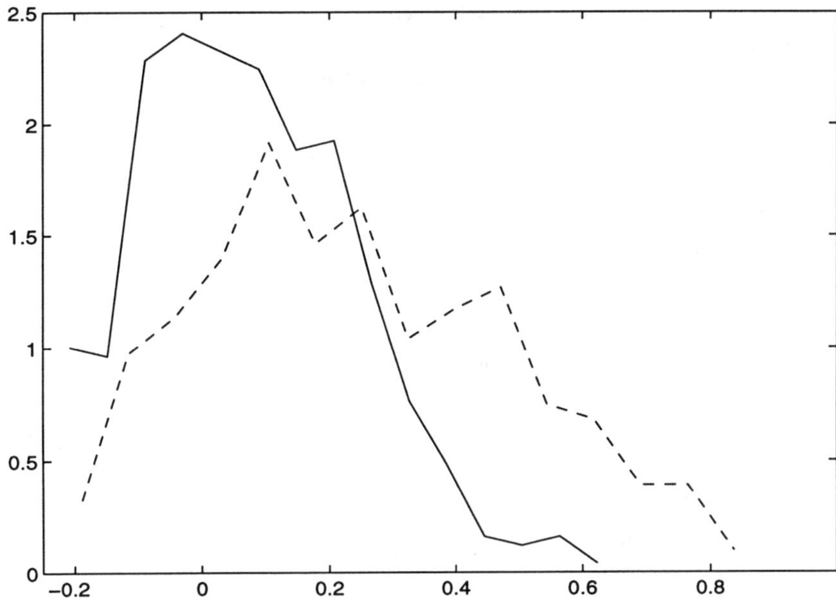

Fig. 14.3. Cross-sectional distribution of adjusted R^2
Output: dashed line. Productivity: solid line.

instead, we would have positive comovements at business cycle frequencies generated by a common monetary shock and substitution effects in the long run. Positive comovements at business cycle frequencies generated by the demand shock would also be predicted by models such as those suggested by Murphy *et al.* (1989) or Cooper and Haltiwanger (1990), whereby sectoral shocks propagate through aggregate demand spillovers and inventories (demand complementarities generated by sectoral shocks). For these models, positive comovements may also prevail in the long run.

A measure of complementarity and substitution effects can be constructed by looking at the spectral density of our panel of sectoral output growth rates and computing the ratio between the sum of the negative values of the co-spectra and the sum of their positive values for different frequencies. This will give us an index of the importance of positive covariances amongst sectors relative to negative covariances. To illustrate our method let us consider an m-dimensional vector y_t of sectoral variables, where $y_t^i = a^i(L)v_t$. Let $S(\phi)$ be the spectral density matrix of y_t. The real part of the off-diagonal elements of this matrix are the co-spectra between the different sectors, which give us information about the cross-correlations between sectors at all frequencies. The co-spectrum is defined as

$$s^{ij}(\phi) = \sum_{k=-\infty}^{\infty} c_k^{ij} \cos(\phi k),$$

where c_k^{ij} is the covariance at lag k between y_t^i and y_t^j. Let us now decompose $s^{ij}(\phi)$ as

$$s^{ij}(\phi) = s^{ij}(\phi)_- + s^{ij}(\phi)_+,$$

where

$$s^{ij}(\phi)_- = [s^{ij}(\phi) - |s^{ij}(\phi)|]/2$$

is the negative co-spectrum at frequency ϕ, and

$$s^{ij}(\phi)_+ = [| \, s^{ij}(\phi) \, | + s^{ij}(\phi)]/2$$

is the positive co-spectrum at frequency ϕ. Our proposed measure of the substitution effect of the common shock v_t on the variables in y_t is the ratio

$$\mathcal{C}(\phi) = -\frac{\sum_{i,j} s^{ij}(\phi)_-}{\sum_{i,j} s^{ij}(\phi)_+}. \tag{14.5}$$

Obviously $\mathcal{C}(\phi) \geq 0$. Moreover, the numerator cannot be greater in modulus than the denominator since

$$\sum_{i,j} s^{ij}(\phi)_- + \sum_{i,j} s^{ij}(\phi)_+$$

is equal to the sum of the entries of $S(\phi)$, i.e. the spectrum of $\sum_i y_t^i$, and therefore cannot be negative. Hence $0 \leq \mathcal{C}(\phi) \leq 1$.

We computed $\mathcal{C}(\phi)$ taking as y_t firstly the common technological component, and secondly the non-technological. Figure 14.4 reports separately the numerator and the denominator of (14.5) for the technology shock and the non-technology shock. The figure illustrates nicely the business cycle features of our data: positive co-spectra have peaks at business cycle frequencies, whereas negative co-spectra are rather flat.

Figure 14.5 reports the ratio $\mathcal{C}(\phi)$ for both the components. The picture emerging is one where technology innovations generate strong negative comovements at low and high frequencies, but induce positive comovements at business cycle frequencies. These results tell us that some source of positive comovements, traditionally associated with the business cycle, is indeed real and that in the long run substitution effects dominate. The other shock has stronger substitution effects in the short run, but generates mainly complementary fluctuations in the long run. Since we have been unable to label this shock, the result is hard to interpret; however, we can say that in the long run there are externalities which are not supply driven.

14.3.2. What is the mechanism that links technological change and growth? Some light on the propagation mechanism may come from the identification of the sectors with the strongest correlation between output growth rates

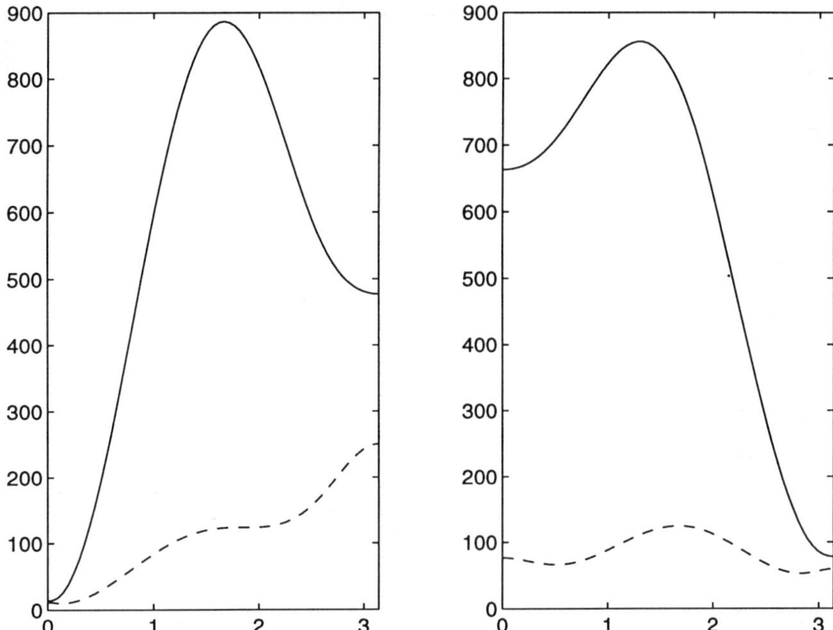

Fig. 14.4. Absolute sum of positive and negative co-spectra. Technological component: left. Non-technological component: right
Positive co-spectra: solid lines. Negative co-spectra: dashed lines.

and the common technological component. Table 14.1 reports the 20 sectors with the highest R^2.

These core sectors are mainly in the industrial machinery and equipment goods group and in primary and fabricated metals, i.e. they are concentrated in sectors producing investment in capital goods and their inputs. This result is consistent with what was noted by De Long and Summers (1991, 1992) who found a strong link between equipment investment and output growth for a broad cross-section of nations; they interpreted this as indicating the presence of externalities in the activity of the equipment investment sectors. Our results, as De Long and Summers's, suggest a view of the propagation of technology innovations which is quite different from that suggested by a real business cycle–Solow growth model. In that framework, the technological innovation is identified with total factor productivity and is purely exogenous. On the contrary, a strong positive correlation between technology innovations and the rate of growth of those key sectors indicates that new technology, requiring new capital goods, is embodied in capital and propagates through investment.

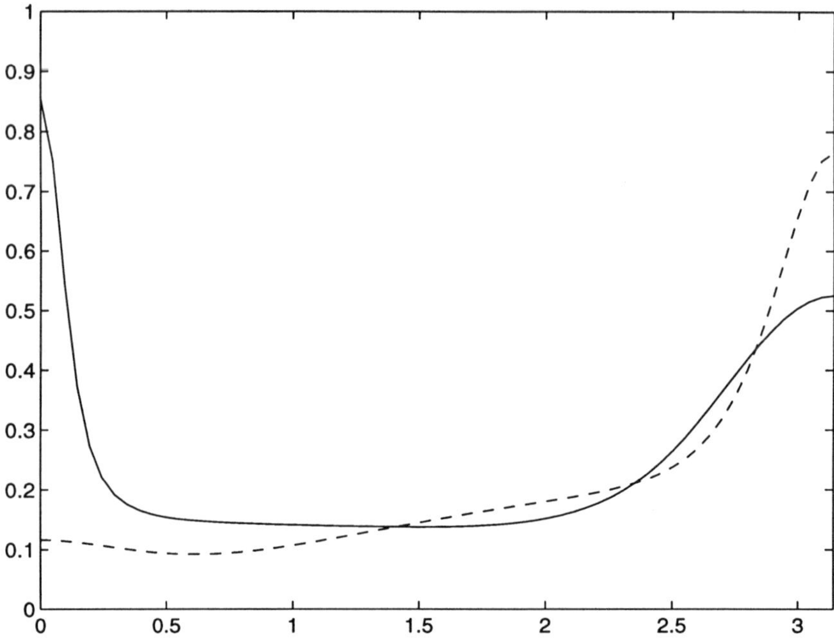

Fig. 14.5. Substitution index

Technology shock: solid line. Non-technology shock: dashed line.

14.4. Diagnostic Checking, Data Sources, and Data Treatment

14.4.1. To check the appropriateness of the statistical specification for the model of the common component we have compared two alternative series of estimated shocks: the technology shocks derived from the estimation of the MA(2) on Δx_t and Δp_t (solid line in Figure 14.6), and the technology shocks derived from the estimation of the same model from aggregation of the odd sectors only (dashed line in Figure 14.6). These two processes are almost identical (the correlation coefficient is 0.95). This is comforting since an implication of the analysis here and in Chapter 3 is that results should be robust to changes in the vector of averages used for estimation.

To verify the orthogonality between the residuals and the u_t's we applied a Q-test as explained in Chapter 3. We found that only 6% of the $[n^2 - (n+1)]/2 = 101025$ couples reject the hypothesis of pairwise orthogonality at the 5% significance level.

To verify whether, under the two-common-shocks assumption, the sectoral component has died out in our sample, we computed the ratio of the variance of the aggregated idiosyncratic component to the variance of the

Table 14.1. Sectors with the highest adjusted R^2: results from OLS regressions of output against the common technology shock

Sectors	SIC	$\bar{R}^2$
Gray and ductile iron foundries	3321	0.68
Machine tool accessories*	3545	0.65
Cement, hydraulic	3241	0.65
Concrete block and brick	3271	0.64
Air and gas compressors*	3563	0.62
Motors and generators	3621	0.61
Power transmission equipment, n.e.c.*	3568	0.61
Ball and roller bearings*	3562	0.61
Structural clay products, n.e.c.*	3259	0.60
Iron and steel forgings	3462	0.56
Internal combustion engines, n.e.c.*	3519	0.56
Synthetic rubber	2822	0.55
Bolts, nuts, rivets, and washers	3452	0.55
Truck trailers	3715	0.55
Speed changers, drives, and gears*	3566	0.54
Steel pipes and tubes	3317	0.54
Blast furnaces and steel mills	3312	0.53
Special dies, tools, jigs & fixtures*	3544	0.53
Saw blades and handsaws	3425	0.53
Pumps and pumping equipment*	3561	0.52

* Starred sectors belong to the broad classification 'industrial machinery and equipment'.

aggregate as explained in Chapter 3. Results are quite encouraging since we obtain ratios of 0.01 for output and 0.05 for productivity.

14.4.2. The data set used is the Annual Survey of Manufacturers (ASM), which is a survey of manufacturing establishments sampled from those responding to the comprehensive Census of Manufacturers. This database contains information for four-digit manufacturing industries from 1958 to 1986.

We have used value-added data for output and deflated them by the value of shipments.

Logs of sectoral data on output and productivity were subject to unit root tests. For all data we were not able to reject the null of a unit root (results available on request) at the 5% level.

The electronic computer sector (SIC 357) was found to have a unit root after detrending by a segmented trend with change in drift in 1972.

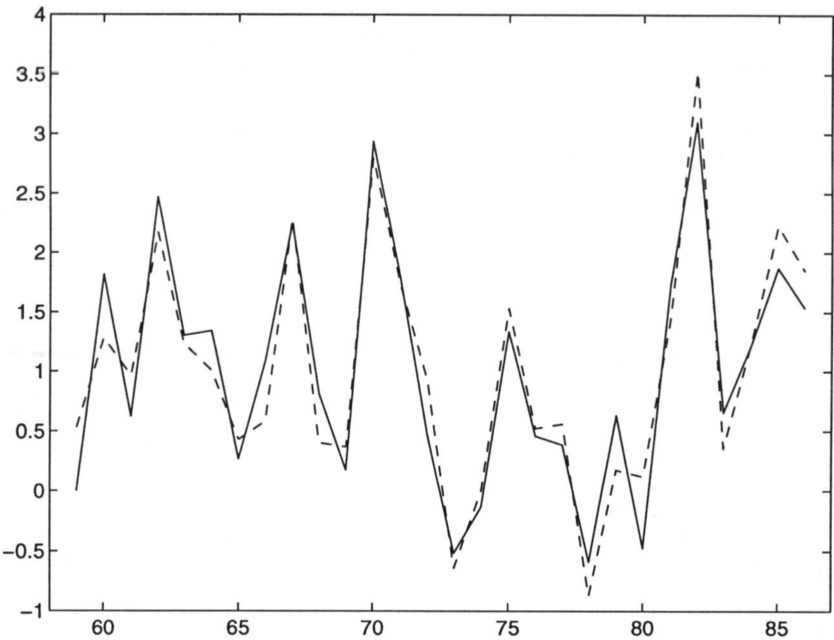

Fig. 14.6. Estimated common technology shock

Estimated using the average of all sectors: solid line. Estimated using the average of odd sectors only: dashed line.

14.5. Summary

In this chapter results from Part I have been exploited to estimate the contribution of technology innovations to output and productivity in 450 US manufacturing sectors from 1958 to 1986.

The technology shock has been identified as that for which the sum of the negative realizations is minimized. This method exploits the least controversial feature of technology innovations, i.e. that technology innovations are mostly positive.

We explored the nature of common movements in output and productivity by looking at the source of common shocks and their dynamic impact over time and across different sectors. For this purpose we developed an index of the substitution versus the complementarity effect of shocks. We found strong complementarities at business cycle frequencies originated by both technology and non-technology innovations, indicating that some, but not all, cyclical movements are real.

Although this result, to a certain extent, supports what is claimed by the real business cycle literature, the additional finding, that the growth rates of the investment in the machinery and equipment good sectors are strongly correlated with the common technological component, suggests a different propagation mechanism of technology shocks.

Conclusions

Let us now try to sum up the results and provide indications for future research that emerge from this book.

In Part I we have taken as a starting point a model of heterogeneity which has been recently employed in the macroeconomic literature: the independent microvariables differ for a constant in front of the same macrovariable, and for an idiosyncratic variable. We have seen that this simplification is strongly at odds with the US state data on income and wages. Thus, if we want to retain the common–idiosyncratic model, the common component has to be modeled as dependent on several macroeconomic shocks and the responses of agents to macroeconomic shocks must be different. For that matter, casual empiricism suggests that microvariables are driven by more than one macro source of variation, and that the intensity and the dynamics of the responses vary across agents. This raises a problem: how many common shocks are necessary to give a convincing representation of the comovements of the disaggregate series? We have proposed a method and shown some applications in Chapters 2, 3, and 14. Our results seem reasonable. However, the method still calls for theoretical refinements and systematic applications to other data sets. In particular, it would be interesting to see whether the estimated number of common shocks varies within reasonable bounds when regional (or sectoral) data for different countries are employed.

The question as to how many common shocks drive the macroeconomic variables is interesting both *per se* and because, with many common shocks and different responses of the agents, aggregation produces the largest range of dynamic effects. Some of them can be analyzed just by looking at the spectral density matrix of the aggregate vector. We found that non-singularity of the aggregate vector is compatible with micromodels having an exact behavioral equation, this being an effect of aggregation and heterogeneity, not of measurement errors corrupting the macrovariables. We also found that cointegration is destroyed by aggregation, unless either the micro cointegration coefficients are equal or there is only one permanent common shock driving the microvariables. Thus, either the micromodel allows the conclusion that the micro cointegration coefficient is a common parameter (as is the case for consumption and total income in Chapter 13), or the estimation of the number of common permanent shocks—which is a non-standard problem with large cross-sections evolving through time—becomes crucial in cointegration analysis of the aggregate variables.

Aggregation has also quite substantial effects on VAR and ARMAX representations. Firstly, the aggregate shocks result from a mixing of both corresponding and non-corresponding micro shocks. In the same way, the aggregate dynamics result from a mixing of both corresponding and non-corresponding micro dynamics; for example, a macroequation can be dynamic even though the corresponding microequations are static, it can contain lagged values of the dependent variable even though the corresponding equation does not, and so on. As a consequence, given an estimated equation or vector equation, we cannot interpret its dynamic shape as revealing the behavior of the agents underlying the macrovariables. Moreover, if the estimated macroparameters fail to fulfill the restrictions obtained within an economic micromodel, this is not a good reason to reject the micromodel. What is needed, both for the interpretation and testing of restrictions, is the other half of the theoretical construction, namely an assumption on the distribution of the microparameters over the population. The latter should be as parsimonious as possible, provided that it is compatible with existing knowledge of micro data. In the empirical exercise of Chapter 13 we have given an example in which standard consumption theory is coupled with micro information on the autocorrelation of micro incomes and our results on the number of common shocks driving micro incomes. We have shown that the theory and the main features of the data can be reconciled. Moreover, at the cost of some oversimplification, overidentifying restrictions for the macro data can be obtained and tested.

Trying to make reasonable assumptions on the distribution of the microparameters is a very difficult task. The microparameters of dynamic models include both the coefficients of the objective functions and the coefficients of the ARIMA independent processes, so that, with a few exceptions, empirical evidence on the microparameters does not exist and would be very difficult to collect. Nevertheless, we do not think that such difficulties should convince us to stick to the representative-agent practice, which amounts to transforming a complete lack of information about a distribution into an assumption that such a distribution is concentrated on a single point of the microparameter space.

Lastly, let us observe that even though our attention has been concentrated on models based on intertemporal optimization and rational expectations, the difficulties of aggregation show up in any economic reasoning on macrovariables. Agents behaving according to rules of thumb and, say, adaptive expectations, do not produce macroequations more easily interpretable than mainstream macromodels.

Appendix

Elements of Discrete Time Series Theory

We assume that the reader is acquainted with the standard tools of linear algebra, Hilbert spaces, real and complex analysis, and random variables. In several cases this appendix does not provide formal proofs but only hints. Detailed references are provided in Section A.9.

Let us begin by considering scalar stochastic processes. A covariance–stationary process is a bilateral sequence of random variables

$$\{x_t\}_{t=-\infty}^{\infty} = \{\ldots, x_{t-1}, x_t, x_{t+1}, \ldots\}, \tag{A.1}$$

with constant mean and constant covariances, i.e. $\mathrm{E}x_t = \mu$ for any t and, given k, $\mathrm{cov}(x_t, x_{t-k}) = \gamma_k$ for any t. To simplify the notation, in the sequel we shall use the symbol x_t to denote both the variable x_t and the process $\{x_t\}_{t=-\infty}^{\infty}$; from the context it should be clear which mathematical object we are referring to.

Denote by $\mathcal{X}^o$ the set of all the finite linear combinations of the unit constant and the variables in (A.1). We define the inner product between two elements z and y belonging to $\mathcal{X}^o$ as the second moment $\mathrm{E}(zy)$, and the norm, or length, of z as $\sqrt{\mathrm{E}z^2}$. The distance between z and y is defined as $\sqrt{\mathrm{E}(z-y)^2}$. Notice that the norm of a constant μ is $|\mu|$, while the norm of a zero-mean variable is its standard deviation.

Two variables are *orthogonal* if their inner product is zero, i.e. if their covariance is equal to the product of their means. If z and y are orthogonal we shall write $z \perp y$. A variable is zero mean if it is orthogonal to the unit constant. If z is zero mean, z is orthogonal to y if and only if $\mathrm{cov}(z, y) = 0$. The null element of the space is the zero constant, which is the only variable that is orthogonal to all the variables in $\mathcal{X}^o$, including itself. A zero-mean process x_t with the property that x_t is orthogonal to x_{t-k} for $k \neq 0$, i.e. a zero-mean process with no autocorrelation, is called a *white noise*.

Convergence of a sequence of variables of $\mathcal{X}^o$ can be defined in terms of the distance. Convergence of the sequence $y_1,\ y_2,\ \ldots$ implies the Cauchy property, i.e. that for any $\epsilon > 0$, there exists an integer n_ϵ such that for $n, m > n_\epsilon$,

$$\mathrm{E}(y_n - y_m)^2 < \epsilon.$$

The inner product and the norm fulfill the inequality

$$|\mathrm{E}(xy)|^2 \leq \mathrm{E}(x^2)\mathrm{E}(y^2).$$

If y_n converges to y then, since $|\mathrm{E}((y_n - y)z)|^2 \leq \mathrm{E}((y_n - y)^2)\mathrm{E}(z^2)$, $\mathrm{E}(y_n z)$ converges to $\mathrm{E}(yz)$, i.e. the inner product is continuous.

However, sequences fulfilling the Cauchy property do not necessarily converge within $\mathcal{X}^o$. For instance, suppose that x_t is a white noise. Then the sequence

$$y_s = x_0 + \alpha x_1 + \alpha^2 x_2 + \cdots + \alpha^s x_s,$$

with $|\alpha| < 1$, fulfills the Cauchy property, but has no limit in $\mathcal{X}^o$, since the latter contains only finite linear combinations. On the other hand, given a Cauchy sequence $\{y_s\}$ in $\mathcal{X}^o$, one can define a stochastic variable y such that $\mathrm{E}(y - y_s)^2$ tends to zero as s tends to infinity. The space obtained by adding the 'limits' of the Cauchy sequences of $\mathcal{X}^o$, call it $\mathcal{X}$, is complete, i.e. Cauchy sequences in $\mathcal{X}$ converge to elements of $\mathcal{X}$. A vector space with an inner product, complete with respect to convergence of Cauchy sequences, is called a Hilbert space.

A.1. Orthogonal Projections

A subset $\mathcal{S}$ of $\mathcal{X}$ is a linear subspace if it is closed with respect to sum and multiplication by scalars. A subspace $\mathcal{S}$ is closed if the limits of convergent sequences of elements of $\mathcal{S}$ lie in $\mathcal{S}$, i.e. if $\mathcal{S}$ is closed in the topology associated to the distance defined above. If y_k, $k = 1, \infty$, is a sequence of variables, the subspace spanned by the variables y_k is, by definition, the set of all finite linear combinations of the variables y_k, plus their limits. The subspace spanned by the variables y_k is closed.

THEOREM A.1. (ORTHOGONAL DECOMPOSITION THEOREM) Let z be an element of $\mathcal{X}$, and $\mathcal{S}$ be the closed subspace of $\mathcal{X}$ spanned by the variables z_k, $k = 1, \infty$. There exists a decomposition

$$z = p + u,$$

where $p \in \mathcal{S}$ and u is orthogonal to (the elements of) $\mathcal{S}$. This decomposition is unique, i.e. if $z = p' + u'$ with $p' \in \mathcal{S}$ and $u' \perp \mathcal{S}$, then $p' = p$ and $u' = u$. Moreover, p is the best linear predictor of z in $\mathcal{S}$, i.e. if $z = p^* + u^*$ with $p^* \in \mathcal{S}$, $p^* \neq p$, then $\mathrm{E}(u^*)^2 > \mathrm{E}u^2$.

Proof. Let us firstly prove that if p and u exist then they are unique. We have $p - p' = u' - u$. Since both p and p' belong to $\mathcal{S}$, then $u - u'$ belongs also to $\mathcal{S}$. Since both u and u' are orthogonal to $\mathcal{S}$, $u - u'$ is orthogonal to $\mathcal{S}$. Hence $u - u'$ is orthogonal to itself, so that $u = u'$ and $p = p'$.

If p and u exist, then p is the optimal linear predictor. Consider the equality $u^* = u-(p^*-p)$. Taking expectations we get $\mathrm{E}(u^*)^2 = \mathrm{E}u^2+\mathrm{E}(p^*-p)^2$, because $u \perp p^* - p$, which belongs to $\mathcal{S}$. Since $p^* \neq p$, $\mathrm{E}(p^* - p)^2 > 0$, so that $\mathrm{E}(u^*)^2 > \mathrm{E}u^2$.

Let us now come to existence. Let $\mathcal{S}_n$ be the subspace spanned by z_k, $k = 1, n$. The projection on $\mathcal{S}_n$, call it P_n, can be obtained by the standard least squares formula

$$P_n = \sum_{k=1}^{n} b_k z_k, \quad b = B^{-1}a, \tag{A.2}$$

where $B_{kl} = \mathrm{E}(z_k z_l)$, $a_k = \mathrm{E}(zz_k)$. By a standard reasoning we can substitute the variables z_k by variables $\tilde{z}_k$ such that $\tilde{z}_k$ has unit norm, $\mathrm{E}(\tilde{z}_k\tilde{z}_l) = 0$ for $k \neq l$, while $\tilde{z}_k$, $k = 1, n$, span $\mathcal{S}_n$. For, consider the orthogonal projection $z_2 = C_1 z_1 + v_2$ and replace z_2 by v_2, then consider the projection $z_3 = C_2 z_1 + C_2 v_2 + v_3$ and replace z_3 by v_3, and so on. The sequence $\tilde{z}_k$ is obtained from the sequence $z_1, v_2, v_3, \ldots$ by dividing each variable by its squared norm. By (A.2),

$$P_n = \sum_{k=1}^{n} c_k \tilde{z}_k,$$

with $c_k = \mathrm{E}(z\tilde{z}_k)$, is the orthogonal projection of z on $\mathcal{S}_n$. The squared norm of P_n is $\sum_{k=1}^{n} c_k^2$. Since the norm of P_n is limited by the norm of z, the sequence $\{c_k\}$ is square summable. Therefore $\sum_{k=r}^{r+q} c_k^2$ can be made smaller than any preassigned positive real. But the last sum is the squared norm of $P_r - P_{r+q}$. Therefore P_n is a Cauchy sequence and converges to a variable p of $\mathcal{S}$. As a consequence $u_n = P_n - z$ converges as well. Call u the limit. Since u_n is orthogonal to z_k, $k \leq n$, then, by the continuity of the inner product, u is orthogonal to $\mathcal{S}$. Q.E.D.

The variable p is called the *orthogonal projection* (or *regression*) of z on $\mathcal{S}$, while u is called the *residual.* By the orthogonality of p and u, $\mathrm{E}z^2$ can be decomposed in the following way:

$$\mathrm{E}z^2 = \mathrm{E}p^2 + \mathrm{E}u^2.$$

Moreover, if the constant belongs to $\mathcal{S}$, u is orthogonal to the constant and therefore is zero mean. Hence $\mathrm{E}z = \mathrm{E}p$ and $\mathrm{E}z^2-(\mathrm{E}z)^2 = \mathrm{E}p^2-(\mathrm{E}p)^2+\mathrm{E}u^2$, so that the above decomposition holds for the variances, i.e.

$$\mathrm{var}(z) = \mathrm{var}(p) + \mathrm{var}(u).$$

The quantity $R^2 = \mathrm{var}(p)/\mathrm{var}(z)$ measures the goodness of p as a prediction of z; it takes on values between zero and unity. Two interesting limit cases are $z \in \mathcal{S}$ and $z \perp \mathcal{S}$. In both cases the orthogonal decomposition is trivial:

in the former case $p = z$ and $u = 0$, so that $R^2 = 1$; in the latter $p = 0$ and $u = z$, so that $R^2 = 0$.

Projections are linear operators. For, let us denote by $P(y|\mathcal{S})$ the projection of y on $\mathcal{S}$. It is easily seen that for any $z \in \mathcal{S}$ and $y \in \mathcal{S}$ and any pair a, b of real numbers

$$P(az + by|\mathcal{S}) = aP(z|\mathcal{S}) + bP(y|\mathcal{S}). \tag{A.3}$$

In fact, from $z = P(z|\mathcal{S}) + u$ and $y = P(y|\mathcal{S}) + v$ we get

$$az + by = aP(z|\mathcal{S}) + bP(y|\mathcal{S}) + w,$$

where $w = au + bv$ is orthogonal to $\mathcal{S}$ (since both u and v are) while $aP(z|\mathcal{S})+bP(y|\mathcal{S})$ belongs to $\mathcal{S}$. Uniqueness of the projection implies (A.3).

Another important property of projections is that if $\mathcal{S}$ is the *direct sum* of the orthogonal subspaces $\mathcal{S}_1$ and $\mathcal{S}_2$, i.e. $\mathcal{S} = \{y : y = y_1 + y_2, y_1 \in \mathcal{S}_1, y_2 \in \mathcal{S}_2\}$, then the projection of z on $\mathcal{S}$ is the sum of the projections on $\mathcal{S}_1$ and $\mathcal{S}_2$:

$$P(z|\mathcal{S}) = P(z|\mathcal{S}_1) + P(z|\mathcal{S}_2). \tag{A.4}$$

To see this, project both sides of $z = P(z|\mathcal{S}_1) + \eta_1$ on $\mathcal{S}_2$. By orthogonality of $\mathcal{S}_1$ and $\mathcal{S}_2$, $P(P(z|\mathcal{S}_1)|\mathcal{S}_2) = 0$, so that

$$P(z|\mathcal{S}_2) = P(\eta_1|\mathcal{S}_2) = \eta_1 - v,$$

where v is the residual of the projection of η_1 on $\mathcal{S}_2$. Hence

$$z = [P(z|\mathcal{S}_1) + P(z|\mathcal{S}_2)] + v.$$

The term in square brackets belongs to $\mathcal{S}$. Moreover, v is orthogonal to $\mathcal{S}_2$ by definition, and is orthogonal to $\mathcal{S}_1$ because $v = \eta_1 - P(\eta_1|\mathcal{S}_2)$. Thus v is orthogonal to $\mathcal{S}$. Equality (A.4) follows from the uniqueness of projection.

The above result can be generalized to the case where $\mathcal{S}$ is an infinite direct sum $\sum_{k=1}^{\infty} \mathcal{S}_k$, with $\mathcal{S}_k \perp \mathcal{S}_l$, $l \neq k$, i.e. the set of all convergent sums of the form $y = \sum_{k=1}^{\infty} y_k$, $y_k \in \mathcal{S}_k$. In this case we have

$$P(z|\mathcal{S}) = \lim_{n\to\infty} \sum_{k=1}^{n} P(z|\mathcal{S}_k) = \sum_{k=1}^{\infty} P(z|\mathcal{S}_k). \tag{A.5}$$

A.2. The Wold Representation

Typically we want to find the optimal linear prediction of the stochastic variable x_t based on the values assumed by x_{t-k}, $k > 0$. This means regressing the variable x_t on the space spanned by its own past, i.e. on the smallest closed subspace of $\mathcal{X}$ containing x_{t-k}, $k > 0$, and the unit constant, call it $\mathcal{X}_{t-1}$. We get the orthogonal decomposition

$$x_t = P(x_t|\mathcal{X}_{t-1}) + \eta_t. \tag{A.6}$$

Notice that since $\eta_{t-k} = x_{t-k} - P(x_{t-k}|\mathcal{X}_{t-k-1})$, then η_{t-k} belongs to the space $\mathcal{X}_{t-k}$. Since: (i) η_t is orthogonal to η_{t-k} for $k > 0$, (ii) η_t is orthogonal to the constant and has therefore zero mean, then η_t is a white noise.

Now let us project x_t on the space $\mathcal{H}_t$ generated by the unit constant and η_{t-k}, $k \geq 0$:

$$x_t = P(x_t|\mathcal{H}_t) + d_t.$$

Since η_t is a white noise, using (A.5),

$$P(x_t|\mathcal{H}_t) = \mu + \sum_{k=0}^{\infty} P(x_t|\eta_{t-k}) = \mu + \eta_t + \sum_{k=1}^{\infty} a_k \eta_{t-k}$$

(where the unitary coefficient of η_t turns out by regressing each side of (A.6) on η_t). Summing up,

$$x_t = \mu + \eta_t + \sum_{k=1}^{\infty} a_k \eta_{t-k} + d_t, \tag{A.7}$$

where η_t is the residual of the projection of x_t on its past, while d_t is the residual of the projection of x_t on the space spanned by η_{t-k}, $k \geq 0$. Equation (A.7) is called the *Wold decomposition* or *Wold representation* or *fundamental representation* of x_t. η_t is known as the fundamental noise of x_t.

Consider now the variable d_t. Firstly, by combining (A.6) and (A.7) we get $d_t = P(x_t|\mathcal{X}_{t-1}) - \sum_{k=1}^{\infty} a_k \eta_{t-k} - \mu$. Thus d_t lies in $\mathcal{X}_{t-1}$. This means that $P(d_t|\mathcal{X}_{t-1}) = d_t$, or that d_t can be predicted without error by knowing only the *past* realizations of x_t. Moreover, the processes d_t and η_t are orthogonal at all leads and lags: in fact, $d_t \perp \eta_{t-k}$, $k \geq 0$, by construction, and $d_t \perp \eta_{t+k}$, $k > 0$, because $d_t \in \mathcal{X}_{t-1}$.

Lastly, lagging (A.7), and defining $\mathcal{D}_{t-1}$ as the smallest closed subspace of $\mathcal{X}$ containing d_{t-k}, $k > 0$, and the unit constant, it is easily seen that $\mathcal{X}_{t-k} \subseteq \mathcal{H}_{t-1} + \mathcal{D}_{t-1}$ for $k > 0$, while from (A.6) and the above observations it should be clear that $\mathcal{X}_{t-k} \supseteq \mathcal{H}_{t-1} + \mathcal{D}_{t-1}$, so that we have $\mathcal{X}_{t-1} = \mathcal{H}_{t-1} +$

$\mathcal{D}_{t-1}$, which is a decomposition of $\mathcal{X}_{t-1}$ into two orthogonal subspaces. Hence

$$d_t = P(d_t|\mathcal{X}_{t-1}) = P(d_t|\mathcal{H}_{t-1}) + P(d_t|\mathcal{D}_{t-1}) = P(d_t|\mathcal{D}_{t-1}),$$

where the last equality is motivated by $d_t \perp \mathcal{H}_{t-1}$. This means that d_t is perfectly predictable as, i.e. *is*, a (possibly infinite) linear combination of the variables d_{t-k}, $k > 0$. Notice that this implies that d_t is a linear combination of the variables d_{t-k}, for $k > \bar{k}$ and any $\bar{k} > 0$.

A random process like d_t is often called *deterministic* because its stochastic nature has no relation with time. The simplest example of a deterministic process is $d_t = d$ for all t, where d is a random variable independent of t. A somewhat more interesting example is

$$d_t = \alpha \cos t + \beta \sin t,$$

where α and β are such that $\mathrm{E}\alpha = \mathrm{E}\beta = 0$, and $\mathrm{E}\alpha\beta = 0$ and $\mathrm{E}\alpha^2 = \mathrm{E}\beta^2 = 1$. Clearly, such a process is covariance stationary since $\mathrm{E}d_t = 0$ for all t and $\mathrm{E}d_t d_{t-k} = \cos t \cos(t-k) + \sin t \sin(t-k) = \cos k$. The key feature of the random variables appearing in both the examples, i.e. d, α, and β, is that they do not depend on time. They are drawn only once, at the beginning of time, so to speak, and never change. Once they have been drawn, there are no innovations which can cause deviations of the process from its predetermined track. Their variance is non-zero, but their variance conditional on their own past is zero.

A.3. MA Representations for Regular Processes

A process x_t which has no deterministic component is called *purely stochastic* or *regular*. From (A.7), a regular process has a representation as a moving average (infinite in general) of a white noise. Notice also that, if x_t is regular, $\mathcal{X}_t = \mathcal{H}_t$, i.e. the present and past of x_t on one hand, and the present and past of the fundamental noise on the other, span the same space. In accordance with all current stochastic macroeconomic literature, in this book we only consider regular processes.

Let us rewrite (A.7) for a regular process:

$$x_t = \mu + \sum_{k=0}^{\infty} a_k \eta_{t-k}, \tag{A.8}$$

with $a_0 = 1$, $\eta_t = P(x_t|\mathcal{X}_{t-1})$. Convergence of the RHS implies that the sequence $\{a_i\}$ is square summable and that

$$\sigma_\eta^2 \sum_{k=0}^{\infty} a_k^2 = \sigma_x^2.$$

On the other hand, suppose that $\{b_k\}$ is square summable and that ϵ_t is a white-noise process. The sum

$$y_t = \mu + \sum_{k=0}^{\infty} b_k \epsilon_{t-k} \tag{A.9}$$

makes sense as a stationary stochastic process. The question is: is (A.9) the Wold representation of y_t?

The answer will be given in Theorem A.2 below. Let us firstly introduce the lag operator notation. Consider the vector space of all bilateral sequences

$$\ldots,\ a_{-2},\ a_{-1},\ a_0,\ a_1,\ a_2,\ \ldots$$

with the condition

$$\sum_{k=-\infty}^{\infty} a_k^2 < \infty.$$

This set is usually denoted by $\mathcal{L}^2(-\infty,\infty)$. Convolution $\{a_k\}\{b_k\}$ is defined as the sequence $\{c_k\}$ such that

$$c_k = \sum_{l=-\infty}^{\infty} a_l b_{k-l}$$

(for the reason why $\{c_k\}$ is square summable see Section A.9). Define L, the *lag operator*, as the sequence having a one at place 1, zero elsewhere. The convolution $L\{a_k\}$ is the sequence having a_{k-1} at place k. We have

$$\{a_k\} = \sum_{k=-\infty}^{\infty} a_k L^k,$$

where L^k is the sequence having a one at place k (with k positive or negative), zero elsewhere. The sum above is also indicated by $a(L)$. The sequence L^{-1} is indicated by F. We have $FL = 1$, i.e. the sequence having a one at place 0, zero elsewhere.

A sequence $a(L)$ is *invertible* if there exists a sequence $b(L)$ such that the convolution $a(L)b(L) = 1$. Suppose that $a(L)b(L) = 1$ and also that $a(L)b'(L) = 1$. Then $b(L)a(L)b'(L) = b(L) = b'(L)$. Thus if $a(L)$ is invertible the inverse is unique and will be denoted by $a(L)^{-1}$.

EXAMPLE A.1. The operator $(1-\alpha L)$ is invertible if $|\alpha| \neq 1$. If $|\alpha| < 1$,

$$(1-\alpha L)^{-1} = 1 + \alpha L + \alpha^2 L^2 + \cdots.$$

If $|\alpha| > 1$,

$$\begin{aligned}(1-\alpha L)^{-1} &= \left[-\alpha L(1-\alpha^{-1}F)\right]^{-1} \\ &= -\frac{1}{\alpha}F\left(1 + \frac{1}{\alpha}F + \frac{1}{\alpha^2}F^2 + \cdots\right).\end{aligned}$$

If $|\alpha| = 1$, the inverse $a(L)$, supposed to exist, should fulfill $a_0 - \alpha a_{-1} = 1$, $a_k - \alpha a_{k-1} = 0$ for $k \neq 0$. The second equation implies that both a_0 and a_{-1} vanish, otherwise $a(L)$ would not be square summable, but this contradicts the first equation. In particular, $1 - L$ has no inverse. The finite polynomial

$$a_0 + a_1 L + \cdots + a_n L^n$$

admits an inverse if none of its roots has unit modulus. In that case,

$$(a_0 + a_1 L + \cdots + a_n L^n)^{-1} = a_0^{-1}(1 - \alpha_1 L)^{-1}(1 - \alpha_2 L)^{-1} \cdots (1 - \alpha_n L)^{-1},$$

where the factors with $|\alpha| < 1$ have an inverse in L, while those with $|\alpha_k| > 1$ have an inverse in F.

A sequence $a(L)$ is *unilateral in* L if $a_k = 0$ for $k < 0$, and unilateral in F if $a_k = 0$ for $k > 0$. Henceforth we shall use 'unilateral' to mean unilateral in L. For example, the sequence $(1 - \alpha L)$ has a unilateral inverse if and only if $|\alpha| < 1$.

Now suppose that $a(L)$ is unilateral and consider the function of a complex variable z defined as

$$a(z) = \sum_{k=0}^{\infty} a_k z^k.$$

The series converges absolutely for $|z| < 1$. In fact, if $|a_k|$ tends to zero geometrically, so does $|a_k z^k|$. If $|a_k|$ tends to zero slower than geometrically, then $|a_k z^k|$ tends to zero faster than $|a_k|^2$, which is summable. Therefore $a(z)$ makes sense and is analytic for $|z| < 1$. We shall often refer to the analytic function $a(L)$, this being a loose way of referring to $a(z)$.

Let us now return to our stochastic variable x_t and to the space $\mathcal{X}$. There is a natural correspondence between the sequences $a(L)$ and a family of operators on the Hilbert space $\mathcal{X}$. Define $Lx_t = x_{t-1}$. Since the elements of $\mathcal{X}$ are linear combinations of x_t, for $t = -\infty, \infty$, or limits of such combinations, the operator L can be extended to the whole $\mathcal{X}$. Moreover, given a sequence $c(L)$, $c(L)x_t$ makes sense if and only if $c(L)$ is square summable. For, firstly observe that

$$d(L)\eta_t = \sum_{k=-\infty}^{\infty} d_k \eta_{t-k},$$

where η_t is the fundamental noise of x_t, has finite variance if and only if $d(L)$ is square summable. Since (A.8) may be rewritten as

$$x_t = a(L)\eta_t,$$

up to the constant term, then write

$$c(L)x_t = c(L)a(L)\eta_t$$

and recall that $\mathcal{L}^2(-\infty, \infty)$ is closed with respect to convolution.

Now we are ready to present an important uniqueness result:

THEOREM A.2. Consider the stationary, regular process x_t and its Wold representation

$$x_t = \mu + a(L)\eta_t,$$

where $a(L)$ is unilateral, $a(0) = 1$. The function $a(z)$ (which is analytic for $|z| < 1$) has no zeros for $|z| < 1$. Moreover, suppose that

$$x_t = \mu + b(L)\epsilon_t,$$

with $b(L)$ unilateral and ϵ_t white noise. If $b(z)$ has no zeros for $|z| < 1$, then $b(L) = ba(L)$, $\epsilon_t = b^{-1}\eta_t$, with b scalar.

We do not give a proof for Theorem A.2. However, the following MA(1) example should be sufficient to provide the reader with a good intuition of its content. Consider

$$x_t = (1 - \alpha L)\eta_t = \eta_t - \alpha\eta_{t-1}, \tag{A.10}$$

with η_t white noise. Consider the decomposition

$$x_t = p_{kt} + \epsilon_{kt},$$

where $p_{kt} = P(x_t | x_{t-1}, x_{t-2}, \ldots, x_{t-k})$. Let us firstly show that

$$\tilde{p}_{kt} = -\sum_{l=1}^{k} \alpha^l \frac{1 + \alpha^2 + \cdots + \alpha^{2(k-l)}}{1 + \alpha^2 + \cdots + \alpha^{2k}} x_{t-l} \tag{A.11}$$

is equal to p_{kt}. By using $x_{t-l} = \eta_{t-l} - \alpha\eta_{t-l-1}$, and rearranging terms, we get

$$\tilde{p}_{kt} = -\alpha \frac{1 + \alpha^2 + \cdots + \alpha^{2(k-1)}}{1 + \alpha^2 + \cdots + \alpha^{2k}} \eta_{t-1} + \sum_{l=2}^{k+1} \frac{\alpha^{2(k+1)-l}}{1 + \alpha^2 + \cdots + \alpha^{2k}} \eta_{t-l},$$

so that

$$\tilde{\epsilon}_{kt} = x_t - \tilde{p}_{kt} = \eta_t - \sum_{l=1}^{k+1} \frac{\alpha^{2(k+1)-l}}{1 + \alpha^2 + \cdots + \alpha^{2k}} \eta_{t-l}. \tag{A.12}$$

One can easily check that $\text{cov}(\tilde{\epsilon}_{kt}, x_{t-l}) = 0$, $l = 1, k$ (while $\text{cov}(\tilde{\epsilon}_{kt}, x_{t-k-1}) \neq 0$), so that, by the uniqueness of the orthogonal decomposition, $\tilde{p}_{kt} = p_{kt}$.

Now let us consider in turn the cases $|\alpha| < 1$, $|\alpha| = 1$, $|\alpha| > 1$.

CASE $|\alpha| < 1$. The process $-\alpha\eta_{t-1} - p_{kt}$ is obtained from the RHS of (A.12) by dropping the term η_t. A standard calculation shows that its variance is

$$\frac{\alpha^{2(k+1)}}{1+\alpha^2+\cdots+\alpha^{2k}}\sigma_\eta^2. \tag{A.13}$$

Since $|\alpha| \neq 1$ the above expression can be written as

$$\alpha^{2(k+1)}\frac{\alpha^2-1}{\alpha^{2(k+1)}-1}\sigma_\eta^2. \tag{A.14}$$

(A.14) tends to zero geometrically as k goes to infinity, so that p_{kt} converges to $-\alpha\eta_{t-1}$. Since $\epsilon_{kt} - \eta_t = -\alpha\eta_{t-1} - p_{kt}$, the residual ϵ_{kt} converges to η_t.

CASE $|\alpha| = 1$. (A.13) reduces to $\sigma_\eta^2/(k+1)$. Hence, p_{kt} tends to $-\alpha\eta_{t-1}$ when $k \to \infty$ and (A.10) is still the Wold representation of x_t. However, convergence is no longer geometrical. Moreover, (A.11) becomes

$$p_{kt} = -\sum_{l=1}^{k}\frac{k+1-l}{k+1}x_{t-l}.$$

The coefficients of this sum tend to unity in modulus. Hence, unlike the case $|\alpha| < 1$, the coefficients of (A.11) do not converge to the coefficients of any square summable sequence. This may be rephrased by saying either that x_t does not possess an autoregressive representation, or that $1 - \alpha L$ is not invertible.

REMARK A.1. Notice that, for $\alpha = 1$, we have proved that the residual

$$\begin{aligned} x_t - p_{kt} &= [1 + k/(k+1)L + \cdots + 1/(k+1)L^k]x_t \\ &= [1 + k/(k+1)L + \cdots + 1/(k+1)L^k](1-L)\eta_t \end{aligned}$$

tends to η_t. Therefore the operator

$$[1 + k/(k+1)L + \cdots + 1/(k+1)L^k](1-L)$$

tends to 1 in $\mathcal{L}^2(-\infty, \infty)$. However, this does not imply that

$$1 + k/(k+1)L + \cdots + 1/(k+1)L^k$$

tends to any element in $\mathcal{L}^2(-\infty, \infty)$. In other words, even though the finite projections tend to the projection on the whole $\mathcal{X}_{t-1}$, the coefficients of the finite projection do not approximate the coefficients of any sensible operator in L.

REMARK A.2. In order to avoid a possible misunderstanding, let us note that the convergence results proved just above are not necessary to show that p_{kt} converges to the projection of x_t on $\mathcal{X}_{t-1}$. This is ensured by Theorem A.1 and is true also when $|\alpha| > 1$. The proofs just above show that if $|\alpha| \leq 1$ then p_{kt} converges to $-\alpha\eta_{t-1}$, i.e. η_t is the fundamental noise for x_t, which is consistent with Theorem A.2.

REMARK A.3. Let us observe that when $|\alpha| < 1$ the fact that (A.10) is the Wold representation of x_t could have been proved by a very simple and direct argument. The operator $1 - \alpha L$ has the inverse $1 + \alpha L + \alpha^2 L^2 + \cdots$, so that

$$-\alpha\eta_{t-1} = -\alpha(1 + \alpha L + \alpha^2 L^2 + \cdots)x_{t-1} = -\sum_{l=1}^{\infty} \alpha^l x_{t-l}. \tag{A.15}$$

Thus $-\alpha\eta_{t-1} \in \mathcal{X}_{t-1}$; since η_t is orthogonal to $\mathcal{X}_{t-1}$, owing to the uniqueness of the orthogonal decomposition, $-\alpha\eta_{t-1} = P(x_t|\mathcal{X}_{t-1})$. However, the derivation obtained above by the calculation of p_{kt} is interesting in its own right. In fact, when regressing x_t on a finite number of lagged values in finite sample situations, we get an estimate of p_{kt}. The latter, as the calculations above have shown, converges to the projection on $\mathcal{X}_{t-1}$ as fast as α^k tends to zero. Moreover, by comparing (A.11) to (A.15), we see that the estimated coefficients of p_{kt} are biased as estimates of the coefficients α^k, i.e. the coefficients of the projection on $\mathcal{X}_{t-1}$, but that the bias tends to zero geometrically.

CASE $|\alpha| > 1$. In this case the variance of $-\alpha\eta_{t-1} - p_{kt}$ is still given by (A.13), but now this expression approaches $(\alpha^2 - 1)\sigma_\eta^2$ as $k \to \infty$. Hence p_{kt} does not converge to $\alpha\eta_{t-1}$. This result does not mean that p_{kt} does not converge or that we have no Wold representation. Simply, (A.10) is not the Wold representation of x_t. To recover the Wold representation rewrite (A.11) as

$$\begin{aligned}
p_{kt} &= -\sum_{l=1}^{k} \alpha^l \frac{1 - \alpha^{2(k-l+1)}}{1 - \alpha^{2(k+1)}} x_{t-l} \\
&= -\sum_{l=1}^{k} \alpha^{-l} \frac{1 - \alpha^{-2(k-l+1)}}{1 - \alpha^{-2(k+1)}} x_{t-l} \\
&= -\sum_{l=1}^{k} \alpha^{-l} \frac{1 + \alpha^{-2} + \cdots + \alpha^{-2(k-l)}}{1 + \alpha^{-2} + \cdots + \alpha^{-2k}} x_{t-l}.
\end{aligned}$$

The last expression can also be obtained from (A.11) by replacing α with $1/\alpha$. A simple symmetry argument should then be sufficient to convince the reader that p_{kt} approaches

$$p_t = -\alpha^{-1} \frac{1}{1 - \alpha^{-1}L} x_{t-1}.$$

Moreover, the residual ϵ_{kt} approaches

$$\epsilon_t = \frac{1}{1-\alpha^{-1}L} x_t = \frac{1-\alpha L}{1-\alpha^{-1}L} \eta_t. \tag{A.16}$$

Hence $p_t = -\alpha^{-1}\epsilon_{t-1}$ and the Wold representation is $x_t = (1-\alpha^{-1}L)\epsilon_t$. Observe that ϵ_t, although a non-trivial infinite unilateral MA of η_t, is a white noise. This is easily seen by looking at its spectral density function, as we will do below.

A.4. Non-Fundamentalness and Prediction

By remembering that η_t is orthogonal to $\mathcal{X}_{t-1}$, we see that η_{t-1} cannot belong to $\mathcal{X}_{t-1}$ when $|\alpha| > 1$, since, if it did, (A.10) would be the Wold representation of x_t. Hence $\eta_t \notin \mathcal{X}_t$. Instead, η_t belongs to the space spanned by the future of x_t, as is easily seen by observing that the operator has the inverse $-\alpha F(1-\alpha^{-1}F)^{-1}$. Thus if $|\alpha| \neq 1$, then η_t belongs to either $\mathcal{X}_t$ ($|\alpha| < 1$), or to the future of x_t ($|\alpha| > 1$). By contrast, when $|\alpha| = 1$, a simple symmetry argument (write $-x_t = \tilde{\eta}_t - \tilde{\eta}_{t+1}$, with $\tilde{\eta}_t = \eta_{t-1}$) shows that η_t is the projection of x_t on the space spanned by the future of x_t, so that η_t belongs both to $\mathcal{X}_t$ and the space spanned by the future of x_t.

A representation $x_t = b(L)\eta_t$, with $b(L)$ unilateral and square summable, in which η_t does not belong to $\mathcal{X}_t$ is called non-fundamental, and the noise η_t non-fundamental with respect to x_t. By Theorem A.2, η_t is non-fundamental if and only if $b(z)$ has zeros of modulus smaller than unity.

We must recall here that the fundamental noise and the fundamental representation of a process x_t play their central role within the problem of predicting x_t on the basis of x_{t-k}, $k > 0$. However, there is no reason to believe that a structural white noise is fundamental. As argued in Sections 1.1 and 12.2, a process like $(1-\alpha L)\eta_t$ with $|\alpha| > 1$ is not less likely in economic models than the case with $|\alpha| < 1$. When $|\alpha| > 1$ the fundamental representation is $(1-\alpha^{-1}L)\epsilon_t$, with ϵ_t non-structural.

Notice that the variance of non-fundamental noises is smaller than the variance of the fundamental noise. To see this, consider that η_t is orthogonal both to x_{t-k} and η_{t-k}, $k > 0$. By the uniqueness of orthogonal decompositions $-\alpha\eta_{t-1}$ is the projection of x_t on x_{t-k} and η_{t-k}, $k > 0$, while η_t is the residual. By contrast, ϵ_t is the prediction error of an observer predicting x_t on the basis of the past of x_{t-k} alone.

A.5. Scalar ARMA Processes

Consider

$$x_t = \mu + c(L)\eta_t,$$

with $c(L)$ square summable and η_t white noise. x_t is an ARMA (AutoRegressive Moving Average) if $c(L)$ is a rational function, i.e. the ratio of two polynomials:

$$c(L) = \frac{a(L)}{b(L)} = \frac{a_0 + a_1 L + \cdots + a_n L^n}{b_0 + b_1 L + \cdots + c_r L^r}. \tag{A.17}$$

In order for (A.17) to make sense it is necessary that $b(L)$ has no roots of unit modulus. ARMA processes can arise as stationary solutions to difference equations. In our case x_t is the process fulfilling, up to a constant term,

$$b(L)x_t = a(L)\eta_t.$$

Notice that the equation $(1 - \alpha L)x_t = \eta_t$ has the solution $(1 - \alpha L)^{-1}\eta_t$ both if $|\alpha| < 1$ and if $|\alpha| > 1$. In the first case x_t is a linear combination of η_{t-k}, with $k \geq 0$, and in the second case with $k < 0$. No stationary solution exists if $|\alpha| = 1$. Roots of $b(L)$ of modulus smaller than unity may arise in economic models. However, the forward terms η_{t+k}, $k > 0$, typically disappear when expectations are introduced (see, e.g., Nickell, 1985).

An important feature of a rational operator $c(L)$ is that its coefficients, when the denominator is expanded, decline exponentially (the speed being determined by the smallest in modulus among the roots of $b(L)$ of modulus greater than unity, and by the biggest in modulus among those of modulus smaller than unity). Thus, for example, the process

$$x_t = \eta_t + \frac{1}{2}\eta_{t-1} + \frac{1}{3}\eta_{t-2} + \cdots,$$

although making sense because $\sum 1/k^2 < \infty$, is not an ARMA. In this example, the function $a(z)$ is analytic for $|z| < 1$ but not for $|z| = 1$: since $\sum 1/k$ is a divergent series, $a(1)$ does not exist. By contrast, if $\mu + (a(L)/b(L))\eta_t$ is the Wold representation of x_t, where $a(L)$ and $b(L)$ are polynomials, then $a(L)/b(L)$ is analytic in a disk of radius greater than unity, for, if the polynomial $b(L)$ had a root of unit modulus, $a(L)/b(L)$ would not be square summable.

The following is the specification of Theorem A.2 for ARMA models:

THEOREM A.3. Let x_t be an ARMA

$$x_t = \mu + \frac{a(L)}{b(L)}\eta_t,$$

and let

$$x_t = \mu + \tilde{c}(L)\tilde{\eta}_t$$

be its Wold representation. Then $\tilde{c}(L)$ is a rational function, $\tilde{c}(L) = \tilde{a}(L)/\tilde{b}(L)$, where: (i) $\tilde{b}(z)$ has no zeros of modulus smaller than or equal to unity; (ii) $\tilde{a}(z)$ has no zeros of modulus smaller than unity. If $x_t = \mu + \hat{c}(L)\hat{\eta}_t$ is any unilateral representation of x_t fulfilling (i) and (ii), then for a scalar d, $\hat{c}(L) = d\tilde{a}(L)/\tilde{b}(L)$, $\hat{\eta}_t = d^{-1}\tilde{\eta}_t$.

A.6. Vector Processes

Let x_t be an n-dimensional stochastic vector. x_t is covariance stationary if $\mathrm{E}(x_t)$ is a constant n-vector μ, and $\mathrm{E}(x_t x'_{t-k}) = \Sigma_k$ is an $n \times n$ matrix depending only on k. Notice that $\Sigma_k = \Sigma'_{-k}$. Define $\mathcal{L}_n^2(-\infty, \infty)$ as the set of all sequences

$$\ldots, A_2,\ A_{-1},\ A_0,\ A_1,\ A_2, \ldots$$

where the A_k's are $n \times n$ matrices fulfilling

$$\sum_{k=-\infty}^{\infty} \sum_{l=1}^{n} \sum_{r=1}^{n} a_{lr,k}^2 < \infty,$$

where $a_{lr,k}$ is the (l, r) entry of A_k. Define L as the sequence having the identity matrix I at place 1, zero elsewhere. Define the convolution $\{C_k\} = \{A_k\}\{B_k\}$ by

$$C_k = \sum_{l=-\infty}^{\infty} A_l B_{k-l}.$$

Using the definitions of L and of convolution:

$$\{A_k\} = \sum_{k=-\infty}^{\infty} A_k L^k = A(L).$$

The matrix-valued function $A(z)$ is analytic for $|z| < 1$. Multiplying $A(L)$ by $A_{\mathrm{ad}}(L)$ we get the matrix having $\det A(L)$ on the diagonal and zero elsewhere. Therefore, $A(L)$ is invertible if and only if $\det A(L)$ is invertible. If $A(L)$ is unilateral in L and is invertible, the inverse is unilateral in L if and only if the scalar $\det A(L)$ has an inverse that is unilateral in L.

Define $\mathcal{X}$ as the space of all finite linear combinations of the components of the vectors x_{t-k} and the constant vectors, for any integer k, completed with their limits. Define $\mathcal{X}_t$ in the same way but with $k \geq 0$. We can take the projection of each of the components of x_t on $\mathcal{X}_{t-1}$:

$$\begin{aligned} x_{1t} &= P(x_{1t}|\mathcal{X}_{t-1}) + \eta_{1t} \\ x_{2t} &= P(x_{2t}|\mathcal{X}_{t-1}) + \eta_{2t} \\ &\vdots \\ x_{nt} &= P(x_{nt}|\mathcal{X}_{t-1}) + \eta_{nt} \end{aligned} \tag{A.18}$$

where η_t is a zero-mean vector white noise, i.e. $\mathrm{cov}(\eta_{lt}\eta_{rt-k}) = 0$, for $k \neq 0$, for any l and r. Now define $\mathcal{H}_t$ as in the scalar case and project the components of x_t on $\mathcal{H}_t$:

$$x_{lt} = P(x_{lt}|\mathcal{H}_t) + d_{lt}.$$

If the vector d_t vanishes we say that x_t is linearly regular.

Regularity will be assumed throughout. Now, unlike the scalar case, complications arise here due to possible linear relations linking the components of η_t. We define the *rank* of x_t as the rank of $\mathrm{E}(\eta_t\eta_t')$: thus the rank of x_t is m if the components of η_t are linked by $n-m$ linear relations, not involving lags. It turns out that if the rank of x_t is m, then $n-m$ linear relations involving lags link the components of x_t. To prove this, firstly write x_t as

$$x_t = A(L)\eta_t, \tag{A.19}$$

where $A(L)$ is square summable and $A(0) = I$. Notice that $A(L)$ is uniquely determined if and only if x_t has maximum rank n. However, since $A(z)$ is analytic for $|z| < 1$ and $A(0) = I$, $\det A(z)$ vanishes only for a subset of $U = \{z : \ |z| < 1\}$ with no accumulation points in U.[1] Now consider

$$A_{\mathrm{ad}}(L)x_t = \det A(L)\eta_t.$$

If B is an $(n-m)\times n$ matrix of rank $n-m$ such that $B\eta_t = 0$, then

$$BA_{\mathrm{ad}}(L)x_t = 0,$$

where the rank of $BA_{\mathrm{ad}}(z)$ is $n-m$ for $|z| < 1$, apart possibly for a subset having no accumulation point in U. When an n-dimensional vector process x_t has rank n we say that x_t has *maximum rank*. When the rank is less than n we say that x_t is *singular*. The following theorem generalizes Theorem A.2.

THEOREM A.4. Let x_t be an n-dimensional, stationary, regular, maximum rank, stochastic process with Wold representation (A.19). Then $\det A(L)$ has no zeros for $|z| < 1$. Moreover, let

$$x_t = \mu + B(L)\epsilon_t,$$

with $B(L)$ unilateral and square summable, and ϵ_t white noise. If $\det B(L)$ has no zeros for $|z| < 1$ then for a non-singular matrix B we have $B(L) = BA(L)$ and $\epsilon_t = B^{-1}\eta_t$.

Starting with the white noise of (A.19), by iterated regressions and normalization (as in the proof of Theorem A.1) one obtains

$$\eta_t = Mu_t,$$

where u_t is an *orthonormal* white noise, i.e. one whose components are mutually orthogonal and of unit norm. From (A.19) we get

$$x_t = \mu + C(L)u_t.$$

[1] This is a well-known consequence of analyticity. See Smirnov (1964, pp. 64–65). See also Chapter 6 in this book, Lemma 6.2.

Naturally, there exists an infinity of representations of x_t with an orthonormal white-noise vector. However:

THEOREM A.5. Under the same assumptions of Theorem A.4, let

$$x_t = \mu + C(L)u_t, \qquad x_t = \mu + \tilde{C}(L)\tilde{u}_t.$$

Assume that u_t and $\tilde{u}_t$ are orthonormal and that $\det C(L)$ and $\det \tilde{C}(L)$ do not vanish for $|z| < 1$. Then, for an orthonormal Q, we have $\tilde{C}(L) = QC(L)$ and $\tilde{u}_t = Q'u_t$.

ARMA vector processes can be defined as stationary solutions of vector difference equations

$$B(L)x_t = A(L)\eta_t,$$

for $A(L)$ and $B(L)$ polynomial matrices, where the existence of a stationary solution requires that $\det B(z)$ has no zeros of unit modulus. ARMA processes can be represented as

$$x_t = C(L)\eta_t, \tag{A.20}$$

where the entries of $C(L)$ are rational functions with no poles of unit modulus.

THEOREM A.6. Assume that x_t is of maximum rank and that it has the rational representation (A.20). Let

$$x_t = \mu + \tilde{C}(L)\tilde{\eta}_t$$

be the Wold representation of x_t. Then $\tilde{C}(L)$ is a matrix of rational functions fulfilling: (i) $\tilde{C}(L)$ has no poles of modulus smaller than or equal to unity; (ii) $\det \tilde{C}(L)$ has no zeros of modulus smaller than unity. Suppose that

$$x_t = \mu + \hat{C}(L)\hat{\eta}_t$$

is a unilateral representation fulfilling (ii). Then, for a non-singular matrix D, $\hat{C}(L) = D\tilde{C}(L)$, $\hat{\eta}_t = D^{-1}\tilde{\eta}_t$.

A.7. The Spectral Density

Given an n-dimensional, stationary, regular stochastic process, we define the matrix function

$$f(\phi) = \sum_{k=-\infty}^{\infty} \Sigma_k e^{-ik\phi}, \tag{A.21}$$

for $\phi \in [-\pi, \pi]$ (we recall that Σ_k is the matrix of covariances between x_t and x_{t-k}). $f(\phi)$ is known as the spectral density matrix of x_t.[2] If x_t has the representation

$$x_t = B(L)\eta_t$$

with η_t white noise and $B(L)$ square summable, then

$$f(\phi) = B(e^{-i\phi})\Sigma_\eta B'(e^{i\phi}), \tag{A.22}$$

where Σ_η is the covariance matrix of η_t. Notice that we are not assuming that the representation of x_t is the Wold representation, or that it is unilateral, or that x_t has maximum rank. We are asserting, as the reader can easily check, that if a valid MA representation of x_t is given, then the spectral density matrix can be obtained by (A.22). Notice also that even if the representation $x_t = \mu + B(L)\eta_t$ is unilateral in L, convergence of $\sum B_k z^k$ is guaranteed for $|z| < 1$, whereas the sum in (A.22) must converge with $z = e^{-i\phi}$, whose modulus is unity. In fact, it can be shown that the spectral density of a regular process exists almost everywhere in $[-\pi, \pi]$ (see Section A.9). No problem arises if $B(L)$ is rational. In that case convergence is guaranteed everywhere in $[-\pi, \pi]$.

A simple inspection of (A.21) is sufficient to prove that x_t is a white noise if and only if its spectral density is constant. Going back to (A.16) and using (A.22), the spectral density of ϵ_t is

$$\frac{|1 - \alpha e^{-i\phi}|^2}{|1 - \alpha^{-1} e^{-i\phi}|^2}\sigma_\eta^2 = \alpha^2\sigma_\eta^2.$$

Therefore η_t is a white noise.

If x_t and y_t are n-dimensional vectors orthogonal at all leads and lags, then the spectral density of $x_t + y_t$ is the sum of their spectral densities.

If $D(L)$ is $m \times n$ and square summable, then the spectral density of the m-dimensional vector $D(L)x_t$ is

$$D(e^{-i\phi})f(\phi)D'(e^{i\phi}). \tag{A.23}$$

THEOREM A.7. Let x_t be a regular process of dimension n. The spectral density matrix $f(\phi)$ has the same rank m, $m \le n$, almost everywhere in $[-\pi, \pi]$, where m is the rank of x_t.

THEOREM A.8. Let x_t be regular and of maximum rank with spectral density $f(\phi)$. There exist a square summable matrix $A(L)$ such that

[2] The standard definition has $1/2\pi$ in front of our $f(\phi)$. In this way the integral of the spectral density over $[-\pi, \pi]$ gives the variance of x_t. Since we do not need this result the factor $1/2\pi$ has been dropped for notational convenience.

(i) $A(0) = I$ and (ii) $\det A(z)$ has no zeros for $|z| < 1$, and a positive definite matrix Σ such that

$$f(\phi) = A(e^{-i\phi})\Sigma A(e^{i\phi}). \tag{A.24}$$

Moreover, if $\tilde{A}(L)$ and $\tilde{\Sigma}$ fulfill (i), (ii), and (A.24), then $\tilde{A}(L) = A(L)$, $\tilde{\Sigma} = \Sigma$.

Uniqueness of $A(z)$ and Σ, uniqueness of the Wold representation, and (A.22) imply that the Wold representation of x_t is $x_t = \mu + A(L)\eta_t$.

If x_t has an ARMA representation, then the entries of $f(\phi)$ are rational functions of $e^{-i\phi}$. On the other hand, if the spectral density is rational then x_t is an ARMA. Precisely:

THEOREM A.9. Suppose that the spectral density $f(\phi)$ of x_t is of maximum rank and rational. There exist a rational matrix function $A(z)$ and a positive definite matrix Σ, where (i) $A(0) = I$, (ii) $A(z)$ has no poles of modulus smaller than or equal to unity, and (iii) $\det A(z)$ has no zero of modulus smaller than unity, such that

$$f(\phi) = A(e^{-i\phi})\Sigma A(e^{i\phi}). \tag{A.25}$$

Moreover, if $\tilde{A}(z)$ and $\tilde{\Sigma}$ fulfill (i), (ii), (iii), and (A.25), then $\tilde{A}(z) = A(z)$, $\tilde{\Sigma} = \Sigma$.

Theorem A.9 implies that, if a vector x_t has rational spectral density, and we manipulate x_t by means of an $m \times n$ matrix $D(L)$, where $D(L)$ is rational, the spectral density of $D(L)x_t$ is rational (see (A.23)). Therefore, by Theorem A.9, $D(L)x_t$ is an ARMA. In particular, aggregation of the components of an ARMA vector produces an ARMA. The proof of Theorem A.9 is a constructive procedure, i.e. the matrices $A(L)$ and Σ can be obtained in a finite number of steps implying rational operations and roots extractions. Such a procedure is described in Chapter 10.

Finally, an observation on some representations of singular vector processes is necessary. Consider

$$x_t = B(L)u_t, \tag{A.26}$$

where x_t is n-dimensional, u_t is an h-dimensional orthonormal white noise, and $B(L)$ is a rational $n \times h$ matrix with no poles of modulus smaller than or equal to unity. Determinants of square submatrices of $B(z)$ vanish either for any complex number or for a finite set of complex numbers. Therefore we can speak unambiguously of the rank of $B(L)$. Let $\text{rank}B(L) = r$. Obviously $r \leq h$. Assume that $h \leq n$. Now consider any Wold representation of x_t (we recall that if x_t is not maximum rank then the Wold representation is not unique):

$$x_t = A(L)\eta_t.$$

The rank of the $n \times n$ matrix $A(L)$ is n (since $A(0) = I$). As a consequence, the rank of η_t must be r. To prove this, notice that the spectral density of x_t has the representations

$$B(e^{-i\phi})B(e^{i\phi}) = A(e^{-i\phi})\Sigma_\eta A(e^{i\phi})$$

(u_t is orthonormal, thus $\Sigma_u = I$) so that, excluding at most a finite number of values for ϕ,

$$\Sigma_\eta = A(e^{-i\phi})^{-1}B(e^{-i\phi})B(e^{i\phi})A(e^{i\phi})^{-1}.$$

Therefore the dimension of the null space of Σ_η must equal the dimension of the null space of $B(e^{-i\phi})$. Now determine an r-dimensional orthonormal white noise $\tilde{u}_t$ such that $\eta_t = C\tilde{u}_t$, where C is $n \times r$. Putting $\tilde{B}(L) = A(L)C$, we have

$$x_t = \tilde{B}(L)\tilde{u}_t.$$

This representation differs from (A.26) in that now the matrix in L is $(n \times r)$-dimensional, the white noise vector is r-dimensional, but both have maximum rank.

A.8. Granger Causality and Sims's Theorem

Let $(y_t \quad x_t)'$ be stationary and regular. We say that y_t fails to *Granger-cause* x_t if the projection of x_t on the past of x_t and y_t coincides with the projection on the past of x_t only:

$$P(x_t|x_{t-1}, x_{t-2}, \ldots; y_{t-1}, y_{t-2}, \ldots) = P(x_t|x_{t-1}, x_{t-2}, \ldots).$$

Now consider the projection

$$P(y_t|\ldots, x_{t-1}, x_t, x_{t+1}, \ldots), \tag{A.27}$$

i.e. the projection of y_t on past, current, and future x_t's. Sims (1972) has proved that y_t fails to Granger-cause x_t if and only if the projection (A.27) coincides with the projection

$$P(y_t|x_t, x_{t-1}, \ldots),$$

i.e. with the projection of y_t on current and past x_t's.

Let

$$\begin{pmatrix} S_y(e^{-i\phi}) & S_{yx}(e^{-i\phi}) \\ S_{xy}(e^{-i\phi}) & S_x(e^{-i\phi}) \end{pmatrix}$$

be the spectral density of $(\, y_t \quad x_t\,)'$. If $S_y(e^{-i\phi})$ has no zeros, i.e. if $S_y(z)$ has no zeros of unit modulus, then the projection (A.27) has the representation

$$p(L)x_t = \frac{S_{yx}(L)}{S_x(L)}x_t.$$

Thus Sims's theorem can be rephrased in the following way: y_t fails to Granger-cause x_t if and only if $p(L)$ is unilateral in L.

REMARK A.4. Notice that Sims's theorem holds irrespective of whether the vector $(\, y_t \quad x_t\,)'$ is singular or not. Consider, for instance,

$$\begin{aligned} y_t &= u_t \\ x_t &= (1+2L)u_t, \end{aligned}$$

where u_t is a white noise. The second equation can be rewritten as

$$x_t = 2y_{t-1} + u_t.$$

Since u_t is orthogonal to the past of both x_t and y_t, the latter is the projection of x_t on the past of both x_t and y_t. Projecting x_t on the past of itself alone yields a residual with a bigger variance since u_t is nonfundamental for x_t (see Section A.4). Therefore y_t Granger-causes x_t. On the other hand, the function

$$p(L) = \frac{1+2F}{(1+2L)(1+2F)} = \frac{1}{1+2L}$$

is not unilateral in L, according to Sims's theorem.

A.9. Bibliographic Notes

For an introduction to Hilbert spaces see Halmos (1951). Square summable sequences and functions whose square has a finite integral in $[-\pi,\pi]$ are linked by an isometric one-to-one correspondence. Precisely,

$$\{a_k\} \to a(e^{-i\phi}) = \sum_{k=-\infty}^{\infty} a_k e^{-ik\phi}. \tag{A.28}$$

Moreover, the convolution of two sequences corresponds to the product of the corresponding functions. Thus the convolution is square summable. Secondly, if an inverse of a sequence exists, then it is unique. Moreover, both (A.21) and (A.22) make sense. Notice, however, that both these formulas define the spectral density up to a function which vanishes on $[-\pi,\pi]$ with the exception of a zero measure subset. For the Fourier transform, i.e.

(A.28), and the Riesz–Fischer theorem, which establishes the correspondence between sequences and functions, see Apostol (1967, pp. 306–11).

For the MA representations of a stationary process, see Wold (1954). Theorem A.7 is proved in Rozanov (1967, p. 58, Theorem 4.1). Theorem A.8 is a consequence of Theorem 4.3, p. 60 (see also Remarks 1, 2, and 3). Theorem A.4 is a consequence of Theorems 4.3 and 4.2. Theorems A.6 and A.9 are consequences of the results of Theorem 10.1, p. 47. Theorems A.2 and A.3 are one-dimensional specifications of Theorems A.4 and A.9 respectively. In Rozanov's book the term 'singular', for stochastic processes, is employed for the processes that in Section A.2 have been called deterministic, whereas, we must recall, in this book 'singular' is used for vector processes which do not have maximum rank. For the spectral density see also Hannan (1970), Priestley (1981).

References

Ahlfors, L. V. (1979), *Complex Analysis: an Introduction to the Theory of Analytic Functions* (3rd Edition). New York: McGraw-Hill.

Altonji, J. G. and Ashenfelter, O. (1980), "Wage Movements and the Labour Market Equilibrium Hypothesis," *Economica,* 47, 217–45.

Anderson, O. D. (1975), "On a Lemma Associated with Box, Jenkins and Granger," *Journal of Econometrics,* 3, 151–56.

—— (1978), "Concerning One of T.W. Anderson's Theorems—A Correction to 'Forecasting Aggregates of Independent ARIMA Processes' by Rose," *Metron,* 36, 99–103.

Ansley, C. F., Spivey, W. A., and Wroblesky, W. J. (1977), "On the Structure of Moving-Average Processes," *Journal of Econometrics,* 6, 121–34.

Apostol, T. M. (1974), *Mathematical Analysis.* Reading, MA: Addison Wesley.

Ashenfelter, O. (1978), "Estimating the Effects of Training Program on Earnings," *The Review of Economics and Statistics,* 60, 47–57.

Attanasio, O. P. and Weber, G. (1991), "On the Aggregation of Euler Equation for Consumption in Simple OLG Models," IFS Working Paper Series no. W92/11, London.

—— (1992), "Consumption Growth and Excess Sensitivity to Income: Evidence from US Micro Data," IFS Working Paper Series no. W92/15, London.

Banerjee, A., Dolado, J. J., Galbraith, J. W., and Hendry, D. F. (1993), *Co-integration, Error Correction and the Econometric Analysis of Non-Stationary Data.* Oxford: Oxford University Press.

Bernanke, B. (1986), "Alternative Explanations of the Money-Income Correlation," *Carnegie–Rochester Conference Series on Public Policy,* 25, 49–99.

Bertola, G. and Caballero, R. J. (1990), "Kinked Adjustment Costs and Aggregate Dynamics," in Blanchard, O. J. and Fisher, S. (eds.), *NBER Macroeconomics Annual,* 1990. Cambridge, MA: MIT Press, 237–95.

Beveridge, S. and Nelson, C. R. (1981), "A New Approach to the Decomposition of Economic Time Series into Permanent and Transitory Components with Particular Attention to Measurement of the Business Cycle," *Journal of Monetary Economics,* 7, 151–74.

Billingsley, P. (1986), *Probability and Measure* (2nd Edition). New York: Wiley.

Blanchard, O. J. and Quah, D. (1989), "The Dynamic Effects of Aggregate Supply and Demand Disturbances," *American Economic Review,* 79, 655–73.

Blinder, A. S. (1981), "Temporary Income Taxes and Consumer Spending," *Journal of Political Economy,* 89, 26–53.

Blinder, A. S. and Deaton, A. S. (1985), "The Time Series Consumption Function Revisited," *Brookings Papers on Economic Activity,* 2, 465–521.

Brillinger, D. R. (1981), *Time Series. Data Analysis and Theory* (Expanded Edition). San Francisco: Holden-Day.

Caballero, R. J. (1990), "Expenditure on Durable Goods: A Case for Slow Adjustment," *Quarterly Journal of Economics,* 105, 727–43.

Campbell, J. Y. (1987), "Does Saving Anticipate Declining Labor Income? An Alternative Test of the Permanent Income Hypothesis," *Econometrica,* 55, 1249–73.

Campbell, J. Y. and Deaton, A. S. (1989), "Why Is Consumption so Smooth?" *Review of Economic Studies,* 56, 357–74.

Campbell, J. Y. and Perron, P. (1991), "Pitfalls and Opportunities: What Macroeconomists Should Know about Unit Roots," in Blanchard, O. J. and Fisher, S. (eds.), *NBER Macroeconomics Annual,* 1991. Cambridge, MA: MIT Press, 141–201.

Caplin, A. S. (1985), "The Variability of Aggregate Demand with (S, s) Inventory Policies," *Econometrica,* 53, 1395–409.

Caplin, A. S. and Leahy, J. (1991), "State-Dependent Pricing and the Dynamics of Money and Output," *Quarterly Journal of Economics,* 106, 683–708.

Chamberlain, G. (1983), "Funds, Factors, and Diversification in Arbitrage Pricing Models," *Econometrica,* 51, 1305–23.

Chamberlain, G. and Rothschild, M. (1983), "Arbitrage, Factor Structure, and Mean-Variance Analysis on Large Asset Markets," *Econometrica,* 51, 1281–304.

Christiano, L. J. and Eichenbaum, M. (1990), "Unit Roots in Real GNP: Do We Know and Do We Care?" *Carnegie–Rochester Conference Series on Public Policy,* 32, 7–61.

Clarida, R. H. (1991), "Aggregate Stochastic Implications of the Life-Cycle Hypothesis," *Quarterly Journal of Economics,* 106, 851–67.

Cochrane, J. H. (1988), "How Big is the Random Walk in the GNP?" *Journal of Political Economy,* 96, 893–920.

Cooper, R. and Haltiwanger, J. C. (1990), "Inventories and the Propagation of Sectoral Shocks," *American Economic Review,* 80, 170–90.

Coutts, K., Godley, W., and Nordhouse, W. (1978), *Industrial Pricing in the United Kingdom.* Cambridge: Cambridge University Press.

Davidson, J. E. H. and Hendry, D. F. (1981), "Interpreting Economic Evidence: Consumers' Expenditures," *European Economic Review,* 16, 177–92.

Davidson, J. E. H., Hendry, D. F., Srba, F., and Yeo, S. (1978), "Econometric Modelling of the Aggregate Time-Series Relationship between Consumers' Expenditure and Income in the United Kingdom," *Economic Journal,* 88, 661–92.

Deaton, A. S. (1987), "Life-Cycle Models of Consumption: Is the Evidence Consistent with the Theory?" in Bewley, T. F. (ed.), *Advances in Econometrics, Fifth World Congress,* Vol. II. Cambridge: Cambridge University Press, 121–48.

—— (1992), *Understanding Consumption.* Oxford: Oxford University Press.

Debreu, G. (1970), "Economies with a Finite Set of Equilibria," *Econometrica,* 38, 387–92.

De Long, J. B. and Summers, L. H. (1991), "Equipment Investment and Economic Growth," *Quarterly Journal of Economics,* 106, 445–502.

—— (1992), "Equipment Investment and Economic Growth: How Strong is the Nexus?" *Brookings Papers of Economic Activity,* 2, 157–99.

Engle, R. F. and Granger, C. W. J. (1987), "Cointegration and Error Correction: Representation, Estimation and Testing," *Econometrica,* 55, 251–76.

Engle, R. F., Hendry, D. F., and Richard, J.-F. (1983), "Exogeneity," *Econometrica,* 51, 277–304.

Evans, G. W. (1989), "Output and Unemployment Dynamics in the United States: 1950-1985," *Journal of Applied Econometrics,* 4, 213–37.

Flavin, M. A. (1981), "The Adjustment of Consumption to Changing Expectations about Future Income," *Journal of Political Economy,* 89, 974–1009.

Forni, M. (1990), "Misspecification in Dynamic Models," Materiali di Discussione n. 65, Dipartimento di Economia Politica, Modena.

—— (1996), "Consumption Volatility and Income Persistence in the Permanent Income Model," *Ricerche Economiche,* 50, 223–34.

Forni, M. and Lippi, M. (1994), "Permanent Income, Heterogeneity and the Error Correction Mechanism," Materiali di Discussione n. 118, Dipartimento di Economia Politica, Modena.

Forni, M. and Reichlin, L. (1995), "Let's Get Real: A Dynamic Factor Analytical Approach to Disaggregated Business Cycle," CEPR Working Papers Series no. 1244.

—— (1996), "Dynamic Common Factors in Large Cross-Sections," *Empirical Economics,* 21, 27–42.

Friedman, M. (1957), *A Theory of the Consumption Function.* Princeton, NJ: Princeton University Press.

Galí, J. (1990), "Finite Horizons, Life Cycle Savings and Time Series Evidence on Consumption," *Journal of Monetary Economics,* 26, 433–52.

—— (1991), "Budget Constraints and Time Series Evidence on Consumption," *American Economic Review,* 81, 1238–53.

Geweke, J. (1977), "The Dynamic Factor Analysis of Economic Time Series," in Aigner, D. J. and Goldberger, A. S. (eds.), *Latent Variables in Socioeconomic Models.* Amsterdam: North-Holland, 365–83.

—— (1978), "Temporal Aggregation in the Multiple Regression Model," *Econometrica,* 46, 643–61.

Geweke, J. and Singleton, K. J. (1981), "Maximum Likelihood 'Confirmatory' Factor Analysis of Economic Time Series," *International Economic Review,* 22, 37–54.

Giannini, C. (1992), *Topics in Structural VAR Econometrics.* Berlin: Springer Verlag.

Gonzalo, J. (1989), "Cointegration and Aggregation," Working Paper 89–30, Economics Department, UCSD.

—— (1993), "Cointegration and Aggregation," *Ricerche Economiche,* 47, 281–91.

Goodfriend, M. (1992), "Information-Aggregation Bias," *American Economic Review,* 82, 508–19.

Granger, C. W. J. (1969), "Investigating Causal Relations by Econometric Models and Cross-Spectral Methods," *Econometrica,* 37, 424–38.

—— (1980), "Long Memory Relationships and the Aggregation of Dynamic Models," *Journal of Econometrics,* 14, 227–38.

—— (1987), "Implication of Aggregation with Common Factors," *Econometric Theory,* 3, 208–22.

—— (1990), "Aggregation of Time-Series Variables: A Survey," in Barker, T. and Pesaran, M. H. (eds.), *Disaggregation in Econometric Modelling.* London: Routledge, 17–34.

Granger, C. W. J. and Morris, M. J. (1976), "Time Series Modelling and Interpretation," *Journal of the Royal Statistical Society,* A, 139, 246–57.

Griliches, Z. (1957), "Hybrid Corn: An Exploration in the Economics of Technological Change," *Econometrica,* 25, 501–22.

Hall, R. E. (1978), "Stochastic Implications of the Life Cycle-Permanent Income Hypothesis: Theory and Evidence," *Journal of Political Economy,* 96, 971–87.

Hall, R. E. and Mishkin, F. S. (1982), "The Sensitivity of Consumption to Transitory Income: Estimates from Panel Data on Households," *Econometrica,* 50, 461–81.

Halmos, P. R. (1951), *Introduction to Hilbert Spaces.* New York: Chelsea.

Hannan, E. J. (1970), *Multiple Time Series.* New York: Wiley.

Hansen, L. P. and Sargent, T. J. (1980), "Formulating and Estimating Dynamic Linear Rational Expectations Models," *Journal of Economic Dynamics and Control,* 2, 7–46.

—— eds., (1991a), *Rational Expectations Econometrics.* London: Westview.

—— (1991b), "Two Difficulties in Interpreting Vector Autoregressions," in Hansen, L. P. and Sargent, T. J. (eds.), *Rational Expectations Econometrics.* London: Westview, 77–119.

Hayashi, F. (1985), "The Permanent Income Hypothesis and Consumption Durability: Analysis Based on Japanese Panel Data," *Quarterly Journal of Economics,* 100, 1083–113.

Hendry, D. F. (1995), *Dynamic Econometrics.* Oxford: Oxford University Press.

Hendry, D. F. and von Ungern-Sternberg, T. (1980), "Liquidity and Inflation Effects on Consumers' Expenditure," in Deaton, A. S. (ed.), *Essays in the Theory and Measurement of Consumers' Behaviour.* Cambridge: Cambridge University Press, 237–61.

Hildenbrand, W. (1994), *Market Demand.* Princeton, NJ: Princeton University Press.

Johansen, S. (1988), "Statistical Analysis of Cointegration Vectors," *Journal of Economic Dynamics and Control,* 12, 231–54.

—— (1991), "The Role of the Constant Term in Cointegration Analysis of Non-Stationary Variables," Institute of Mathematical Statistics, University of Copenhagen.

Jovanovic, B. and Lach, S. (1989), "Entry, Exit and Diffusion with Learning by Doing," *American Economic Review,* 79, 690–99.

—— (1990), "The Diffusion of Technology and Inequality among Nations," Mimeo.

Kaplansky, I. (1972), *Fields and Rings.* Chicago: The University of Chicago Press.

King, R. G., Plosser, C. I., Stock, J. H., and Watson, M. W. (1991), "Stochastic Trends and Economic Fluctuations," *American Economic Review,* 81, 819–40.

Kirman, A. P. (1993), "Ants, Rationality, and Recruitment," *The Quarterly Journal of Economics,* 108, 137–56.

Lee, K., Pesaran, M. H., and Pierse, R. G. (1990), "Aggregation Bias in Labour Demand Equation for the UK Economy," in Barker, T. S. and Pesaran, M. H. (eds.), *Disaggregation in Economic Modelling.* London: Routledge, 113–49.

Lewbel, A. (1992), "Aggregation with Log-Linear Models," *Review of Economic Studies,* 59, 635–42.

—— (1994), "Aggregation and Simple Dynamics," *American Economic Review,* 84, 905–18.

Lilien, D. M. (1982), "Sectoral Shifts and Cyclical Unemployment," *Journal of Political Economy,* 90, 777–93.

Lillard, L. A. and Willis, R. J. (1978), "Dynamic Aspects of Earning Mobility," *Econometrica,* 46, 985–1012.

Lippi, M. (1988), "On the Dynamic Shape of Aggregated Error Correction Models," *Journal of Economic Dynamics and Control,* 12, 561–85.

—— (1989), "A Short Note on Cointegration and Aggregation," Materiali di Discussione n. 49, Dipartimento di Economia Politica, Modena.

—— (1990), "Issues on Aggregation and Microfundations of Macroeconomics," Paper presented to the Workshop "Rational Behavior and Aggregation: Theory and Tests", EUI, Florence.

Lippi, M. and Forni, M. (1990), "On the Dynamic Specification of Aggregated Models," in Barker, T. S. and Pesaran, M. H. (eds.), *Disaggregation in Economic Modelling.* London: Routledge, 35–72.

Lippi, M. and Reichlin, L. (1993), "The Dynamic Effects of Aggregate Demand and Supply Disturbances: Comment," *American Economic Review,* 83, 644–52.

—— (1994a), "Diffusion of Technical Change and the Decomposition of Output into Trend and Cycle," *Review of Economic Studies,* 61, 19–30.

—— (1994b), "Common and Uncommon Trends and Cycles," *European Economic Review,* 38, 624–35.

Long, J. B. and Plosser, C. I. (1983), "Real Business Cycles," *Journal of Political Economy,* 91, 39–69.

Lucas, R. E. (1972), "Expectations and the Neutrality of Money," *Journal of Economic Theory,* 4, 103–24.

—— (1973), "Some International Evidence on Output-Inflation Tradeoffs," *American Economic Review,* 63, 326–34.

—— (1976), "Econometric Policy Evaluation: A Critique," *Carnegie–Rochester Conference on Public Policy,* 1, 19–46.

Lütkepohl, H. (1982), "Non-Causality Due to Omitted Variables," *Journal of Econometrics,* 19, 367–78.

—— (1984), "Linear Transformations of Vector ARMA Processes," *Journal of Econometrics,* 26, 283–93.

—— (1987), *Forecasting Aggregated Vector ARMA Processes.* Berlin: Springer Verlag.

Mansfield, E. (1973), "Determinants of the Speed of Application of New Technology," in Williams, B. R. (ed.), *Science and Technology in Economic Growth,* Proceedings of a Conference held by the International Economic Association. New York: Wiley, 199–226.

Mas-Colell, A. (1985), *The Theory of General Economic Equilibrium. A Differentiable Approach.* Cambridge: Cambridge University Press.

Murphy, K. M., Shleifer, A., and Vishny, R. W. (1989), "Industrialization and the Big Push," *Journal of Political Economy,* 97, 1003–26.

Nerlove, M., Grether, D. M., and Carvalho, J. L. (1979), *Analysis of Economic Time Series.* New York: Academic Press.

Nickell, S. (1985), "Error Correction, Partial Adjustment and All That: an Expository Note," *Oxford Bulletin of Economics and Statistics,* 47, 119–29.

Osterwald-Lenum, M. (1992), "A Note with Quantiles of the Asymptotic Distribution of the Maximum Likelihood Cointegration Rank Test Statistics," *Oxford Bullettin of Economics and Statistics,* 54, 461–72.

Phillips, P. C. B. and Ouliaris, S. (1988), "Testing for Cointegration Using Principal Components Methods," *Journal of Economic Dynamics and Control,* 12, 205–30.

Pischke, J.-S. (1995), "Individual Income, Incomplete Information, and Aggregate Consumption," *Econometrica,* 63, 805–40.

Priestley, M. B. (1981), *Spectral Analysis and Time Series.* New York: Academic Press.

Quah, D. (1990), "Permanent and Transitory Movements in Labor Income: an Explanation for 'Excess Smoothness' in Consumption," *Journal of Political Economy,* 98, 449–75.

Quah, D. and Sargent, T. J. (1993), "A Dynamic Index Model for Large Cross Sections," in Stock, J. H. and Watson, M. W. (eds.), *Business Cycles, Indicators and Forecasting.* Chicago: The University of Chicago Press, 285–309.

Rose, D. E. (1977), "Forecasting Aggregates of Independent ARIMA Processes," *Journal of Econometrics,* 5, 323–45.

Rozanov, Y. A. (1967), *Stationary Random Processes.* San Francisco: Holden-Day.

Runkle, D. E. (1991), "Liquidity Constraints and the Permanent Income Hypothesis," *Journal of Monetary Economics,* 27, 73–98.

Salmon, M. (1982), "Error Correction Mechanisms," *Economic Journal,* 92, 615–29.

Sargent, T. J. (1978), "Estimation of Dynamic Labor Demand Under Rational Expectations," *Journal of Political Economy,* 86, 1009–44.

—— (1987), *Macroeconomic Theory* (2nd Edition). New York: Academic Press.

—— (1989), "Two Models of Measurements and the Investment Accelerator," *Journal of Political Economy,* 97, 251–87.

Sargent, T. J. and Sims, C. A. (1977), "Business-Cycle Modeling Without Pretending to Have Too Much *A Priori* Economic Theory," in Sims, C. A. (ed.), *New Methods of Business Cycle Research.* Minneapolis: Federal Reserve Bank of Minneapolis, 45–109.

Shapiro, M. and Watson, M. W. (1988), "Sources of Business Cycle Fluctuations," in Fisher, S. (ed.), *NBER Macroeconomics Annual,* 1988. Cambridge, MA: MIT Press, 111–48.

Sims, C. A. (1971), "Discrete Approximations to Continuous Distributed Lags in Econometrics," *Econometrica,* 39, 545–64.

—— (1972), "Money, Income and Causality," *American Economic Review,* 62, 540–52.

—— (1974), "Seasonality in Regression," *Journal of the American Statistical Association,* 69, 618–26.

—— (1980), "Macroeconomics and Reality," *Econometrica,* 48, 1–48.

Smirnov, V. I. (1964), *A Course in Higher Mathematics,* Vol. III, Part II. Oxford: Pergamon Press.

Stock, J. H. and West, K. D. (1988), "Integrated Regressors and Tests of the Permanent Income Hypothesis," *Journal of Monetary Economics,* 21, 85–95.

Stoker, T. M. (1982), "The Use of Cross-Section Data to Characterize Macro Functions," *Journal of the American Statistical Association,* 77, 369–80.

—— (1984), "Completeness, Distribution Restrictions, and the Form of Aggregate Functions," *Econometrica,* 52, 887–907.

—— (1986), "Simple Tests of Distributional Effects on Macroeconomic Equations," *Journal of Political Economy,* 94, 763–95.

Theil, H. (1954), *Linear Aggregation of Economic Relations.* Amsterdam: North-Holland.

Tiao, G. and Wei, W. (1976), "Effects of Temporal Aggregation on the Dynamic Relationships of Two Time-Series Variables," *Biometrika,* 63, 513–23.

Trivedi, P. K. (1985), "Distributed Lags, Aggregation and Compounding: Some Econometric Implications," *Review of Economic Studies,* 52, 19–35.

Waerden, van der, B. L. (1953), *Modern Algebra.* New York: Frederick Ungar.

Watson, M. W. and Engle, R. F. (1983), "Alternative Algorithms for the Estimation of Dynamic Factor, MIMC and Varying Coefficient Regression Models," *Journal of Economctrics,* 23, 385 400.

West, K. D. (1988a), "The Insensitivity of Consumption to News about Income," *Journal of Monetary Economics,* 21, 17–34.

—— (1988b), "Dividend Innovations and Stock Price Volatility," *Econometrica,* 56, 37–61.

Wold, H. (1954), *A Study in the Analysis of Stationary Time Series* (2nd Edition). Stockholm: Almquist and Wicksell.

Zeldes, S. P. (1989), "Consumption and Liquidity Constraints: an Empirical Investigation," *Journal of Political Economy,* 97, 305–46.

Index

agent-specific parameters 68, 72, 80, 125–26
aggregate model 105, 107, 126, 140
aggregation weights 10, 45–46, 48–49, 53, 105, 107, 110, 113, 123, 128
Ahlfors, L. V. 103
Alternative Principle 90, 92, 93, 103, 110, 117, 124, 129, 130–37, 147
Altonji, J. G. 18, 176 n.
analytic functions 82, 85–90, 103, 131–32, 135–36
Anderson, O. D. 62
Ansley, C. F. 62
Apostol, T. M. 80, 84, 224
ARIMA 82, 103, 108, 112
ARMA 53, 62, 215–16, 219, 221
ARMAX 76, 149–51, 152
Ashenfelter, O. 18, 176 n.
Attanasio, O. P. 186, 188

Banerjee, A. 41
Bernanke, B. 78
Bertola, G. 18
Beveridge, S. 171
Billingsley, P. 92
Blanchard, O. J. 77, 145, 153
Blinder, A. S. 161 n., 165
Brillinger, D. R. 37 n., 41

Caballero, R. J. 18
Campbell, J. Y. 29 n., 41, 164, 165, 167, 185, 186, 187
Caplin, A. S. xiii, 18
Chamberlain, G. 18
Christiano, L. J. 187
Clarida, R. H. 188
Cochrane, J. H. 170, 171
cointegration 26–30, 122–29, 150, 164–67, 180, 182
common:
  component 4, 68–70, 106–8, 120, 126, 140, 198
  parameters 68, 80, 83, 125–26
  shocks 4, 19–42, 81, 95–100, 120, 126, 180, 188–89, 198
complete information 172–73, 180
consumption volatility 170–72
Cooper, R. 195
Coutts, K. 76
covariance generating function 57, 88–89, 102, 131, 138–40, 144
covariance–stationary processes 204

Davidson, J. E. H. 164, 165, 186, 187
Deaton, A. S. 161 n., 165, 170, 186, 187
Debreu, G. 103
De Long, J. B. 197
dependent variables, *see* dependent–independent variable model
dependent–independent variable model 100–3, 109, 118–20
deterministic processes 208–9, 224
disaggregated model 84, 105
distributions over the microparameter space 110–12
dynamic factor models 5, 189
dynamic principal components 35–38, 46, 190

Eichenbaum, M. 187
Engle, R. F. 18, 41, 154, 164, 187
error correction mechanism 73–75, 164, 182–83
Evans, G. W. 78
excess sensitivity 160–63, 174, 175, 178
excess smoothness 170, 178

Flavin, M. A. 161, 186
Forni, M. xii, xiii, 18, 52, 140, 153, 154, 159, 187, 188
Friedman, M. 76, 115, 164
fundamentalness 6–7, 52, 59 n., 143, 145, 146, 148–49, 173, 174, 215
  and aggregation 54
fundamental:
  noise 6, 208
  polynomial 6
  representation 6, 208

Galí, J. 186, 188
general equilibrium 77, 109–10
Geweke, J. 18, 153, 154
Giannini, C. 153
Gonzalo, J. 129
Goodfriend, M. xiii, 18, 187
Granger, C. W. J. xiii, 16, 18, 41, 62, 114, 140, 164, 187, 222, 223
Granger causality 52, 102, 138–40, 222–23

Griliches, Z. 193

Hall, R. E. 68, 78, 159, 160, 161, 164, 186
Halmos, P. R. 223
Haltiwanger, J. C. 195
Hannan, E. J. 224
Hansen, L. P. 78, 121, 154, 187
Hayashi, F. 186
Hendry, D. F. 75, 78, 186
heterogeneity 3–5, 32, 39, 60, 71, 121, 172, 173, 183
Hilbert space 204, 205
Hildenbrand, W. xiii

identification 142, 145, 152–53, 190–93
  of the common shocks 51–52
  of the microparameters 59–62
idiosyncratic:
  component 4, 68–70, 106–8, 120, 126, 140, 151, 173, 179
  shocks 4, 81, 126, 173, 179, 180
incomplete information 179
independent variables, *see* dependent–independent variable model
individual model 4, 44, 84
information set 68, 73, 171, 172, 174, 176
invertibility of operators in L, *see* operators in L

Johansen, S. 41
Jovanovic, B. 193

Kaplansky, I. 103 n.
King, R. G. 193
Kirman, A. P. xiii

Lach, S. 193
lag operator, *see* operators in L
large numbers 7–14, 106–8
Leahy, J. 18
Lee, K. 154
Lewbel, A. xiii, 61 n., 63, 114, 129, 154
life cycle, permanent income theory of consumption 68–70, 159–72
Lilien, D. M. 194
Lillard, L. A. 18
Lippi, M. xiii, 18, 129, 140, 153, 154, 159, 187, 188, 193 n.
local:
  component 44
  shocks 44
log-linear models 126–28, 129
Long, J. B. 194
Lucas, R. E. 18, 154, 194
Lütkepohl, H. 62, 140, 154

Mansfield, E. 193
Mas-Colell, A. 103
matrices of rational functions 93
maximum rank 218, 224
  see also rank
micromodel 81–83, 85–90, 107, 120, 126, 140
microparameter space 80
Mishkin, F. S. 186
Morris, M. J. 62
Murphy, K. M. 195

negligible subsets 90–91
Nelson, C. R. 171
Nerlove, M. 140
Nickell, S. 73, 74, 154, 183, 187, 216
non-fundamentalness, *see* fundamentalness
non-redundancy, *see* redundancy
non-singularity, *see* singularity

open regions 80, 92, 134, 136
operators in L 210–12
  invertibility of 210
  unilateral 211
orthogonal projections 205–7
orthonormal white-noise vectors 144, 218
Osterwald-Lenum, M. 29 n., 41
Ouliaris, S. 42
overidentifying restrictions 72, 152–53

permanent:
  common shocks 28
  component 180
  shocks 27–28, 32, 123, 129, 182
permanent income 68, 159
Perron, P. 29 n., 41
persistence 171
Phillips, P. C. B. 42
Pischke, J.-S. xiii, 18, 161, 176 n., 187
Plosser, C. I. 194
population space 83, 113–14
Priestley, M. B. 224

Quah, D. 52, 77, 145, 153, 154, 187

rank:
  of the aggregate vector 116–21
  of vector processes 31, 33, 218
rational expectations 68, 71
rational spectral density 221
redundancy 95–100, 118–20, 123–25, 129, 147, 181
regional model 43–46
regression, *see* orthogonal projections
regular processes 209
Reichlin, L. xii, xiii, 52, 154, 193 n.
representative agent 68, 172, 173, 179

Rose, D. E. 62
Rothschild, M. 18
Rozanov, Y. A. xiv, 62, 137, 224
rules of thumb 75–77
Runkle, D. E. 186

Salmon, M. 78, 183, 187
Sargent, T. J. 18, 52, 71, 76 n., 78, 121, 154, 187
sectoral component 194, 198
Shapiro, M. 78
Sims, C. A. 18, 138, 140, 149, 154, 222
Sims's theorem 222–23
Singleton, K. J. 18
singularity 24–26, 116–21, 150, 167–70, 179–82, 218, 224
  see also rank
singular processes, *see* singularity
Smirnov, V. I. 103, 218 n.
Solow growth model 197
spectral density 36–38, 55, 56, 108, 131–32, 137, 151, 171, 178, 190, 195–96, 219–22
spectrum, *see* spectral density
Stock, J. H. 186
Stoker, T. M. 63, 114, 154
structural VAR models 77–78, 141–48, 152
Summers, L. H. 197
superior information 171

technology shocks 190–93
Theil, H. 154
Tiao, G. 140, 154
transitory:
  component 180
  shocks 27–28
trend stationary processes 163
Trivedi, P. K. xiii, 62, 154

Ungern-Sternberg, T. von 75

VAR models, *see* structural VAR models

Waerden, B. L. van der 104
Watson, M. W. 18, 78
Weber, G. 186, 188
Wei, W. 140, 154
West, K. D. 186, 187
white-noise processes 204, 220
Willis, R. J. 18
Wold, H. 224
Wold decomposition, *see* Wold representation
Wold representation 53–58, 103, 131–34, 141, 147, 151, 208–9, 217–19

Zeldes, S. P. 186